Challenges and Issues in Knowledge Management

a volume in
Research in Management Consulting
Series Editor: Anthony F. Buono

Research in Management Consulting

Anthony F. Buono, Series Editor

Challenges and Issues in Knowledge Management

edited by

Anthony F. Buono
Bentley College

and

Flemming Poulfelt
Copenhagen Business School

INFORMATION AGE
PUBLISHING

Greenwich, Connecticut
www.infoagepub.com

*Published with
support from*

Library of Congress Cataloging-in-Publication Data

Challenges and issues in knowledge management / edited by Anthony F. Buono
and Flemming Poulfelt.
   p. cm. -- (Research in management consulting ; v. 5)
 Includes bibliographical references.
 ISBN 1-59311-419-2 (pbk.) -- ISBN 1-59311-420-6 (hardcover)
 1. Knowledge management. 2. Consulting firms--Management. I. Buono,
Anthony F. II. Poulfelt, Flemming. III. Series.
 HD30.2.C4715 2005
 658.4'038--dc22

                        2005017306

Printed in the United States of America

CONTENTS

INTRODUCTION

Anthony F. Buono and Flemming Poulfelt

The field of knowledge management (KM) lies at the heart of management consulting, as "knowledge has become *the* resource rather than *a* resource" (Drucker, 1995, p. 31). Indeed, as knowledge has replaced capital, natural resources, and labor as the key competitive resource, consultancies are investing significant time and organizational capital—for themselves as well as for their clients—in an attempt to capture, identify, retrieve, and utilize knowledge across all areas of their firms (Management Consulting International, 2004a, 2004b). An increasingly demanding business environment is also forcing consultants to respond to market forces faster and with deeper insight than ever before (Kennedy Information, 2004; Sharif, 2003), and knowledge creation and knowledge sharing—in terms of exploration, development, and exploitation—have become increasingly important in delivering true value to the client (see Davenport & Prusak, 2004). Many of the top consultancies also offer KM services for their clients, focusing on how they can develop their internal knowledge management practices, increasing the value of established knowledge systems, procedures, and processes.

In general, the basic idea of knowledge management refers to the ways in which organizations capture, process, share, and use information. In contrast to simply managing the flow of information, the basic goal of knowledge management is to leverage and disseminate information, insights, and knowledge that already exist in an organization so that its members will be able to seek out, utilize, and enhance their activities and processes, and, based on that experience, create new knowledge that ulti-mately improves organizational performance. The resulting literature—both conceptual and empirical—runs the gamut from the view that knowledge is a *thing*, an explicit collection of identifiable objects, some-thing that can captured and stored in databases and repositories, to the polar perspective that knowledge is more of a *process*, much more tacit and embedded in the mental schemas and exchanges that occur within social networks (cf. Alvai & Leidner, 2001; Lissack, 2000; Nonaka & Takeuchi, 1995; Polanyi, 1969; Shariq, 1999; Szulanski, 1996).

While *explicit knowledge* is relatively easily expressed in words and num-bers and easily communicated (e.g., hard data, codified procedures, scien-tific formulae), *tacit knowledge* is much more difficult to formalize, communicate, and share with others. Yet it is estimated that roughly 90% of the knowledge in any organization is tacit in nature, in essence con-tained in the heads of its members (Wah, 1999). Indeed, although the rapid growth of information technology (IT) has prompted many organi-zations and their consultants to envision a new world of easily "leveraged" and codified knowledge, to their dismay many have found little more than "information junkyards" in their wake (McDermott, 1999). Some cynics (e.g., Skyrme, 1997) even suggest that the very idea of knowledge management is an oxymoron—that in far too many organizations there is little, if any, real knowledge and attempts to manage what knowledge there is falling well short of aspirations.

Within this context, consulting services can be arrayed along a knowl-edge continuum, from those practices that can be captured and codified, producing proprietary tools that provide fine-tuned solutions to standard-ized problems, to more personal, highly customized solutions to unique and novel problems (Dunford, 2000; Hansen, Nohria, & Tierney, 1999). While it is difficult to fully separate these two perspectives and in practice the two approaches often blur, their differences capture the essence of the KM challenge (Petersen & Poulfelt, 2002). While we may be able to orga-nizationally embed knowledge in methods, processes, procedures, and products, its core—its very essence—resides in the minds of people and their tacit ability to put that knowledge into practice. Although this ten-sion between systems and people has been recognized for years, it still remains a puzzle as to how to strike and optimize the balance in practice.

FIRST- AND SECOND-GENERATION KNOWLEDGE MANAGEMENT CHALLENGES

This volume captures many of the issues and challenges surrounding what might be thought of as the transition between first- and second-gen-

Table I.1. First- and Second-Generation Knowledge Management (KM) Perspectives and Challenges

First-Generation Knowledge Management	Second-Generation Knowledge Management
Knowledge as possession (knowledge as a thing)	Knowing-in-action (knowledge as a socially embedded phenomenon)
KM as largely a technical issue: • Complex management information systems • Data repositories—databases and documents • Support structures largely mechanistic	KM as a sociocultural, political, and technical issue: • Complex human systems • Communities of practice and knowledge zones • Support structures largely organic
Desire for knowledge sharing as key driver	Need for boundary spanners and cultural "map makers" to guide knowledge sharing
KM as planned change	KM as guided changing

eration knowledge management within the field of management consulting. As illustrated in Table I.1, a first generation perspective, which was the underpinning of most early KM initiatives, is the *knowledge as possession* view (see, e.g., McElroy, 2000; Ruggles, 1998). This perspective assumes that knowledge is something that people possess, an entity that can be made explicit, captured and transferred from one person or group to another. As John Doyle, the former head of Hewlett-Packard Labs, purportedly reflected, "If HP only knew what HP knows" (reported in Davenport & Prusak, 2003, p. 189). The underlying assumption is that if an organization can capture the insights and experiences of key organizational members, it can enhance knowledge sharing across a wide range of individuals and groups and improve its performance.

Many companies that invested heavily in IT-based KM systems, however, lacked a sufficient understanding of their internal abilities and the necessary requirements to administer and support these systems. In fact, studies suggest that organizations frequently overestimate the abilities, availabilities, and commitment of their internal staff to effectively implement and support KM initiatives (see, e.g., Davis, 2004) and practice suggests that knowledge is often context bound. Thus, while the processes underlying knowledge transfer can be facilitated by computer-mediated communication (Sussman & Siegal, 2003), success depends much more fully on the human element (Petersen & Poulfelt, 2002). Indeed, simply offering "best practice" solutions and prescriptions to specific business problems—a hallmark of the consulting field—often confuses rather than enlightens clients because they often fail to see the "bigger picture"

(Sharif, 2002). Thus, a second-generation perspective on knowledge management underscores that knowledge is socially constructed, which makes it difficult for individuals to fully know, understand, and transfer tacit knowledge from one context to another. *Knowing-in-action* suggests that knowledge is not so much possessed as embedded in practice. True *knowing*, therefore, has to be generated within its own context, and the focus moves from simply capturing and supplying knowledge within a planned change framework, to creating and maintaining the conditions required for guiding the knowing process (see Kerber & Buono, in press).

Since knowledge is often viewed as a scarce resource, rather than assuming a basic desire and openness to sharing information, organizational members may be tempted to hoard their knowledge base, especially if they feel insecure in the organization or if they believe that keeping knowledge increases their competitive value to the organization. In fact, one view is that companies and their members are *inherently hostile* to knowledge sharing (Husted & Michailova, 2002). From such mildly hostile attitudes as a reluctance to spend time on knowledge sharing to far stronger orientations (e.g., attempts to survive power games, fear of hosting "knowledge parasites," trying to maintain the status quo in the face of change), a second-generation view is that organizations need to actively intervene to encourage and support knowledge sharing. As many of the chapters in this volume emphasize, a fundamental challenge is to develop a culture that values people and fosters knowledge sharing, encouraging, supporting, and rewarding organizational members to openly share and utilize what they know. As such the real challenge in knowledge management is to bring knowledge and management into a concerted action.

Challenges and Issues in Knowledge Management—the fifth volume in the Research on Management Consulting series—presents 16 chapters that explore these various perspectives, focusing on knowledge management within the context of the management consulting industry, the dynamics associated with knowledge sharing and dissemination, methodological approaches to studying knowledge in organizations, and reflections on knowledge management and management consulting. As the chapters underscore, it is important to ensure that KM initiatives are aligned with the needs of the organization and its members, that the KM system is "owned" by organizational members with particular emphasis on executive sponsorship and team member acceptance, and that it be understood as an ongoing process rather than simply another management objective or faddish consulting tool. The focus, therefore, should be on how knowledge processes can be facilitated, leveraged, and utilized in organizational value creation.

KNOWLEDGE MANAGEMENT AND THE MANAGEMENT
CONSULTING INDUSTRY

The initial section in the volume contains five chapters that examine how management consultancies have attempted to capture, build on, and exploit their knowledge bases. In the first chapter, Jan Mouritsen and Per Nikolaj Bukh present a case study of KM practices in a professional services firm, drawing a distinction between knowledge management and intellectual capital as a mechanism to integrate various kinds of KM activities. Drawing on KM practices at COWI, a Northern European consulting group, Mouritsen and Bukh argue that knowledge can be made more manageable through the use of intellectual capital statements that reflect the portfolio of, investments in, and effects of knowledge.

Building on COWI's KM principles, the chapter illustrates how an intellectual capital statement can "capture" and present organizational knowledge in a way that allows analysis and interpretation of what *is* happening and what *could* happen in the KM arena. The authors argue that to be truly useful such intellectual capital statements must be interpreted and managed in the larger organizational context, and their ensuing discussion illustrates how intellectual capital statements can sufficiently structure knowledge so that it can be assessed, debated, managed, and directed toward the strategic concerns of the firm.

Chapter 2 by Anne Bang investigates some of the practical problems related to such attempts to capture and manage knowledge. Using a comparative case study of KM issues in two consultancies—one of the pioneers in the KM field noted for its "best practices" and a smaller Denmark-based consultancy—Bang explores the tensions between the initial intent of many KM initiatives (e.g., global knowledge production) and the pressures and concerns (reflective of organizational, cultural, and technological differences) at the local level.

Noting that the two firms studied represent very different approaches to knowledge management, the chapter explores a range of tension points, including the distinction in many management-consulting firms between "productive" and "nonproductive" time (i.e., serving clients vs. doing anything else), the hopes pinned to best practice initiatives, and the need for knowledge-based forums that place KM efforts in the unique context of the particular organization. Bang argues that a significant body of KM theory and practice tries to reduce knowledge into a mere commodity, which ultimately decontextualizes it and leaves it on a distant and abstract level. Drawing on illustrative examples from her cases, the chapter explores the limitations of implementing KM systems as a shortcut to "solve" complex, organizational knowledge-based problems. The chapter ends with questioning these KM frameworks, noting that an underlying issue concerns the extent to which we attempt to control, measure, and evaluate those factors that actually add value or simply focus on those things that we are able to measure.

The next chapter by Sue Newell raises questions about the efficacy of an increasingly popular consulting offering. Although many consultants sell their services on the premise that they can facilitate the transfer of "best practices" into their client organizations, Newell argues that this is more fallacy than reality as it based on an overly simplistic view of knowledge. She suggests that the idea of best practice transfer is grounded in the knowledge as possession view, in essence something that can be captured and directly transferred to others. By understanding the situated nature of knowledge—knowledge as practice and the difference between knowledge and *knowing*—actual "best practice" transfer is far more problematic.

Drawing on a case study of a hospital-based project team in the United Kingdom, Newell examines how the team worked together to transform a time-consuming, inefficient, and problematic process. Yet, although the new process was widely disseminated throughout the hospital system as a "best practice," professionals in the other hospitals dismissed it as impractical and unworkable. Exploring the underlying reasons why the transfer was not successful, she suggests that an important dimension of the problem-solving process was the creation of a community of practice and significant changes in the social relations in the workplace—changes that did not occur in other parts of the system. In the absence of this holistic generation of knowledge and changed relationships, the templates and the new practice made little sense.

The chapter concludes with an insightful discussion of the role that consultants can play in facilitating *knowing* in practice. Since practice is socially constructed, Newell suggests that a key task is to facilitate dialogue and discussion in each new context so that those involved can develop new understandings and become knowledgeably skilled as a full participant in the particular sociocultural practice.

Continuing this theme, Chapter 4 by Elena Bou and Alfons Sauquet focuses on how members of a global consulting firm carry out their practice, "knowing" and "acting" simultaneously. Exploring the idea of "knowing-in-practice," their study compares and contrasts expert and novice consultants, illustrating how these two groups rely on different "bundles of knowledge" and how that evolves as organizational members engage in "real work" in a particular context or "situated practice."

Using direct observation and in-depth interviews, Bou and Saquet present a detailed vignette that illustrates the consulting firm's formal and informal processes for business development and securing an engagement contract. Their analysis shows how the actual practice of selling consulting products is far more complex than the one reflected in formal organizational procedures, relying on extensive tacit understandings between the actors. The discussion draws out the different types of knowledge involved—from individual-explicit and individual-tacit, to collective-explicit and collective-tacit knowledge—and how these different forms interact in practice. The chapter concludes with the authors' reflections on the complex interaction between different types of knowledge and the dynamics involved in different levels of knowing and learning in practice.

The final chapter in this section, by Antti Ainamo, presents a historical overview (mid-1940s to the mid-1990s) and analysis of the evolution of knowledge management in the Jaako Pöyry Group (JPG), a highly successful Finnish engineering and consulting firm. Utilizing co-evolutionary and personalized exchange perspectives on knowledge management, Ainamo's social history and ethnographic analysis explores how "good" KM cultures are created and sustained over time. The chapter illustrates how Jaako Pöyry, JPG's founder, imported ideas and practices from abroad, recombining them with his own insights and leveraging them to trigger a partly sequential and partly co-evolutionary process that included (1) exploration of global state-of-the-art knowledge and efforts to "imprint" this insight at the core of JPG's KM system; (2) successful entrepreneurial entry into new markets by leveraging this core knowledge base; and (3) codification and exploitation of both core and new markets and experiences.

Drawing on a combination of oral history, ethnographic research, and archival material, Ainamo illustrates how firms can function as a global knowledge broker in countries that are largely isolated from international processes of convergence—in essence, bridging over "structural holes" in their social landscape. Reflecting on JPG's history, the chapter concludes with the lessons for and insights into the growth and development of KM systems over time. As Ainamo suggests, through efforts to develop a "global broker role," knowledge exploration and creation can be socially embedded in an organization and developed into a growing body of experience that can be codified and exploited, going from personalized exchange at the individual level to process knowledge at the organizational level.

DYNAMICS OF KNOWLEDGE SHARING AND DISSEMINATION

The second section in the volume contains four chapters that examine the challenge of sharing and disseminating knowledge within and across organizations, focusing on the obstacles and factors that hinder and facilitate knowledge sharing. Chapter 6 by Stefan Heusinkveld and Jos Benders supports the critique that consultants and their firms are often presented as important suppliers and propagators of management knowledge. According to the authors, although consulting firms seek to develop an internal knowledge repertoire that supports the commercialization and implementation of their services, researchers have not paid much attention to the ways in which such knowledge repertoires are developed and internally disseminated within the consultancies themselves. As they suggest, most accounts point to the abundant possibilities of knowledge creation and transfer in consultancy firms, neglecting the significant barriers to realizing these possibilities.

Drawing on interviews with 40 management consultants in 24 different consultancies, Heusinkveld and Benders argue that the actual transfer of management knowledge within consultancies goes well beyond simply constructing a useful method and making it available to colleagues. Rather, efforts to internally disseminate a repertoire are often accompanied by considerable struggles, from the fear of losing ownership of the new repertoire and the need for sufficient internal training to enable others to competently apply the knowledge, to the challenge of persuading others to incorporate it into their practice. As they conclude, the consultancy skills required to disseminate a new repertoire *within* a firm are part of an intricate process that is just as significant as those needed to widely propagate the new knowledge commodity in the external corporate marketplace.

This theme continues in Chapter 7 by Lotte Henriksen in her assessment of knowledge sharing processes and dynamics in "ServCo," a large accounting and consulting firm. Henriksen explores the management challenges in such knowledge-intensive firms, drawing out the factors that promote and inhibit intrafirm knowledge sharing and utilization. Her in-depth case study allows us to "step inside" a firm that has explicitly chosen to focus on knowledge sharing as a management tool. The chapter underscores the importance of combining the use of existing systems and forms of work (exploitation) with the development of new ways to do things (exploration) in creating truly useful frameworks for knowledge sharing.

As Henriksen's analysis emphasizes, while knowledge sharing is clearly beneficial and of interest to firms like ServCo, many of their practices and cultural orientations work against knowledge sharing in practice. Time pressures, a reward system that differentiates between "productive" and "nonproductive" time (similar to Bang's earlier observation of time spent on serving the client vs. literally anything else), physical distance, and a culture that emphasizes excellence and professional pride all interact to create an environment where people are reluctant to share their knowledge. Despite good intentions and IT-based systems intended to facilitate knowledge sharing and dissemination, Henriksen argues that true knowledge sharing requires a much more concerted effort by upper-level management. Because organizational knowledge is primarily stored in individuals, organizations need to design social structures that support an internal sharing of that experience. The capacity to convert individual knowledge to organizational knowledge, therefore, is dependent on those factors that affect the development and exchange of knowledge on the interpersonal level—in essence, cultural change.

The chapter concludes with an assessment of what can be done to facilitate knowledge exploration and exploitation in organizations, emphasizing the importance of adapting knowledge activities to fit local conditions within the framework of the firm's overall knowledge strategy. Emphasis must be placed on establishing frameworks within which knowledge can be developed, shared, integrated, and applied. Within this context, management can be seen as a matter of coordination rather than control, as knowledge sharing and knowledge management come to be about managing knowledge processes and dynamics within the firm.

The next two chapters examine these dynamics in the context of mergers and acquisitions. In Chapter 8, Markus Ejenäs and Andreas Werr focus on interorganizational exchanges within the context of a consulting firm merger. Although they suggest that mergers between consulting firms are typically rationalized by knowledge-based arguments (e.g., enhanced capabilities, expanded service range), the actual alignment of the merger partners' knowledge systems is fraught with difficulties. While the integration of explicit knowledge systems (e.g., migrating the contents of one database into another) is relatively straightforward, the complex interrelationship between explicit and tacit knowledge makes it difficult for consultants to fully benefit from the methods, cases, and tools of their merger partner. In essence, these individuals lack the specific expertise and organization-specific context necessary to interpret and effectively apply this knowledge.

Based on an in-depth case study of a merger between a multinational management consultancy and an IT-based consulting firm, Ejenäs and Werr examine the challenge of integrating the knowledge bases of the two consultancies. While high hopes were initially placed on the potential of joint consulting projects as an integrating mechanism, they found that there were relatively few projects that actually provided opportunities for meaningful interaction and exchange. The authors explore the intricate process of creating a supportive context for knowledge sharing, the tensions involved in such efforts, and the highly vulnerable nature of KM processes—especially in the context of organizational combination. As they conclude, the integration of knowledge bases and KM systems in consulting firm mergers involves a unique set of challenges and dilemmas that creates significant barriers for the creation of a shared consulting practice.

Chapter 9 by Kenneth Husted, Jens Gammelgaard, and Snejina Michailova continues this theme, exploring the tensions surrounding knowledge sharing in an acquisition context and suggesting that the resulting inability to achieve anticipated synergy effects during post-acquisition integration is a significant determinant of acquisition failure. While existing studies of acquisition failure draw from economics, finance, strategy, organization theory, and human resource management, the authors apply insights from knowledge-sharing behavior. Husted and his colleagues argue that much of the knowledge-sharing literature is based on an implicit assumption that people are generally willing to share their knowledge, especially when given the right incentive. Rather than being relatively simple and straightforward, however, they suggest that sharing knowledge in and across organizations is anything but a smooth and self-propelled process. They argue that people have a deeply-rooted resistance—*knowledge-sharing hostility*—not only to sharing the knowledge they possess, but also to reusing knowledge from others.

The chapter establishes a conceptual link between obstacles during the post-acquisition period and individual knowledge-sharing behavior as related to knowledge transmitters (*knowledge hoarding*) and knowledge receivers (*knowledge rejecting*). Husted and his colleagues suggest that the due diligence process should be expanded to include such knowledge-sharing resistant behavior, especially when acquisition-related synergies are dependent upon such sharing. The chapter concludes with recommendations for management consultants and how they can intervene in an attempt to reduce the tensions between knowledge transmitters and receivers, contributing to the potential for framing and capturing crucial knowledge-based synergies in an acquisition.

METHODOLOGICAL APPROACHES TO STUDYING KNOWLEDGE IN ORGANIZATIONS

This section comprises three chapters that develop and illustrate a novel methodological approach to KM research—using pictures and videos to capture KM processes and dynamics. In Chapter 10, Nicoline Jacoby Petersen and Sille Østergaard discuss the use of photography as a research methodology within organizational studies in general and knowledge management in particular. The chapter begins by offering a framework that describes the various ways in which photography can be used in organizational research, drawing out the underlying assumptions and implications of these different approaches. The authors then focus on one of these methods—Group Photo Views—where photos of an organization are used as stimuli—in essence visual questions—during interviews with small groups of employees.

Drawing on their empirical KM studies in a number of Danish management consulting firms, the chapter illustrates how Group Photo Views can be used as a *means* to create research data rather than using the photos as research data in and of themselves. Petersen and Østergaard illustrate the process of conducting Group Photo Views, drawing out the various methodological issues, problems, and potential of this approach in studying knowledge management.

Continuing this theme, in Chapter 11 Sisse Siggard Jensen explores reflective practices and "knowing in action" through the interpretive lens of "video-views"—digital video data. Based on her analysis of 22 video-views that capture the dynamics surrounding knowledge sharing in a development department, Jensen presents three stories that provide insights into the department's professional practice when "running code" within the context of a complex IT project. The chapter explores the intricate system of knowledge sharing and learning practices as they unfold within a series of knowledge zones that emerge and evolve through the observations and interactions of the developers and managers.

Jensen's descriptions reveal the multifaceted interaction between explicit and tacit knowledge among the developers, noting the critical task of bringing knowledge that is "out of context" (e.g., explicit documentation in programmer "bibles") into context through shared experience and programmer intuition (the tacit knowledge that creates the code). As she suggests, however, such intuition and tacit knowledge are of limited organizational use without the ability to explain and document that knowledge within its new context, in essence making the code explicit once again. Jensen traces the ensuing development and exchange through a complex system of organizational knowledge zones, underscoring the need to build such learning into professional practice.

In Chapter 12, Mette Mønsted explores how knowledge-based organizations involved in innovation and product development utilize an array of strategies to exchange knowledge and create meaning from that knowledge. Her analysis focuses on small high-tech firms and how they manage their R&D processes, dealing with internal complexity and external relations through an entrepreneurial leadership and communication style. Drawing on these insights, she argues that the ways in which these smaller firms manage their projects under high levels of uncertainty can help us to better understand the challenges faced by product development units in larger knowledge-based firms, especially communities of practice working on the "boundary of knowledge."

Drawing on a series of video-scenes, Mønsted illustrates the fundamental differences between knowledge at the organizational ("what a firm knows") and individual ("who knows what") levels. The challenge of capturing organizational knowledge and sharing that knowledge across individuals and project teams (which she describes as "loosely-coupled networks") underscores the role of power and leadership. She suggests that traditional project management tactics, which are based on linear thinking and concrete production tasks, fall well short of the demands posed by the complex, parallel development of tools and applications that she observed. The chapter concludes with an assessment of how entrepreneurial behaviors in smaller firms can provide insight into ways to enhance communication across these communities of practice and appropriate managerial roles and interventions for managing knowledge workers.

REFLECTIONS ON KNOWLEDGE MANAGEMENT AND MANAGEMENT CONSULTING

This final section contains four chapters that delve into the theoretical underpinnings of knowledge and knowledge management, drawing out the ramifications for the management consulting arena. In Chapter 13, Stephen Gourlay and Andrew Nurse offer a critical analysis of Nonaka's popular theory of organizational knowledge creation—the SECI model (i.e., modes of knowledge conversion: socialization, externalization, combination, internalization). They argue that although the SECI framework has been increasingly cited since its publication, the core of the theory is flawed. After noting some partial criticisms of this framework, Gourlay and Nurse examine the survey and case study evidence on which it is based, concluding that this material does not support the theory.

As part of their analysis, Gourlay and Nurse also examine the key theoretical assumptions and ideas underlying the SECI model, focusing particularly on tacit knowledge, the SECI process of knowledge conversion, and Nonaka's definition of knowledge. They conclude that although the theory has been of heuristic value, a new approach to knowledge creation is needed if we are to learn *whether* and, if so, *how* knowledge might be managed. They call for systematic reviews of existing KM research, with a view to determining the extent to which new areas are actually being studied—drawing out their dimensions and characteristics—as a way of expanding our understanding of this complex area.

Continuing this theme, Chapter 14 by Nicolas Rolland, Alice Guilhon, and Georges Trepo reflects on the last decade of KM research and practice. Rolland and his colleagues provide a synthesis of the contributions of

KM researchers and practitioners, providing insights into the gap between theoretical approaches and practitioner perspectives. The authors trace the progression of knowledge management through several key stages, from explorations of the concept of knowledge, its dimensions, and its role, to how knowledge can be shared and its relation with organizational learning and strategy formation, to knowledge's social networks and the concomitant need to nurture communities of practice and manage organizational space.

Drawing on their own 5-year study of KM practice in 102 international companies, Rolland and his colleagues explore the underlying organizational motivations, strategies, foci, and expectations for KM initiatives. They argue that there is still a wide gap between KM intent and practice, pointing to the need to fully integrate organizational structure, culture, management practices, and related tools with desired outcomes and results. As they conclude, however, the KM field is continuing to evolve, progressing from being a search for information toward becoming a management philosophy based on a realization of the importance of communicating, sharing, and disseminating information and knowledge throughout the organization.

In Chapter 15, Peter Holdt Christensen questions the value of theoretical perspectives on knowledge management, raising the issue as to whether KM theory really adds value to the practice of managing knowledge. Based on a content analysis of 50 recent journal articles on knowledge management, Christensen explores seven KM outcomes: integrating (exploiting existing knowledge), producing (increasing productivity), creating (innovation and new ideas), transferring (dissemination), measuring (efforts to link initiatives with outcomes), retaining (documenting knowledge and keeping organizational members), and reflecting (concept building). He also identifies a number of central KM drivers from a theoretical perspective and compares them with the drivers that managers identify as important for KM success.

As Christensen argues, from a theoretical perspective KM is conceptualized in almost endless ways, and he questions whether the burgeoning work in this area enhances practitioner understanding of knowledge management or simply increases their confusion. Comparing his theory-based content analysis with visual images of KM held by practicing managers (see the earlier section on methodological approaches), he suggests that theorists and practitioners generally point to the same KM drivers but at different levels of abstraction. For example, while theorists emphasize the critical role of trust, culture, and social ties, practitioners point to more practical enablers that reflect these concepts—ongoing social relationships with coworkers, facilitative social structures, and seminars. He also found that practicing managers have a difficult time differentiating between KM initiatives and other organizational activities, since the two blend together in practice. As he concludes, there is reason to believe that KM theory does reflect its practice, but there is still ample room for improvement.

In the final chapter, Hans Siggard Jensen explores an issue that often emerges when discussing knowledge and the knowledge-based claims made by consultants—the difference between research and consulting. Looking at the similarities and differences between the practice of medicine (as done by the general practitioner) and management consulting, Jensen examines two different modes of knowledge production: Mode 1, in which researchers provide the scientific theories that are applied by practitioners (as found in the medical model), and Mode 2, in which knowledge production and knowledge application are intertwined (as found in management consulting).

Using this distinction, Jensen argues that management consultants, through processes of reflection and analysis, tend to become researchers, while those researchers who are involved with actual problems tend to become consultants. This view, which he suggests is a Mode 2 partnership-type approach, can provide us with a new understanding of the relationship between research, knowledge, and consultancy. Because the problems in organizational life are seldom sufficiently simple to be solved by a single theory, we have to be able to handle a broad range of knowledge types. Jensen calls for a Mode 2 orientation to such knowledge production, emphasizing knowledge about *how* to do a certain thing, with insight into *what* is involved and *why* a given procedure works. As he concludes, while there may be a lingering preference for abstract conceptualization and model building as a basis for research, we need to move much closer to a Mode 2 approach to truly enhance knowledge in management consulting.

CHALLENGES AND ISSUES IN KNOWLEDGE MANAGEMENT

This volume has explored a range of challenges and issues about knowledge, knowledge sharing, and knowledge management in management consulting. Despite all the work that has been accomplished in this field, as Davenport (1999) has suggested, it is still not clear whether the KM realm is the "next fad" or "yesterday's fad."

As the chapters in this book have illustrated, knowledge is quite different from information, and the ability to share and utilize knowledge requires a rich array of concepts, tools, and processes. Knowledge flows through communities (McDermott, 1999) much more than it resides in databases and information systems. As Lissack (2000) suggests, perhaps we will ultimately realize that KM initiatives are best suited for the domain of the corporate anthropologist and architect rather than IT specialists and database managers. From a management consulting perspective, as the contributors to this book have underscored, this orientation has a number of ramifications for how we conceptualize and implement KM-related interventions.

Since new knowledge is suggested to be created "at the boundaries of the old" (McDermott, 1999, p. 109), it is our hope that the analyses and discussion in this volume have provided new insights into the theory and practice of knowledge management, especially in terms of how knowledge can be created, captured, shared, and utilized in a value-adding manner. We would like to thank the book's contributors for their good-natured colleagueship and willingness to accept our constant queries and proddings in moving this volume to completion. Our own knowledge and insights into the KM arena have been enhanced by their willingness to share their knowledge and insights into this complex and fascinating area. We hope that the volume has demonstrated that knowledge management in practice is about how managers and consultants put knowledge processes into action, and how they can facilitate and develop processes around knowledge creation, sharing, and application in organizational life.

REFERENCES

Alvai, M. & Leidner, D. E. (2001). Knowledge management and knowledge management systems: Conceptual foundations and research issues. *MIS Quarterly, 25*(1), 107–136.

Davenport, T. H. (1999). Knowledge management, round two. *CIO, 13*(5), 30–33.

Davenport, T. H., & Prusak, L. (2003). *What's the big idea? Creating and capitalizing on the best management thinking.* Boston: Harvard Business School Press.

Davenport, T. H., & Prusak, L. (2004). Knowledge management in consulting. In L. Greiner & F. Poulfelt (Eds.), *Handbook of management consulting: The contemporary consultant—Insights from world experts* (pp. 305–326). Mason, OH: Thompson South-Western.

Davis, C. (2004). A roadmap for long-term knowledge management success. *AIIM E-Doc, 18*(1), 36–38.

Drucker, P. F. (1995). *Managing in a time of great change.* Oxford: Butterworth Heinemann.

Dunford, R. (2000, August). *Key challenges in the search for effective management of knowledge in management consulting firms.* Paper presented at the Academy of Management, Management Consulting Division, Toronto.

Hansen, M. T., Nohria, N., & Tierney, T. (1999). What's your strategy for managing knowledge? *Harvard Business Review, 77*(2), 106–116.

Husted, K., & Michailova, S. (2002). Diagnosing and fighting knowledge-sharing hostility. *Organizational Dynamics, 31*(1), 60–73.

Kennedy Information. (2004). *The global consulting marketplace, 2004–2006: Key data, trends and forecasts.* Peterborough, NH: Kennedy Information Research Group.

Kerber, K. W., & Buono, A. F. (2005). Rethinking organizational change: Reframing the challenge of change management. *Organization Development Journal.*

Knowledge Management Review. (2001). A day in the life of a knowledge management practitioner. *Knowledge Management Review, 4*(5), 11.

Lissack, K. M. (2000). Knowledge management redux: Reframing a consulting fad into a practical tool. *Emergence, 2*(3), 78–89.

Management Consulting International. (2004a). How leading firms manage knowledge. *Management Consulting International,* 179 (August), 1, 3–5, 9.

Management Consulting International. (2004b). How leading firms manage knowledge. *Management Consulting International,* 180 (September), 1, 4–7.

McDermontt, R. (1999). Why information technology inspired but cannot deliver knowledge management. *California Management Review, 41*(4), 103–117.

McElroy, M. W. (2000). Integrating complexity theory, knowledge management and organizational learning. *Journal of Knowledge Management, 4*(3), 195–210.

Nonaka, I., & Takeuchi, H. (1995). *The knowledge-creating company: How Japanese companies create the dynamics of innovation.* New York: Oxford University Press.

Petersen, N. J., & Poulfelt, F. (2002). Knowledge management in action: A study of knowledge management in management consultancies. In A. F. Buono (Ed.), *Developing knowledge and value in management consulting* (pp. 33–60). Greenwich, CT: Information Age.

Polanyi, M. (1969). Tacit knowing: Its bearing on some problems of philosophy. In M. Grene (Ed.), *Knowing and being: Essays* (pp. 159–180). London: Routledge & Kegan Paul.

Ruggles, R. (1998). The state of the notion: Knowledge management in practice. *California Management Review, 40*(3), 80–89.

Sharif, A. M. (2002). Professional services organizations and the role of consulting in the new economy. *Information Systems Management, 19*(2), 19–30.

Shariq, S. Z. (1999). How does knowledge transform as it is transferred? Speculations on the possibility of a cognitive theory of knowledgescapes. *Journal of Knowledge Management, 3*(4), 243–251.

Skyrme, D. (1997). Knowledge management: Oxymoron or dynamic duo. *Managing Information, 4*(7), 24–26.

Sussman, S. W., & Siegal, W.S. (2003). Informational influence in organizations: An integrated approach to knowledge adoption. *Information Systems Research, 14*(1), 47–66.

Szulanski, G. (1996). Exploring internal stickiness: Impediments to the transfer of best practice within the firm. *Strategic Management Journal, 17*(Winter), 27–44.

Wah, L. (1999, May). Making knowledge stick. *Management Review,* pp. 24–29.

PART I

KNOWLEDGE MANAGEMENT AND THE MANAGEMENT CONSULTING INDUSTRY

CHAPTER 1

MANAGING ORGANIZATIONAL KNOWLEDGE NETWORKS IN A PROFESSIONAL SERVICES FIRM

Interrelating Knowledge Management and Intellectual Capital

Jan Mouritsen and Per Nikolaj Bukh

The professional services firm (PSF) is undoubtedly the example *par excellence* of a knowledge-based organization (Alvesson, 2004; Löwendahl, 1997; Sveiby, 1997). Its services are intangible, typically in the form of information or advice, and its employees are well educated with specialized, highly cognitive skills. Insight, reflexivity, and ideas are the main resources of production—and the main outcomes of the production process. As professional services firms, consultancies offer knowledge as a means to provide solutions to its customers, often with the goal of enhancing the profitability of the client firm. Since knowledge is essential for PSF growth and performance, management control activities are oriented toward allocating knowledge for an economic end. Firms also try to make knowledge and its related processes more manageable through the application of a variety of technologies and devices.

Challenges and Issues in Knowledge Management, 3–21
Copyright © 2005 by Information Age Publishing
All rights of reproduction in any form reserved.

Contemplating firms that exist in the so-called knowledge society, Drucker (1993, p. 7) formulated a major challenge for researchers as well as managers in knowledge-intensive firms: "How knowledge behaves as an economic resource we do not yet fully understand.... We need an economic theory that puts knowledge into the center of the wealth producing process." Drucker suggests that while knowledge is related to the production of wealth, how this is done in practice continues to escape our insights. Questions linger with respect to how the translation between knowledge (management) and wealth production actually takes place.

The chapter attempts to engage this question, as we focus on the translation between knowledge and wealth production, drawing out the distinction between knowledge management and intellectual capital. As part of this discussion, we distinguish between (1) the mechanics of developing, distributing, and interpreting information and knowledge, which we characterize as first-order knowledge management (KM), and (2) the control of knowledge resources through economizing, organizing, and modularizing knowledge, which reflects second-order KM concerns (Kreiner & Mouritsen, 2003: Mouritsen & Flagstad, 2004). As an illustration of these points, the chapter draws on material from COWI, a northern European consulting firm,[1] and its efforts to manage knowledge and develop intellectual capital statements.

The chapter begins with a brief overview of the role and functioning of knowledge in the context of intellectual capital. The discussion then turns to COWI as an example of an innovative approach to knowledge management and the implications for KM practices in professional services firms. When looking through the lens of intellectual capital, the individual seems to lose some glamour compared with KM rhetoric, as attention is increasingly placed on the development of a *constellation of knowledge resources* as a network rather than on the development of knowledge in and of itself.

KNOWLEDGE MANAGEMENT AND THE EFFECTS OF KNOWLEDGE

From a managerial perspective, knowledge is a peculiar resource. It is obviously important, especially in knowledge-based organizations. We could even argue that knowledge is "good" because more knowledge intuitively is better than less knowledge. Knowledge as such, however, is an abstraction without an object. Out of context, it is not clear exactly what it is that managers should do to effectively deal with "knowledge." Typically, therefore, the management problem—which might be thought of as first-order knowledge management—is framed in terms of how to find knowledge, share it, and/or store it rather than thinking about what actually constitutes knowledge.

This orientation toward knowledge raises a series of concerns about how knowledge can be managed. As suggested above, all too often the literature is oriented toward handling knowledge more than identifying its object. Nonaka (1994), for example, focuses on the relationship between tacit and codified knowledge and between personal and organizational knowledge. He and his colleagues (e.g., Nonaka & Takeuchi, 1995) describe four modes for knowledge conversion between tacit and codified knowledge, and arrive at the conclusion that knowledge can be managed either through socialization, externalization, combination, or internalization. The clear emphasis here is on the different possibilities of where knowledge is located and how it might be captured and shared rather than on the object of the knowledge. In Nonaka's view, tacit knowledge is the main source of creativity and motivation to engage, which is necessary for the knowledge-based organization to thrive. Yet, while this is an inspiring and compelling proposition, it is not clear that it will always work.

March (1991) distinguishes between exploration and exploitation, of which exploration reflects Nonaka's version of creativity, but he also cautions that creativity is a very difficult mode for a firm to constantly entertain (see also Kreiner, 2002). Since creativity develops new things—typically things that have not been seen before—such novelty, by definition, is often met with reluctance. A dominant sentiment in organization after organization is that the status quo works, so why change it. Since creativity can also be met by the response of stupidity, there can be personal costs to creative endeavors. March also suggests that creativity, if it works, can be detrimental to coordination and thus to productivity and coherence. If all processes are creative and in a state of flux, they can be unpredictable and unreliable. As such, they cannot be part of an organized setting. So, even if a certain amount of creativity is doubtlessly important, the organization would deteriorate if creativity were the only operating principle.

Similarly, if exploitation was introduced as the main principle for management and all processes were engineered to "best practices," there would be no learning. The organization would gradually stifle, and opportunities (e.g., in the form of introduction of new products, services, or processes) would be forgone. In practice, of course, it might be easier to accept some form of exploitation rather than exploration, because something that can be demonstrated by successful examples is more readily acceptable. However, we cannot know the consequences of forgone opportunities because the possible opportunity cost cannot be observed, only inferred.

The problem, therefore, is not just to strike a balance between exploration/creativity and codification/exploitation. To merely attempt to achieve an "optimal balance" between these perspectives is an insufficient proposition, largely since it appears to be a moralizing statement rather than a step toward a solution to see how processes of exploration and exploitation can function simultaneously in the organization. Conventional wisdom suggests that this is difficult or almost impossible to achieve. For example, Hansen, Norhia, and Tierney (1999) distinguish between a personification strategy and a codification strategy. They argue that some professional services firms are characterized by a repetitive set of tasks and could therefore benefit most from adopting a codification strategy of knowledge management, while others might benefit more from personalization. The authors suggest that the right mix depends on the markets in which the firms operate: a heterogeneous marketplace requires a personification strategy while a homogeneous set of customers and services makes a codification strategy more effective.

Both Nonaka's (1994) and Hansen and colleagues' (1991) suggestions imply that knowledge under different circumstances has different fundamental properties, and are thus different things that require different forms of management. Even if there are relationships between Nonaka's four modes of knowledge management and Hansen and colleagues' two types of strategies, they are still understood as having separate foci. Each of the forms has a separate existence from the others. But even when inscribed in processes and strategies, it is not possible to conclude that knowledge is an object, because when functioning in organizations—in essence, attempting to be productive—it becomes part of an extensive network of producers, users, mediators, gatekeepers, formalizers, doers, and destroyers, all of which keep certain kinds of insights and information in place organizationally, technologically, politically, and strategically.

No knowledge is "on hold," even if it is "waiting" in a technology or integrated into an IT system. Likewise, no knowledge could exist only as feelings, emotions, or cultural expressions. To suggest that the question of knowledge can be squeezed down to an ontological discussion, as is done in most of the literature on knowledge management, is to overlook the essential part of knowledge—the way it makes a difference. The further we take knowledge out of its context, the less likely we are to understand how it works. Rather, attention could be directed toward the process and networks where tasks are accomplished and where knowledge is embedded in something. When knowledge unfolds, its productive capabilities, which are inscribed by different "containers of knowledge," still have to operate on something else to make a difference. Knowledge is a process of applying, developing, and stabilizing certain insights at the same time. As Latour (1987, p. 248) eloquently argues:

> No one has ever observed a fact, theory or machine that could survive outside the networks that gave birth to them. Still more fragile than termites, facts and machines can travel along extended galleries, but they cannot survive one minute in this famous and mythical "out-thereness" so vaunted by philosophers of science.

The point is that knowledge exists in a network. This network is heterogeneous, incorporating a vast array of elements from people and facts, to intranets and extranets, to "small talk" and interpersonal exchanges. The elements cannot exist separately as containers, and therefore the challenge is to create a perspective that allows the *relationships* between these "containers of knowledge" to develop. This perspective must incorporate both the items of knowledge and the strategizing involved in developing and maintaining a purpose of the knowledge that has to be developed, applied, and stabilized. Otherwise, the network would have no orientation.

This is where intellectual capital—a second-order KM challenge—separates itself from our initial foci on (first-order) knowledge management. The idea of intellectual capital opens and incorporates more knowledge containers than was possible through a limited view of the mechanics of developing, distributing, and interpreting information and knowledge. It also provides knowledge with a purpose, whether strategic or political, and orients it toward effects that go beyond the mere accumulation of knowledge. By focusing on intellectual capital, knowledge is about making a difference to something or somebody. Within the context of professional services firms, the idea of intellectual capital goes beyond the limiting assumption that people occupy the central container of knowledge or that codified knowledge will only work in certain kinds of markets. Rather, it highlights that knowledge functions in a network, where facts, aspirations, employees, clients, stabilized insights, and other phenomena travel together—and this networked interaction is exactly that which makes knowledge powerful and enables it to be broadly disseminated.

KNOWLEDGE MANAGEMENT AND INTELLECTUAL CAPITAL AT COWI

COWI is a northern European consulting group that provides services within the engineering, environmental science, and economics fields. The organization has roughly 3,400 employees of whom approximately 2,100 are graduate engineers, planners, sociologists, biologists, doctors, agronomists, economists, and other university graduates. COWI is viewed as a knowledge-intensive firm because of its heavy reliance on people and their areas of specialization. The firm integrates various types of expertise, symbolized by its diverse employee backgrounds and skill sets, toward meeting client needs.

First-Order Knowledge Management Challenges

As depicted in Table 1.1, COWI's management has adopted an official policy that provides a good overview of its KM orientation. As its first principle, COWI heralds the primacy of its employees. It suggests that since knowledge development goes through employees, they have to be motivated and engaged. This, of course, was a challenge to organizations in the "pre-knowledge" society. Its focus is on stabilizing knowledge, since it favors an organizational space constituted by a more networked organization, where dialogue and collaboration are central. Managers are thus put under scrutiny to conduct a particular type of work, and the manager—not primarily the employee—is called to accountability.

The manager has to sustain a development focus through particular kinds of investments, whose objectives are to communicate values, secure

Table 1.1.   COWI's Principles of Knowledge Management

Sharper Focus on People

We regard knowledge management as the latest challenge to management. It is a concept that brings important changes to the traditional industrial and system-oriented management philosophy—changes that put a much sharper focus on people and their living and working conditions, their well-being and job satisfaction, and their potential for development. It is a concept that applies to client, employee, or any other interested party.

This shift in focus is, quite simply, essential if the dialogue with our clients is to function at its best and if we are to continue to give the best possible consultancy service. For us as consultants, knowledge lies at the very heart of the services we provide and is therefore our most important raw material. Ensuring our knowledge resources are developed optimally, therefore, is of particular importance.

Dynamic Interplay with the World

Knowledge is best developed by being applied and shared in a dynamic interplay with the world around us. Human relations and dialogue must be strengthened, first and foremost to create the greatest possible value for our clients.

But knowledge can only be disseminated through the staff. It is the individual employee who possesses that knowledge and experience that, taken together, represents our very reason for being. The introduction of knowledge management is an important step in our efforts to create the best possible framework for staff development and working life, at the same time as securing the platform for the Group's continued growth.

sharing of knowledge, make relevant information available, and ensure that corporate development and personal development are conducted simultaneously. Such ambitions put the employee at the heart of corporate strategy and suggest that employees constitute the only "raw materials" from which the firm can grow and prosper. This perspective is in line with the idea of the "knowledge-creating company" (Nonaka & Takeuchi, 1995).[2]

The second principle is that managers also have to include employees *outside* organizational work units and departments; to make them part not only of the organization but also relate them to the clients. Employees must experience clients' needs and must be encouraged and supported in interunit cooperation. Therefore, the notion of hierarchy is weak, and the manager has to be able to act on corporate rather than departmental or work unit goals and ambitions. The knowledge-based firm is in this exposition also an entity, where different kinds of alignments have to be performed simultaneously for corporate and individual development to be effectively integrated. This integration stems from two main integrative mechanisms: a focus on the client's needs and the capitalization of cross-specialization insight from the organization as a whole.

There are different orientations—and potential tensions—between these two KM principles. The first principle directs attention inward in the organization, as knowledge is presumed to be located in the employee. The supposition that knowledge is in the "heads of people" implies that the crucial management problem is to motivate people to use it properly. Thus, a central KM task becomes education, and people must be managed so they will be properly aligned with corporate objectives and development. Incentives to create knowledge sharing are therefore important concerns of managers.

The other principle implies that knowledge is oriented outside the person and, to some degree, outside the organization. Not all knowledge attracts the same kind of attention when an external element is added in the form of a client. The introduction of a client differentiates relevant and nonrelevant knowledge. Knowledge, according to the first principle, is in the person and has to pass a logic or objective criterion like "truth." The second criterion suggests that it also has to "perform" (i.e., to make sense) in the eyes of others. This kind of knowledge is not only personal, but also related to others' ambitions about what knowledge can or should be able to accomplish. Since clients would probably often want the firm to mobilize knowledge from different departments, suddenly the organizational mechanisms of knowledge integration become knowledge producers themselves. This principle indicates that integration mechanisms also perform knowledge services, and in particular they create new knowledge by combining and recycling existing knowledge. Within this context, managers' concerns focus on relating items of knowledge to each other.

The complexities involved by the second principle should not be underestimated, especially since important containers of knowledge exist beyond individuals per se. For example, relationships between employees and clients produce insights; relationships between employees across the firm create new knowledge; and relationships between various kinds of internal employees and clients give rise to yet new knowledge.

A new layer or dimension of creativity in the professional services firm is introduced here. Individual knowledge is rarely, if ever, acknowledged merely because it is most recent, most advanced, or the most true knowledge. Its relevance is not judged by its standing in terms of truth; individual knowledge, which is professional, is not surprisingly interesting if it has agreeable effects (e.g., for the development of client relations). It has to *perform* in the world rather than merely describe the world (Lyotard, 1984). This implies that expertise in the form of true technical knowledge and insights into a professional area do not suffice as adequate knowledge. The individual also has to know about clients, their needs, and organizational arrangements that allow knowledge development and sharing to take place. This includes, at the very least, that technical knowledge has to be intertwined with knowledge about corporate ambitions, so that the development of individuals' knowledge—even their technical knowledge—has to pass a test of relevance that then establishes the contours of performative knowledge, which may not always be true or best knowledge in a technical sense.

A lingering question focuses on how such complexities can be managed. COWI's KM guiding principles suggest this to be done through *dialogue*. The organization's culture brings coherence and direction to this dialogue. The organization becomes a place where people can experience each other, interact, and, importantly, act in situations of co-presence. Collective learning becomes an effect of learning opportunities pursued by individuals—employees and clients—who are engaged in learning activities made possible by the common understanding of the "rules of the game" established by a community of people. Such ambition is implied by COWI's management principles. However, the entire construct of integration through dialogue is founded on a fragile form of knowledge management. Learning exists only when a breach of community ambitions has been made—that is, when people experience a mismatch between what they do and what they are compelled to do by the situation they are in. Learning is thus developed locally and compared with cultural ideas of ambition and direction. Yet COWI seems to react negatively toward this notion of knowledge management, especially in the context of its intellectual capital ambition.

Intellectual Capital and Second-Order Knowledge Management

While first-order knowledge management is concerned with the mechanics that hold a community of inquirers together, intellectual capital adds a new dimension by creating a managerial agenda on the basis of the firm's knowledge resources. Thus, second-order knowledge management implies new types of questions that go beyond the sharing of knowledge among people. Rather, questions are raised about economizing (i.e., how much should be invested in knowledge development and sharing), organizing (i.e., where should knowledge be located), and modularization (i.e., what knowledge should be reused). When these questions are raised within the framework of an intellectual capital statement, they become managerially oriented issues.

While first-order knowledge management raises questions about relevance from the perspective of a culture—the certainty of a community—the intellectual capital statement focuses on relevance from the perspective of "reflexivity"—the uncertainty of the adequacy of performance. Reflexivity is a different mode of inquiry than what follows from the mere sensing of "disorder" in the community. Reflexivity characterizes and raises questions about the status quo, often with a view to its (possible) transformation. As Giddens (1990, p. 38) suggests, "The reflexivity of modern social life [is] that social practices are constantly examined and reformed in the light of incoming information about those very practices, thus constitutively altering their character." Consequently, information about knowledge is used to alter knowledge—it transforms practice.

The intellectual capital statement is a management technology aimed at allowing such reflexivity to occur. It does so by constructing a "non-community" image of the firm that presents it in a form that is outside the conventions of corporate culture. As such, it illuminates concerns about knowledge, not in terms of their fit with organizational culture or community, but with managerial questions based on insights that are partially decontextualized or at least removed from the cloud of groupthink that a community is likely to produce (Mouritsen & Flagstad, 2004).

As suggested in Table 1.1, COWI attempts to monitor its performance as part of its KM efforts, which creates this type of reflexivity. The monitoring system regarding intellectual capital is part of the organizational routines used for internal management purposes, but parts of it (as shown

Table 1.2. Quantification of COWI's Intellectual Capital Statement

Resource

	Budget 2003	Accounts 02/03	01/02	00/01
CLIENTS & MARKETS				
1 Public clients		45%	46%	45%
2 Semi-public clients	↑	14%	15%	16%
3 Private clients		31%	27%	24%
4 Other clients		10%	11%	15%
5 Number of clients		1,622	1,438	1,484
6 Projects abroad		29%	29%	30%
7 Clients abroad		15%	16%	17%
ORGANISATION				
13 Professional networks, number(*)	↑	49	45	32
14 Staff participating in professional networks(*)		20%	15%	13%
15 Best practise on the Intranet, number(*)	↑	964	894	773
16 Projects/employee, number		17	18	18
17 Ongoing projects, number		5,774	5,410	5,102
18 Average turnover/project (dkk '000)		1,157	1,030	1,010
STAFF				
29 Number of employees	↑	1,972	1,643	1,581
30 Average age		43.6	42.5	42.1
31 Length of education, year		6.4	6.6	6.7
32 Length of education, written down, year		4.3	4.5	4.6
33 Employees with highest education (PhD, etc.)		4.1%	4.7%	4.70%
34 Higher education: technical		52%	55%	56%
35 Higher education: natural sciences		5%	5%	4%
36 Higher education: social sciences		9%	9%	10%
37 Other higher education		4%	4%	5%
38 Work experience, year		15.4	16.1	16.2
39 Seniority in COWI, year		9.7	9.7	9.8
40 Project management capacity, all projects		58%	61%	57%
41 Project management capacity, major projects		35%	37%	37%
42 Project management capacity, international projects		24%	26%	27%

Processes

	Budget 2003	Accounts 02/03	01/02	00/01
8 Lectures/100 employees, number(*)	→	13	10	13
9 Professional publications/100 employees, number(*)		10	11	6
10 Client inflow		32%	16%	24%
11 Client outflow		19%	19%	8%
19 Inter-disc. cooperation; technical		18%	16%	16%
20 Inter-disc. cooperation; natural sciences		55%	51%	50%
21 Inter-disc. cooperation; social sciences		46%	45%	44%
22 Trade within COWI Group(*)	←	6.4%	3.5%	2.7%
23 Staff exchange with COWI Group		0.6%	0.7%	1.1%
24 Long-term postings	←	6.4%	2.8%	2.8%
25 Development activity, externally financed		5.9%	6.5%	4.2%
26 Development activity, internally financed		0.9%	1.2%	1.7%
43 International travelling experience in COWI	→	21%	28%	26%
44 Supplementary education(*)		0.6%	0.8%	1.1%
45 Staff inflow		31%	17%	17%
46 Staff outflow		11%	13%	11%
47 Travel abroad		6.0%	6.3%	6.4%

Results

	Budget 2003	Accounts 02/03	01/02	00/01
12 Media exposure, millions number(*)	→	149	110	131
27 QA audits completed/100 employees, No(*)	↑	2.3	5.7	5.0
28 Costs attributable to external faults(*)		0.4%	0.1%	0.3%
48 Staff satisfaction index(*)		67.7%	n/a	68.0%
49 Sick leave		2.5%	2.7%	2.6%
50 Staff owning COWI shares (*)	↑	48%	62%	70%
51 Engineering students' preferred place of work, no.(*)	2/1	3/2	5/1	2/2
52 Business students' preferred place of work, no.(*)	207	309	36/11	50/13

in Table 1.2) are also communicated externally as part of the company's annual report.

The intellectual capital statement in Table 1.2 presents a new expression of knowledge management. First, it defines a framework of interest, which is larger than the one stipulated in COWI's KM policies (Table 1.1). A series of new objects have been added that go beyond employees per se focus on two additional types of resources or knowledge containers: customer relations and organizational processes. While the principles outlined in Table 1.1 do mention them, their actual role in the overall KM framework is much more substantial in Table 1.2. Thus, COWI's intellectual capital statement suggests that knowledge is translated into knowledge resources, which are objects, or in our terminology containers of knowledge. These containers not only enable the circulation of knowledge, but they are also objects that can be acted upon from a managerial perspective. Suddenly, we see that knowledge is transformed from something in the heads of people to various types of bodies or containers.

The framework introduced with the intellectual capital statement also identifies three managerial challenges, differentiating resources, processes, and results. In general management language, it focuses on the constitution of a portfolio of knowledge resources (just like the financial balance sheet is interested in the constellation of assets and liabilities), the investments in process improvement (just like the financial statement talks about investments), and outcomes (just like the financial statement pinpoints financial effects). The intellectual capital statement thus superimposes a set of general management questions on KM efforts.

Second, the intellectual capital statement creates a grid that allows the organization to quantify its resources. For each knowledge resource, the grid numerically captures these three managerial concerns (resources, processes, results), and the firm is provided with documentation that, over time, indicates the direction and magnitude of development. The statement allows a general reading of what is going on and provides a decontextualized understanding (i.e., from outside the community or the culture) of the current state of affairs.

Looking at the indicators in Table 1.2, the firm appears stable, especially in terms of client relationships and employee resources. At the same time, the organization's intranet seems to encompass more and more best practices. The portfolio, thus, indicates an effort to try to stabilize knowledge as best practices. Examining the investments in processes, there is more uncertainty in the client portfolio than might be initially apparent, because the separate indications of in- and outflows of clients suggest more clearly that the firm's relations with clients are constantly in flux and are being reformed. This introduces a measure of risk in understanding the portfolio of customers. Furthermore, the low level of intrafirm processes is somewhat surprising, especially considering the ambition of the firm stated in its KM principles (Table 1.1).

Third, management is able to use the intellectual capital statement to indicate (through the use of arrows in Table 1.2) where changes are desired, focusing on the need for more international and private sector clients, more engagement in networks outside the firm, more attention to the intranet, and more media attention. Obviously this focus goes well beyond first-order KM activities. From the perspective of second-order knowledge management, the firm is networked. The intellectual capital statement expands knowledge management from a relatively narrow focus, offering a broader view so that the client and the network are central parts of the firm's KM activities.

These three observations characterize how intellectual capital or second-order knowledge management can work. By inscribing knowledge resources and making them amenable to analysis through quantification, knowledge is suddenly something that can be evaluated generally rather than only from the perspective of the organizational culture favored by first-order knowledge management. Thus, in the intellectual capital statement knowledge is presented in a way that allows an analytical interpretation of what is happening and what *could* happen in the KM arena. The intellectual capital statement also invokes a normative proposition, raising questions about *how* the firm develops its knowledge containers in which insight, information, and knowledge are found, shared, changed, critiqued, and integrated.

This approach and its quantification allow a decontextualized and general interpretation of the firm—just like an annual financial statement presents a one-sided and preliminary view of the firm's economic value. Thus, to be useful, the intellectual capital statement must also be interpreted and managed in an organizational context, which can raise significant challenges. As illustrated by COWI's intellectual capital statement:

1. The language of knowledge is connected with the language of growth and profitability. In analyzing the firm's project-management capacity, for example, it is suggested that "we will concentrate project management on relatively fewer key employees and thus optimize the use of project management experience." The challenge is to actually *optimize* "project management expertise" in practice.

2. A composition of capabilities and knowledge resources is presented as conducive to the changes in the marketplace: "our strategy is focused on international activities … [executed by] project management capacity on international assignments." This indicates that the specific challenges in putting knowledge together is

prioritized and that building certain capabilities are more important than other ones in the specific situation of the firm. In effect, not all types of knowledge are managerial concerns all the time.

3. The firm's new portfolio of potential employees indicates that "the survey of engineering students' preferred places of work ranks COWI in second place." While favorable, this perspective also suggests that individual employees are transformed from concrete individuals to elements in the labor market. The person becomes a type, and individual competency development is transformed into a portfolio decision.

These points are, of course, subject to interpretation. By drawing on this information in COWI's intellectual capital statement, our intent was to illustrate how knowledge can be structured, debated, and managed. In a sense, there is an element of displacement in this approach, where individuals' characteristics are developed into appendices of other things and transformed into a broader concern for the corporate agenda.

As knowledge is made "manageable," the individual becomes less significant and emphasis is increasingly placed on the knowledge fit with the corporate strategy. The person fits this framework, it increasingly appears, *if* he or she can understand the client and align his or her aspirations with those of the client. The person is viewed as particularly well functioning if he or she can operate in the context of the firm's best practices, becoming part of organizational capital—just like a particular category of people will be given background and training (knowledge) to become project managers. In this instance, project managers—not individuals—constitute the particular kind of capability that is able to form a network with the client, the organization, and its employees. Thus, knowledge management is taken out of the context of the individual and made a corporate concern through which the individual is interesting only for certain skills that make sense in a network involving other organizational entities, global competition, client structure, and the means of collaboration (e.g., in the form of information and project management systems) (Larsen & Mouritsen, 2001).

We see here a new form of reflexivity in relation to knowledge. The firm not only needs to be capable, but also capable of doing *something* (Mouritsen, Larsen, & Bukh, 2001). This "something" must be strategic, because it concerns what the firm is able to achieve with the competencies that it puts in place. This strategic focus, for example, could be a narrative about how knowledge functions in the firm, what its objectives and objects are, and what kinds of efforts (i.e., concrete KM mechanisms) should be put in place. This is the way that the intellectual capital statement can help to survey not only what knowledge *is*, but also how it *devel-*

ops. Concerns can then be raised as to the most interesting constellation of knowledge resources and their connections. This is, at least, what the intellectual capital statement "promises."

Looking at COWI's intellectual capital statement and its narrative (according to the principles introduced in the Danish guideline for intellectual capital statements; see Mouritsen, et al., 2003), for example, a number of relationships can be suggested. As discussed earlier, first-order knowledge management concerns developing, disseminating, and storing knowledge (i.e., the mechanics of knowledge creation and knowledge sharing). As a second-order KM technology, however, Table 1.3 focuses on the logic of knowledge and creates a strategy for what knowledge is to accomplish and how that knowledge narrative, as well as a set of durable management challenges, unfolds. Together these elements outline COWI's business model of knowledge, a set of first-order KM efforts and a set of associated indicators. The business model and first-order KM activities place knowledge management firmly within the culture of organizational learning and require knowledge sharing in a community. Here knowledge is embedded. The indicators do quite different things. They disembed KM concerns because they distance them from the culture/community and introduce a new layer of reflexivity. The numbers speak more to a general "production function," where general questions about development in the portfolio of knowledge resources, the development of investments in developing knowledge, and the development of effects can be raised. These concerns are not tied to the specific organizational culture or community; they speak more generally to resources possessed in principle by any firm.

Table 1.3 illustrates a translation of the intellectual capital statement. It creates a framework, which interacts with the reader's logic, to question the extent to which the firm is well functioning, successful, and sustainable. As a way of guiding an analysis of these indicators, COWI presents the purpose of intellectual capital as the development of an appreciation of the user's value of the service through a particular offering that requires certain knowledge resources. The presentation in Table 1.3 explains how the translation between this ambition and certain activities takes place. The ambition to create "interdisciplinary solutions," for example, translates into such management objectives as "cooperation with the customer," "project management," and "knowledge sharing." These initiatives, in turn, translate into specific management mandates, such as the need to "develop markets," "increase cooperation between groups," and "control quality." These initiatives can then be visualized by a series of indicators that reflect the actions, such as "customer profiles," "level of interdisciplinary cooperation," and "quality audits." The translations show how these ideas are actualized, and the various elements help

Table 1.3. Second-order Knowledge Management in COWI

Knowledge Narrative	Durable Management Challenge	Actions	Indicators/Information
Use value (purpose) COWI offers interdisciplinary solutions integrating engineering, finance, and the environment by combining front-line competencies in these fields	Supply of "total and complete" solutions in close contact with customers	Develop international and international private markets	• Customer profile • Proportion of international customers • Proportion of international projects
		Enhance image with customers	• Number of speeches • Number of articles • Customer satisfaction
	Competent handling of project activities	Increase cooperation among group companies	• Interdisciplinary cooperation (time) • Cross-organizational cooperation (time) • Intergroup trade
Service/product COWI supplies comprehensive consulting services--analysis, planning, and design		Improve project management processes	(no indicator)
		Improve development processes	(no indicator)
Knowledge resources In order to supply these services we need a high level of disciplinary competencies and the ability to combine them into an interdisciplinary solution		Install quality control at all organizational levels	• Quality audits • Number of errors and expenses
		Optimize management systems	(no indicator)
	Mix of competencies and skills	Make internal and external competencies visible	• # Internal and external networks • # Best practices • Staff educational profile • Staff experience

to refine and redefine each other. As proposed by COWI, for example, we can trace how "interdisciplinary solutions" relate to "quality audits" and ultimately in turn to quality management initiatives.

KNOWLEDGE MANAGEMENT AND INTELLECTUAL CAPITAL IN PROFESSIONAL SERVICES FIRMS

The COWI case illustrates a dilemma in managing knowledge resources in professional services firms. The translation between first- and second-order knowledge management centers on the extent to which a firm's knowledge managers can (or should) allow individuals to be categorized as a "production resource." An organizational member, as part of a firm's intellectual capital, is only meaningful when he or she is part of a broader network of concern. This does not mean that a professional services firm will not benefit from looking at the quality of its staff. It just means that the very idea of staff quality depends on relationships with clients, other staff, organizational procedures, and even IT systems.

As illustrated by the COWI case, in this instance project management was a central factor in understanding how individuals are attached to other objects both inside and outside the firm. Project management capabilities, of course, may not be universally the critical KM challenge in all professional services firms. Project management is singled out as a concern among other concerns, and reflects a prioritization of the possible ways in which knowledge can be developed in the firm. COWI's intellectual capital statement indicates that project management capabilities reflect a current barrier in the development of the firm's knowledge. Other possible avenues to develop knowledge are viewed as less rewarding in the situation. This can be seen from two things in the intellectual capital statement:

1. COWI lacks project management skills, particularly in international projects, which is the challenge to be addressed.
2. COWI has a good reputation in the eyes of students (possible employees) and therefore the labor market is seen as favorable.

The priorities in knowledge management can be analyzed and pointed out in this way, illustrating how the intellectual capital statement can help navigate between different types of efforts. In this instance, project management is seen as a current barrier, but recruitment is not a concern because there is a good supply of qualified candidates. Investments in project management are thus a managerial response to the situation. In other situations it may be that recruitment would be singled out as a domain for managerial concern. The intellectual capital statement helps to identify priorities in the management of knowledge resources. Therefore, the intellectual capital statement becomes a means to make priorities and decisions about the development of knowledge management, and it helps to prioritize the various courses of action that can be pursued.

The employees in a professional services firm are typically highly educated. Looking at the descriptive statistics of COWI, the number of such educated and skilled employees approaches 3,400. Although this has been taken as a signifier of a firm's knowledge base and intensity, the chapter suggests that the KM challenges facing the professional services firm are far more complex. This recognition marks the differences between what we have referred to as first- and second-order knowledge management:

1. Rather than seeing the individual as the object of management of knowledge, the network of knowledge resources, including both human and nonhuman objects, should be recognized.

2. Rather than mainly focusing on the cultural-based community of people, attention should be directed to the networks between different parties inside or outside the community—and to what the network implies.

3. Rather than merely suggesting that knowledge development is an end goal, there should be attention to how knowledge makes a difference.

4. Rather than accepting that knowledge is manageable only as processes involving people, knowledge management should also be oriented toward management concerns that emphasize economizing, organizing, and modularizing knowledge.

5. Rather than suggesting that knowledge about the firm's knowledge base can only be captured by intuition and reflection, attention should also be placed on a KM portfolio that attempts to capture and quantify a firm's knowledge resources—thus enhancing reflexivity.

In the transition from first- to second-order knowledge management, the professional services firm will experience disruptions and surprises. It is a novel approach in people-intensive firms, especially where the employee has traditionally been the center of concern. Even if some aspects of second-order knowledge management are present in many professional service firms, they are generally not fully implemented. Of course, some critics might argue that this approach to knowledge and knowledge management is not needed. On the other hand, this perspective could translate knowledge management into a more reflexive praxis that addresses Drucker's (1993, p. 7) question about how knowledge behaves as an economic resource. If this is the case, perhaps the development of the professional services firm would be far more professional.

NOTES

1. Further information on the COWI can be found at www.cowi.dk.
2. Our description of COWI is clearly a simplification of the multitude of activities that go on in relation to knowledge management and intellectual capital. However, our analysis is designed to make the points clear rather than to cover all the practices that a full coverage of COWI would require. We pay only scant attention to the particulars of COWI's "best practices," knowledge-sharing practices, competency databases, project information databases, internal networks, project-management courses, and so forth. We suggest that these are all part of the elements that make up the intellectual capital of the firm, but we do not show in detail how they work as practices. These are items of knowledge management that are made to cohere through intellectual capital, as we explain in the chapter.

REFERENCES

Alvesson, M. (2004). *Knowledge work and knowledge-intensive firms.* Oxford: Oxford University Press.

Drucker, P. (1993). *Post-capitalist society.* Oxford: Butterworth-Heinemann.

Giddens, A. G. (1990). *The consequences of modernity.* Stanford, CA: Stanford University Press.

Hansen, M. T., Norhia, N., & Tierney, T. (1999). What's your strategy for managing knowledge? *Harvard Business Review, 77*(2), 106–116.

Kreiner, K. (2002). Tacit knowledge management: The role of artifacts. *Journal of Knowledge Management, 6*(2), 112–123.

Kreiner, K., & Mouritsen, J. (2003). Knowledge management as technology: Making knowledge manageable. In B. Czarniawska & G. Sevon (Eds.), *The northern lights* (pp. 223–248). Copenhagen: Copenhagen Business School Press.

Latour, B. (1987). *Science in action.* Milton Keynes, UK: Open University Press.

Larsen, H., & Mouritsen, J. (2001). Videnledelsens 2. bølge: En recentrering af videnledelsen gennem videnregnskabet. *Ledelse & Erhvervsøkonomi, 65*(1), 5–16.

Lyotard, J.-F. (1984). *The postmodern condition: A report on knowledge.* Manchester, UK: Manchester University Press.

Löwendahl, B. (1997). *Strategic management of professional service firms.* Copenhagen: Handelshöjskolens Forlag.

March, J. G. (1991). Exploration and exploitation in organizational learning. *Organization Science, 2*(1), 71–87.

Mouritsen, J., & Flagstad, K. (2004). Managing learning and intellectual capital. *International Journal of Learning and Intellectual Capital, 1*(1), 72–90.

Mouritsen, J., Larsen, H. T., & Bukh, P. N. (2001). Intellectual capital and the "capable firm": Narrating, visualizing and numbering for managing knowledge. *Accounting, Organizations and Society, 26*(7), 735–762.

Mouritsen, J., Bukh, P. N., Flagstad, K., Thorbjørnsen, S., Johansen, M. R., Kotnis, S., Larsen, H. T., Nielsen, C., Kjærgaard, I., Krag, L., Jeppesen, G., Haisler, J., & Stakemann, B. (2003). *Intellectual capital statements: The new guideline.* Copenhagen: Ministry of Science, Technology and Innovation. Available at www.vtu.dk/icaccounts

Nonaka, I. (1994). A dynamic theory of organizational knowledge creation. *Organization Science, 5*, 14–37.

Nonaka, I., & Takeuchi, H. (1995). *The knowledge-creating company.* Oxford: Oxford University Press.

Sveiby, K. E. (1997). *The new organizational wealth: Managing and measuring knowledge-based assets.* San Francisco: Berrett-Koehler.

CHAPTER 2

KNOWLEDGE MANAGEMENT IN PRACTICE

Examining Knowledge as Modes of Production

Anne Bang

"Nothing disturbs a Bishop as much as having a saint in his diocese ...
Bishops within all religions praise the dynamic quality
with all kinds of static statements, as demanded by culture.
But these statements become as gilded wins, which are hanged on a living tree,
they close out the sunlight and in the end strangles it."

—R. M. Pirsig (1991, p. 416)

Very frequently one sees such slogans as "Knowledge is the road to the future" or "Knowledge is our competitive advantage." In fact, knowledge has become one of, if not *the* most important, components in contemporary society. While discussions about the true nature and character of knowledge can be traced back to early Greek writing, knowledge management (KM) has only recently become a popular field of interest to both academic scholars and business practitioners. Yet, based on the number of books, journals, and articles dedicated to the subject—which have multi-

Challenges and Issues in Knowledge Management, 23–49
Copyright © 2005 by Information Age Publishing

plied substantially over the past decade—KM is clearly among the fastest growing concepts in the management literature.

Knowledge management has developed into a rather easily recognized discourse, in which we continuously incorporate such concepts as knowledge managers, knowledge departments, knowledge consultants, and knowledge processes, products, objects, and services. These institutionalized configurations are seen as specific approaches to improving objectives and attempts to solve (almost any kind of) problem in modern organization. It is even argued that in order to further improve or maintain competitive advantages in complex and dynamic markets, companies need to fundamentally alter the ways in which they manage knowledge (cf. Davenport & Prusak, 2000; Nonoka & Takeuchi, 1995; Nonaka, Toyama, & Boyosiére, 2001). However, in many cases the extended focus on knowledge or even an entire reevaluation of the organization from a knowledge-based perspective fails to lead to the intended and stipulated results (Fahey & Prusak, 1998).

The theoretical field occasionally offers new definitions and typologies in order to deal with and arrange the chaotic reservoirs of company knowledge—in the context of what is referred to as the *knowledge society*. Many have argued that the knowledge society reflects turbulence, change, and complexity, and *knowledge* itself is a fluid, immaterial mix of everything from past experience, personal and company values, written material, qualifications, and competencies, to the ability to learn new things. The new challenge of modern organization is thus to become better at leveraging this complicated mix and its competitive advantages, upon which new forecasts, predictions, and plans can be made.

One of the main contributors to the practical arrangement of KM thus far is the consulting industry. Here, KM has largely been undertaken and conceptualized as a product/service, used both as an internal solution and an external sales tool. Theoretical definitions, typologies, and techniques are used, and new tools, guidelines, and empirical models are developed on the basis of (or desire to become) new best practices.

KNOWLEDGE MANAGEMENT IN PRACTICE

By drawing on case material from one of the market leaders within the KM field, with particular emphasis on a consulting department in the firm, the chapter examines tensions and challenges underlying different approaches to knowledge management. At the firm level, the company sought to establish clarity, transparency, and stability on a global level. From an analytical perspective, the chapter focuses on the central elements in this systematic model that facilitate an identification of key KM challenges. Since the firm's comprehensive model was also widely recognized as a "best practice" in the KM field, the discussion will also briefly touch on the concept of *best practice* and its implications for KM initiatives. As will be discussed, without significant effort to analyze the unique company conditions and its modes of production, "best practice" will simply become yet another rigid and abstract reductionism.

The case data point to two decisive elements in creating new KM processes: the need to (1) alter the firm's system of time evaluation and (2) recreate an employee-driven knowledge forum. First, altering a firm's system of time evaluation involves the definition of and distinction between "productive time" (utilization) and "nonproductive time." The idea of "productive time" must be expanded to include time spent working on KM-related activities, even if those activities are not directly linked to fulfilling client needs. Second, employee involvement through the recreation of a knowledge forum that focuses on knowledge-related problems in that particular organization enables the firm to detect and analyze problems with respect to the specific organizing of the company and its modes of knowledge production. This effort frees knowledge management from a universal solution, moving KM efforts closer to very specific, local, and constantly moving arrangements of production.

The analysis focuses on the unfolding knowledge strategy of a global consulting company, with an emphasis on (1) the *aspects* of knowledge that were intended to be created and leveraged and (2) *how* this task was initiated and managed. The discussion explores the tensions between the initial intent of the KM initiative (global knowledge production) and the pressures and concerns—which reflected organizational, cultural, and technological differences—at the local level.

A brief discussion of KM concepts from a few central academic scholars (Davenport & Prusak, 2000; Nonaka & Takeuchi, 1995) follows the case analysis. The discussion will explore the concepts of *knowledge, change,* and *process* as they are transformed from academic concepts to an operational level. Drawing on the theoretical contributions of Chia (1996, 1999, 2003) and Styhre (2003), it will be argued that these concepts (*knowledge, change,* and *process*) are problematically reduced within much of the KM literature, which makes it difficult to effectuate the goals suggested by the KM literature in practice.

The chapter concludes with an exploration of the dangers of implementing KM systems as a shortcut to "solve" the complex organizational problems concerning knowledge. As many organizations have experienced already, when KM is formalized on an operational level it naturally reduces knowledge into a mere object or commodity, which can (1) create severe practical problems in changing and complex environments, and

(2) constrain knowledge production to the short-sighted lens of instrumentality.

A Leading KM System in a Global Consulting Firm: Global Intensions and Local Problems

In the beginning of the 1990s, knowledge management was a fairly new discourse, and Global Consulting[1] (GC) was viewed as one of the field's pioneers. The company had just launched a strategic plan in which knowledge management had been identified as a key component of the consulting firm's corporate strategy. The focus on KM was intended to give Global Consulting a sustainable competitive advantage by better leveraging its own intellectual capital and, as a result, better meet its consultants' and clients' knowledge needs. These anticipated advantages were linked to a new technological infrastructure that connected individual consultants to GC's "KnowNET," which included a repository of over 100 "powerpacks" (an enormous clearinghouse of knowledge), online contact to a network of subject-matter experts, and a central clearinghouse of tools and methodologies.

An organizational infrastructure was also created that separated GC's KM strategy into three main knowledge centers. These three centers were to become the core of the firm's KM system. One center was responsibile for *generating new knowledge*. Another was responsible for *translating knowledge into methods and automated tools*, and the GC Department of Knowledge Management (DKM) was tasked with *gathering, storing*, and *synthesizing* the firm's *internally generated* knowledge as well as *external* knowledge and information.

Later in the process, the technological infrastructure was supported by implementing Departments of Knowledge Management (DKM) in the local countries with additional sets of knowledge roles, knowledge responsibilities, and knowledge assignments in order to support the development of a knowledge culture. Apart from a local Knowledge Manager in each country, approximately six to eight knowledge workers were employed in the Danish DKM. Two to three of the knowledge workers were to assist the Consulting Department, whereas the rest were assigned to the Audit Department.

Denmark's Local Center of Business Knowledge: Knowledge as Commoditized Objects

At the end of the 1990s, Global Consulting had an almost fully implemented KM system in Denmark that was connected to the firm's global KM system, which was primarily located in the three centers in the United

States. The local Department of Knowledge Management (DKM) was created with the mission to secure professional local service and implement centralized initiatives (e.g., maintain KnowNET, ensure that knowledge bases containing tools and methodologies were continually updated) in Denmark.

One of the services provided by Denmark's DKM was *business research and analysis*. The center created reports on specific subjects, clients, competitors, or markets, and gathered specific information on request. The time spent by the DKM on each internal client was tracked and billed accordingly. The DKM's success was measured by its amount of billable time—and DKM's utilization rate was 33%. As costs were connected to DKM's service, most orders had to be discussed with the appropriate department manager, which resulted both in fewer requests by the end of the day and also some service denials. This led to a lower rate of support than was initially intended.

Another problem, especially among the consultants, was the time gap between the need for the information and the time it was finally provided. The employees in Denmark's DKM often had requirements at the last minute, and without very clear and precise requests, what was typically provided at short notice fell well short of what was needed and expected. As a result, paying for a service that failed to meet their needs and requirements further contributed to low usage of the service.

A Clearinghouse of Company Knowledge: Intent versus Reality

The employees at Denmark's DKM were also faced with the challenge of *knowing about* GC's knowledge (i.e., *what* was being stored and *where* the information was housed). Since the GC knowledge base had over 100 powerpacks, each one filled with filtered knowledge about specific topics—including the company's best work products, such as proposals and deliverables from previous client engagements—and a repository with over 30,000 unfiltered documents, such insight amounted to a rather large, frustrating, and often impossible task. In the different departments of GC's consulting arm, the sheer amount of information and the difficulty of working through the system resulted in the development of department-specific databases. Since these databases were part of the consultant's personal interface rather than part of the global infrastructure, Denmark's DKM unit was of little assistance in dispersing and transferring usable database information across the departments. Thus, the local databases were used for storing information and the global Know-NET system (including powerpacks, information links, and leading practices) was mainly used to draw information from.

Locating and Submitting Knowledge Objects: Decontextualized Objects

The local databases also confronted the employees at Denmark DKM with other problems. Denmark DKM was expected to assist consultants with the local submission process of information into the global infrastructure. But since each department had its own separate database to store documents, it didn't push the consultants to go through the difficult and laborious task of submitting their information into the global infrastructure. In addition, the Danish engagement documents were rarely written in English, which further limited their utility in the global database. Moreover, it was necessary to have sufficient knowledge about the systemic order of categories and topics to submit information into the system, which further compounded the problem. Thus, there would often be a discrepancy between Danish and U.S. consulting assignments.

A similar problem existed in the use of specific objects—often referred to as "knowledge" objects (e.g., tools, techniques, models, PowerPoint presentations, and reports) in the system. If a consultant wanted to use one of these objects, he or she was faced with language barriers and cultural differences in how and where the information would be categorized. Though many initiatives from the United States were made precisely to equalize differences, Danish and U.S. approaches were often quite different in practice. Thus, what might be considered as identifiable knowledge in one context was seen as largely incomprehensible, with many meanings, in another. Yet the basic issue of relying on clear, transparent, and well-understood language as a founding KM system premise, especially in global firms, is something that is not fully discussed in the KM literature. Even when an attempt is made to ensure such consistency, dependence on translation, interpretation, and reduction of natural language remains a problem. In this instance, it resulted in very few submissions from the Danish consulting group that were intended to renew the global knowledge base.

Barriers to Organizational and Cultural Knowledge Initiatives

Apart from the implementation of local DKMs, another important initiative in building the GC knowledge culture was the implementation of a balanced scorecard model and the implementation of different knowledge roles. The balanced scorecard model was founded on the identification of five mega-processes: strategy, service, sales, people, and knowledge. These mega-processes were implemented as a central part of the firm's Performance Evaluation Review (PER) system, across all levels of the hierarchy. Performance indicators were measured out on the company level, department level, and on an individual level in alignment with the mega-processes. On a company level, this indicates that the firm was trying to broaden its business focus both internally and externally to include other variables that were just as important as *sales* and *service*. Each department had concrete sales goals, which were also identifiable for some of the consultants (not all consultants had direct sales goals). On a personal level, the consultants discussed their assignments and goals in each of these mega-processes with their department manager. Additionally, it was relatively easy to identify measurable goals on the service level—each consultant was expected to reach a level of 75% billable time.

When it came to identifying measurable goals with respect to *people* and *knowledge* processes, however, it was much more difficult. Since sales and service were still regarded as the two most important processes, the identification of goals for the people and knowledge processes were naturally seen as less important. As a result, consensus began to emerge as to the number of knowledge objects that should be submitted, the amount of time that should be spent on people and knowledge forum activities, and even the importance of being updated on one or several themes or areas within one's service area. A related outcome was the potential to become a *subject-matter expert* (SME)—one of the new roles that were created in accordance with the overall GC KM system.

Apart from the knowledge manager and knowledge workers at Denmark's DKM, employees and managers were recognized and announced as SMEs on both a global level and local country level. As SMEs, these individuals were identified according to their knowledge about a specific topic, which could be a tool, a method, an industry, or a business area. These individuals and their topic of expertise were listed in the technological infrastructure to enable other consultants to quickly get in direct contact with an appropriate SME when facing a problem or question when dealing with a client. While such expert systems have an initial appeal, the GC experience points to their underlying difficulties. Apart from the basic (and often problematic) time lag between posting a question and receiving an answer, Davenport and Prusak (2000, p. 137) suggest that a related difficulty is "that it can be difficult to extract knowledge from an expert in the first place—either because the expert doesn't know what he or she knows or because he or she doesn't want to surrender the knowledge." Even though it is recommended by Davenport and Prusak that users of expert systems engage in a "dialogue" with the system, in essence, entering information about a problem or situation implies that *knowledge* is something that one person can choose to give away as an object, resource, or commodity and can likewise be received as such by another person.

However, on an operational level and in order for such a system to have a chance of having a practical impact, there are myriad unresolved issues and questions. What is in fact an expert? Can someone be an expert in knowledge management? And, if so, is the *expert* then an expert in the

KM process, in managing the KM process, in KM implementation, or in KM preinvestigation? Is that "expert" also an expert with respect to all company sizes, in all industries, and in all cultures in one or several of these topics? While it might appear attractive both to clients and internal organizational members that the company has a large number of SMEs, the low level of use of the GC system was linked with its inherent limitations. In reality, very few questions were seen as appropriate to pursue or able to be sufficiently captured to put into the system, especially given that most of the problems were entangled in a specific complex organizational arrangement with its own unique texture. Such dynamics make it very difficult to become an *expert* in the first place. As a result, the system of global and local-level SMEs was rarely, if ever, used by the Danish consultants.

In line with the new processes and roles, a series of employee forums were put in place. The *Knowledge Forum* was intended to stimulate involvement, motivating employees by sharing knowledge ideas and initiatives and focusing on improving the overall knowledge processes in the company. The *Knowledge Forum* was to meet every month. The firm's time evaluation system, however, continued to distinguish between billable hours (productive time) and nonbillable hours (nonproductive time). Since utilization rate goals for the consultants were set at 75% of their time, any consultant who was busy with external projects did not have any incentive to prioritize nonbillable internal activities. As a result, the forums were regarded as unimportant, and it was more prestigious and advantageous to spend one's time on client-focused billable activities rather than on internal, nonbillable initiatives. In addition, the actual prospects of influence were considered to be very small, as the overall KM system together with most of the tools, models, and working standards, were pregiven from the United States and were not to be altered significantly.

The Challenge of KM Transfer

In the beginning of the new millennium, GC sold its worldwide Management Consulting (MC) groups. Global Consulting Denmark MC (Danish MC) was bought by a European company. As a result, Danish MC became more self-governing in respect to the internal organizing of the company than it had been under the overall influence of Global Consulting.

Being a part of a large global consulting company like Global Consulting contributed significant economies of scale to the Danish consulting department, especially in terms of exposure to large international clients, a well-known brand, and global marketing. In the wake of its divestiture from Global Consulting, the Danish firm now had to build up competences in a number of areas that had previously been taken for granted. The GC local Departments of Knowledge Management (DKM) in Denmark remained part of Global Consulting.

In this new institutional setting (the Danish MC), a large KM project was initiated together with several smaller KM initiatives as part of other focus areas, including economics, strategy, and business services. Business services and KM issues were of crucial importance, as company deliverables depended on the methodologies, tools, and knowledge developed independently by the newly acquired Danish firm. First steps in the KM process focused on mapping the KM process itself (e.g., what components did the knowledge process consist of) on a practical level. Here the entire *working process* of the consultant in his or her daily *practice* was taken as a point of departure. This was done in order to investigate whether the Global Consulting KM *process* in the overall Global Consulting KM *system* was in coherence with the Danish *practices*—or if it simply looked better than it worked.

The Concept of Best Practice

The second step in the KM initiative included two different levels of outlining methods, tools and "best practices." The first level concerned the methods and tools developed by Danish consultants in general and their "best" practices in particular. *What, which,* and perhaps *how much* could, in fact, be said to belong to the GC knowledge framework. An underlying question is when does an idea, technique, tool, or method become an independent "best practice," thereby separating itself from its original theoretical restriction and intellectual property right? This step suddenly made it very clear that there was a big difference between perceptions of "best practice" as gathered experiences concealed in different documents, notes, and reports, and "best practice" as something written down in method-like terms. This basic difference forced many of the business units to begin to write down their individual techniques, approaches, and experiences and make concrete decisions on what were essential business services. Many found that "best practice," as something that was frequently used in a daily common-sense manner in conversations with other consultants and clients, was actually very difficult to conceptualize and capture on paper. *What* was, in fact, variable and what was constant, especially in the context of different experiences from three or four projects under the same theme? What is the legitimate level of formalization? The same challenge or problem was also influencing the work of the KM project team on the company level. The KM project team was initially assigned with outlining what KM "best practices" were available for use and implementation in the company.

Outlining, using, and implementing such *best practice* may seem to be a relatively straightforward task, especially since this is done literally every day by consultants and is used throughout the business sector as a way of improving and implementing different activities. Moreover, as Davenport and Prusak (2000) suggest, focusing on such *best practices*—identified either inside or outside the company—is an effective way for companies to get started with knowledge management. Yet, while this approach may be popular and appear to provide a good foundation for building a KM system, most best practices–oriented KM programs only deal with those practices that are clearly articulated and documented. As Davenport and Prusak have suggested: "More tacit knowledge about how work is done is not easily summarized into a best practice, and broader knowledge management initiatives are usually required to incorporate certain kinds of complex expertise into organizational knowledge" (p. 169).

As noted earlier, Global Consulting's comprehensive KM system was largely regarded as a best practice. From the perspective of the Danish MC group, however, it was far from a best *local* practice, as it simply didn't work as prescribed or intended.

Although Davenport and Prusak's concern might initially seem to be little more than a detail, especially on a general level, they (2000, pp. 169–170) also argue that "firms should not underestimate the difficulties of importing best practices ... [as best practices] may be so contextual and specific to an organization that they don't take in their new environment." This point links to an additional problem in working with knowledge management from a *best practice* perspective: the tendency to focus implementation efforts on the model's broader elements, forgetting or leaving out the specific nature of assumptions and premises in a given company (i.e., the conditions under which something can be meaningfully effectuated or implemented). Leaving out the specific elements or the underlying *tacit knowledge*, which according to Davenport and Prusak (2000) is not easily summarized, is exactly what makes any model, tool, theory, or method "general." And as general knowledge, it becomes abstract (something that needs more explication) when it is taken away from the context that exclusively decides whether or not it works effectively. Again, it seems that much of what is made into "small details" by KM mainstream theorizing is what can endanger the whole outcome of a KM focus. In essence, when only the "big picture" is emphasized, with little regard for the "smaller details," the particular conditions (i.e., tacit knowledge) that allow sufficient formalization to conceptualize "best practice" are lost. Within this context, it seems only natural that a company would overlook the analytical effort necessary to thoroughly analyze its own conditions in order to actually implement a best practice. This way of plasticizing KM seems only to endeavor a trial-and-error learning strategy.

The Global Consulting Denmark MC group experienced the tensions between the ideal and real impact of the overall GC KM system. The challenge of capturing and writing down best practices on all business service levels in the company made it necessary to begin a broader analytical investigation into the different modes of service production in the company and how these were connected to KM-related issues.

LESSONS FROM THE FIELD:
REFLECTIONS ON KOWLEDGE MANAGEMENT IN PRACTICE

Reflecting on the KM experience of Global Consulting and Danish MC, a number of lessons about the challenges and difficulties involved in effectuating knowledge management begin to emerge. Drawing on Danish MC's approach to knowledge management, the discussion draws out two specific examples of changes in the overall KM approach from Global Consulting to Danish MC to more clearly draw attention to the main argument of the chapter: when *knowledge* is conceptualized into general KM models, it is at the same time reduced to nothing more than an instrumental object. As illustrated by the following vignette, this often creates an empty feeling of control, one that can endanger the entire outcome of efforts to improve company efficiency from a knowledge perspective:

> The new knowledge manager was approached by one of the department managers, who said, "Since you are the new knowledge manager of this place, would you come and tell my department about these knowledge issues—as we are now being evaluated on them." An agreement was made regarding time and place and plans to follow up on the specific content of the meeting with the department. Several times the knowledge manager approached the department manager in order to discuss the specific needs of the department, but to no avail. When the day for the meeting arrived, there had still not been any communication between the knowledge manager and the department manager. While the knowledge manager was concerned, the department manager simply said, "You are the knowledge manager, you will know what to say and do." The knowledge manager went to the meeting, sat down, and said, "Your department manager asked me to come today and tell you about knowledge issues. As you know, you are going to be evaluated on these issues. As he and I haven't spoken since our first conversation, and in order for this meeting to be relevant, rather than talking about something as abstract as *knowledge* issues, I will talk about Queen Victoria's sexuality in the 19th century. I am sure that this makes much more

sense than to discuss knowledge issues as such…. Or, I could simply ask you 'what are *you* doing?'."

From Global and Generalized Standards to Local Attention

Instead of starting out with yet another normative outline of a best practice—an attempt to formulate an "ideal" KM strategy or develop "new" company knowledge definitions and evaluation standards—Danish MC began its KM initiative with a realistic assessment of possibilities and limitations, especially in the context of how the company operated on a day-to-day basis. Special attention was placed on different modes of knowledge production and how they were related to different consulting services. An underlying problem, of course, is that gaining access and insight to how knowledge actually organizes production, influences different arrangements, and becomes effectual on an everyday work basis is far easier said than done. It is almost impossible without engaging the entire organization in problem investigations, creating a different consideration of the knowledge production and utilization process.

Performance Evaluation: From Utility to Productivity

In order to capture local attention and insight, it was necessary to first and foremost provide incentives for a broader part of the consultant group to get involved in the internal build-up of the company. In order for this to happen, management had to reevaluate the most ingrown and profound way of evaluating the performance of the consultants. Instead of using categories to distinguish between "productive" and "nonproductive" time, Danish MC excluded the notion of nonproductive time and expanded its evaluation system to include a wide range of internal processes. These internal categories were also directly included in the yearly appraisal system. Such reorganization and reenvisioning of time and evaluation systems, of course, take time, and do not transform attitudes and organizational culture overnight. By restructuring the performance evaluation system, however, the firm was able to initiate a questioning of the underlying cultural attitude and the firm's orientation that differentiated "good from bad" and "right from wrong."

At Danish MC, time was configured into the five main mega-processes: strategy, sales, service, people, and knowledge. Each of these categories had different activities attached and new projects could be located within them. For example, the internal Knowledge Management project got its own "project number" within the overall *Knowledge* category, and under this specific project a number of different topics were attached to it. The time spent on Knowledge Strategy, Analysis, Information Technology, Knowledge Culture, and so forth could be indicated separately. In this new system, it was possible to legitimize the role of the consultants, even if they did not have a rate of 75% billable time. Much attention was placed on creating a flexible system, one that would be continually updated and renewed as needed. When one project was finished, its project number was closed and filed. An obvious downside of these systems, of course, is that they are heavy on administration.

Expanding the evaluation system to include time spent on internal knowledge processes as "productive time" is only the first step. Once this is done, the very real problem of *how* various actions and activities in this area should be evaluated must be delineated. Many of our known systems of evaluation that include knowledge issues attempt to evaluate the consultant by the number of yearly-submitted knowledge objects or by a number of predefined knowledge contributions (Petersen & Poulfelt, 2002). While seemingly straightforward, this approach to knowledge evaluation creates a number of practical problems. First, it puts primary attention on quantity rather than quality. Second, this method of evaluation often results in submitting "anything" rather than nothing, and there is often a peak of activity just before the individual's yearly performance evaluation. Companies using this approach often install a quality control function in an attempt to minimize the risk of an overfilled, outdated systemized databank. Such quality control is intended to ensure that the knowledge objects submitted to the system have sufficient quality and that outdated objects are deleted from the system. Making this quality control function work productively in practice, however, requires the ability to distinguish "good" from "poor" knowledge in literally every production area of the company. A related challenge is having the competency to be able to diagnose future market trends and organizational needs. In practice, most firms use an automatic delete function, which purges knowledge objects after a given period of time (typically 1–2 years).[2]

The Knowledge Forum: Revitalizing Employee Input

The reconfiguration of Danish MC's time evaluation system and its renewed emphasis on the need to develop internal knowledge competencies set the stage for a reinvigorated employee-based Knowledge Forum. An important incentive for participating in the forum was the potential influence it would have in reforming and improving the firm's knowledge processes. A cross-sectional team of experienced and relatively new consultants were brought together to explore possibilities. The opportunity to discuss knowledge issues with representatives from different parts of the company—which brought together insights from different projects, initiatives, and key stakeholders—made it clear that different people used the *concept of knowledge* in very different ways. Apparently *knowledge, as a concept*, was not something that many of the consultants speculated about on a daily basis—in essence, they were too enmeshed in their existing projects.

Early in these discussions, the Knowledge Forum found out that in order to create better conditions for a new KM system it was not very productive to begin with knowledge concepts such as *knowledge processes, knowledge objects,* or linking the daily problems to *knowledge* as a specific defined concept. In fact, when directly asked about knowledge-specific issues—for example, "*How* does the *knowledge process* look in your department?"—the consultants were inclined to try to recall distinctive elements about knowledge from prior policies, definitions in the GC KM policy, or in a KM book. This tendency made the discussions abstract and immediately took the focus away from the challenges of creating value for clients.

Thus, instead of attempting to apply a "known" and potentially constraining definition of knowledge, which might (or might not) grasp the specific modes of knowledge production in the firm, a broader notion of knowledge began to emerge in the Knowledge Forum. Discussions in the Knowledge Forum took KM-related issues away from abstract KM terms, definitions, and models, and instead focused on the different modes of production in the company on a daily, operational level. Each member of the Knowledge Forum went back to their respective groups, departments, and projects and observed *how* their colleagues sought to create *value* and the types of *obstacles* that made this difficult. The goal was to capture and investigate *different modes of work production* in the firm and how *knowledge* and *value* was actually effectuated, instead of simply trying to follow a mechanistic and normative process developed by someone else and for someone else.

Discussions in the Knowledge Forum regarding the knowledge-creating process—across different lines of production, projects, departments, and individuals—encouraged the members of the Forum to think about knowledge in practical terms. An underlying intent was to ensure that their understanding of knowledge was not separated from the various thresholds and contexts in which it was embedded. Rather than beginning with such questions as *which* knowledge objects have value, how *many* knowledge objects each consultant should submit, or *where* different knowledge objects should be placed, the discussion focused on discussing *how* knowledge or value was produced and for *whom*, comparing the circumstances where something "new" was produced with the circumstances that produced repetition of known (existing) objects. The exercise here was to uncover the often hidden premises (in each case) that others who we do not think of or take for granted could reveal possibilities and limitations that are inherent in a specific production mode. Such broader realization was intended to facilitate the process of developing new specific tools, techniques, or models and adapting existing organizational practice to fit if possible.

On a firm level, this had several advantages. First, through the direct involvement of the members in the Knowledge Forum, who represented many differences in the company, it was possible to create a "living" picture of the company. Knowledge Management was now being directly linked to daily work processes. By examining the problems and challenges involved with daily work, the Knowledge Forum facilitated the ability of the consultants to determine whether a problem was linked to a local obstacle or a more general one. Solutions to local problems were subsequently discussed in the Knowledge Forum, and were often resolved by directly involving the consultants in creating a solution. When more general problems and solutions were discussed, one of the directors of the company was invited to participate, in order for the Knowledge Forum to get direct feedback and possible support from upper management.

REFLECTIONS ON KNOWLEDGE AS A SIGNIFIED COMMODITY: ABSTRACT AND DECONTEXTUALIZED

Regardless of where knowledge is designated, contemporary KM experiences and theorizing have the tendency of converting the arrangement of knowledge into little more than a commodity, a short-sighted view that regards knowledge in a utility-value context.[3] The commoditization of knowledge as an abstract and empty analytical signifier can be found in a number of elements: The KM field was born out of the fast developing information technology arena, in which knowledge has abusively and repeatedly been mistaken for documents to be filed in a system. The concomitant structural and systematic submission and retrieval processes to be followed are by no means innocent. Instead they seem to penetrate and organize both cultural and organizational aspects of company procedures, techniques, and standards, including systems of time, rewards, and evaluation.

This commoditization of knowledge can also be found in part of the theoretical field, which limits the view of knowledge management to the mere use and benefits of information technology. Some of the critics of this KM perspective (e.g., Nonaka & Takeuchi, 1995; Nonaka et al., 2001; Prusak & Davenport, 1998) are particularly relevant in their emphasis on application and practitioner concerns, and have become the foundation of the many normative KM approaches implemented in today's companies. Davenport and Prusak (2000, pp. 5, 25) suggest the very broad and at first sight complicated notion of knowledge as a

> fluid mix of framed experience, values, contextual information, and expert insight that provides a framework for evaluation and incorporation of new experiences and information ...[which can be converted to knowledge that] can be exchanged, bought, found, generated, and applied to work.... There is a genuine market for knowledge in organizations. Like markets for goods and services, the knowledge market has buyers and sellers who negotiate to reach a mutually satisfactory price for the goods exchanged.

However, also in this definition we find that knowledge is transformed into distinctive measurable objects, and thus, is transformed into nothing more than a commodity to be defined and utilized at the organization's direct discretion.

Viewing knowledge in this way bears the risk of disregarding a range of valuable components that cannot be immediately recognized within a logic of instrumentality. According to Culler (1983), among others (e.g., Cetina, 2001; Chia, 1996, 1999, 2003; Styhre 2003), there is a more profound reason underlying the reduction of knowledge into a commodity. They argue that our approach to knowledge is a consequence of our dominant managerial orientation, which calls for ongoing reduction by implementing systemic models of representation. As Culler argues (1983, p. 152),

> A theory of representation that seeks to establish as foundations must take as given, must assume the presence of, that which accurate representation represents. There is thus always a question whether a supposed given may not in fact be a construct or product, dependent, for example on the theory which it purports to support.

The underlying question concerns the extent to which we control, measure, and evaluate those factors that actually add value or simply measure those things that are measurable. It appears that knowledge, no matter how well defined and how transparent it may seem, in the end always seems to escape our firm grip. There is no easy way to manage and control the essence of what adds value or makes a profound difference. Instead, based upon what have become the general and static symbols of knowledge, we create rather rigid and fragile systemic walls, which have to be nursed, administrated, and rebuilt again and again. An example of this type of problem appears when departments change names, organizations reorganize, and companies merge and divest—and they spend significant resources administrating the resultant daily changes.

According to Alversson (2001), the idea of *managing* knowledge—which is shaped by our dominant business model—is reduced to another attempt at management instrumentalism. The complexity, ambiguity, and fluid nature of knowledge, he argues, is reduced into fixed measurable objects. A distinct problem with this kind of knowledge schematic is that it locates and classifies, but limits a great deal of organizational practice in the process. It blocks the production of noncausal, nonhierarchical, and nonlinear knowledge. The "lines of flight" (creativity and innovation without an instrumental end), which eventually slip by, are instantaneously reduced to known material. Thus, "knowledge management" often contains no real change or creation, and simply reflects a reorganization of processes and procedures. In fact, knowledge management, as suggested by Styhre (2003, p. 25) and Chia (1999, p. 224), is an oxymoron. One part is aimed at controlling and ordering (management), whereas the other (knowledge) is fluid and processual. Styhre argues, "Knowledge is much more complex and elusive than almost any other organisational resource and thus the reductionist view of knowledge, provided by many knowledge management theorists is complicated to maintain" (p. 25).

Whereas "mainstream" KM theories presuppose, and therefore give priority to, the notion of knowledge as managerial (orderable and controllable) on the organizational and individual level, Styhre's (2003) strategy shows how the supposedly rational and stable aspects of organizational and individual knowledge require a specific reduction of the concept. The concept of knowledge becomes incomprehensible as it takes on many meanings—and the meaning we give the concept seems to vary according to when, by whom, and under which circumstances it is used. Styhre addresses this problem when he explores the different interpretations of knowledge as it has been used and expressed through time.[4] The key issue for Styhre, however, is to show how theorists within the KM literature have taken an extremely difficult and complicated concept and reduced it to contain only a few of its components. In contrast to this instantaneous reduction into a measurable commodity, Styhre finds inspiration in Cetina's (2001, p. 181) view on knowledge:

> Objects of knowledge appear to have the capacity to unfold infinitely. They are more like open drawers filled with folders extending indefinitely into the depth of the dark closet. Since epistemic objects are always in the process of being materially defined, they continually acquire new properties and change the ones they have. But this also means that objects of knowledge can never be fully attained, that they are, if you wish, never quite themselves.

Here we address a concept of knowledge that can never be fixed at a single point, but *continuously unfolds* as it is used, discussed, and examined. In fact, as Styhre argues, the model offered by "mainstream" KM theorizing is of little or no practical use.

Following this line of thinking, one can say the same about knowledge in practice—*knowledge as praxis*—as Nonaka and Takeuchi (1995, p. 7) lament the "void of understanding *knowledge creation* from all the talk about knowledge." Talking about knowledge and the management of knowledge doesn't get us any closer to knowledge as it unfolds in practice—its modes of production or organizing. No matter how broad and apparently vague we start out addressing the issue of knowledge in KM, we obviously end up approaching knowledge as a temporal generic, mechanic, and static object, resource, mean, or product. This way of thinking about *knowledge* must be addressed as a serious problem. Main contributors within what here is termed "mainstream" KM conceive of the world as uncertain, unstable, and basically changeable. In this perspective, it can seem as a paradox that knowledge can also be formed and identified as objects for efficient production. According to Chia (1999, p. 210), this can be seen as a consequence of the way our entire understanding of the social world is conceived. Throughout the theorizing of social arrangements, not many contributions have endeavored to understand the *nature of change*, but repeatedly articulated the *social world* and *change* from "dominant static categories that obscure a logic of observational ordering based on the representationalist principles of division, location, isolation, classification and the elevation of self-identity." Thus, as a way of exploring such paradoxical thinking, it is necessary to explore the underlying essential components such as *change* and *process* in "mainstream" KM theory.

Processes and Change in Knowledge Management

Nonaka and Takeuchi (1995) criticize most organizational studies for being static and passive in their view of organizations. Thus, they argue for a new theory of organizational knowledge creation, in which knowledge creation can be understood as a process of converting *tacit* knowledge into *explicit* knowledge and back again into *tacit* knowledge. According to Nonaka and Takeuchi, the process of knowledge creation takes as its point of departure the assumption that we are working with two different types of knowledge. These two types of knowledge can easily be observed as isolated and separated elements, as explicit knowledge is easily communicable. They take the reader through the different philosophers of knowledge (e.g., Plato, Aristotle, Descartes, Locke, Kant, Hegel,

Marx) and end up in the 20th century in order to argue against the validity of the Cartesian split between a subject and an object (i.e., the split between mind and body).

In practice, however, Nonaka and Takeuchi (1995) draw upon other configurations that are just as rigid as those that they confront with their criticism, as they maintain several assumptions about organizations, cultures, and individuals as entities, identities, and subjects (Nonaka & Takeuchi 1995; Nonaka et al., 2001). These categories are expounded as preestablished categories valid for organizational analysis, and thus, they remain trapped in the very discourse they set out to criticize. Moreover, their process-based view suggests that it is possible to transfer knowledge from tacit to explicit and from individuals to the larger organization for the benefit of the organization *as a whole*.

This way of perceiving organizations and individuals has a profound effect on the way Nonaka and Takeuchi (1995) (and later Nonaka et al., 2001) are able to comprehend two central components in knowledge management: *processes* and *change*. The criticism made by Tsoukas (1996, p. 14), suggesting that tacit knowledge is immanent in explicit knowledge at all times, is directed precisely at this aspect: "Tacit knowledge is the necessary component of *all* knowledge; it is not made up of discrete beans which may be ground, lost or reconstituted."

Nonaka and Takeuchi (1995) propose a normative model of knowledge creation and by creating a dualistic view of knowledge and contending its preestablished purpose (i.e., the process of transforming tacit to explicit and back again), makes the process of knowledge creation instrumental. The process has an end or goal outside itself—the goal of creating new knowledge. In order to maintain a normative view of knowledge management, Nonaka and his colleagues have installed a classification that itself is not changeable.

Processes and Change: Implications and New Openings for KM

In contrast to "mainstream" KM theory, there are critical voices (notably Chia, 1996, 1999, 2003) on perspectives of change and process that are useful to reflect on the limitations and new possibilities for KM practice. As Chia (1999) argues: "There is a growing realization that our current theories of change are not sufficiently 'process-based' to adequately capture the dynamics of change."

This critical view has two dimensions. First, Chia is a profound critic of organizational theory, which tends to look at change from an "organization as entity" vantage point —in essence, form with specific content. This way of thinking about change, according to Chia (1999), limits our view of "change" to already established categories and classifications such as culture, environment, and departments. As Chia (1996, p. 40) notes, this is

> a fundamental ontological posture which asserts that reality pre-exists independently of observation and as static, discrete and identifiable "things," "entities," "events," "generative mechanisms," etc. This version of realism underwrites the dominant academic predisposition which takes unproblematic commonsensical notions such as 'the organisation, its "goals," "culture," "environment," "strategies," "lifecycles," etc., as theoretically legitimate objects of analyses.

The essence of Chia's argument is not to claim that there are no such things as organizations, departments, products, or individuals. His point is that these categories, when preestablished as oversimplified entities, function as a nondisputed truism that produces crucial limitations on how *change, process,* and *knowledge* can become effectuated. Problems, activities, services, and so forth more often cross these organizational orders, as they *continually "explode"* and *"mutate"* (Cetina, 2001). These explicit formulated orders and structures try to obtain (often false and misleading) a sense of safety, internally as well as externally, to customers and other stakeholders. However, in practice we often see a constant displacement between the order and structure of the company and its disorganizing modes of production. This dynamic is what Cooper (1986) refers to as constant organizing/disorganizing production. We never know exactly *why, what,* and exactly *to what* something changes, if we follow the modes of production, which do not follow the organizational order and structure per se. Rather, modes of production follow the *questions* that we are able to pose and the *challenges* we see ourselves faced with at a given time, place, and situation. As such, they do not limit themselves to the organization as an entity, but rather reach out in a social collectivity, combining assemblages of artifacts into products, services, and knowledge. They are, as Chia (1996, p. 150) suggests, "loosely emergent sets of organizing rules which orient interactional behaviour in particular ways within a social collectivity."

If, as a point of departure, we think of organizations as not *partially stable* entities, we alter the conditions under which *change* and *knowledge* can be understood and effectuated. This view stands in start contrast to the world as described by many KM theorists. As Chia (1999, p. 222) argues:

> A metaphysics of change acknowledges the existence of an external fluxing reality, but denies our ability to accurately represent such a reality using established symbols, concepts and categories precisely because real-

ity is ever-changing and hence resistant to description in terms of fixed categories.

Thinking about change as something that already and always exists as a basic condition, efficient practice can no longer become something organizations must implement and which requires external intervention. Viewed this way, change is something that occurs naturally and of its own volition once the invisible hand of cultural intervention is removed (Chia, 1999).

What is needed, according to Styhre (2003), is a critical view of the notions of knowledge and management that will be able to offer a new conceptual framework containing a new vocabulary, which brings "knowledge back down from heights of abstraction and idealization" (p.157). In organizational theory, several contributors have argued that our language poorly captures the complexity and multiplicity of reality—and seemingly the concept of knowledge itself. Chia's (1999) criticism is aimed at organizational theorists at large when he argues that none of our contemporary organizational models are sufficiently "process-based" to adequately capture the dynamics of change. As Chia argues:

> We are not good at thinking movement. Our instinctive skills favor the fixed and the static, the separate and the self-contained. Taxonomies, hierarchies, systems and structures represent the instinctive vocabulary of institutionalized thought in its determined subordinating of flux, movement, change and transformation. Our dominant models of change in general and organisational change in particular are, therefore paradoxically couched in the language of stasis and equilibrium. (p. 209)

Although knowledge management may be striving for dynamic planning, we are dealing with a concept of knowledge based on a very limited rational framework. What seems to be given much less attention is trying to work with the notion of *knowledge* in its specific complex assemblage— its practical unfolding and the problems it contains on a day-to-day work basis, which, however, cannot be viewed as a simple act of declaration. On the contrary, trying to work with knowledge on a day-to-day work basis is trying to unfold the terms on which "problems of knowledge" is stated in order to alter these.

Implications for Practice

The alchemistic definitions within much of the KM literature, which in essence signify commodities on an operational level, invoke severe difficulties when put into practice. As more companies undertake KM initiatives—including the application of empirical and conceptual models, various techniques and tools, and investigations into the actual practice of knowledge management—knowledge itself seems to become increasingly difficult to map out and maintain as a clear and unambiguous concept. During the last decade, we have witnessed everything from the implementation of entirely new and very expensive information and KM systems, to organizational "yellow pages," expert findings, and informal discussion groups. In many cases, an extended focus on knowledge—or even an entire reevaluation of the organization from a knowledge-based perspective—fails to lead to the intended and stipulated results. Thus, what may seem to be a well-developed field is also embedded in mystery and continues to prove to be very difficult to manage in practice.

It seems as if we have allowed ourselves to be blinded by the claims and potential—and the seemingly legendary results—promised by different techniques, tools, typologies, and models. We seldom truly investigate the extent to which the basic conditions for using these fashions actually fit the organizing conditions in the specific company in question. How often do we spend the resources to analyze these conditions before implementation? Do "fit-it-all solutions," with their abstract rules of demarcation, meet organizational needs?

This chapter has attempted to illustrate how "mainstream" KM (both in practice and in theory as "best practices" and recipes) has become just another abstract model in which *knowledge* is reduced to an object, a resource, or a commodity. When complex and changing companies engage in complex and changing markets, a vast production of information is produced on a daily basis. Knowledge management has "come to the rescue" as a way of categorizing, ordering, and controlling this vast production. But there is a danger in blindly trusting the effectiveness of the defined and classified as something concrete. On the contrary, it seems the concepts of KM have "already" moved far away from working processes on an operational level, and it is becoming more time consuming than productive to follow these paths.

The intent of this chapter was not to denigrate the importance of necessary initiatives to reduce information overload in order to become effective and productive, but merely to discuss *how* this reduction can become more effective and productive in changing and complex conditions when attempted without the truism of axiomatic abstractions. In essence, how can something be *indefinite* yet *concrete* rather than *signified* yet *abstract*? Or as Fuglsang and Ljungstrøm (1999, p. 27) writes, *essentia*, is designated by

> that which already falls in the shine of the field vision without considering how inaccurate this is, as it is already presumed to be defined, ... for which reason we maintain and are maintained in the belief of the determinable

and substantial form of identity, and thus, we are given comfort, tranquillity and confidence in the unambiguous rather than in becomings.

The challenge in most of the KM literature takes as a point of departure the assumption that society is moving *from* an industrial *to* a knowledge society, from one synthesized and coherent story to yet another. However, the practical challenges seems to surpass this oversimplified story: competition in contemporary society is at once local, international, and global, it is fast and it is slow, it is rigid and flexible, and it is full of meaning and full of nonsense. It does not move by our rational and oversimplified models, but rather it cuts in between, it connects and disconnects, and often takes us by surprise. This reality poses severe challenges and demands that we move KM away from its present abstractions and general frameworks. The challenge is one of constantly breaking existing forms and inventing new ones on the basis of each concrete problem—and these problems can only be brought to light by digging up their roots. There is no easy way out, especially given the abstraction that is implied in "current state" diagnosis. The extent to which such abstraction is necessary raises questions about the validity of any current state assessment—and to that extent, perhaps we will recognize that "weapons and tools are consequences, nothing but consequences...that a weapon is nothing outside of the combat organization it is bound up with" (Deleuze & Guattari, 2002, p. 398).

CONCLUSIONS

"He even knew that the reminiscences of the piano distorted the image he had of the music, that the field which is accessible for the musician isn't a poor scale of seven tones, but an infinite, yet almost completely unknown scale where only here and there, separated from each other by a close, unexplored darkness, few of those millions of nuances of love, passion, strength of the soul and sublime calmness which it consist of, each of them as different from the other as one universe from another, has been discovered by some great artists, who favour us by rousing that feeling in us, that correspond to that motive they have found, and thereby showing us what richness and variety, without us knowing, is hiding in the great, unexplored and depressing night which fills our soul, and which we confuse with Emptiness and Nothingness."

—Proust (1983, p. 376)

Contemporary KM theory, with its clear emphasis on knowledge as a commodity, has surely contributed to the creation of many analytical tools, techniques, and typologies intended to help companies further develop their competitive advantage. Through the axiomatic reduction to a commodity-based concept of knowledge, however, leveraging knowledge and its consumption have been reduced to another management fad with severe practical problems. Recognizing that knowledge cannot be captured in generalized and transparent definitions and typologies, or implemented as best practice, puts severe pressure on the need to constantly reexamine the dynamic and changing conditions in an organization. There is a need to look at the production of knowledge in much wider contexts, where arrangements of knowledge emerge through the interaction of consultants, customers, markets, and unpredictable events. Clearly, we need to go beyond the normative techniques, tools, and models at hand.

As this chapter has hopefully illustrated, it is necessary to constantly examine the specific conditions of each mode of production, going beyond the blind trust we place in yet another axiomatic KM model based on the idea of knowledge as a mere commodity. Emphasizing modes of knowledge production expands the potential usability of different techniques and tools, as we try to explore and invent rather than merely adopt and implement a best practice–based, "fit-it-all" solution. Global Consulting seemed mired in a utility-based time evaluation system that blocked many of its innovative KM initiatives. Although the company was viewed (from the outside) as having one of the most profound and consistent KM systems, the view from inside the firm was quite different. Many of the firm's "best practice" tools and techniques were not used or were seen as administrative burdens, creating substantial practical problems with submission, working conditions, and conflicts with the competence and development of the consultants. Altering the fundamental time evaluation system in Danish MC enabled the firm to make its internal initiatives more productive, providing incentives and motivating its consultants to become more fully involved in the actual modes of knowledge production in the company. Ultimately, the most productive techniques emerged from the revitalized Knowledge Forum, where participants were encouraged to localize problems, analyze these, and thus connect their solutions to the firm's modes of knowledge production; sometimes these were group, project, or department specific and sometimes the problems could be located on a firm level. Success seemed grounded in the firm's willingness to go beyond the implementation of generalized definitions, generalized solutions, and evaluations standards.

In a society where change is regarded as a fundamental condition for most companies, we still seem to seek "solutions" by simply reinstalling temporary static classifications and typologies. On the surface, best practices, general models, and the implementation of a broad array of "knowledge" techniques seem to fulfill our immediate need for order and control. As we actually try to implement these models, however, we are increasingly discovering that "knowledge" is something that cannot be simply reduced to a resource, an object, or a commodity that fits into these generalized forms. When we try to compress the created value from production into knowledge objects, we merely create problems on an operational level, especially when the organization is faced with constant ambiguity and uncertainty. While it often seems as if uncertainty suggests something dangerous or even destructive, something that must be settled or clarified in order to reach a new state of equilibrium, this often creates no more than a false image or another empty signifier. In and of itself, however, it appears that our deeply rooted and inborn habit of favoring what Chia (1999) calls "the fixed and the static, the separate and the self-contained" can be more dangerous and destructive than uncertainty in and of itself. In essence, our ability to create and appreciate new approaches to knowledge is limited by our bias toward what is already known.

NOTES

1. The name Global Consulting is a pseudonym. The real name of the Global Consulting company has been changed in order to protect the rights and claims of professional secrecy. Consequently, all identifying names of cities, departments, and so forth have been altered.

2. When the Balanced Scorecard was implemented in GC Denmark, it was still a fairly new concept in Denmark but widely recognized in the United States. Since the publication of Kaplan and Norton's (1996) book, there have been many experiments in Denmark that have expanded the classical economic focus of financial measures with systems of performance measurement in areas such as customer variables, internal variables, and development variables (e.g., growth, knowledge, innovation).

3. During a period of one year, Danish MC bought up several management consulting, IT, and Internet companies. None of these companies had a sophisticated, developed system for reducing information in the databases. One of the Internet companies did Internet/intranet development for one of the larger firms in Denmark, where the same problem could be found. Student projects (interviews and observation) dealing with knowledge sharing in another large firm supports this claim. The Knowledge Management Team in Danish MC developed a system of *personal database responsibility*, where each person or function had a responsibility of maintaining a high knowledge level in a specified number of databases. This approach produced a number of problems: apart from unwanted administrative tasks, the person responsible for the database was also responsible for deleting submitted documents by other individuals, a responsibility no one seemed to be willing to take. In practice, placing the responsibility on each individual for his or her own submissions only seemed to water down the principle of responsibility.

4. Beginning with the *Oxford Dictionary*, Styhre (2003) examines the different concepts of knowledge through the philosophy of knowledge starting with

the Greeks. In Greek philosophy, we find at least three concepts of knowledge: *Episteme*, *Techne*, and *Phronesis*. He analyzes these three knowledge concepts in order to investigate their origin and to relate them to interpretations provided in the French, German, and English languages.

REFERENCES

Alversson, M (2001). Knowledge works: Ambiguity, image and identity. *Human Relations*, *54*(7), 863–886.

Cetina, K. K. (2001). Objectual practice. In T. R. Schatzki, K. K. Cetina, & E. Savigny (Eds.), *The practice turn in contemporary theory* (pp. 175–188). London: Taylor & Francis.

Chia, R. (1996). The problem of reflexivity in organizational research: Towards a postmodern science of organization. *Organization*, *3*(1), 31–59.

Chia, R. (1999). A Rhizomatic model of organizational change and transformation: Perspective from a metaphysics of change. *British Journal of Management*, *10*, 209–227.

Chia, R. (2003). Ontology: Organization as "world-making." In R. Westwood & S. Clegg (Eds.), *Debation organization: Point-counterpoint in organization studies* (pp. 98–113). London: Blackwell.

Cooper, R. (1986). Organization/disorganization. *Social Science Information*, *25*(2), 299–335.

Cortada, J. & Woods, J. (Eds.) (2000). *The knowledge management yearbook 2000-2001*. Boston: Butterworth Heinemann.

Culler, J. (1983). *On deconstruction: Theory and criticism after structuralism*. London: Routledge & Kegan Paul.

Davenport, T. H., & Prusak, L. (2000). *Working knowledge: How organizations manage what they know*. Boston: Harvard Business School Press.

Deleuze, G., & Guattari, F. (2002). *A thousand plateaus: Capitalism and schizophrenia*. London: Continuum.

Fahey, L., & Prusak, L. (1998). The Eleven Deadliest Sins of Knowledge Management. *California Management Review*, *40*(3), 265–281.

Fuglsang, M., & Ljungstrøm, A. C. (1999). *Det nøgne liv—en poetik for det sociale*. København: Samfundslitteratur.

Kaplan, R. S., & Norton, D. P. (1996). *The balanced scorecard: Translating strategy into action*. Cambridge, MA: Harvard Business School Press.

Nonaka, I., & Takeuchi, H. (1995). *The knowledge creating company: How Japanese companies create the dynamics of innovation*. New York: Oxford University Press.

Nonaka, I., Takeuchi, M., & Byosiére, P. (2001). A theory of organizational knowledge creation: Understanding the dynamic process of creating knowledge. In M. Dierkers, A. Berthoin Antal, J. Child, & I. Nonaka (Eds.), *Handbook of organizational learning and knowledge* (pp. 491–517). Oxford: Oxford University Press.

Petersen, N. J., & Poulfelt, F. (2002). Knowledge management in action: A study of knowledge management in management consultancies. In A.F. Buono (Ed.),

Developing knowledge and value in management consulting (pp.33–60). Greenwich, CT: Information Age.

Pirsig, R. M. (1995). *Lila: En undersøgelse af moral*. Århus: Schønberg.

Proust, M. (1981). *Swann's way* (C.K.S. Moncrieff & T. Kilmartin, Trans.). London: Chatto & Windus.

Styhre, A. (2003). *Understanding knowledge management: Critical and postmodern perspectives*. Copenhagen: Copenhagen Business School Press

Tsoukas, H. (1996). The firm as a distributed knowledge system: A constructionist approach. *Strategic Management Journal, 17*, 11–25.

CHAPTER 3

THE FALLACY OF SIMPLISTIC NOTIONS OF THE TRANSFER OF "BEST PRACTICE"[1]

Sue Newell

One of the oft-quoted reasons for using consultants is because they can enable an organization to adopt "best practice" in a particular area. This notion is premised on the assumption that "best practice" can be identified in one place and the knowledge about this practice can be transferred to another place in order to transform practice there. Many consultants sell their services precisely on this basis. Consultants selling Enterprise Resource Planning (ERP) software, for example, market their services on the basis that their ERP software supposedly embodies "best practices." Thus, when a company buys this software the underlying message is that they are also buying the practices and processes that are embedded in the software.

This chapter explores the limitations of this idea through a knowledge perspective that views knowledge as socially constructed and embedded in practice. This perspective suggests that the situated nature of knowledge makes it literally impossible to transfer "best practice" in such a direct way. Rather, knowledge has to be generated in its own context, perhaps using ideas from elsewhere, but essentially requiring the reconstitu-

Challenges and Issues in Knowledge Management, 51–68
Copyright © 2005 by Information Age Publishing
All rights of reproduction in any form reserved.

tion of existing practice in any given context rather than simply involving the transfer of knowledge from one place or situation to another. As illustrated by a case example, recognizing the situated nature of knowledge has practical implications for the role of consultants as they attempt to encourage the transfer of ideas across organizations.

DEFINING KNOWLEDGE AND KNOWLEDGE MANAGEMENT

Today, knowledge is seen as one of, if not *the*, most valuable aspects of an organization (Grant, 1996). Yet, despite its importance, the conventional wisdom is that such knowledge is typically not well managed within many organizations. This observation has given rise to many companies instigating knowledge management initiatives. In this sense, "knowledge management" (KM) has become one of the latest management fashions (Abrahamson, 1996), with many companies attracted by the suggestion that they can gain significant advantage by better managing their knowledge. The perceived advantage is premised on the assumption that if organizations were able to better use what they, or at least their employees, already knew, then they would be able to operate much more effectively. There would be less "reinventing the wheel" as novice employees facing a problem or opportunity in one situation would not have to learn how best to deal with the situation but would instead reuse the knowledge of expert employees who had previously successfully dealt with the situation. Indeed, even if others had previously been unsuccessful in dealing with the situation, this knowledge could somehow be transferred so that the same mistakes were not continuously remade. In this way, organizations would become more efficient—better exploiting their existing knowledge.

Given the dynamic environments in which organizations now operate, KM is viewed not only as a way to enhance efficiency but also as a way to enhance the ability to innovate—to develop new products, services, and organizational processes. If an organization was able to use all the potentially available knowledge—external as well as internal—it should be able to create new ideas. So, knowledge is seen to be crucial both for (1) exploring (creating) new knowledge—creating "best practice"—to enhance innovative capability and (2) exploiting what is already known—reusing "best practice"—whether originally developed internally or externally (March, 1991). From this perspective, consultants, whether internal or external, are seen as an important resource in helping organizations to explore and in particular exploit knowledge through the transfer of "best practice" knowledge across situations.

While this view of the importance of knowledge is widely accepted in the management literature, there is much debate about what constitutes "knowledge." These debates have been ongoing for centuries, with ancient philosophers such as Aristotle and Plato focusing very much on this question. More recently, with the acknowledgment of the importance of knowledge for organizational competitive advantage, these debates have emerged very potently within the management literature. The two most prominent views of knowledge in the management literature are knowledge as "possession" and knowledge as a "socially embedded phenomenon."

Knowledge as Possession

The most common view of knowledge, and the view underpinning the most widespread organizational KM initiatives that are being implemented today, can be described as the *knowledge as possession* view. This perspective assumes that knowledge is a possession—of individuals in particular. Thus, just as I own a football that I can give to someone else who will then "possess" the football, I have knowledge that I can pass to another. Knowledge is seen as an entity that can be made explicit and transferred from one person or group to another. Thus, if a particular retail company appears to have developed some good practices for managing its warehouse-to-store distribution system, the belief is that the knowledge underpinning such practices can be made explicit and codified (written down) and transferred to another organization. The second organization will subsequently acquire this knowledge and begin to operate the same good distribution practices. This dynamic is essentially what is meant by the transfer of best practice.

The organizational KM initiatives that have been widely adopted are often premised on this knowledge as possession view. Such initiatives often involve the implementation of information and communication technologies (ICT), which are aimed at capturing, storing, searching, retrieving, and reusing knowledge. For example, Ruggles (1998) reports on a survey of 431 organizations that had adopted initiatives to "manage knowledge." The four most common activities that were reported by the organizations were all ICT-type initiatives: creating an intranet, implementing data warehousing, adopting decision-support tools, and developing groupware capability. Alavi and Leidner (1999) report very similar findings.

This dominant view of knowledge, then, sees knowledge as a resource that is possessed—mostly by individuals but also by groups, organizations, or even societies. McElroy (2000) refers to this approach as first-genera-

tion knowledge management and the focus is on strategies that emphasize dissemination, imitation, and exploitation of knowledge—in essence,
the transfer of best practices.

Knowledge as a Socially Embedded Phenomenon

There has been a recent shift in the KM literature, as some writers have
begun to recognize the situated and embedded nature of knowledge. The
alternative to the knowledge as possession view is that knowledge (or
rather knowing) is not so much possessed as *embedded in practice* and as
such is *inherently social*. Those who adopt the view that knowledge is
embedded in practice would argue that direct knowledge transfer, as suggested in the best practice literature, is not possible because knowledge is
socially constructed and inherently sticky (Szulanski, 1996). Therefore,
transferring knowledge of any "good" practice from one situation to
another, where those involved possess different knowledge and engage in
different practices, will not be straightforwardly effective. McElory (2000)
labels these more recent approaches as second-generation KM, and the
focus is on approaches that promote education, innovation, and exploration.

In second-generation KM, the focus moves from the supply of knowledge to creating and maintaining the conditions required for the production of *knowing* (Blackler, 1995). Second-generation KM recognizes that
knowledge is context-dependent, since "meanings" are interpreted in reference to a particular paradigm (Marakas, Johnson, & Palmer, 2000). As
Shariq (1998) notes, in order to make sense or create understanding,
humans bring prior knowledge and context to the information. Without
the human context the information by itself does not have any meaning.
Given differences in contexts, alternative interpretations or understandings are inevitable, even when people are presented with the same explicit
knowledge. Thus, first-generation KM is based on the view of knowledge
as possession, while second-generation KM is based on the view of knowledge as based in practice.

Knowledge Management Typologies

Other writers have similarly identified a distinction in the way knowledge is understood and applied in organizational KM initiatives. Table
3.1 summarizes some of these typologies related to managing knowledge
in organizations. This section briefly considers each of these typologies in

Table 3.1. Comparative Knowledge Management Typologies

	Knowledge as Possession	Knowing as Embedded in Practice
Hansen et al. (1999)	Codification strategy	Personalization strategy
Swan et al. (1999)	Cognitive view	Community view
Alavi (2000)	Repository model of knowledge management systems	Network model of knowledge management systems

turn, drawing out the distinction between knowledge as possession and knowledge as embedded in practice.

Hansen, Nohria, and Tierney (1999) observed two KM strategies used by different companies: codification and personalization. Companies using the *codification strategy* essentially attempted to make all knowledge explicit, storing it on a database and encouraging others to search this database as a way of acquiring knowledge from others rather than developing this knowledge through their own experience (the knowledge as possession view). In contrast, other companies used a personalization strategy, encouraging employees to develop networks with each other and use these networks to engage in discussion and dialogue. This strategy accepts that knowledge is closely tied to the person who developed it and needs to be shared mainly through face-to-face contacts between people. Knowledge sharing can therefore be encouraged through discussion, dialogue, and shared practice (the knowing as embedded in practice view).

Swan, Newell, Scarbrough, and Hislop (1999) distinguish between a cognitive and community view of knowledge management. The cognitive view equates knowledge to objectively defined concepts and facts that can be transferred through text, using ICT. This approach is used to enhance the exploitation of knowledge—ensuring that knowledge is reused in different contexts across an organization so "reinventing the wheel"–type behaviors are minimized. The community view, on the other hand, sees knowledge as socially constructed and based on experience. From this view, much knowledge will always remain largely tacit and as such can only be shared through joint experiences in social networks and groups. This approach focuses more on the creation or exploration of knowledge, seeing the transfer of knowledge as an inherently problematic idea.

Alavi (2000) focuses explicitly on KM systems—IT-based systems developed to enhance knowledge exploitation and exploration—and distinguishes between two approaches to the development of such systems: repository and network approaches. The *repository model* of KM systems is based on the knowledge as possession view, and focuses on building knowledge repositories and retrieval technologies. Emphasis is placed on the development of relational databases and document management systems so that data, both internal and external, can be stored and searched. The *network model* of KM systems, in contrast, is based on the situated view of knowledge, and focuses on using technology to connect or link people. Companies, for example, might develop a corporate "yellow pages" directory that lists individuals and their expertise, creating a "knowledge map'" of the organization that depicts where certain expertise is located. The key difference between these two approaches is that the network model focuses on providing information on the sources of knowledge while the repository model focuses on supplying the knowledge itself.

Two Different Epistemologies

The typologies summarized in Table 3.1 emphasize the basic dichotomy between the two ways of viewing knowledge. Our focus now turns to possible ways of integrating these different views. While the two traditions—knowledge as something possessed versus knowing as something practiced—remain distinct, Cook and Brown (1999) have recently tried to bring them together. They suggest that both are useful perspectives and simply represent two different, albeit related, epistemologies: (1) the epistemology of possession (knowledge) and (2) the epistemology of practice (knowing). It is the "generative dance" between knowledge and knowing that, they argue, is important. Thus, knowledge as something possessed must be practiced in a specific context to be meaningful. In this sense, knowledge is a "tool of knowing" (Cook & Brown, 1999), making knowledgeable action possible.

Another way of looking at this distinction is to recognize that knowledge is always a combination of tacit and explicit knowledge (Polanyi, 1958). While the knowledge as possession school of thought tends to argue that tacit knowledge can be made explicit, Cook and Brown (1999) make it clear that tacit and explicit knowledge are inherently different and cannot simply be converted from one to the other. They use the example of learning to ride a bike to illustrate this point: the tacit knowledge of riding a bike, which enables one to maintain one's balance on the bike, will always remain tacit. Even if one explains balance in explicit terms, this knowledge will not, on its own, allow a person to learn to balance—knowing how to balance can only be acquired through practice. Tsoukas (1996) frames this view differently when he argues that tacit and explicit knowledge are mutually constituted. We need both tacit and explicit knowledge to be able to complete any given activity or practice.

The recognition that knowledge is a possession and yet is also inherently embedded in practice is helpful and suggests that both views of knowledge are correct, albeit they focus on different aspects of knowledge and the knowing process. The *knowledge as possession* view focuses on explicit knowledge that can be transferred between people, while the *knowing as practice* view focuses on how the practices, experiences, and tacit understandings of individuals in particular sociocultural contexts will inevitably influence the ways in which explicit knowledge is made meaningful and actually used. However, the situated view of knowing—knowledge as practice—is often ignored in much contemporary debate and many KM initiatives, particularly by those involved in the attempt to transfer best practices. We consider the knowing as practice approach in more detail in the next section.

THE PRACTICE OF KNOWING

Tsoukas and Vladimirou (2001, p. 981) define organizational knowledge as "the set of collective understandings embedded in a firm, which enable it to put its resources to particular uses." While they note that much of this organizational knowledge may be formal and explicit, there is always and inevitably an informal and tacit aspect to this knowledge that is generated in action or practice. Collins (1990) refers to this as *heuristic knowledge*, the knowledge that arises as individuals engage in their daily routines and improvise (Orlikowski, 1996) in response to particular situations that are encountered. While this insight may or may not be shared with others, heuristic knowledge based in action has been found to contribute significantly to efficient working (e.g., Orr, 1996). From this perspective, organizational knowledge is embedded in practice and is both dispersed and ambiguous.

In terms of *dispersion*, as Nelson (1991) notes, knowledge of a particular practice or process does not form a complete and coherent body of knowledge that can be precisely documented or even articulated by a single individual. Rather, it is a form of knowing that exists only through the interaction among various collective actors (Gherardi & Nicolini, 2000; Lave & Wenger, 1991). In terms of the *ambiguity* of knowledge, it is also clear that each individual has only a partial view of what constitutes a particular organizational process, since knowledge is inherently indeterminate (Tsoukas, 1996). Each individual sees the organizational process through a particular interpretive lens, which means that another individual may see that organizational process differently. In particular, individuals from different departments or functions are likely to see an organizational process differently because departments have different "thought worlds" and focus on different aspects of a process (Dougherty, 1992).

Importantly, this suggests that holistic knowledge of a particular activity or practice does not exist prior to its documentation, so collective knowledge of that activity has first to be generated through interaction and communication. Moreover, mere access to, or possession of, explicit or codified knowledge is only the starting point, because the ambiguity of knowledge means that information may not resolve misunderstandings (Weick, 1995). Rather, people need to communicate, assimilate cognitive frameworks, and develop shared understandings (Becker, 2001). This indicates that any given work practice is culturally mediated. The practice is the outcome of a web of knowledge formed through social participation, material working conditions, and negotiated interpretations (Star, 1996). To transfer knowledge from one context to another will therefore be limited by preexisting ideas about "normal practice" in the "other" context. In particular, the transfer of knowledge will be limited by the absorptive capacity of those involved (Cohen & Levinthal, 1990), the capacity of a recipient of knowledge to take in and use knowledge. Most importantly, absorptive capacity is a function of preexisting knowledge and practice.

Situated Practice and the Problems of Knowledge Transfer: A Case Example

To illustrate this point, we will draw on a study of a project team that was set up in a hospital in the United Kingdom to redesign the process for diagnosing and treating cataracts (see Newell, Edelman, Scarbrough, Swan, & Bresnen, 2003). A person is said to have a cataract problem when the lens of the eye has become sufficiently "dirty" that their vision is blurred. Essentially, a film builds up on the lens through simple exposure to particles in the air. Once this film gets too dense and sight is significantly impaired, the treatment is to remove the lens and replace it with an artificial lens. Most people who have cataract problems, however, do not realize that this is the problem, but rather assume that they need new glasses. A visit to their optician typically results in a diagnosis very different from the one they expected—one requiring an operation to replace the lens rather than new glasses. In the UK, what happens next usually involves a long series of visits to various professionals before the required treatment is finally provided—the operation. The chronology of typical events is:

1. The patient visits the optician with the intent of getting new glasses, but the optician makes a preliminary diagnosis of cataracts. However, opticians cannot officially diagnose the problem because they do not have the authority to do so, despite the fact that they are well trained and have the technical equipment to do this.

Rather, the optician tells the patient to visit their general practitioner (GP).

2. The patient visits the GP and tells the GP what the optician has said. The GP, however, does not have the expertise or equipment to either confirm or deny this preliminary diagnosis. The GP must therefore refer the patient to a specialist—the hospital consultant.

3. There is a waiting list for the specialist, so the patient has to wait to be seen, often for 3 to 6 months. When the patient does finally get to see the specialist, they will normally confirm the diagnosis earlier made by the optician. The patient, however, cannot yet be placed on the waiting list for the actual operation because they first need to have a general health check to ensure that they are fit enough for the operation. The patient is, therefore, referred to a nurse.

4. The patient gets an appointment and visits the nurse who does a relatively routine health check and confirms that the patient can have the operation. At this stage, the patient can move on to the waiting list for the operation by the hospital specialist.

5. The waiting list is often another 3 to 6 months, but once the patient gets to the top of the list they are given an appointment to have the operation and, assuming all goes well, will finally get the needed operation to improve eyesight. After the operation, many patients will still need glasses, but different ones to those they have previously had. They will, therefore, need to return to their optician.

6. However, before they do this they will first need to return to the hospital specialist who will confirm that the operation has been successful—this visit will also, of course, pick up those very few cases where there has been a problem, which is the reason for the visit.

7. Finally, the patient can return to the optician for the new glasses that will return their sight to perfect vision.

As described, this process is long and drawn-out and often takes 12 months in total—for what should be a relatively simple and routine operation. Recognizing this problem, one hospital created a team involving the various professionals involved—hospital specialists, local opticians, local GPs, and local nurses as well as an internal consultant who was a part of a specialist change management group. The internal consultant led the team through the redesign and change implementation process, and the team successfully managed to redesign the steps involved. The new process for patients living within this hospital area would now entail:

1. A visit to the optician, where the cataract problem will be diagnosed. Now, the optician has the authority to officially make this diagnosis and can directly place the patient on the waiting list of the hospital specialist, after going through a simple self-completion health-check form with the patient. Patients in good health are then given an appointment for the operation.

2. The day before the scheduled operation, the patient will be phoned by a nurse to check that their health is still good. The patient is also invited to ask any questions they may have about the operation. As long as everything seems fine from the perspective of both the nurse and the patient, the patient is instructed to show up for the hospital appointment and the operation. The hospital specialist's waiting list is now significantly reduced because they do not have to see patients for either the pre-operation diagnosis or the post-operation check-up (see below). The patient therefore now has to wait only 6 to 12 weeks for the operation.

3. After a few days the patient is told to return to the optician for new glasses. At this appointment, the optician will check that the operation was successful and, where there seems to be any problems, refers the patient back to the hospital specialist. If no problems are diagnosed, the patient will be given new glasses and the process is terminated.

As described, the new process is much simpler and quicker. Everyone involved was more satisfied with the new process: the patients because the procedure was shorter and involved fewer visits; the opticians because they now had more responsibility and were compensated accordingly; the hospital specialists because they could satisfy patients better and have more time to spend on problem cases; the GPs because they did not have to waste their time on a problem in which they had no expertise; and the nurses who could cut out unnecessary visits and reduce their heavy workload. The new practice was widely publicized by the internal change consultant across other hospital authorities in the UK. Since many of these individuals expressed interest in the changes that had been made, this "best practice" was codified (described in a written document) by the change consultant and circulated to the other hospitals. Upon reading the new practice, however, the professionals in the other hospitals dismissed the new practice as "unworkable."

Why did this new "best practice" not transfer easily across to the other hospitals? In order to understand why the transfer was not successful, it is important to reflect on how the initial team was successful in designing the new practice. As those involved in the project exchanged ideas and information, new meanings and insights were generated. In particular, through the process of interaction and deliberation, a holistic under-standing of the diagnostic and treatment practice was created. Before the project team was established, each professional group had only a partial view of what constituted the overall cataract diagnosis and treatment rou-tine or process (see Shani, Sena, & Stebbins, 2000; Tsoukas, 1996); they each knew what their role was but they did not know what others did across the process. In particular, through the exchange within the project team, all of the professional groups involved in the process started to rec-ognize the value of and underutilization of the opticians' skills and exper-tise. Through working together on the project and sharing their professional knowledge, the hospital specialists involved learned to respect and trust the competencies of the opticians. Moreover, the build-ing of relationships, facilitated by membership on the project team, meant that now an optician could telephone a specialist working at the hospital and directly ask his or her advice. The hospital specialists were providing regular feedback to the opticians, so the opticians could con-tinue to learn how to make diagnoses that were acceptable to the special-ists. In essence, an important outcome from involvement in the cataract project team was the creation of a *community of practice* (Brown & Duguid, 1991) in which shared meaning was being continuously constructed through a process of narration and joint work. Through interactions that occurred during the process of redesigning the cataract practice, the landscape of social relations had been changed.

The new work practice, however, could not be directly transferred to other hospital contexts where the proposed recipients had not been through this change process. These latter individuals had not generated the requisite holistic knowledge and broader understanding of skills; and the relations between the hospital specialists, opticians, GPs, and nurses had not changed. In the absence of this holistic generation of knowledge and changed relationships, the templates and the new practice made little sense. In other words, it was not possible to transfer the templates and knowledge of the new diagnostic and treatment process to other contexts where the holistic knowledge generation process had not taken place. The barriers between the sociocultural practices of the professional groups involved still existed, obstructing best practice transfer. In the initial project team, micro-level shifts in the relative power of the different pro-fessionals occurred through engaging in the project process itself. In other contexts, those involved would not share the new reality about prac-tice that had been generated at the focal hospital (Rowley, 2000). Existing professional boundaries and the concomitant distribution of knowing among those involved meant that the new practice was rejected as unworkable. Thus, within each new context, the various professionals involved need to generate the collective knowledge that was the basis of the redesigned practice at the focal hospital.

In effect, knowledge of the practice of the diagnosis and treatment of cataracts was sustained by the interaction of the various collective actors, and the knowledge existed only through this social interaction (Gherardi & Nicolini, 2000). As Cook and Brown (1999) observe, groups not individuals possess the "body of knowledge," and not everybody within a group possesses everything that is in this body of knowledge. Knowledge of the routine, therefore, had to be generated through interaction and communication within the project team (Weick, 1995). Attempts to transfer knowledge of this new best practice to another situation where those involved had not been through this process of knowledge generation could not be and were not effective.

In this "other" context, preexisting ideas about normal practice limit the absorptive capacity of those involved (Cohen & Levinthal, 1990). Since absorptive capacity has been found to be the biggest impediment to the internal transfer of knowledge (Szulanski, 1996), it appears that any given work practice must be viewed as culturally mediated. Thus, for hospital specialists who have not been through the "conversion" process that those in the case team had been exposed to, their prior knowledge is likely to tell them that "opticians cannot accurately diagnose cataracts." Thus, acceptance of a new practice, which renders obsolete these taken-for-granted assumptions, is unlikely in the absence of situated learning (Orlikowski, 2000).

This does not mean that the templates and description of the new "best practice" produced by the focal hospital will not be useful to those in other contexts. In understanding how they may be used, it is helpful to see the developed templates as *boundary objects* (Star, 1989). Since boundary objects have interpretive flexibility (Hildreth, 2000), we should expect then that the templates designed at the focal hospital will be modified in each new context as those involved attempt to make sense of this explicit knowledge. During this process, knowledge will be shared and blended with these existing templates in order to generate new knowledge in each new context. Thus, the knowledge embedded in the templates must undergo what Czarniawska and Joerges (1996) refer to as a *process of traveling*, whereby the knowledge must be legitimated in each new context. Given differences in contexts, alternative interpretations or understandings are inevitable, even when people are presented with the same information. Thus, the templates and practices developed at the focal hospital will be interpreted differently in other contexts. As Dervin (1998, p. 38) states: "reading about a best practice ... makes little sense without an understanding of the struggle and gaps it was invented to traverse."

While this example emphasizes the situated nature of knowing, it is also clear that formal knowledge possessed by the various participants was also important. Each member of the cataract project team had particular professional knowledge that was important to the diagnosis and treatment of cataracts. They each used their respective knowledge as a tool to make sense of what was happening in the existing process of diagnosis and treatment and, more importantly, as a tool to discuss how the process could be changed to satisfy the different needs of the various stakeholders involved. A group of individuals who did not first possess this body of knowledge could not have redesigned the cataract process in a meaningful way. The team that made the changes possessed the necessary knowledge, knowledge that was distributed across the different professionals involved, which enabled the team to know how it could change the practice. In this sense, we can see the generative dance played out between knowledge and knowing—knowledge was the tool through which those involved could know and so change the practice of diagnosing and treating cataracts.

THE ROLE OF CONSULTANTS IN FACILITATING KNOWING IN PRACTICE

The internal consultant in the cataract project team case was extremely important in bringing together the various representatives of the different professional groups and facilitating a dialogue between them. This interaction enabled them to generate the holistic understanding of the cataract diagnosis and treatment process, which helped to break down the barriers between the independent sociocultural practices of the different professional groups. The resultant insight and relationships led to the changed practice and improved service. Without the facilitation by the internal consultant of a social process of interaction and dialogue, each professional group would have remained entrenched in its own set of existing practices and taken-for-granted assumptions. The consultant, however, was not successful in simply transferring the knowledge about this new practice to other hospitals, largely due to the realities in the other contexts. Those involved were blinded by their taken-for-granted assumptions and tacit understandings about the role and expertise of the different professionals involved.

In these situations, the role of the consultant cannot be to simply transfer explicit knowledge of a new, so-called "best practice." Rather, the most important role of the consultant is to facilitate dialogue and discussion in each new context so that those involved can similarly develop new understandings of the role and expertise of the others involved. It is the resulting interaction and the knowledge it develops that will ultimately allow them to change their overall practice. It is helpful, of course, for consultants to share the templates and explicit description of new practices with professionals in other contexts as they can facilitate their engagement in this social process of interaction. However, it is important to avoid suggesting that what has been done elsewhere is *the* best practice since this stance does not allow room for negotiation in each new context. Moreover, presenting a very fixed idea of *the* best practice is likely to lead to resentment and resistance from those in new contexts, especially initially when the new practice appears so alien. In this sense, preventing reinvention is not the goal of the consultant. Indeed, the goal of the consultant is, to some extent at least, to encourage reinvention, albeit reinvention that is informed by what has been done in other places, and to facilitate interaction and dialogue among key stakeholders.

Drawing on the cataract project team case, it is clear that recognizing the situated nature of knowing is crucial to understanding why a best practice identified in one situation is difficult to simply transfer to another context. The mere possession and dissemination of knowledge is not enough to change practice because practice can only be changed when the barriers between the sociocultural practices of the different communities involved are broken down. That said, tasks and practices do differ in the extent to which the mere possession of knowledge allows one to knowledgeably engage in the practice. As illustrated in the bike-riding example, the mere possession of knowledge (how to ride a bike) does not necessarily allow one to simply and successfully apply that knowledge (immediately be able to ride a bike). In this case, practice is paramount to develop the tacit knowledge that underpins this activity. Similarly, few of us would be comfortable performing an intricate surgery on someone, however much we read about the operation and "possessed" the necessary explicit knowledge. We would want instead to have a skilled surgeon perform the operation—someone who was practiced in the performance of the operation, with the requisite tacit understanding that must accompany the explicit knowledge about how and why to do certain things.

Lave and Wenger (1991) refer to this as *knowledgeable skill*—learning that is configured through the process of becoming a full participant in a particular sociocultural practice. Thus, for those practices where knowledgeable skill is fundamental, there can be no transfer of knowledge about best practice that will straightforwardly change the practice. In these instances, the role of the consultant is to facilitate interaction, which will help to create shared understandings that can provide the space for change.

The challenge is different for those tasks and practices where the possession of knowledge allows one to accomplish the task fairly readily, without having to develop unique tacit knowledge through extensive practice. For example, we can follow instructions and build a desk from a set of pre-shaped and preprepared pieces; we can follow the instructions in a recipe book and make a reasonably sophisticated meal for a dinner party; or, in a work context, we can follow a set of instructions in order to process a customer order. It is not that these types of activities do not contain any tacit knowledge. Of course they do, but they contain the kind of tacit knowledge that most of us possess as an outcome of our daily life experiences. For such practices, there may be more scope for encouraging change through the transfer of knowledge about best practice. Unfortunately, there are relatively few practices in the context of work where the tasks involved can rely almost exclusively on explicit knowledge and commonly held tacit knowledge. As we suggested earlier, improvisation in action is commonplace and most even moderately complex practices typically involve a number of people, each engaged in their own particular part of the activity, with little understanding of the overall process. Moreover, even a simple procedure like taking a customer order may vary across organizational cultures because of different expectations and norms, so that the transfer of knowledge about a so-called "best practice" may be inappropriate and ineffective.

CONCLUSION

Many organizations are keen to improve the ways in which they exploit and explore knowledge so that they can improve existing products and services and develop new ones that will add value and better satisfy their customers. The idea that an organization can do this through the acquisition of knowledge about a new best practice that will allow them to change existing practices is appealing. Certainly it is an idea that many consultants promote, selling their services on the premise that they can help a company adopt such "best practices." This chapter explores the limitations of this view by examining the ways in which practice is socially constructed. Individuals only become knowledgeably skilled by becoming a full participant in a particular sociocultural practice (Lave & Wenger, 1991). Moreover, knowledge of any given sociocultural practice is distributed across individuals and groups, with no one individual or group understanding the overall practice. To change practice will typically require that those involved develop a common understanding—holistic knowledge—of the overall practice. Such an understanding depends on social interaction and discussion among those involved so that each can appreciate how their own practice can change to facilitate an overall improvement in the process.

Given this context, the straightforward transfer of knowledge about a new practice is unlikely to be helpful since changing practice involves a renegotiation of what it means to be knowledgeably skilled. In this context, the possession of knowledge alone will not change practice, but will rather be a tool through which participants in the practice can rethink and reevaluate how best to operate. This dynamic suggests that consultants should not attempt to directly transfer "best practice," trying to reduce reinvention either within or across organizations. Rather, the role of consultants, for anything but the most simple practice, is to actively encourage reinvention by helping participants in each context engage in the discussion and dialogue that will enable them to understand the overall practice. Only then will the participants be fully able to reconsider the roles and responsibilities of both their own group and the roles and responsibilities of others.

NOTE

1.   The case on which this chapter is based is published in S. Newell, L. Edelman, H. Scarbrough, J. Swan, and M. Bresnen, "'Best practice' development and transfer in the NHS: The importance of process as well as product, "*Journal of Health Services Management, 2003*, vol. 16, pp. 1-12. The research was based on a project supported by the United Kingdom EPSRC.

REFERENCES

Abrahamson, E. (1996). Management fashion. *Academy of Management Review, 21*, 254–285.

Alavi, M. (2000). Managing knowledge. In R. Zmud (Ed.), *Framing the domain of IT management* (pp. 15–28). Cincinnati, OH: Pinnoflex Educational Resources Ltd.

Alavi, M., & Leidner, D. (1999, February). Knowledge management systems: Issues, challenges and benefits. *Communications of the Association for Information Systems, 1*, 5.

Becker, M. (2001). Managing dispersed knowledge: Organizational problems, managerial strategies and their effectiveness. *Journal of Management Studies, 38*(7), 1037–1051.

Blackler, F. (1995). Knowledge, knowledge work and organizations: An overview and interpretation, *Organization Studies, 16*, 1021–1046.

Brown, J. S., & Duguid, P. (1991). Organizational learning and communities of practice: Towards a unified view of working, learning and innovation, *Organization Science, 2*(1), 40–57.

Collins, M. (1992). *Artificial experts: Social knowledge and intelligent machines.* Cambridge, MA: MIT Press.

Cohen, M., & Levinthal, D. (1990). Absorptive capacity: A new perspective on learning and innovation. *Administrative Science Quarterly, 35*(1), 128–152.

Cook, S. D. N., & Brown J. S. (1999) Bridging epistemologies: The generative dance between organizational knowledge and organisational knowing. *Organization Science, 9,* 381–400.

Czarniawska, B. (1996). Travels of ideas. In B. Czarniawska & G. Sevon (Eds.), *Translating organizational change* (pp. 13–48). Berlin: De Gruyter.

Dervin, B. (1998). Sense-making theory and practice: An overview of user interests in knowledge seeking and use. *Journal of Knowledge Management, 2*(2), 36–45.

Dougherty, D. (1992). Interpretive barriers to successful product innovation in large firms. *Organization Science, 3*(2), 179–202.

Gherardi, S., & Nicolini, D. (2000). The organizational learning of safety in communities of practice. *Journal of Management Inquiry, 9*(1), 7–18.

Grant, R. (1996). Prospering in dynamically-competitive environment: Organizational capability as knowledge integration. *Organization Science, 7,* 375–387.

Hansen, M., Nohira, N., & Tierney, T. (1999). What's your strategy for managing knowledge? *Harvard Business Review, 77*(2), 106–116.

Hildreth, P. (2000). Communities of practice in the distributed international environment. *Journal of Knowledge Management, 4*(1), 27–38.

Lave, J., & Wenger, E. (1991). *Situated learning: Legitimate peripheral participation.* Cambridge, UK: Cambridge University Press.

March, J. G. (1991). Explorations and exploitations in organizational learning. *Organization Science, 2*(1), 71–87.

Marakas, G. M., Johnson, R. D., & Palmer, J. W. (2000). A theoretical model of differential social attributions toward computing technology: When the metaphor becomes the model. *International Journal of Human Computer Studies, 52*(4), 719–750.

McElroy, M. (2000). Integrating complexity theory, knowledge management and organizational learning. *Journal of Knowledge Management, 4*(3), 195–203.

Nelson, R. (1991). Why do firms differ, and how does it matter? *Strategic Management Journal, 12* [Winter Special Issue], 61–74.

Newell, S., Edelman, L., Scarbrough, H., Swan, J., & Bresnen, M. (2003). 'Best practice' development and transfer in the NHS: The importance of process as well as product knowledge. *Journal of Health Services Management, 16,* 1–12.

Orlikowski, W. (1996). Improvising organizational transformation over time: A situated change perspective. *Information Systems Research, 7*(1), 63–92.

Orlikowski, W. (2000). Using technology and constituting structures: A practice lens for studying technology in organizations. *Organization Science, 11*(4), 404–428.

Orr, J. (1996). *Talking about machine.* Ithaca, NY: ILR Press/Cornell University Press.

Polanyi, M. (1958). *Personal knowledge.* Chicago: University of Chicago Press.

Rowley, J. (2000). From learning organization to knowledge entrepreneur. *Journal of Knowledge Management, 4*(1), 7–15.

Ruggles, R. (1998). The state of the notion: Knowledge management in practice. *California Management Review, 40*(3), 80–89.

Shani, A. B., Sena, J. A., & Stebbins, M. W. (2000). Knowledge work teams and groupware technology: Learning from Seagate's experience. *Journal of Knowledge Management, 4*(2), 111–124.

Shariq, S. Z. (1998). Sense making and artifacts: An exploration into the role of tools in knowledge management. *Journal of Knowledge Management, 2*(2), 10–19.

Star, S. L. (1989). The structure of ill-structured solutions: boundary objects and heterogeneous distributed problem-solving. *Distributed Artificial Intelligence, 2*, 37–54.

Star, S. L. (1996). Working together: Symbolic interactionism, activity theory and information systems. In Y. Engestrom & D. Middleton (Eds.), *Cognition and communication at work* (pp. 296–318). Cambridge, UK: Cambridge University Press.

Swan, J., Newell, S., Scarbrough, H., & Hislop, D. (1999). Knowledge management and innovation: Networks and networking. *Journal of Knowledge Management, 3*(4), 262–275.

Szulanski, G. (1996). Exploring internal stickiness: Impediments to the transfer of best practices within the firm. *Strategic Management Journal, 17*, 27–43

Tsoukas, H. (1996). The firm as a distributed knowledge system: A constructivist approach. *Strategic Management Journal, 17*, 11–25.

Tsoukas, H., & Vladimirou, E. (2001). What is organizational knowledge? *Journal of Management Studies. 38*(7), 973–993.

Weick, K. (1995). *Sensemaking in organizations*. London: Sage.

CHAPTER 4

"KNOWING" IN THE CONSULTANCY FIRM

Exploring Knowledge, People, Context, and Tools in Action

Elena Bou and Alfons Sauquet

In recent years, the practitioner and academic communities have placed significant attention on the study and management of knowledge in organizations. Although the study of knowledge has been sustained by different theoretical trends, two main discourses are becoming consolidated in the knowledge management (KM) domain. The first discourse, which is based on *knowledge*, reflects what Tsoukas (1996) refers to as a "taxonomic perspective," emphasizing types and characteristics of knowledge. Adopters of this perspective pay particular attention to knowledge conversions (e.g., Boisot, 1995; Crossan, Lane, & White, 1999; Davenport & Prusak, 1998; Gupta & Govindarajam, 2000; Myers, 1996; Nonaka & Takeuchi, 1995; Probst, Raub, & Romhardt, 2000). They agree that knowledge, as any other company asset or input, should be captured, stored, distributed, and applied. Much of this focus is on the challenge of knowledge transformation since, according to this view, knowledge should be "ready to

Challenges and Issues in Knowledge Management, 69–106

use." Only when it is "captured" by the organization and made explicit it will be a competitive advantage. This trend has been the prevalent perspective in the KM field.

So-called knowledge-intensive firms (KIFs) have not been an exception, and management consultancies have been pioneers in developing and implementing KM systems that were based primarily on capturing information, making it accessible and/or connecting people (e.g., KPMG: Alavi, 1997; Andersen Consulting: Davenport & Hansen, 2002; Ernst & Young: Chard & Sarvary, 1997; PricewaterhouseCoopers: McCauley, Fukagata, Lovelock, & Farhoomand, 2000). These approaches are sustained under the belief that relevant knowledge can be captured and that, once knowledge is captured, it will be made accessible and eventually, people will act according to the application of that knowledge.

During the last decade, scholars shifted toward framing theoretical approaches focused on sustaining practical initiatives, emphasizing *knowing* over knowledge per se (e.g., Blackler, 1995; Brown & Duguid, 2000; Cook & Brown, 1999; Lave & Wenger, 1991; Newell, Robertson, Scarbrough, & Swan, 2002; Orlikowski, 2002). This approach leans on the central consideration of action—practice—and focuses on the coexistence of learning and action and the context in which it takes place. More importantly, context is not a landscape or a container, but a "territory" to travel through. It is a constituent element. Besides, as practice becomes the focal point of attention, the boundaries between learning and knowing become less relevant. Consequently, knowledge and its types are conceded little or no attention for they are not appreciated as action antecedents.

Learning is not just described as the result of a cognitive process but as a phenomenon that derives basic properties from its context. In other words, learning is situated (Lave & Wenger, 1991). Practitioners have echoed these theories and KM approaches were increasingly based on social approaches, fostering communities of practice in the organization and paying special attention to organizational culture (Alvesson & Karreman, 2001).

The underlying premise of this chapter is that by disregarding knowledge and its types, researchers have, in essence, been prevented from studying the *interaction* between different knowledge types and knowing. Cook and Brown (1999), for example, have suggested that it is in the interplay between knowledge and knowing that generativity can be found. Yet, while their model provides a good framework to study the interplay between knowledge and knowing, or what might be thought of as the interplay between knowledge and action, some authors have pointed to some shortcomings (e.g., Bou, Sauquet, & Bonet, 2004; Orlikowski, 2002). First, Cook and Brown highlight the fact that different types of knowledge are combined when we are acting and knowing, scant explanation is given about how this combination takes place. Second, although Cook and Brown's theory has been used as a reference by many scholars (e.g., Bechky, 2003; Castillo, 2002; McNulty, 2002; Merali, 2000), there is a lack of empirical research that illustrates, sustains, or delves deeper into the model (for an exception, see King & Ranft, 2001). Finally, we anticipate that discussing neglected factors—such as idiosyncratic aspects of practice, organizational structure, and the role of the knower and actor—could enrich the model. Indeed, as contingency issues have been conceded relatively little attention, considering these variables may shed light on questions that could potentially lead us to a more comprehensive vision of the interplay of knowledge and knowing.

Drawing on the study of knowing and practice as a reference, the chapter explores the following issues and questions:

- The relationship between practice and "knowing" is still unclear—how do we engage in knowing-in-action?
- The current "knowing" discourse has conceded little or no attention to knowledge, which has prevented researchers from studying the interaction between different knowledge types and knowing. What is the role of different types of knowledge in organizations, how are they articulated in practice, and what are the key knowledge dynamics in action? Are there key aspects that may help to reconcile both approaches in theoretical and practical ways?
- To what extent do organizational elements exert an influence on knowing (e.g., organizational structure, see Lam, 2000; characteristics of practice, see Schön, 1983)?

The chapter explores these issues through an in-depth case study of AKUA, a global management consulting firm. However, before delving into the empirical study and our description of "real" practitioner work in the KM arena, the discussion clarifies the main theoretical aspects considered, the research setting, and methodology. The chapter concludes with a preliminary examination of our findings and the implications for our thinking about knowledge management.

THE STUDY OF PRACTICE, KNOWING, AND BUNDLES OF KNOWLEDGE

A practice-based discourse has increasingly been adopted by many scholars in the KM domain. However, one of the main problems we face is that the terms "knowing" and "practice" are unclear. Indeed, many authors present their work based on the study of "knowing" and "practice" without defining the terms or blurring them in their research (e.g., Atherton, 2003; Lanzara & Patriotta, 2001; Shin, Holden, & Schmidt, 2001). Table 4.1, for example, illustrates the different ways in which these concepts have been used.

Based on an analysis of these definitions, a number of observations can be drawn. First, all the authors agree that knowing and action are interwoven, although the nature of that relationship is not always the same. For instance, some authors argue in favor of an intimate relationship between both terms (e.g., Schön, 1983), suggesting that knowing and acting are mutually constituted. This view challenges the foundations of Cartesian dualism as it sharply distinguishes between mind and body and, more importantly, its natural inference according to which knowledge precedes action. In turn, Schön's work is indebted to the antimentalist claims of Ryle (1949), who questioned efficient performance on the basis of logical and empirical reasoning, and Polanyi (1958), who explored the role of knowledge in relation to action.

Second, some authors stress the fact that knowing implies "relations" (Lave & Wenger, 1991) and/or "interactions" (Cook & Brown, 1999; Orlikowski, 2002). Indeed it is important that in addition to acknowledging the centrality of practice we do not lose sight of the thinking subject (Clancey, 1995) and provide room for epistemological agency. In other words, stressing situatedness does not mean dissolving the agent in the practice; on the contrary, it involves understanding a dynamic interaction between the agent, knowledge, and practice and this is only feasible through providing evidence of how knowledge and knowing mutually constitute each other.

Third, knowing is implicit in our actions. Our "doing" is the evidence of that "knowing,'" and, most of the time, knowers or actors remain unaware of the existence of this knowing phenomena. Finally, some authors stress the fact that knowing has to do with the epistemic work inherent in action, and therefore "knowledge" is also present and considered. All these perspectives will be considered when we refer to *knowing* in the chapter.

Taking into account the different definitions of "practice" that are summarized in Table 4.1, we refer to *practice* as the typical situations encountered by practitioners when they are doing "real work" in a particular context framed by time and space. This definition captures some crucial characteristics, which underscore that practice is a group of activities situated in a specific context with historical influences.

Although these authors share a lot of common aspects, their focus differs when studying practice and knowing. For instance, Schön (1983) focuses on the practice of different professionals, comparing the "rational

**Table 4.1. Definitions of "Knowing"
and "Practice" in the KM Literature**

Authors	Knowing	Practice
Schön (1983)	"Our knowing is ordinarily tacit, implicit in our patterns of action and in our feel for the stuff with which we are dealing … our knowing is our action" (p. 49). "we are usually unable to describe the knowing which our action reveals" (p. 54).	"performance in a range of professional situations" (p. 60). "preparation for performance" (p. 60).
Lave & Wenger (1991)	"Knowing is activity by specific people in specific circumstances" (p. 52). "Knowing is inherent in the growth and transformation of identities and it is located in relations among practitioners, their practice, the artifacts of that practice, and the social organization and political economy of communities of practice" (p. 122).	
Cook & Brown (1999)	"'Knowing' refers to the epistemic work that is done as part of action or practice" (p. 387). "'knowing' is about relation: it is about interaction between the knower(s) and the world" (p. 388). "knowing is to interact with and honor the world using knowledge as a tool" (p. 389).	"we intend the term "practice" to refer to the coordinated activities of individuals and groups in doing their 'real work' as it is informed by a particular, organizational or group context" (p. 316).
Gherardi (2000; 2003)	"Knowing is a collective accomplishment which depends on a range of spatially and temporally distributed local practices lying outside the control of any organization and within a network of relationships" (2003, p. 352).	"practice is a system of activities in which knowing is not separate from doing" (2000, p. 215). "practice connects 'knowing' with 'doing'" (2000, p. 218).
Orlikowski (2002)	"knowing is not a static embedded capability or stable disposition of actors, but rather an ongoing social accomplishment, constituted and reconstituted as actors engage the world in practice" (p. 249). "knowing is an enacted capability" (p. 256).	"When practices are defined as the situated recurrent activities of human agents, they cannot simply be spread around as if they were fixed and static objects" (p. 253).

technician" who applies rules and procedures to the "reflective practitioner." He argues that not only does this practitioner reflect on action, but he or she also reflects *in* action in order to face uncertainty and complexity. This reflection-in-action is a "conversation" with the situation and is linked to the ability of being aware of what is happening and being able to find the best solution in order to achieve one's purpose or goal. Yet, while Schön's contribution is key to the study of knowing and practice, his examples are mainly problem-solving situations where the practitioners are able to control certain aspects of the situation. For instance, in his examples the practitioners stopped to review or comment about a difficult case or a difficult problem to solve. Second, the context is considered, but it is more of a container than an active player. Schön does not consider how contextual variables affect this knowing-in-action. Finally, Schön's model is centered in the agent or actor and his activities. Most of his work is based on the study of activities in which a single individual plays a predominant role.

Based on her anthropological studies, Lave (1993) defends a perspective based on situated activity, stressing the role of contextual issues and claiming that situated activity is closely linked with changes in knowledge and action (i.e., learning). According to Lave, learning, therefore, is ubiquitous in practice and there are difficulties in providing a differential status for knowledge. Lave and Wenger (1991) framed their theory of situated learning and legitimate peripheral participation along these same lines. In contrast with Schön's theory, Lave and Wenger emphasize contextual and collective aspects, but they stress that the processes by which individuals get an identity in a social web undermine the individual's capacity. Apparently, it is sociology without an actor or, as Clancey (1995) argues in a very sound way, Lave's characters "do not think."

Another group of authors, under the umbrella of activity theory (e.g., Blackler, 1995; Engeström, 1987), also draw attention to knowing and make the activity or practice their object of study—situated in the activity's historical context.

As noted earlier, while Cook and Brown's (1999) model is valuable to study the interplay between knowledge and knowing, it is not comprehensive enough as it still pays too large a tribute to the taxonomic perspective, has not been empirically grounded, and does not acknowledge an evolving dynamic. This point is well taken by Orlikowski (2002) who offers a framework drawing out the evolution of the study of "knowing" and the idea of knowing as "enacted capability." However, her study of practice is solely based on in-depth interviews lacking observation of the actual practice. Also, it is difficult to see how what Orlikowski identifies as "practices" in her empirical work in a specific firm may apply to other organizations. From our point of view, once practice is defined by way of its situatedness,

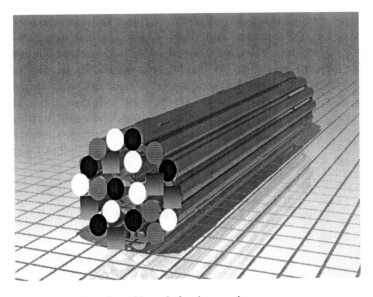

Figure 4.1.   Bundles of knowledge in practice.

it has inherent contextual and idiosyncratic aspects and may not be broadly generalizable.

Drawing on these different contributions, the chapter explores the idea of "knowing"-in-practice. Thus, *situated practice* becomes our object of analysis. Taking practice as our starting point, we will explore "knowing" without omitting the role of knowledge and the learning that is inherent in it. In examining the relationship between knowledge and knowing, we consider that in practice the combination of different types of knowledge constitutes a "bundle of knowledge" (see Figure 4.1). We may know its ingredients, but we do not know its different forms, combinations, or shapes. A metaphor would be a palette of primary colors (different types of knowledge), which are combined to form a picture (the action). Different pictures may have different combinations of colors and different shades.

The chapter explores how this bundle of knowledge ("knowing") is formed, trying to distinguish different variables that may alter this combination. Our hypothesis is that the bundle of knowledge that is used in practice may vary depending on the idiosyncrasy of the practice and the organizational structure where it takes place. As Lam (2000) argues, different organizational structures may foster different types of knowledge: the professional bureaucracy sustains the development of individual explicit knowledge, the machine bureaucracy fosters collective explicit knowledge, the operating adhocracy harbors individual tacit knowledge, and the J-form organization supports collective tacit knowledge. Thus, depending on the practice and organizational form, this "bundle of knowledge" can be formed in different ways with potentially different epistemic dynamics. In other words, different organizations may foster or prioritize different types of knowledge. However, not only are types of knowledge affected, but it also may vary their dynamics in action. For instance, in some organizations reflection-in-action may be privileged over other forms of epistemic work. Subsequently, organizations are conceptualized as a combination of different types of knowledge with different ways of "knowing."

RESEARCH SETTING AND STUDY DESIGN

Our exploration into "knowing" and learning is based on a study of experts and novices in the consulting practice in a specific firm, referred to as AKUA. Within this context, the "experts" are the senior managers who have been in their position for at least 3 years and the "novices" are the individuals who have recently taken on a managerial role. According to the formal organization, their basic functions are nearly identical. While a longitudinal analysis of knowledge development within a group of individuals might be the ideal approach to studying how "knowing" evolves, a comparison between experts and novices enables us to study the interplay between knowledge and knowing that entails a learning situation.

AKUA is a global management consulting firm that delivers industry-focused assurance, legal, and advisory services. As an organization, AKUA is quite hierarchical: there are eight main professional positions and several subdivisions within each group with vertical "ladders." It is expected that successful consultants will climb as high as possible in the organization. The research for this chapter focuses on the firm's advisory or consulting division.

The consulting process starts when a business opportunity has been identified (see Figure 4.2). A service proposal is written and presented to the customer. If the negotiation is successful, the project is internally registered and planning is initiated. At this point, the project is developed. During this phase, agreed deliveries are created and presented to the client. There is also project follow-up and evaluation, with working hours and expenses controlled and registered. Once the work is done, the project is closed and there is a final review and evaluation of the team.

Each project is undertaken by a group of consultants with different positions, and the members of the team usually vary from one project to another. The different activities of the projects are assigned to the con-

-AKUA BUSINESS PROCESSES-

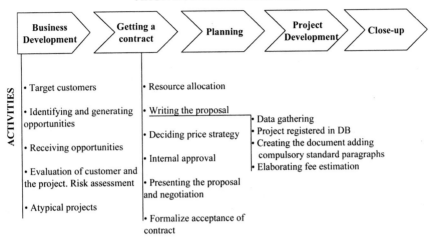

Figure 4.2. Standard AKUA processes.

Table 4.2. Data Collection Methods

Documentation	Archival data
Direct Observation	Five consulting projects:
	11 meetings
	26 hours of recorded data
	22 people
	Informal conversations
	Field notes
Structured, in-depth interviews	15 interviews

sultants according to their hierarchical position in the company, which reflects AKUA's clear and formalized division of labor.

Our study draws on direct observation and in-depth interviews with the expert and novice consultants. The direct observation is based on data from five consulting projects and their group meetings. After observation, in-depth interviews were conducted to inquire about their practice. Data were collected through tape recordings, the researcher's observation notes, and analysis of company documentation and tools (see Table 4.2).

KNOWING-IN-ACTION AT AKUA

This section provides a vignette that captures the way in which the consultants at AKUA attempt to sell their offerings. Although this material consists of a single exchange and it does not comprise the whole practice of the consultants, it is representative of a typical situation at the firm. The vignette is intended to (1) provide the reader with the "flavor" of practice, which will facilitate the subsequent analysis, and (2) illustrate our empirical approach in the field. The analysis "zooms" in and out of the field data, providing an in-depth example of the practice, and an examination and explanation of what is happening.

According to AKUA procedures, the firm's approach embraces two different business processes: "Business Development" and "Getting a Contract" (see Figure 4.2). Although each process explicitly outlines its objective, formalized activities, and who should perform each activity, the vignette shows that the actual practice of selling consulting products is much more complex than the one reflected in the formal organizational procedures, drawing on tacit understandings between the actors. The data in the vignette are verbatim, with the exception of the bracketed comments, which are from the researcher's field notes.

Vignette: Selling Consulting Services in AKUA

Researcher:	Who prepared the proposal?
Senior Manager 1:	(1) The seniors, Consultant A, and me. [Consultant A is the director of this project]
Researcher:	How did you make the proposal?
Senior Manager 1:	(2) Ah, well. Yes, I am allowed to show you that… we use some databases. [The Senior Manager moves toward his laptop and shows a screen with access to corporate databases, where previous business proposals are attached. These proposals have been evaluated and chosen as "best practice."]
	(3) However, we usually use the word-of-mouth system. You get to know who has done a similar project before. In this case, Consultant A had done the other project. We made it based on that proposal. [He takes out a document, which is the proposal for the project.]
	(4) Good, well, as I was telling you, here is the background that we wanted to show them we knew. Then the senior consultant compiled the information and, with the data he compiled, I prepared info on the denomination of origin. We talked about the region, also about the characteristics of the olive groves, which type of

olive they had. And we even made a first diagnosis, on the basis of the information we'd gathered, where we told them what problems we thought they might be facing. In fact, we were right, and that quite surprised them.

Researcher: Of course, because I imagine that they were also testing you.

Senior Manager 1: (5)   Yes, but you have to show them that you're not a greenhorn, that you most certainly know what you're talking about, to give them confidence, because if not, they'll say, "Hold on! What's this idiot on about! I'm the expert, and this guy is telling me fairy stories—no way...." Then we had already spotted that there'd been a problem of demand, that there's an excess of supply and that the positioning of their image was bad. They had a very good reputation, in fact it was the second best-known, but as the positioning was on low segments of products, you know, it was bad.

(6)   We talked first for a bit about them, then we told them what was going on in the olive sector worldwide, that we were well informed, that Consultant A already had this in his data and knowledge bases. Above all, we talked about Australia—the case of Australia is a curious one—and, well, not only Australia ..., we'd got it already for another proposal, but we did show them. We told them that we have the capacity to analyze what happens in the world, and that we know what we're talking about.

(7)   We focused on it from three viewpoints: supply, demand, and organization. And we did it like this because these are the three points we consider we have to cover in the strategic plan.

(8)   And then we threw in some questions.... And then we gave the answers. We said that these things are what must be taken into account when preparing a strategic plan, and then we said, "On a world scale, these questions were dealt with in different countries.... And what about Spain? In Spain there's this, ..., this..., this..., that..., and this one." And then

we told them, "We did all these—this, this, and this." So they could see we had experience and we knew what we were talking about. And, in fact, it was one of the things that decided them, led them to go for us, because they could see that this reference helped us more than anything else.

Researcher: And who were the other consultants competing for the job?

Senior Manager 1: (9)   BP. It has a lot of experience in strategic sector plans, but in this industrial sector they don't have as much as we do.

(10)   BP also has a name and its reputation to rely on. They could do this service, I think they're as capable as we are. The problem is that our strong point was our experience in the sector, and we had to emphasize it to have a competitive advantage against BP, because if not, they could take it off us just the same. Then, the annoying thing was that even if it went to price, then that's when ... and in fact, we were quite nervous when setting the price strategy. At the first meeting we never talk about price. This is the rule we have, because you want to leave them with a good taste in the mouth, and if you say price, they.... On the subject of price, I can tell you my experience, that it's better to negotiate in *petit comité* ..., you can't go to a meeting and say, "Well, that's so much."

Researcher: And what you told me before, the questions you replied to. Is this what you normally use?

Senior Manager 1: (11)   Yes, increasingly. The questions to make them think, yes. Not only on issues of strategy, but even proposals we're offering, and above all when you put them to the people there, you ask them questions that will make them reflect, that will make them say, "Well, I hadn't thought about that, he's right, this fellow."

Researcher: And how did that turn out?

Senior Manager 1: (12)   It turned out well. Consultant A and I said, "We are going to look at what issues could catch them." And based on that, we both began to ask questions, and the ones we liked [*laughs*] we asked them.

Researcher: But the idea of asking questions in this type of presentation, it's just that in other projects, you were already doing it.

Senior Manager 1: (13) Yes, we'd already done it before. And it gave good results. Who thought it up? I don't know. Since here proposals are transmitted from one person to another, and you see one and you say, «hey, this is great, I like it, and so on», and you apply it in another. Someone must have thought it up, but I don't know who. (14) I tell you this because to prepare this document—which has 52 pages—we had 4 days. So you either use this, you know, or you have something similar you've already done. It'll never be the proposal you would have wanted, but either you take stuff from various sources or, if not, you don't have time. (15) Then we explained all the phases that we were going to do, from the point of view of internal and external analysis and all the things that we were going to analyze, the summary of the SWOT, putting forward the alternatives. But practically, we did this because it got through to them better. And really…, these are the methodological things and the activities that we were going to do. (16) The three of us [Partner A, Consultant A, and Senior Manager 1] went to the presentation. And this was good, because with BP, the partner didn't go.

Researcher: Was that decisive?

Senior Manager 1: (17) We haven't asked them, but really, it shows your involvement and your willingness to do the project. But it's not the same having the partner responsible for the sector, who is a heavyweight in the organization, as having a senior manager or a director.

Researcher: And in this presentation, did you all present one part, or was there anyone earmarked to make the presentation?

Senior Manager 1:   (18)   Consultant A took on making the first phase of the presentation, because the truth is, he's the expert with experience in oils.... By the end of this project, I'll have become an expert in the olive sector, but not yet. Although, and this is also true, we sell ourselves as if I was a specialist in the olive-growing sector. At times you have to lie, you take the risk, but ... at times. Until you learn [the particular area of expertise], they are just white lies, but you learn to tell them so convincing that the client believes it. Consultant A presented the first part, I presented the part on methodology, and the partner was..., well, the first part was him, because we told him, to convince the customer why it had to be AKUA. But we had prepared this. Consultant A came in with the part on the sector, and I came in with the part on methodology.

(19)   The important thing is that you transmit self-confidence and that you know what you're doing and know the sector.... When we talked to them about the sector and the knowledge we had of their situation, and of what was happening in Spain and of what had happened in the world. About the world they had no idea, I'm convinced. It rang a bell, but what's happening in Spain, what's happening in their region, that's their daily bread, that's what they know about, and we set it out and no one complained and said no, on the contrary: then they saw that we had understood the problem.

(20)   Then, at the time of the sale, the partner tells them that we can offer them the best service, that we are involved, that we are going to be here, that we wanted to do it. This had considerable importance. And then, above all that, they saw that we knew about the sector, and that we understood their problem. The methodology, that is the part that I presented, and I sincerely think that we have no differences about anything over BP because, in fact, I would bet anything that if I see their methodol-

ogy and ours, there would not be much difference....

(21)   The partner has to see the proposal to put in the dots and commas. If you give a proposal to the partner and the partner says, "I don't like this," you're lost. Before it reaches the partner—hey, I tell you because the partner, apart from this, has to be concerned with thousands of projects and thousands of commercial actions in other places—we have to get organized.

(22)   Normally, the manager or a senior manager, the difference between manager and senior manager is length of service, a senior manager is normally in charge of bigger projects and a manager is given smaller projects. First-year managers sometimes act as project manager on one of the large projects, but the commercial team has a partner; if it's a large project, it will always have a partner; if it's a smaller project, perhaps a partner isn't needed. In that case, there'll be a director. This was a large project, and we had a partner, a director, and me, a senior manager.

(23)   I took charge of making the proposal, with the help of a senior consultant and an assistant for researching information on the background—but then he didn't take part in the project because he was involved in something else. The rest [of the material] I already had, I have databases and other proposals, depending on the problem they want to deal with, and I sit down beforehand with Consultant A, the director, to focus the subject. He tells me, "This is what we want, this is what has to be done, and this is the problem to go through, and so on." When we have it clear, I set to work on the proposal.

(24)   The team helps me find the information, I process that information, and when I've got a first draft I argue it through with the director. Then it's the director who makes changes, and says, "This we will have to focus on, perhaps

from that angle, or this yes, the other no." This is what we discuss among ourselves and produce the document. And when the final document is ready, this is when you pass it on to the partner. But the partner, as I told you, has to see it once it's perfect, because if it's not perfect he tells you, "This is useless. This is [expletive deleted]!"

Researcher: And how can he see if it's perfect or not so quickly?

Senior Manager 1:   (25)   Because he reads it, he begins to read, if, suddenly ..., he has already shaped it in his head, based on his experience, he knows the problem. We've spoken before and he knows the problem, and also knows how it has to be focused. If he begins to read and suddenly doesn't like what he's reading, he says, "Hey, this isn't good enough, turn it over twice mate, because I'm certainly not going to read this," and he gives it back so you just have to sort it out. He tells you the points and, well, he doesn't tell you explicitly, but you simply have to look a bit at where he's going.

(26)   The director has previously sat with the partner and he already knows where he has to go. It's all very hierarchical and very structured. The partner can sit with me, but normally he won't, not to go over the director's head.

(27)   There have been partners who have even said to me, "My part is to dot the i's and cross the t's, or correct the odd mistake that has got past you." Otherwise, they don't have time to start drawing up the proposal. They only touch it up a bit, you know, what you have to think about is this, that, and the other. They say, "Think about it and when you've got it right, come back."

(28)   I don't like it at all if the partner tells me this, so I make sure he doesn't come back. Now, have I been told this? Yes, I have, above all when I was a manager, with less experience. Yes, they have said this to me.

(29)   I've been a manager for 3 years, this is my fourth year as senior manager. Of course, the first year, when you make your first proposals, you don't do it very well. Well, it's not that you don't do it well, maybe you do it well but it's not the standard that AKUA wants, or the standard the partner is looking for. But that can be learned. When I have to present a proposal now, I know the points I have to cover and already have my idea of how I should present it to comply with the standard. I know what I have to do to understand and make the customer understand that I understand their problem. That's tricky to get over.

Researcher: And what happens sometimes is that, perhaps, depending on the partner you're working with, depending on each project, you know that Partner A has such and such a mania, well, not mania, but...

Senior Manager 1:   (30)   Too true! There are certain partners, well for example ... directors too, it doesn't have to be a partner—and I also have my own manias, I have to say. If they give me a bullet point, without respecting the margin, as soon as I see it, it's out—these are manias.... There are other partners who don't like bold [print], they just don't like it. There are others who when you use blue, they want it in ochre. In other words, yes, everyone has their own [preferences]. What happens is that you work more or less with the same people because we are organized by sectors. Then you already know what they want, their weak points. The same as the seniors, they know what my weak point is, and the consultant knows the weak point of the senior. And if he doesn't know, he'll learn.

(31)   In fact, we have part of our remuneration fixed and the other part variable, depending on compliance with objectives. And what has the highest weighting among these is sales.

(32)   I think that Partner A, the partner of this project, might have an objective, I don't know, of 1,500 million pesetas. But of course, he has

> to make it alone…, or go to the people he has below him, lean on them, and give them objectives at their level, or if not, how is it going to work?

Researcher: I see. In other words, this was how you managed to get the project, and then you did the contract letter.

Vignette Commentary: Analyzing the Data

This next section delves into the vignette, drawing out lessons and observations about the overall process and practice in the consulting firm, taking into account the data obtained by different practitioners in the interview phase.

Putting Things Together

Once one of the AKUA partners and his commercial team (usually a director and/or a senior manager) get in touch with a potential customer, the next step is writing the business proposal and presenting it to the customer. According to the firm's formalized procedures, the manager or senior manager is supposed to gather all the relevant data, register the project in the database, and create the document (the "Proposal") by adding compulsory standard paragraphs (see Figure 4.2). Although these actions are generally followed, the process is more complex in practice.

"Writing the business proposal" is not an individual activity. There are a number of different people and positions involved in its creation. In this case, a partner, a director, a senior manager, and two senior consultants were all involved in the process. The division of labor, which is an aspect of the organizational structure of AKUA, is a relevant dimension because it affects the actual practice. For instance, one crucial requirement is that the proposal should reflect the customer's problems and needs. However, the division of labor prevents all the actors from having direct contact with the customer. As a consequence, the senior manager has to transfer the customer's needs to the manager. This activity is apparently effortless for the senior manager, but it is really crucial for the novice manager, who usually is absent in the meeting with the customer. As a manager explains:

> Kicking off a project is very difficult for a manager if he has been absent in the commercial phase…. Senior managers are always there from beginning…. You could ascertain, you can get information from the person who has been present, but there is always a limit. I have realized that when I participate in the initial data gathering, prepare the proposal, and defend it, my success rate is really very high. If I am in the middle of the process, it

decreases.... Therefore, it is very important to realize that you're winning their confidence and to be involved during the whole process. This is important in capturing what the customer wants. Once you know what he wants, you give it to him, and a bit more ... but that feeling only comes when you are present.

Consultants need to detect if they're being hired because somebody told them to "hire you," because [the client] really has a need, or because he wants to defend something internally but he cannot do it by himself and he needs your help. They need to realize if the client is committed or not, if he is in favor or against [the project], if he has been obliged or not. I think all this is important so you can reflect it in the proposal. It is not the same when someone really needs you than someone who has been obliged to work with you. In the last case, you have to give him other things. In the proposal, you have to try to make him see the benefits for him.... And a good salesman doesn't sell at a distance, he doesn't sell on behalf of others. He needs to be with his customer. So, here, I don't see very clearly how we are organized.

For the senior manager, capturing the client's needs is relatively straightforward, largely because he was present in the meeting. However, for the manager, it is a more complex task as he was not involved in the customer meeting and he has to rely on the senior manager's interpretation and communication. Although transferring the information itself is not particularly problematic, according to the practitioners, capturing the needs of the client also involves detecting the unsaid. It involves "feeling" and intuition, which are forms of individual and tacit knowledge. For these practitioners, having physical access to the customer and participating in the entire process are important for a double reason. While the client contact allows them to do perform the task better, it also legitimates their role within the company. Based on the vignette, apparently the manager and senior manager are supposed to do the same tasks (see section 22). The official difference between them is that the senior manager in an "expert" who has been in the position longer than the (novice) manager. The senior manager has access to the whole process, while the newer manager is left on the periphery. As Lave and Wenger (1991) suggest, legitimate participation is a crucial aspect of becoming a member of a community, and the lack of involvement of the newer managers/consultants limits their learning process.

According to AKUA's standardized procedures, "writing a proposal" entails gathering all the relevant data. This task, however, is not performed by the senior manager, as he guides the other members of the team to where relevant information can be found (e.g., sections 23 and 24). In pursuit of this objective, organizational databases and knowledge repositories of previous business proposals and best practices play an important role (e.g., section 24).

As the vignette illustrates, previous business proposals are key tools for the practitioners. They are a good reference and learning tool. In this framework, learning is produced by analogy. The previous document guides the practitioners (e.g., structure, format, type of letter, methodology) and guides the development of the new proposal (e.g., sections 3 and 6). Resorting to previous work done in the past—by either the individual involved with the proposal or others in the firm—not only saves time (e.g., section 14) but it also helps to spread innovations in an informal way (section 13). Time is crucial for practitioners and it exerts a constant pressure on them, a reality that is underscored by the fact that most consultants participate in more than one project at the same time. This is another distinctive feature of their work, that they have to cope with overlapping projects (section 21).

Despite the value of documentation from previous projects, the vignette captures some of their limitations in practice. Sometimes, having access to the explicit document itself is not enough. In these instances, the practitioners attempt to identify who was involved in the previous project and/or locate the appropriate experts (section 3). These data seem to confirm previous works in which authors have stated that explicit documentation is of limited use when it comes to specific, real situations (e.g., Bou & Sauquet, 2004; Clancey, 1992; Tsoukas, 2003). The information needs to be interpreted, largely through the guidance, understanding, and assistance of the consultants who were actually involved in the earlier project.

On other occasions, the consultants also turn to other colleagues from inside and outside the firm to obtain useful information and practical guidelines—as one of the managers illustrated.

Manager: We have a department with very good sources, you can search through them or through the Internet. Then, people tell you, "Well, I read this and that..." You can draw on a worldwide knowledge management database, ... you can even ask a question and someone from another country will answer, 'Well, I have done something similar." There is a lot of information in many places.

Researcher: However, when you had this problem, you didn't resort to the database. You asked the people you knew had worked on a similar project. And so?

Manager: Well, the truth is that I was assigned to the project on Thursday. On Friday, I was introduced to the client as an expert. I thought [the KM department] could give me the theory of this subject, but I thought it was going to be more valuable to get others' experience.

> They could show me similar models in other compa-
> nies and it was going to be more useful than the the-
> ory I could find about the [project]. Why? Perhaps
> because of the time pressure. The first thing that
> comes into your head is to say "What do I do?"
> Instead of losing 10 hours searching and reading
> things, I am going to see who has done it.

As the above excerpt illustrates, time pressures are a key reason why the practitioners turn to their colleagues rather than explicit resources in the firm's database. The respondents also felt that the others' experiences had significant value, especially since it embraced the type of applied, practical knowledge that will facilitate their efforts.

Another crucial aspect of "writing a proposal," which is not reflected in the formalized procedures, is that the proposal needs to be adapted to the partner who is in charge of the project (section 30). This is only possible if one "knows the partner," which implies more than having a superficial idea of the person's expertise and preferences. It also means that the manager must have sufficient knowledge of the partner to be able to appropriately consider the partner's habits, likes, and dislikes, and to truly understand his messages.

Understanding messages, and therefore, language and meanings, are especially relevant in AKUA. According to some authors (e.g., Werr & Stjernberg, 2003), methods and tools used by consultants provide them with a common language and a common knowledge structure (e.g., concepts, theoretical models). For instance, the senior manager assumes that the researcher knows what SWOT is (section 15), the concept of stakeholders, and so forth. Methods or methodologies are standard and common for the whole company (section 7), and even for other consulting firms (section 20), which fosters understanding among practitioners.

As suggested in this practice, however, it is still necessary to know the specific company jargon to understand what is going on. AKUA's jargon embraces a group of words that only have meaning if you belong to this organization. For instance, the practitioners refer to the "meadow," a metaphor that refers to the layout of the corporate offices. The meadow is the open space where scholars, junior and senior consultants, and managers interact. AKUA has a "big meadow" and a "small meadow" (where just managers are located). Within this context, layout and privacy are symbols of hierarchy. The higher you are in the organizational structure, the more privacy and space you will have (e.g., directors have an office of their own, while senior managers share offices). Indeed, hierarchical aspects are very present in the actual practice of these respondents, and they have to resort to implicit norms to cope with it (e.g., circumventing hierarchical position—section 26).

In order to fully capture messages, you also have to be able to "read between the lines." The meaning in a message is often not explicit, and being able to capture this subtle aspect of the message is crucial. This ability becomes especially important for those consultants climbing the corporate ladder, as this type of knowledge is especially relevant when interacting with the partners. As Senior Manager 1 remarked (section 21), "If the partner says 'I don't like it,' you are lost." This collective tacit knowledge has a lot to do with the "genre" in question (Cook & Brown, 1999) as the same statement in another company might have a different meaning or connotation. In the same way, if a partner says to you, "Turn it over twice, mate" (section 25), the message implies that you have made some error and you should not waste the partner's time. In this instance, the consultant can be in an awkward and risky situation, especially if the subtle warning behind the statement is overlooked.

Complexity increases when the actual practice requires anticipating future events. This is the case when the practitioner has to prioritize relevant information. In order to write the proposal, data and information must be gathered, but questions linger as to how to select the key aspects. According to Senior Manager 1, a key aspect is anticipating customer priorities (see section 12), where Consultant A and Senior Manager 1 have to think about which questions will be relevant for the particular client.

Anticipating customer reactions is also crucial when deciding about the pricing strategy. This activity implies an estimation that considers the budget, workload, and previous experience and expenses with similar projects. However, as the discussion with Senior Manager 1 indicates, there are other less objective aspects that are also considered. In this instance, the partner in charge of the project wants to bring in as much profit as possible in order to meet his annual sales objective (section 32). Moreover, higher incomes in the organization imply more money for the partner at the end of the year—clearly, a strong motivator. At the same time, it is important to take into account how much the customer is willing to pay for the project, something that is not typically made explicit by the client. As a senior manager explained,

> Price estimation is important, because if you propose a price that meets [the client's] expectations, you don't have any problem. We always say that if we are around 10 or 20% up on a customer's expectations, then it is not a problem. If the price is much higher, the door is closed and he will tell you no. If the price is 10% higher, we can negotiate and in the end we can arrange a deal.... But if the price is 20 or 30% higher, even if the client is interested, you run the risk of his going to another firm for their services. Then you are really lost.... Hence, price is an important variable, one that should be cal-

culated very carefully. You have to make the customer see the importance of what you are doing and the fact that what you are proposing to him cannot be done just like that. It implies that a lot of work is involved and the fees are justified.

For instance, we don't fix the fees, but we make the so-called "fee estimate" based on our experience in similar projects. We know—taking into account the size of the customer and his characteristics—the hours we will need. We budget for hours and each hour has a price, depending on the positions of the members of the team. Over that price, you calculate the final fees.... The more experience you have, and the more repetitive the project is, the more you guess correctly. When they ask you something that you are not sure of, then you are a bit "blind."

As the senior manager continued,

Well, for instance, here's an anecdote with a customer. I was talking with the partner, and he told me that he could not come to the meeting with the customer. He told me to go to the meeting by myself. He then asked me if I had done the budget. I said yes, and he asked me how much it was. I told him 66,000 Euros. He told me to "ask him 80." "For heaven's sake!," I thought, "Eighty! That's too much." And he told me to ask him [the client] for 80. He told me he knew the customer and that he would try to bargain over it, but wouldn't think it was too much. To sum it up, I thought, "Well, I am going to tell him that, but we will see what happens at the end." I went to the meeting and made my speech.... The customer took some minutes for his thinking and said, "You have convinced me, I think it is reasonable. I am going to support it in the executive committee." ... Of course, the fellow left me puzzled, because I said "I was scared to ask for 66, he [the partner] asked for 80 and they'll [the customer] give us 80 without batting an eyelid." And why? Well, I don't know. I don't know if it was because he [the partner] knew the customer, or because he had had other similar experiences and he knew it was something the customer needed urgently and he could take advantage of it.

Thus, estimating the price for a consulting service is a complex process, based on experience, knowing the customer, getting a "feel" for the client's needs, and anticipating the client's reactions. This reality clearly exceeded the objectivity suggested in the firm's formalized procedures. It is a process that involves both individual (e.g., section 10 refers to "my experience") and collective (e.g., collective rules: section 10) dimensions.

The Moment of Truth

Once the consultants prepare the written documentation for the proposal, decide on the price, and receive internal approval to move forward, the moment of truth arrives. At this stage, the consultants are "on stage," in front of the client. There is a limited time, and they cannot stop to reflect on or think about the underlying process. At the same time, however, this activity involves a complex amalgam of challenges.

According to the practitioners in our study, there is much more to presenting the proposal than simply explaining the written document. They also have to defend the proposal and convince the customer, being aware of client reaction and instilling a sense of confidence. For this last purpose, they resort to AKUA'S brand image, helping the customer to value their proposal against competitors (section 10), using the client's terminology and jargon, speaking with self-confidence, showing they understand the customer's problem, helping customers to reflect (section 10), illustrating their expertise by presenting team members as experts by pointing out specific aspects of their industrial sector, and emphasizing the commitment of AKUA for that specific project. The discourse employed with the client is, therefore, highly complex with plenty of rhetorical forms. Among these, it is especially relevant how consultants resort to forms of *ethos*. These are discourse constructions that are used by the consultants to demonstrate their credentials and legitimate their role in front of the client audience (e.g., sections 6 and 17). For instance, in section 6 the consultants design a discourse in which they initially present worldwide data about the industrial sector. This is not by chance. If they can prove that they can manage and handle worldwide problems, they will lead the customer to think that they will also be able to manage their problem.

While this exchange is part of the process of convincing the customer, practitioners note that this is not enough. Specific knowledge plays a key role, as clients do not seem attracted by general knowledge like theories or methodologies. Customers value the specific knowledge that the consultants are able to show in the presentation, and it is a differential competitive factor (section 9). Moreover, this specific industrial knowledge points to a difference among AKUA's team members since this type of knowledge is obtained through participation in different projects. As the senior manager noted, "By the end of this project I will have become an expert in the olive sector, but not yet" (section 18).

Although there is a fair amount of latitude involved in this process, the consultants are expected to stay well within organizational norms and AKUA's standards. Everything is expected to be completed within an hour and a half. In these situations, applying steps or adhering to rules can be rather difficult. Our respondents manage this situation by taking for granted certain aspects that they have developed through practice, improvising as events unfold during their presentation. As illustrated by the following comments from Senior Manager 1, the key is "doing" the practice:

And in the end it is like everything else. I remember that at the beginning when I had to present something in public, speak in front of people, it was really a burden. You don't feel secure. But right now, I surprise myself with my ability to improvise and make a presentation. Sometimes, you don't even have time to prepare them. Well, at the end you get so much experience that you know. Of course, at first it's madness. You have to prepare everything. The day before you are there, suffering. You don't sleep for nerves. But then, it is like everything else, you get the hang of it and it works out. It is not that I have got up and got in there, but it's bit by bit … that comes with practice.

Selling Internally: The Underlying Internal Practice

During the course of their practice, we observed the respondents behaving in ways that were not directly related to the formal assigned tasks. For instance, they devoted considerable time to gathering information about new consultants or promotions within the existing group, paying especial attention to rumors and provoking informal conversations. Inquiring about these behaviors, we realized that these were not minor actions. In the same way there is a formal process involved in (external) selling to their clients, there is also a complex informal process of internal selling to colleagues.

"Selling oneself within the company" means to look for an appropriate project and then offering to work with someone on it. A basic question, of course, is why the consultants undertake this course of action since there is already a formal procedure that assigns people to projects. However, this procedure assigns consultants to projects according to organizational needs, without considering the practitioners' preferences. Through this "internal selling," consultants try to meet their individual motivation to work on specific projects. Moreover, in order to have a successful project, senior managers typically look for members they already know. When selecting team members, they first choose among the people they trust. In the same way, the senior manager has been chosen for that project because the director or the partner relies on him. As this dynamic suggests, in addition to winning the customer's trust it is also important to win one's superiors' and colleagues' trust.

There are additional organizational factors that exert an influence. AKUA has a matrix structure. Practitioners belong to both a technical division (where they are specialized in different solutions) and an industry or sector group. However, not all the different solutions or industry groups have the same power and possibilities of growth, and, as a result, promotion. Therefore, the practitioners try to approach certain groups or individuals who, according to them, can facilitate their professional careers.

These are some of the reasons why practitioners devote so much time to making themselves visible *within* their firm. While the "internal selling" game is one way of winning such visibility, the consultants also show their willingness by participating in company events—workshop, meetings, and so on—as a way of getting their superiors to know them.

Winning visibility legitimates one's position within the organization, even to a point that places (legitimates) consultants in a higher status position than the official one they have. In the vignette, for example, Consultant A had been introduced to the researcher (section 1) as a director. However, at the moment of the research he was *not* a director yet. After some months, promotions were announced and he was promoted to the director level, but when the vignette occurred he was still a senior manager. Rather than attempting to mislead the researcher, the individual was unofficially considered as a director. He was already doing the functions of a director, and other organizational members assumed he was in that role—before it was officially announced. In essence, the practitioners "read" a subtle, unofficial company message.

Based on this assessment, it should be clear that actual practice is much more complex than the one reflected in formal procedures and documentation. Table 4.3 reflects this complexity and how the idea of practice can vary depending on one's position within the company.

EXPLORING "KNOWING" IN PRACTICE

The preceding discussion points to a number of different factors that influence consulting in practice. Our analysis of the case vignette draws out the different types of knowledge employed by the practitioners, special characteristics of the nature of their work, and individual, contextual, and organizational aspects of their practice. Moreover, data also suggest differences in the practice of expert managers and novices. This section explores those differences in more detail.

Identifying the Bundle of Knowledge

As illustrated in the vignette, the consultants resorted to myriad forms of knowledge to perform their practice. Using Collins's (1993) classification based on ontological and epistemological criteria, we can distinguish four types of knowledge: individual-explicit, individual-tacit, collective-explicit, and collective-tacit knowledge. In our assessment of practice within AKUA, we identified examples of each type (see Figure 4.3).

Table 4.3.   Practice 1 at AKUA: Commercial Activity/Selling Services

Formalized Process of Getting a Contract

Formalized Activities	*Experts Managers (Senior Managers)*	*Novice Managers (Managers)*
Resources Assignment	• Estimating resources • Assigning people to projects/ choosing the right team • Having trust in someone	• Assigning people to projects • Having trust in someone • Internal selling
Preparing Business Proposal • Data gathering • Project registered in database • Documentation/ adding compulsory paragraphs	• Communicating what customer needs • Locating useful information • Supervising • Anticipating customer reactions: knowing *who* the client is • Adapting the information for the partner	• Understanding what superiors are telling about customer needs • Having a "feeling"/intuition to see what customer wants • Detecting what client really wants/to "see" the unsaid → reading between the lines • Creating the document: trans-lating from official documentation
Deciding Price Strategy	Estimating the price • Anticipating customer reactions • Knowing the partner	
Presenting Business Proposal and Negotiation	• Defending the proposal • Convincing the customer • Giving confidence to the customer: □ Brand image □ Differentiated solutions from competitors □ Using customer's jargon □ Lying in a convincing way □ Speaking with self-confidence □ Showing you understand the problem → prioritizing □ Showing possible threats and offering a solution □ Helping them to reflect □ Selling the team members as experts □ Showing they know about the specific industrial sector □ Showing implications for the firm • Being aware of customer reactions	Giving confidence to the customer/winning customer's trust □ Using customer's jargon □ Showing you understand the problem □ Knowing how to connect with someone
Obtaining Formal Agreement	Negotiating the price: □ Making customer value the offer	

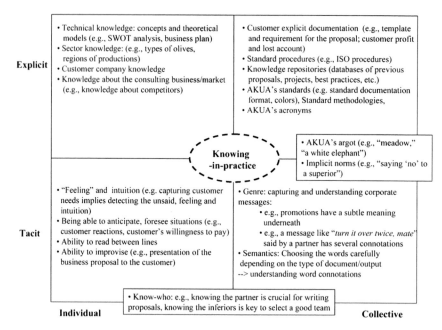

Explicit	• Technical knowledge: concepts and theoretical models (e.g., SWOT analysis, business plan) • Sector knowledge: (e.g., types of olives, regions of productions) • Customer company knowledge • Knowledge about the consulting business/market (e.g., knowledge about competitors)	• Customer explicit documentation (e.g., template and requirement for the proposal; customer profit and lost account) • Standard procedures (e.g., ISO procedures) • Knowledge repositories (databases of previous proposals, projects, best practices, etc.) • AKUA's standards (e.g. standard documentation format, colors), Standard methodologies, • AKUA's acronyms

Knowing -in-practice

• AKUA's argot (e.g., "meadow," "a white elephant")
• Implicit norms (e.g., "saying 'no' to a superior")

Tacit	• "Feeling" and intuition (e.g. capturing customer needs implies detecting the unsaid, feeling and intuition) • Being able to anticipate, foresee situations (e.g., customer reactions, customer's willingness to pay) • Ability to read between lines • Ability to improvise (e.g., presentation of the business proposal to the customer)	• Genre: capturing and understanding corporate messages: • e.g., promotions have a subtle meaning underneath • e.g., a message like *"turn it over twice, mate"* said by a partner has several connotations • Semantics: Choosing the words carefully depending on the type of document/output --> understanding word connotations

• Know-who: e.g., knowing the partner is crucial for writing proposals, knowing the inferiors is key to select a good team

Individual   **Collective**

Figure 4.3. Bundles of knowledge in practice.

Individual-explicit knowledge is particularly relevant in consulting companies. Indeed, individuals who have more of this type of knowledge are considered the formal "experts" within the organization. This would reinforce Lam's (2000) idea that the professional bureaucracy sustains the development of individual-explicit knowledge. Within this form of knowledge, it is worthy to stress the existence of both general (e.g., technical) and specific (e.g., industrial) knowledge. Even though both aspects are part of the individual's explicit knowledge base, the latter is gaining more importance in practice.

Since AKUA is a global company, formalization and standardization play a role in ensuring order and homogeneity, which suggests the additional existence of collective-explicit knowledge. Our empirical data strengthen this premise, and illustrate that this type of knowledge is especially useful in providing the consultants with a common language and the ability to reuse knowledge. Gaining this knowledge is especially relevant for newcomers.

As previously mentioned, however, such organizational artifacts have some limitations. While they typically focus on "what to do" or "what *not* to do," they do not really facilitate practice. For instance, in AKUA written procedures were not very important—even for newcomers. They know about their existence, but time pressures often limit their ability to draw on them. Moreover, the consultants seemed to feel that overlooking these procedures did not comprise the integrity of their practice. As one of the consultants in the study noted, "The methodology tells you what steps to follow, but not how to do it. For instance, it tells you that you have to design a questionnaire, but how should the questionnaire be designed?"

Moreover, explicit documentation cannot be applied without interpretation. Capturing, storing, and distributing this type of knowledge in and of itself may not be difficult, but it is at the moment of practice when difficulties emerge (Bou & Sauquet, 2004; Clancey, 1992; Tsoukas, 2003). As a consequence of these limitations, practitioners usually resort to other colleagues or experts (within or outside the company) who can help them to interpret the procedures or guide their practice.

Despite the amount of written norms and documentation, the most important rules are not written down. They are implicit, shared through informal conversations, and are more crucial than the written guidelines. For instance, although not written in any official AKUA policy, it is "understood" that subordinates cannot say "no" to a partner. Moreover, it is also understood by members of the firm that they "cannot fail to meet a deadline. If you don't sleep, you don't sleep" and that each person has to make him or herself "visible." These statements are examples of unwritten, unofficial norms that are crucial for the survival of the consultant within the company since they are related to the internal organizational system and are expected to be considered in daily practice.

However, writing and acknowledging these norms is not enough. In order to fully understand them, collective-tacit knowledge is also required. For instance, according to the junior consultants, "It's key to know how to say 'no' without putting yourself in hazard." This implies that the practitioners should be able to identify when it is possible to refuse an order and how it might be done without running undue risk. In this instance, the ultimate purpose is to break the unwritten rule of "never say 'no' to a superior's order" in a way that the superior is unaware the individual is breaking the unofficial norm.

As consultants begin to move up the corporate ladder, this type of knowledge becomes increasingly important as they interact with partners. This collective-tacit knowledge has a lot to do with "genre." It is a very contextual knowledge and it only has meaning in a particular scenario. The same statement or sentiment in another company might have a different meaning or connotation.

Individual-tacit knowledge also plays a role, although its nature varies depending on the consultant's experience. Junior consultants need to learn how to work in groups and especially how to work under pressure. Once a consultant has achieved higher status, tacit knowledge shifts to the customer and the need to sell engagements. As illustrated earlier, at AKUA it is understood that it is very important to be able to give confidence to a client and win his trust. Senior managers also need to be able to win their superiors' trust, and one of their tasks is to "free" the director or partner of some of their duties. Other relevant knowledge is being able to anticipate events, for which one's previous experience with customers, colleagues, and projects and also one's own intuition are crucial. Moreover, improvisation is apparently very useful, especially when handling unexpected situations.

Both newcomers and experts agree that consultants should get to know the different individuals. As one of the consultants pointed out, it is important to be observant and to distinguish "who knows and who doesn't, who will support you and who won't, who values your efforts and who doesn't." We have referred to this knowledge as "know-who" (as opposed to know-how) and it implies both an individual skill and explicit and tacit collective knowledge.

The Interplay between "Knowing" and Knowledge: Comparing Experts and Novices

As the preceding discussion has indicated, different types of knowledge exist in AKUA. These different types of knowledge coexist and there is not a conversion. As illustrated earlier, for example, in the practice of "selling consulting products" the practitioners employed different forms of knowledge at the same time (see Figure 4.3). Thus, "knowing-in-practice" appears both in the center of the diagram as well as in a discontinuous line. This means that in the performance of their actual work, the practitioners resort to different forms of knowledge simultaneously and there is an interplay between the enabler (knowledge) and "knowing."

According to AKUA's official documentation, there are not many differences between the practice of senior managers (experts) and managers (novices). Our data, however, suggest that their practice is, in fact, quite different. As we have seen in Table 4.3, their activities do vary and even in the case of common activities, the expert takes into account many more factors. For the expert, practice implies more complexity. As summarized in Table 4.4, this is not the only difference.

Taking into account that AKUA is a highly structured, professional bureaucracy, it could be assumed that the role of explicit knowledge—both individual (Lam, 2000) and collective—should be more relevant than others. However, our data suggest otherwise as individual and collective tacit knowledge are especially relevant for the experts' practice. For

Table 4.4.   Differences and Commonalties Between Experts and Novices

Experts (Senior Managers)	Novices (Managers)
• Practice is more complex. It takes many variables into account.	• Not as many variables are considered
• Anticipates, foresees some situations.	• None, or scarce anticipation
• Improvisation (although they feel awkward to admit it)	• If possible, everything prepared in advance (avoid improvisation)
• Prioritizes between aspects and as a consequence they speed up practice	
• Technical knowledge is subsidiary, it is instilled in them. This makes them self-confident and they pay attention to other aspects.	• Technical knowledge is critically important in their daily practice.
	• Feeling insecure when handling customer's demands.
• Usually resorts to tacit-individual knowledge (to interact with customers) and to tacit-collective knowledge (to interact with partners)	• Usually resorts to formal training.
• Know-who more complex and subtle, tacit components prevail	• Know-who
• Gives "orders" in a subtle way	
• Storytelling to subordinates is frequent	• Sometimes storytelling to subordinates
	• Making themselves visible is more crucial for them.
• Winning superiors' trust in order to "free" them	
• Assess/evaluate subordinates	
• Reading "between the lines": organizational events and messages	

experts, individual-explicit knowledge (i.e., technical knowledge) is not as crucial and it remains subsidiary.

Novices, in contrast, rely more heavily on their technical knowledge, but still employ a type of knowledge constituted by implicit unofficial norms. These unwritten rules mainly focus on the interaction between colleagues, superiors, and subordinates, and on how to break the official standard rules that constrain their practice. They are complex rules that imply a combination of explicit and tacit collective knowledge. Figure 4.4 shows the two different bundles of knowledge in AKUA's consulting practice.

Taking into account these preliminary findings, it appears that an important aspect of relevant knowledge within AKUA is related to the interrelationships between the different practitioners. Many unwritten rules, for example, guide the interactions between the partners, experts and novices, reflecting the reality that practice reflects collective knowledge. Although the tasks are completed by teams, there is still a strict division of labor within the company and everyone has their assigned tasks.

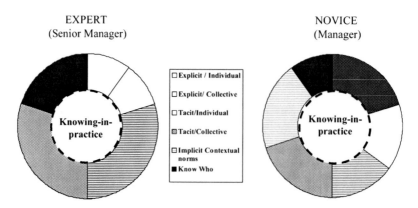

Figure 4.4. Different bundles of knowledge in the consulting practice.

From the very beginning, the novice practitioners have to learn how to interact with other consultants from different hierarchical positions. This dynamic underscored the importance of "knowing," which, as illustrated in the previous sections, emerges from relationships and interactions between individuals.

Contextual, Organizational, and Practice Variables

While the analysis thus far provides insights into some of the differences between knowledge and knowing, questions linger with respect to the ways in which the senior managers' bundle of knowledge evolves in the consulting practice. For example, to what extent do some forms of knowledge prevail over others? Why does collective tacit knowledge appear to play such a crucial role? Why is it so important to be able to "read between the lines"? Based on our analysis, it appears that to a large extent the answers to these questions rest on certain characteristics of the specific consulting practice and its organizational features.

As we have seen, organizational characteristics are ubiquitous throughout our study of practice. Although the case vignette is not intended as a thorough analysis of this issue, there do appear to be a number of recurrent variables. Organizational structure, for example, plays a key role in practice. AKUA has a matrix structure with two axis, and consultants are grouped by the solutions/products they offer and by industry/sector. As a result, it appears that from the company perspective, one's technical and industry knowledge takes prevalence over other forms of knowledge. The concomitant dominant position of individual-explicit knowledge has far-reaching implications for the definition of experts within the company, hiring policies focused on employing knowledgeable individuals, professional development and formal training that foster this type of explicit knowledge, and so on.

The practitioners in the study also stressed that AKUA is highly structured and hierarchical. These features also affect practice, especially in terms of the tacit knowledge that the consultants develop. For example, practitioners devote a lot of time in capturing the implicit norms that allow them to cope with hierarchical pressures. They also attempt to develop the ability to "break away" from the formal structure and its rules in ways that allow them to appear as if they are conforming to expectations. Indeed, as similar analyses have suggested, practitioners attempt to transition from canonical practice to more noncanonical ones (Brown & Duguid, 1991). The canonical practice groups all the formal descriptions of work (e.g., procedures, manuals, job descriptions). The noncanonical refers to the actual practices of the organization's members. Brown and Duguid's (1991) discourse on communities of practice is strongly supported by their analysis of a gap between those formalized procedures and actual practice.

Organizational size also affects practice. AKUA is a global company and therefore it resorts to standard and explicit artifacts to maintain control and homogeneity. However, the large size also fosters the need for visibility: practitioners must take the initiative to make themselves visible and it is important to go where power resides (e.g., decision centers). In spite of the fact that AKUA is highly structured and hierarchical, power is often found away from formal and official structures and systems. It resides in certain individuals, certain business divisions, certain branches, and so forth. As a consequence, the consultants have to "read between the lines" to assess where the power centers are located and what the best way would be to approach them. This is the reason why individual and collective tacit knowledge and, more specifically, the so-called "know-who" knowledge have such a prevailing role in AKUA.

Focusing on the nature of the practice and its characteristics, it is important to note that consulting is a professional service (Schemenner, 1986). This means that the service has a high degree of labor intensity and a high degree of interaction with the customer, with significant customization of the offering. The output, therefore, varies depending on the customer and the process—in which the client also plays a role as co-producer, which leads to further variation. It is in this context that consultants must be able to draw on their own discretion. As a consequence, this practice is characterized by its complexity and the relatively large number of variables that cannot be controlled. These factors make generic and theoretical (explicit) knowledge of limited use from the vantage point of the individual consultant, and they must reply on their ability to improvise and anticipate future situations that are expressions of individual-tacit knowledge.

In this light, the organization's premise that homogeneity and coherence in a global company derives from the available common stocks of knowledge does not remain unchallenged. Clearly, it applies best for newcomers who tend to lean more on explicit knowledge. But in the case of old-timers, who acquire professional expertise as they develop tacit knowledge, it is doubtful that explicit knowledge keeps providing internal coherence. Indeed, coherence is based more on specific rules such as "up or out," which in turn reinforce specific types of knowledge (e.g., know-who). This creates a considerable gap between what the organization perceives as crucial to become a good consultant and the knowledge necessary to acquire such a profile and what the individual consultants perceive as central.

Another relevant characteristic is the effect of time. Time exerts significant pressure and, as a consequence, practitioners must resort to previous work and experience in an effort to reuse existing knowledge or, even better, look for unofficial experts who can guide their actions in practice. These unofficial experts may be within or outside the company and they constitute real "communities of practice." These actual communities, which transcend organizational boundaries, tend to be fueled by previous work experience in the consultants' history or by informal ties. In a sense they constitute a light version of an ecology of practice within which knowledge flows based on personal friendship and/or previous work ties developed in other organizations.

In sum, these various dynamics raise questions about who really is an expert in this practice. Officially, expert in AKUA are the individuals who are able to draw on their individual-explicit knowledge, and they are formally identified in the firm's database as "experts" for an industrial sector or a solution. In actual practice, however, it appears that the real experts are those consultants who are able to identify all the relevant individuals within the organization and interact with them in such a way that will ensure their survival and enable them to climb the ladder of the firm. These experts are able to "read between the lines" in organizational messages, recognizing "key" participants, realizing who will (or will not) support them, and understanding how to develop a good rapport with them. In essence, these individuals are able to reframe the system according to their goals. The expert practitioners appear to be skilled political players.

Types of "Knowing"

Our preliminary observations in this study point to the existence of not only different bundles of knowledge but also of different types of "knowing." In a number of instances, the practitioners resorted to "tacit know-ing." Here, we are referring to the term coined by Polanyi (1966), in which this type of knowing implies an application of theoretical and prac-tical knowledge. Part of this knowledge is indwelled in us in our subsid-iary awareness, while our focal awareness may be concentrated on other factors. This dynamic is seen in the case of the senior managers (experts) when they present business proposals. They leave aside the theories or explicit documentation and focus on the reactions of the audience. At this moment, theories and explicit documentation, while helpful in guiding their responses, are secondary to their (tacit) ability to read the situation and improvise as necessary.

As Schon (1983) suggests, the practitioners turn into reflective practi-tioners and they reflect-in-action. In the case of customized and non-standard projects, this type of knowing is especially relevant and it is enacted in conversations with the customers and the consultants. In these instances, problems are reframed, hypotheses are tested, and a constant inquiry is maintained until a final solution can be achieved.

A last point can be made on the influence of human resource policies in relation to knowledge in AKUA. We have thus far made reference to the importance of considering organizational structure and specific practices vis-à-vis knowledge. It appears though that there are also important con-sequences that can be derived from a human resource perspective. Cer-tain features—such as a hierarchical structure in combination with evaluation procedures that encourage consultants to strive for visibility and/or a culture of continuous ladder progression—can readily hamper the ability of AKUA to turn into a more reflective mode. Indeed, as con-sultants are supposed to get appreciative evaluations and these are par-tially based on the kinds of projects they are involved with, a hidden competence is sought that might prevent them from developing other kinds of expertise. While this in turn might be functional for AKUA, it also has a differential effect in that "successful" consultants will be finally selected in terms of their ability to read the internal organization (know-who). This competence may not be officially recognized, but it appears to be a crucial one for AKUA. The point here is that as long as this practice remains unacknowledged, the organization is privileging an *internal focus* rather than a client or service perspective.

CONCLUSIONS AND FUTURE CONSIDERATIONS

In light of the different trends in the study of knowledge, this chapter began by raising questions about "knowing" and practice, the relationship between knowledge and knowing, and the various dynamics that could affect "knowing"-in-practice. Based on this initial stage of our research, our data suggests that, in practice, "knowing" clusters around a range of elements that are interwoven. "Knowing" implies an epistemic work and, hence, knowledge is an enabler, a "bundle of knowledge"-in-practice that is constituted by different expressions of knowledge. However, the articulation of this bundle is not stable. It varies between experts and novices and with the contingent nature of practice. It is dynamic. As the case vignette indicates, context also plays an active role in "knowing-in-practice." It is a constitutive element and not a mere container.

Questions linger as to how experts become "experts," which is an interesting issue to explore more fully. In the study, we identified and analyzed the differences between experts and novices, but did not explore *how* the relations between the experts and novices and their bundles of knowledge evolve over time. This is a fruitful field of inquiry in which knowledge types, knowing, practice, and learning are interwoven.

The interaction between explicit and tacit knowledge at the individual and collective levels also suggests the need to reexamine and potentially reconsider a host of existing managerial practices. Currently, explicit and abstract knowledge play a prominent role in both the theoretical and practical fields. According to our analysis, although these explicit artifacts and abstract knowledge do play a role in practice, other types of tacit knowledge should also be considered. Of course, conceding such attention to other expressions of knowledge and "knowing" would involve reconsidering important managerial practices, from leadership and managerial style to the hiring and training of employees. Such reflection, however, is well worth our time and effort.

REFERENCES

Alavi, M. (1997). *KPMG Peat Marwick U.S.: One giant brain*. Case study, Harvard Business School.

Alvesson, M., & Kärreman, D. (2001). Odd couple: Making sense of the curious concept of knowledge management . *Journal of Management Studies*, *38*(7), 995–1018.

Atherton, A. (2003). The uncertainty of knowing: An analysis of the nature of knowledge in a small business context. *Human Relations*, *56*(11), 1379–1398.

Bechky, B. A. (2003). Sharing meaning across occupational communities: The transformation of understanding on a production floor. *Organization Science*, *14*(3), 312–330.

Blackler, F. (1995). Knowledge, knowledge work and organizations: An overview and interpretation. *Organizational Studies*, *16*(6), 1021–1046.

Boisot, M. (1995). *Information space: A framework for learning in organizations, institutions and Culture*. London: Routledge.

Bou, E., & Sauquet, A. (2004). Reflecting on quality practices through knowledge management theory: Uncovering grey zones and possibilities of process manuals, flowcharts and procedures. *Knowledge Management Research and Practice Journal, 2*(1), 35–47.

Bou, E., Sauquet, A., & Bonet, E. (2004). *Exploring the generative dance in action: An empirical study of service practices comparison.* Conference Proceedings of the 20th EGOS Colloquium, Ljubljana, Slovenia.

Brown, J. S., & Duguid, P. (1991). Organizational learning and communities of practice: Toward a unified view of working, learning, and innovation. *Organization Science, 2*(1), 40–57.

Brown, J. S., & Duguid, P. (2000). *The social life of information.* Boston: Harvard Business School Press.

Castillo, J. (2002). A note on the concept of tacit knowledge. *Journal of Management Inquiry, 11*(1), 46–57.

Chard, A. M., & Sarvary, M. (1997). *Knowledge management at Ernst & Young.* Case study, Graduate School of Business, Stanford University.

Clancey, W. J. (1992). Practice cannot be reduced to theory: Knowledge, representations, and change in the workplace. In S. Bagnara, C. Zuccermaglio, & S. Stucky (Eds.), *Organizational learning and technological change* (pp. 16–46). Berlin: Springer.

Clancey, W. J. (1995). A tutorial on situated learning. In J. Self (Ed.), *Proceedings of the international conference on computers and education (Taiwan)* (pp. 49–70). Charlottesville, VA: AACE.

Collins, H. M. (1993). The structure of knowledge. *Social Research, 60*(1), 95–116.

Cook, S., & Brown, J. S. (1999). Bridging epistemologies: The generative dance between organizational knowledge and organizational knowing. *Organization Science, 10*(4), 381–400.

Crossan, M. M., Lane, H. W., & White, R. E. (1999). An organizational learning framework: Fom intuition to institution. *Academy of Management Review, 24*(3), 522–537.

Davenport ,T. H., & Hansen, M. T. (2002). *Knowledge management at Andersen Consulting.* Case study, Harvard Business School.

Davenport, T., & Prusak, L. (1998). *Working knowledge: How organizations manage what they know.* Boston: Harvard Business School Press.

Engeström, Y. (1987). *Learning by expanding: An activity-theoretical approach to developmental research.* Helsinki: Orienta-Konsultit.

Gherardi, S. (2003). Knowing as desiring: Mythic knowledge and the knowledge journey in communities of practitioners. *Journal of Workplace Learning, 15*(7-8), 352–358.

Gherardi, S. (2000). Practice-based theorizing on learning and knowing in the organization. *Organization, 7*(2), 211–223.

Gupta, A. K., & Govindarajan, V. (2000). Knowledge management's social dimension: Lessons from Nucor Steel. *Sloan Management Review, 42*(1), 71-80.

King, A. W., & Ranft, A. L. (2001). Capturing knowledge and knowing through improvisation: What managers can learn from the thoracic surgery board certification process. *Journal of Management, 27*(3), 255–277.

Lam, A. (2000). Tacit knowledge, organizational learning and social institutions: An integrated framework. *Organization Studies, 21*(3), 487–513.

Lanzara, G. F., & Patriotta, G. (2001). Technology and the courtroom: An inquiry into knowledge making in organizations. *Journal of Management Studies 38*(7), 943–971.

Lave, J. (1993). The practice of learning. In S. Chaiklin & L. Lave (Eds.), *Understanding practice: Perspective on activity and context* (pp. 3–32). Cambridge, UK: Cambridge University Press.

Lave, J., & Wenger, E. (1991). *Situated learning: Legitimate peripheral participation.* New York: Cambridge University Press.

McCauley, M., Fukagata, M., Lovelock, P., & Farhoomand, A. (2000). *Pricewater-houseCoopers: Building a global network.* Case Study, Centre for Asian Business Cases, University of Hong Kong.

McNulty, T. (2002). Reengineering as knowledge management: A case of change in UK healthcare. *Management Learning, 33*(4), 439–458.

Merali, Y. (2000). Individual and collective congruence in the knowledge management process. *Journal of Strategic Information System, 9*(2-3), 213–234.

Myers, P. S. (1996). *Knowledge management and organizational design.* Boston: Butterworth-Heinemann

Newell, S., Robertson, M., Scarbrough, H., & Swan, J. (2002). *Managing knowledge work.* London: Palgrave Macmillan.

Nonaka, I., & Takeuchi, H. (1995). *The knowledge-creating organization.* Oxford: Oxford University Press.

Orlikowski, W. J. (2002). Knowing in practice: Enacting a collective capability in distributed organizing. *Organization Science, 13*(3), 249–273.

Polanyi, M. (1966). *The tacit dimension.* London: Routledge & Kegan Paul.

Polanyi, M. (1958). *Personal knowledge.* Chicago: University of Chicago Press.

Probst, G, Raub, S., & Romhardt, K. (2000). *Managing knowledge: Building blocks for success.* Chichester, UK: Wiley.

Ryle, G. (1949). *The concept of mind.* Chicago: University of Chicago Press.

Schmenner, R. W. (1986). How can service business survive and prosper? *Sloan Management Review, 27*(3), 21–32.

Schön, D. A. (1983). *The reflective practitioner: How professionals think in action.* New York: Basic Books.

Shin, M., Holden T., & Schmidt, R. A. (2001). From knowledge theory to management practice: Towards an integrated approach. *Information Processing and Management, 37*(2), 335–355.

Tsoukas, H. (1996). The firm as a distributed knowledge system: A constructionist approach. *Strategic Management Journal, 17,* 11–25.

Tsoukas, H. (2003). Do we really understand tacit knowledge? In M. Easterby-Smith & M. A. Lyles (Eds.), *Handbook of organizational learning and knowledge* (pp. 410–427). Oxford, England: Blackwell.

Werr, A., & Stjernberg, T. (2003). Exploring management consulting firms as knowledge systems. *Organization Studies, 24*(6), 881–908.

CHAPTER 5

CO-EVOLUTION OF KNOWLEDGE MANAGEMENT PROCESSES

Drawing on Project Experience in a Global Engineering Consulting Firm[1]

Antti Ainamo

From an American perspective, the fact that a Finnish firm could both emerge as one of the world's leading knowledge brokers in its chosen field in the 1970s and maintain that position after the collapse of the Soviet Union in the 1990s is an interesting phenemenon.[2] After all, during the 1970s, Finland was considered by many in the United States to be a satellite of the Soviet Union, or "just about" (Bailey, 1969; Jakobson, 1984). Yet a Finnish engineering and consulting firm—the Jaakko Pöyry Group—was successful throughout the rise and fall of Soviet influence in its home country. Competences developed in the knowledge-based engineering consulting firm during this period should have lost their value with the fall of the Berlin Wall and the collapse of the Soviet Union, but this has not proved the case.

Challenges and Issues in Knowledge Management, 107–129
Copyright © 2005 by Information Age Publishing
All rights of reproduction in any form reserved.

To examine the processes behind this development, the chapter first briefly reviews literature on the dynamics of organizational knowledge management from a co-evolutionary perspective, which is operationalized with the use of social-history methodology. The description and interpretation of this social history reveals how the imprinting conditions and history of Jaakko Pöyry Group (JPG) from 1946 to 1980 were to have a decisive impact on the future of the firm—in essence, the company went through a partly sequential and partly co-evolutionary process. The chapter then turns to discussions of (1) how JPG could function as a global knowledge broker in a country otherwise largely isolated from an international process of convergence, (2) the generalizable lessons this particular combination of individual agency and globalization contains, and (3) the extent that knowledge management (KM) will generally be based on an imprinting first experience in the field.

KNOWLEDGE MANAGEMENT

The benefits of reusing information time after time without major reinvestment has long suggested why managers have been interested in the business of acting as a knowledge intermediary between their firms and other businesses (Sarvary, 1999; Shapiro & Varian, 1999). Recently, scholars have been able to provide an explanation for the reuse of information with such constructs as "economies of knowledge" (McKenna, forthcoming) and "learning to learn" (Cohen & Levinthal, 1990). Modern KM research refers to the acquisition, assimilation, and interpretation of knowledge (Cohen & Levinthal, 1990) to create new knowledge-intensive solutions (Sutton & Hargadon, 1996), sharing of knowledge about problems and solutions (Dixon, 2000), and exploitation of knowledge-based solutions (Sarvary, 1999).

According to Maister (1997), there are at least three different kinds of knowledge elements at play:

- *Expertise or new knowledge:*   Knowledge is "new" when it provides answers on how to act in a situation that is experienced in a totally novel situation. Often called *expertise*, new knowledge provides what appears as an in-depth and fundamental perspective on the novel situation. Typically, this kind of knowledge takes the form of quite abstract laws and rules, making it less than straightforward to apply. Transferring expertise is often linked to a highly advanced repertoire of skills in terms of communication with the aid of symbols, analogues, language, and "skeumorphs" (see Hargadon & Douglas, 2000; Sutton & Hargadon, 1996).

- *Experience-based knowledge:*   When one is fully comfortable with some "old" or well-worn knowledge, the knowledge appears familiar and well known. Within this context, it is valuable to be able to contextualize the knowledge in terms of cognitive or mental models.[3] Typically referred to as *experience*, this form of knowledge is transferred in the form of concrete examples and stories (Brown & Duguid, 2000; Sutton & Hargadon, 1996).

- *Process or efficiency knowledge:*   Concrete experience that illustrates an abstract model provides a dataset of processes, practices, and routines that can be codified as *information* (Brown & Duguid, 2000). Process knowledge is often linked to operational improvements and rationalization (see, e.g., Hammer & Champy, 1993). This kind of codified data can be readily analyzed, cross-tabulated, and tested in spreadsheets, laboratory experiments, and so forth.

These three kinds of knowledge seldom exist in pure form. Since organizational learning appears to differ across time (i.e., according to an organization's stage of development; see Greiner, 1972; Kim, 1993; Steinmetz, 1969), hybrid forms of knowledge emerge. Events and developments are often uneven and "lumpy." While learning by individuals and by the organization as a whole do "grow" knowledge, this occurs incrementally and often unevenly across parts and levels of the organization (Levitt & March, 1988; March, 1991). Previously successful firms have been found to begin to perform poorly or suboptimally, when a mechanism and KM system that earlier was successful breaks down in terms of knowledge exploitation, new-knowledge creation, or the dissemination of various forms of knowledge and information where these would be needed (Dixon, 2000; Levinthal & March, 1993; Pfeffer & Sutton, 2000). Critical individuals and small groups have been found to become "bottlenecks" that hamper optimal knowledge flows (Gailbraith, 1977; Pfeffer & Salancik, 1978; Thompson, 1967).

Humans have natural propensities for social interaction and collective achievements that would be impossible for any single person (Abell, 2003). Modern information technology can amplify these propensities through enabling distributed learning and efficient knowledge creation and sharing to penetrate or bypass individuals who are bottlenecks (Davenport & Prusak, 1993; Kukko & Ainamo, 2004; Sarvary, 1999). On the other hand, people can also be so selfish that they will not let others benefit from knowledge without some form of exchange (Abell, 2003). Many men and women will not ask others for help, especially if the costs of such help appear greater than the benefits.

Within this context, KM has emerged as a school of research that focuses on how organizations identify, assess, and develop approaches

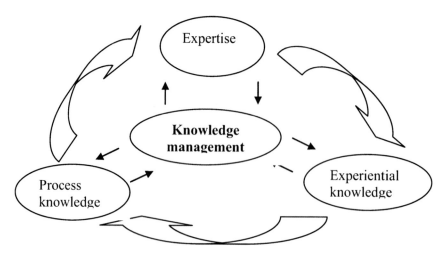

Figure 5.1.   Linkages between different types of knowledge.

that enable them to create and share knowledge effectively, taking into consideration both long-term and new methods (Davenport & Prusak, 1993). Some KM researchers have found that some organizations are able to create "an attitude of wisdom" (Brooking, 1999, p. 109) where organizational members readily access and share knowledge (Hargadon, 1998; Sutton & Hargadon, 1996). This kind of culture appears to facilitate a transfer of knowledge and experience, including both known and new and valuable practices (Sutton & Hargadon, 1996). When accomplished in this way, knowledge creation and sharing simultaneously provide benefits to the individual, to the organization as a whole, and to key stakeholders (Kukko & Ainamo, 2004). The replication of new or old knowledge in such organizations has been argued not to depend only on personal knowledge or its fit with the knowledge of others, but also on the cyclical interaction of various forms of knowledge with one another (Hargadon & Fanelli, 2002). As shown in Figure 5.1, the literature suggests that exemplary firms have what can be called a *dynamic knowledge-management culture*, that is, a cycle of expertise, experience, and process knowledge feeding the next stage sequentially with process knowledge, in turn, providing "food" for expertise.

In partial contrast, other knowledge management researchers have found that the KM cycle is seldom fully optimal: various kinds of intermediate pools and slack in between the phases of the cycle continually appear, even in very successful cycles (Fiol, 1996). A research gap in and around KM cycles raises questions as to whether these cycles—in the case of some individual firms—might be far more optimal over the long term than available benchmarks would suggest. This chapter argues that this dynamic may be related to how KM cycles are initially triggered into existence and how they change over time. Co-evolution of a firm and its environment, with personalized exchange as its change generator, provides a framework to address this research gap.

CO-EVOLUTIONARY RELATIONSHIPS AND PERSONALIZED EXCHANGE

Despite the spate of KM research, significant questions linger as to *how* "good" KM cultures are created. In other words, how do the cultural rules of knowledge management form and change over time? This section explores this question through the perspectives of co-evolution and personalized exchange.

Co-evolution

Originating from evolutionary biology, co-evolution occurs when any two species adapt to a particular ecological niche and have cycles of development that are parallel and interdependent. It has been found in biology that a flower species and its pollinator species, for example, represent a case of co-evolution, where at least one depends on the other. Predator and prey species and parasite and host species represent cases of co-evolution where any change in one will result in an adaptive response in the other, although once in a while a parasite species may be able to jump to an entirely different line of hosts. In evolutionary biology, what is true for internal parasite species is equally true for external parasite species, such as fleas (Mayer, 2001, pp. 233, 312).

Whether studying any co-evolutionary phenomenon in biology or in some other research domain, there are at least two levels of analysis: (1) the "species" that are being studied and (2) the environment in which these species are embedded. When the local environment is isolated from other environments due to natural or other barriers, the evolution of the species will normally either co-evolve with respect to changes within the environment, or one or another of the species will become extinct.

In organizational studies, research on cultural "species" (Lewin & Volberda, 1999, 2003; Weeks & Galunic, 2003) has shown that hierarchical organizations are sometimes so tightly interconnected internally that they are, for all practical purposes, isolated from their external environments (Coleman, 1990). When there is an absence of a critical link with the external environment it is called a "structural hole" (Burt, 1992). The structural hole can represent a similar barrier as a natural barrier in a bio-logical environment.

Structural holes may trigger opportunities to successfully spread knowledge among more conservative species, even if they do not always make it easy or straightforward for the task brokers. As implied by studies of "punctuated equilibrium" (see Gersick, 1991), when there is a systemic context for an organism, such as a particular species of trade or brokerage organization, the organism can be very successful (Ainamo & Tienari, 2002). Moreover, with a local market for a new idea or knowledge already populated by its ideas, the broker species may try to spread or expand its habitat (North, 1981). Especially when there is a removal or barriers in the form convergence of landscape, habitat, or the industry or interna-tional standard, the previously small trade can spread or radiate "by jumping hosts" at a pace that may appear surprising for the noninitiated observer. The reorientation of the broker species is faster and more effi-cient in smaller populations that are in the process of spreading.

The basic distinction between a biological or cultural species is that a cultural species is, in large part, socially constructed. In turn, what is socially constructed in one way can also be socially constructed in another way by social agency. A select social group can function as a bridge between organizations, acting as a hub that enables these organizations to form a network (Djelic & Ainamo, 1999; Godfrey-Smith, 1998; Hargadon, 2002).

The business of such cultural species as brokers of professional business services (e.g., consultants, industrial designers) in the economic field is to bridge over structural holes, effectively changing the cognitive landscapes for other cultural species. The broker species act much like pollinators, moving knowledge that is well known in one domain to a new domain where the knowledge is new and valuable (McKenna, forthcoming; Sutton & Hargadon, 1996). Broker species that trade in ideas can fluidly operate not only locally but also in a global environment because they trade in innovative ideas and experiences rather than heavy goods, for example, that are less mobile (McKenna, forthcoming; Sarvary, 1999).[4]

Personalized Exchange

"Tradesmen" in the long term have always been quicker to benefit from transformations in the world economy than industrialists (Braudel, 1982). Ideas are their objects of trade and exchange, and they are a species par-ticularly evolved for such trade (Braudel, 1982). Architects who serve as consultants in the construction industry, for example, have been found to internationalize through different paths than industrial-manufacturing

firms (Skates, Tikkanen, & Alajoutsijärvi, 2000). What is true for architects is probably also true for other forms of professional knowledge brokers.

The more competition is diluted in hierarchical organizations, "the
greater the necessity for formal rules and elaborate monitoring devices to
measure performance" (McCraw, 1995, p. vi; cf. Normann, 1971). In partial contrast, when ideas are objects of trade, *personalized exchange* includes
repetitive dealings and personal contacts, and "minimizes the need for
formal rules and compliance procedures since reciprocity and consensus
ideology constrain behavior" (McCraw, 1995, p. iv).

As argued by McCraw (1995), taken to the extreme, transformative
change does not require organizations or networks as such, but individuals who have the energy, will, purpose and capacity for strenuous toil to
propel extremely tightly knit networks into processes of variation or
recombine existing ideas and create solutions for the creation of prosper-
ity for themselves and for others (see North, 1981). While research has
begun to forge links between brokers and other innovative groups or individuals and the systems or fields that they change (Hargadon & Douglas,
2000), these studies have not been directly linked with knowledge management.

METHODOLOGY

The chapter draws on the concepts of co-evolution and personalized
exchange to study the Jaakko Pöyry Group, an engineering and consulting firm that has been phenomenally successful from its beginnings. The
analysis focuses on the roles that broker species, tradesmanship, and personalized exchange can have in explaining knowledge management in an
organization that is consistently more successful than comparative firms.

Braudel (1980, p. 27) has coined the methodology of how to study the
long term or *longue durée*. Within this approach, the idea is to study events
in the short term to gauge "the time of the chronicler or newspaper man"
(Braudel, 1980, p. 80). The role of these event histories is to provide a
platform for *conjecture* (medium-term analysis) to show how "social time
grows out of the time of the individual ... that in turn links with ... relative
permanent relationships, in comparison to the events, only" (Peltonen,
1988, p. 102). In essence, in the study of long-term events, the history of
the "social" (Braudel, 1980) "grows" (Peltonen, 1988) out of the history of
the individual.

In the Braudel tradition, the particular emphasis in historical research
is on *mentalities* rather than ideologies (see Hutton, 1981), focused on
writing a "history of a people with politics left out" (Trevelyan, 1942, p.

vii). The typical design matrix to study social mobility is a quantification of "inflow, outflow and total flow" (Haapala, 1989, pp. 68–69; see also Kaelble, 1981). "Inflow" explains the formation of a new social group, "outflow" focuses on the migration away from this group, and "total flow" examines mobility, the generalizability of the change process. Within this context, the approach is based on the collection, analysis, and interpretation of various historical narratives by informants who were present and participated in the events and processes under inquiry (Stone, 1979; Thompson, 1978).

This kind of methodology is not empiricist in the British tradition, but is driven by theory. The idea of embeddedness in favorable conditions over the long term is a research strategy that transcends the traditional dichotomy in research inquiry between the objective and the subjective. It allows for the "spatial study of society" (Braudel, 1982, p. 19); the idea is that thought and action are embedded in "certain economic and social conditions which [have] either prepared or facilitated its progress" (Braudel, 1982, p. 600). The researcher in this research direction will blend "descriptions, narratives, images, developments, regular patterns and breaks in those patterns... but... refrain from the urge to describe everything" (Braudel, 1982, p. 17). The challenge is to choose the data in such a way as to succeed in reconstructing the past. Studies that have included documents in their datasets that date back to the time being studied have generally been more likely to avoid the traps of eclecticism (Heinonen, 1994, pp. 16–21; Lloyd, 1986) and succeed in the goal of historical research—to explain why events took place as they did (Hobsbawn, 1971, p. 25).

A case study is a form of qualitative research where a focal phenomenon is studied in a situation where the boundaries of the phenomenon and its context are not clear, and where many kinds of sources of data are utilized (Yin, 1989). A qualitative study attempts to describe life as it is "in reality." Participant observation is a method often used in case research, with the researcher, in one way or another, participating in the activities of the organization or community where the phenomenon is embedded (Eskola & Suoranta, 1999, pp. 99–100; Kukko & Ainamo, 2004).

Scholars of history, especially in explaining social mobility, have used oral history. In the present study, in addition to observation and participation, I also carried out systematic interviews with members of the "knowledge creating personnel" (Eskola & Suoranta, 1999, p. 87; Hirsjärvi & Hurme, 2001, pp. 47–48; Nonaka & Takeuchi, 1995, pp. 151–158). The ages of the interviewed people ranged from 24 to 79 years. The majority of the interviewees were male, as was also the case for JPG as a whole. However, the share of female employees was increasing. All of the respondents had a minimum of a college-level education, with most having a master's degree in engineering or economics. All of the interviews were done in JPG's offices in Helsinki, London, and New York. The distribution of interviews was skewed toward JPG's forest industry practice and top management. The interviews helped to collect data on events before the period of ethnographic study.

For purposes of collecting key documents about JPG's history, I became an inside participant in the firm's operations in August 2002 in Forest Industry Consulting, one of the company's four business groups. As a member within that JP Management Consulting (Europe) unit, I was given access to archival material and permission to study and systematically record project management practices and organizational and management cultures, both within the business group and JPG as a whole. They provided me with access to personnel, historical documents, archives, and the firm's databanks. Building on Braudel's (1982) methodology, I embraced the subjective—the role of the individual and the interaction of the firm and its members to study JPG's history. The research design was to begin with historical description and analysis, attempting to capture the social reality of the firm, and proceed to an elaboration of the model or a crystallization of that reality, developing a tool for comparison, thought, and control (see Bourdieu, 1980, p. 45).

The chapter is thus based on unique access to oral history, ethnographic research (Van Maanen, 1988), and archival material from the Jaakko Pöyry Group. When there was evidence that the ideas for a new product or service came from another country, as was the case of JPG, the "country of origin" and its related dynamics became complex issues, worthy of investigation as both a separate entity and in unison with JPG. Alternative research choices would have allowed for studies of such important issues as service design and development, organizational networks, and global project management, but the quality of the historical record would have been "spotty" and fragmented.

The way the archives were organized at JPG encouraged me to focus on the role of entrepreneurial capabilities in terms of creating and exploiting social networks in the process of internationalization, focusing on knowledge management in this global engineering and consulting firm. The story of JPG begins with how Jaakko Pöyry, the founder, imported ideas and practices into Finland from abroad, and recombined them, adding his own insights. The analysis traces how he founded the engineering company, gradually diversifying the company's client and service base internationally, and growing the firm, today known as the Jaakko Pöyry Group, into a global market leader by 1980.[5] The historical account begins with a description of the historical and geopolitical context in which Pöyry was embedded.

The ethnographic phase of the study (from 2002 to 2004) consisted of participant observation and taking notes *in situ* in an iterative and continuous process (see Confer, 1992; Hargadon & Sutton, 1997; Sutton & Hargadon, 1996). Special emphasis was placed on following events and processes related to knowledge management. Apart from the appearance of individuals being critical in the process of creating, sharing, and exploiting knowledge, no other major themes surfaced, even when I maintained openness and sensitivity to such possibilities.

In sum, the research process took the form of a historical case study (Yin, 1989) where oral history (interview data) played an important role over alternative sources of historical evidence. In analyzing the data, I performed triangulation of the available sources of evidence (comparisons across interviews, across documents, and across interviews and documents). As agreed with the founder of the firm, Dr. Jaakko Pöyry, he did not comment on the manuscript. Other key informants, including Teuvo Salminen, the number two man in JPG, and Jukka Nyrölä, the head of the Forest Industry business group, made useful comments on the manuscript. Partly based on their comments, I chose not to undertake a direct comparative analysis of the complementarities and tensions between models of production, marketing, and finance originating from countries in Sweden, the United States, and Finland. Instead, the focus was on the role of individuals and social networks working with complementarities and around tensions. I made a choice to leave developments from the 1980s to the 1990s and JPG's diversification into energy, infrastructure, and environment for future research.

The chapter focuses on the early history of the Jaakko Pöyry Group. This research choice allowed for a unified set of data and promoted generalization into other research settings better than a collection of studies based on different methodologies (Eerola, 1997).[6] The data collection, analysis, and interpretation focused on how the conditions for knowledge management were initially created and how they evolved over the *longue durée*. The study was designed to capture the subjective interpretations of the actors and to compile a systemic interpretation in Braudel's research tradition.

THE EVOLUTION OF THE JAAKKO PÖYRY GROUP

The American model did not uniformly diffuse across the Nordic countries in the period immediately following World War II (Hjerppe, 1989, p. 142). The resettlement of refugees from areas lost in the war to the Soviet Union, the resettlement of servicemen returning from the front, residential construction, and much-needed construction work on transportation networks and industrial plants all placed their demands on the nations' scarce resources. Within this context, compared to the other Nordic countries, Finland was a latecomer to the process of Americanization. Sweden, in contrast, which was never directly involved with the war and had its industry and society fully intact, was quick to take in this influence. Norway received American Marshall Aid and transformed her institutional orders in the process of European integration with great speed. Finland would join the European Union only in 1995—4 years after the collapse of the Soviet Union. In hindsight, at a time of rapid economic growth across the Western world (Hobsbawn, 1994), Finland's slow and peculiar process of adapting the "global" American and European model would prove to be a structural hole. It was also an entrepreneurial opportunity for an individual willing to broker and able to bridge the chasm between local and global forms of engineering and management knowledge.

In 1946, at the Helsinki University of Technology, Jaakko Pöyry, age 20, was writing his master's thesis on a radically new kind of diesel engine. Ever since he had been a young boy, he had been interested in global, state-of-the-art technology. After World War II, a friend of his late father secured him a job as a summer trainee at SCA's sulphite pulp mill in Svartvik, Sweden. Pöyry did not hesitate. He did not want to miss the opportunity—technology in Sweden was much more advanced than in Finland. He became enthralled with the pulping process and interested in the pulp and paper industry as a whole.

In 1948, Pöyry started to work in Wärtsilä's Pulp and Paper Machinery department in Finland. Quickly showing his competence, he was put in charge of the department by the time he was 25. In 1953, his superiors at Wärtsilä gave him a mission to visit 60 factories in America and Canada, where he had an ideal opportunity to explore the most advanced technologies of the industry. World War II had never interrupted industrial and technological development in the United States and Canada, and their technology and operations in the pulp and paper industry were well ahead of even Sweden.[7] In 1954, when Pöyry returned home, he was full of ideas about how to develop Finland's domestic forest industry—from wood handling and storage to pulping processes and papermaking. His plans, however, were seen by others in the company as too radical and initially failed to attract or mobilize support.[8]

Just as Pöyry was disillusioned by this state of affairs, two Swedes, a father and his son, contacted him. John Spangenberg was a leading scientific expert with many patents in his name and international experience from many projects in the Americas. His son, Sven Spangenberg, was technical director at Sweden's Fiskeby pulp and paper mill. They asked Pöyry to show them around Finnish pulp and paper mills, and to explain to them how they worked. In 1955, Pöyry resigned from Wärtsilä. As advisor to the Spangenbergs and representative of Tekno-Invest, the Finnish subsidiary of Projecting Ab, a Swedish engineering solutions provider for the forest industry, he sold more than 70 cleaner-installation solutions to Finnish pulp and paper mills. In essence, he controlled the Finnish cleaner-installation market in the industry.

By 1958, Pöyry had established a successful track record in the industry. At that point, the Finnish Forest Owners' Association asked him and Jaakko Murto, a paper technology professor at the Helsinki University of Technology, to design and supervise the basic engineering work for a new sulphate pulp mill at Äänekoski in central Finland. The two Jaakkos had expertise and good knowledge of recent advances in paper and pulp technology. They were also endowed with solid backgrounds in mechanical engineering and hands-on experience in the machine and equipment supply business.[9]

Leveraging the Äänekoski Experience

Before the Äänekosti project was completed, Murto and Pöyry started to work on another project in Sweden, at Fiskeby, where Sven Spangenberg worked. Äänekoski represented the pilot project that was to be replicated. This kind of entrepreneurial drive for designing and implementing new technical solutions and learning from these developments would set the pace for the success of decades to come. A characteristic feature of Pöyry's entrepreneurial drive—reflected in his active participation in the management of the company from 1958 to 1994—was a combination of his interest and readiness to expand in new directions and a stout intent to stick to original core competencies and knowledge. The architecture of this matrix of totally new directions with the development of existing competencies produced dynamic capabilities for learning new knowledge and exploiting the knowledge gained from earlier projects.

Jaakko Murto, however, did not share Pöyry's cosmopolitan readiness to operate in the Swedish market. For Murto, Swedes were also "rivals" and not simply clients. Based on interview data, it was clear that Murto was also engineer and "artist," who preferred to plan alone, rather than as part of a planning team. Given this development, Pöyry took over full ownership of the Murto & Pöyry business, renaming it Jaakko Pöyry & Co.[10]

Very quickly, Jaakko Pöyry & Co. became known for its ability to quickly grasp the nature of a problem, recruit highly competent individuals, and delegate power to them. The 1960s were a period of great expansion for the Nordic forest industry, and Pöyry's timing to grow and expand the business beyond Finland could not have been better.[11] The services of all independent engineering and consulting services firms were in high demand. Among these firms, Jaakko Pöyry & Co. established itself as a significant competitor to the other engineering consultancies with a more international base of clientele and operations.

Norwegians were impressed by Jaakko Pöyry & Co.'s work in Fiskeby. In 1963, the company started to work for *Nordenfjelske Treforedling* (the Norwegian Forest Owners Association, later to transform into *Norske Skog*). The cascade of experience and good references from completed projects in Finland, Sweden, and Norway triggered a self-reinforcing pattern of international growth. A Portuguese company, *Industrias Klabin do Paraná*, approached Pöyry with a proposition that would lead to the planning and engineering of a pulp mill in Portugal, later to be known as Portucel, a project that Jaakko Pöyry & Co. completed in 1965. Pöyry soon had offices in multiple locations across Europe, not only in Finland and Sweden but also in Portugal, Italy, France, and Germany.

In the mid-1960s, Borregaard, a Norwegian forest industry firm, approached Pöyry because it was interested in a prefeasibility study about harvesting trees in Brazil. The interest developed to include a proposition to build an unbleached-pulp mill. Pöyry visited Brazil personally in 1966 "to see how it looks like in that part of Brazil." Jaakko Pöyry & Co.'s share of the workload grew, in comparison to other firms in Borregaard and the other Norwegian and Brazilian subcontractors. With such growth in scale and scope, there was a need to develop a new competence in how knowledge was systematized and codified.

Developing Process Knowledge

With the experience of the myriad projects already underway in many countries and the possibility of more international projects to follow, Pöyry hired Risto Eklund, who had worked on assignments in Rome for 20 years for the Food and Agricultural Organization (FAO) of the United Nations on African Affairs. Eklund began to systematically build data banks out of technical knowledge gained during the company's assignments, integrating any knowledge that could also be gained about assignments performed by competitors.

Pöyry and Eklund felt that an important key to success for their engineering firm was the capacity for decision making and support across national borders: "From engineers to business advisors ... an engineering organization... [must be able] to contribute to the client's strategic planning and support their decision-making process" (Jaakko Pöyry Group, 2002). When Pöyry & Co. set up operations in Brazil, Per Gundersby and a team of 15 Finnish engineers, with their families, were sent to the site to take care of three things: (1) "project management at the site" (that would later be called Riocell), (2) "the actual start-up" of the project, and (3) "so forth." Gundersby and the engineers worked closely with the local Brazilian engineers and workers, familiarizing themselves with the Brazilian culture and learning at least elementary Portuguese.

The firm's reputation continued to grow with the completion of the project for Borregaard in Brazil and it opened doors for Jaakko Pöyry & Co.'s expansion into Canada. There were joint governance problems between Enso-Gutzeit, Tampella, and Kymi, three Finnish firms that owned a manufacturing operation in Kitimat, British Columbia. Jaakko Pöyry & Co.'s engineers were able to rationalize and reorganize the operations at the mill.

When Gundersby returned to Finland in 1972, SIDA, a Swedish development-aid agency, was experiencing major problems with a large development aid project in Baibang, Vietnam. Gundersby was able to transfer the "Brazilian experience" to the SIDA project, providing the agency with a "new spin," successfully arguing that development-aid experts had to be paid salaries at least equal to what the industry would pay. Soon, Gundersby had the previously disagreeing firms in the project "around a common table" and, one by one, critical problems were solved. The Baibang project was ultimately a success and it became very profitable for Jaakko Pöyry & Co.

Before the year was over, the company had also become the principal engineering firm for a new pulp mill to be built in Brazil, with concepts and technological choices radically different from those at the Borregaard project in that country. The speed and efficiency of the company's engineers soon earned the respect of both the financiers and of the local stakeholders of the project. Like the Äänekoski, Fiskeby, and Riocell assignments, this new project, called Aracruz, became a model both within Jaakko Pöyry & Co. and for its clients on how to carry out major projects. Word of the firm's engineering skills and capabilities reached Mondi, a South African forest industry firm, the same year, and it became an important client.

At this point, a decision was made at JPG about an information technology system that would be installed to support the idea of being able to combine the advantages of globalization and local presence. By 1981, Pöyry's engineers began to use e-mail in their correspondence and exchange of technical information. By 1982, telefaxes came into use. A computer-aided design system was also installed by 1983 (Rennel, 1984). The firm expanded in the 1980s, reorganizing its new subsidiaries in the United States, Asia, Australia, and southern Africa on the basis of its company-wide slogan, "Local Presence—Global Resources." The era of rapid internationalization was over and the company was established as a truly global firm.

With a large part of his insight and knowledge integrated into the firm, Pöyry began a gradual withdrawal from day-to-day management. In 1985, he found a suitable candidate for his successor in the then 31-year-old Henrik Ehnrooth. The two men began to expand and diversify the firm from the forest industry into energy-, infrastructure-, and environment-related businesses. Two years after Finland's full membership in the European Union (in 1995), the newly renamed Jaakko Pöyry Group was quoted on the Helsinki Stock Exchange. As founder, Pöyry continued to be owner and participated on the Board, but let his professional staff increasingly take over top management responsibilities. Being quoted on the Stock Exchange served to further spread the reputation of JPG as an expert in its chosen fields, in both the financial community and throughout the industry.

KNOWLEDGE MANAGEMENT AT THE JAAKKO PÖYRY GROUP

Reflecting on the history of the Jaakko Pöyry Group, there appear to be a number of trends that have implications for the development of knowledge management at the company. The event history and conjectures about the long term are summed up in Table 5.1.

Despite the absence of an American agency, such as Marshall Aid, to facilitate its operations, JPG managed to successfully import Swedish and American state-of-the-art knowledge to the point that it was able to develop sufficient expertise that it was reexported back to Sweden, one of the countries of origin. JPG's expertise and experiences accumulated and were recombined with local knowledge elements—project by project, time and time again—in various locations around the world. Pöyry was able to bridge across like-minded international cosmopolitans to create an "addictive" network that was open and expansive, with few redundancies. Only 5 years after he took on the ownership role in the company (originally founded as a partnership), the firm was mapping possibilities to move into Latin America. Within 10 years, the firm had an institutionalized market position in North America with Eurocan, British Columbia, and in Asia with SIDA's Baibang, Vietnam. Pöyry implemented a rapid succession of first moves in the forest industry until he and his firm had developed a unique combination of local presence and global resources. The recombination of technologies, models, and knowledge found in Sweden, the United States, and elsewhere helped the firm gain a "first-mover" advantage as a global knowledge broker. Pöyry, Gundersby, and many other JPG members created "jungle guerrilla" narratives within the

**Table 5.1.   Event History of Jaakko Pöyry and the
Jaakko Pöyry Group from 1948–1980**

Year	Key Events
1948	Jaakko Pöyry works in SCA's pulp mill in Svartvik, Sweden
1953–1954	Jaakko Pöyry visits the United States
1958	Murto & Pöyry is established
1959	First project abroad: Fiskeby, Sweden
1961	Murto & Pöyry is transformed into Jaakko Pöyry & Co.
1963	Nordenfjelske treforening, Norway; Portucel, Portugal
1966	Risto Eklund joins Jaakko Pöyry & Co; Riocell, Brazil
1972	Baibang, Vietnam; Aracruz project begins, Brazil
1979	Mondi, South Africa
1980	Global reorganization: "Local Presence—Global Resources"

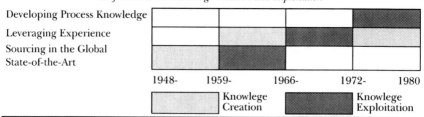

Conjecture about Knowledge Creation and Exploitation

firm that encouraged others to entrepreneurially take on assignments on short notice in geographically remote and isolated locations.

It did, however, take a rather substantial amount of time before Pöyry's visits to Sweden and the United States materialized into state-of-the-art knowledge capable of changing traditional mental patterns in Finland. Once the firm entered an era of dynamic stability, in which its growth and possibilities for exploitation arrived, a key element in JPG's success was the systematic minds of other players in the company, such as Risto Eklund, who developed the firm's knowledge management systems. From the 1970s, it was only through the co-evolution of entrepreneurship and systematic management that the histories of Jaakko Pöyry, the man, and Jaakko Pöyry, JPG, became "models of clockwork precision in terms of mastering timing" (SKOL visio, 2001). Before that time, it appears that personalized exchange between Pöyry and his clients and business partners appears to have played the decisive role.

JPG embraced the ideal of translating technical engineering into business advice, while still keeping the firm's original core competences in technical engineering. These contradictory and complementary sides of the firm—development and patience with the rapid succession of first-mover diversification—helped JPG's clients to forge the forest industry into a globally thriving industry, capable of exploring diversification beyond the industry's traditional boundaries,[12] during a period when many other similarly resource-based industries have declined. Given that the forest industry is a capital-intensive industry, it is interesting that it took a consultant and tradesman such as Jaakko Pöyry to become a prime mover. The history of JPG illustrates how expertise and knowledge creation can become seeds for the growth and internationalization of experience and processes of an industrial field into a highly focused, successful company. In this way, it provides an illustration of the knowledge cycle captured in Table 5.1.

CONCLUSION

In an attempt to add to our understanding of knowledge management, this chapter explored how co-evolution, a concept originating in evolutionary biology, can help to explain how companies bridge over "structural holes" in their social landscape. While co-evolution has been implied to be an important explanatory mechanism in analyzing a plethora of phenomena, there has been little research on long-term processes of knowledge management in highly successful individual firms. The Jaakko Pöyry Group emerged as one of the world's leading consulting and engineering firms in the forest industry. Illumination of the firm's social history, development of its competences, and emergent expansion of its areas and domains appear to present us with some historical lessons on the growth and development of knowledge management in practice.

Pöyry developed a global broker role in the forest industry, despite the fact that his firm originated in Finland, a country geopolitically isolated from the center stage of international commerce. This finding strengthens arguments in literature that in times of industrial transformation, a tradesman or consultant can rise to the center stage via personalized exchange—repetitive dealings and personal contacts—since reciprocity and consensus ideology can shape and influence behavior and minimize the need for formal rules and compliance procedures.

Based on JPG's experience, it appears that global state-of-the-art expertise in the *longue durée* could be developed into a growing body of experience that, in turn, can be exploited and codified. Further research to replicate this type of historical, long-term research is needed to further specify the conditions under which personalized exchange would be more effective than codified and institutionalized rules of the game and economies of scale and scope. JPG's case suggests that process knowledge dominates at the end of a *longue durée*, while personalized exchange dominates at the beginning. Of course, progress from the initial model to the latter might not always be the case, even if JPG's history appears to imply such co-evolution of diverse forms of knowledge.

In contrast to prior studies of knowledge management, this chapter has attempted a dynamic recombination of expertise, experience, and process knowledge over the *longue durée*. Within this view, expertise becomes true knowledge only when it is embedded within a given context, with the act of its transfer or transmission. Expertise is largely meaningless "raw data" without an ability to meaningfully contextualize it. JPG's experience shows how expertise can be eventually refined into experience and process knowledge. It also shows how such knowledge must be socially embedded in order to be useful. Those who possess both expertise and experiential knowledge of the array of contexts in which the expertise has been successfully applied in earlier projects will be at an advantage over those who do not possess such a combination of expertise and experience. Given that there is also an ability to develop processes that efficiently and continuously recombine expertise and experience, a substantial first-mover advantage may be gained.

NOTES

1. This chapter is based on a paper presented as part of the Management Consulting Division program at the 2004 Academy of Management meeting in New Orleans. It also draws on Ainamo (2005) for its empirical data and co-evolutionary perspective. The author gratefully acknowledges funding for this study from the Jenny and Antti Wihuri Foundation and the Marcus Wallenberg Foundation, as well as access to data from colleagues. Discussions with Andrew Hargadon and Marianne Kukko provided ideas on how to carry out the study, while those with Risto Tainio, Tapio Koivu, Johanna Nummelin and Sampo Tukiainen improved the chapter. Any misconceptions presented in the chapter remain the sole responsibility of the author.

2. In the first three decades after World War II, most of Western Europe experienced a process of convergence of ideas and techniques about production, marketing, and finance in a process that was in large part built on the American model and driven by American agents of change (see Djelic, 1998; Fligstein, 1990; Kipping & Bjarnar, 1998; McKenna, forthcoming). The Western European experience in the 1940s and 1950s of Americanization was not uniform, however. Finland, for example, was not among the recipient countries of American Marshall Aid to Western Europe (Djelic & Quack, 2003; Kipping & Engwall, 2002). The chapter refers to the forest industry, which is an amalgam of industries and activities, ranging from forestry to pulping, converting, wholesale, end use, energy, and other infrastructures, as well as environmental protection, planning, and policy. However, in line with established use of language, the field is commonly

called the forest industry, rather than "industries," both in practice and in scientific literature (see Jaakko Pöyry Group, 2002; Laurila & Lilja, 2002).

3. A mental model determines what kind of a situation is worthy of attention, acting as a trigger for action and how to act (see Kim, 1993).

4. For evidence of innovation in networks, see Hargadon (2002), Hargadon and Sutton (1997), and Tuomi (2001). For evidence particular to the large-scale forest industry in Finland about the lack of innovation, see Näsi, Lamberg, Ojala, and Sajasalo (2001).

5. Sonnenfeld (1999) notes, "Chief among early contemporary Nordic corporate travelers in Southeast Asia was the Jaakko Pöyry Co. The Jaakko Pöyry Group of consulting, contracting, and manufacturing companies based in Helsinki, Finland, founded by a pulp and paper engineer of the same name, has been of *singular* importance in the shaping of the forest-related industries not only in Southeast Asia but also throughout the world" [Italics to "singular" added here]. See also Hass (1978) and Marchak (1995).

6. See Eerola (1997) for an in-depth study of the creation of expert knowledge in the Jaakko Pöyry Group in the 1990s.

7. At the time of writing this chapter, none of the paper machine makers are left in the United States.

8. Interestingly, despite the initial rejection of his ideas, Jaakko Pöyry's 1954 plan about the international restructuring of the industry has since largely become reality.

9. This information is based on an interview with Jyrki Kettunen, Research Director of M-Real, June 14, 2003.

10. Already while in Murto & Pöyry, Jaakko Pöyry had a talent for identifying and hiring engineers he respected and trusted, such as Esko Mykkänen. Upon starting Jaakko Pöyry & Co., he also hired Erik Ehrnrooth, who was to become one of the leading engineering minds of what was to become JPG.

11. This information was drawn from Jaakko Pöyry's databanks, which include the breakdowns and histories of forest industry factories, their machines, and the components within these machines from the 19th century (the beginning of the modern forest industry) to the present.

12. In the 1990s, UPM-Kymmene, a Finnish and the world's third largest forest industry firm, developed into a successful business in RFID (radio frequency identification) tags by applying traditional competences in paper-based price tags to new material bases, such as telecommunications and plastics. StoraEnso, a Finnish and the world's largest forest industry firm, developed liquid board packaging, combining traditional paper board with plastics to create a hybrid material base.

REFERENCES

Abell, P. (2003). On the prospects for a unified social science: Economics and sociology. *Socio-Economic History, 1*(1), 1–26.

Ainamo, A. (2005). Coevolution of individual and firm-level competences: Imprinting conditions and globalization at the Jaakko Pöyry Group, 1946 to 1980. *Scandinavian Economic History Review, 53*(1), 19-43.

Ainamo, A., & Tienari, J. (2002). The rise and fall of a local version of management consulting in Finland. In M. Kipping & L. Engwall (Eds.), *Management consulting: An emerging knowledge industry* (pp. 70–87). Oxford: Oxford University Press.

Bailey, B. (1969). *The captive nations.* Chicago: Chas Hallberg & Co.

Bourdieu, P. (1980). *Les sens pratique.* Paris: Editions de Minuit.

Braudel, F. (1980). *On history* (S. Matthews, Trans.). Chicago: University of Chicago Press.

Braudel, F. (1982). *Wheels of commerce: Civilization and capitalism* (Vol. 2) (S. Reynolds, Trans.). London: William Collins & Co.

Brooking, A. (1999) *Corporate memory: Strategies for knowledge management.* London: International Thomson Business Press.

Brown, J. S., & Duguid, P. (2000). *Social life of information.* Boston: Harvard Business School Press.

Burt, R. (1992). *Structural holes.* Cambridge, MA: Harvard University Press.

Coleman, J. (1990). *Foundations of social theory.* Cambridge, UK: Belknap Press.

Cohen, W., & Levinthal, D. (1990). Absorptive capacity: A new perspective on innovation and learning. *Administrative Science Quarterly, 35*(1), 128–152.

Confer, F. R. (1992). The case study method: A case study. In J. D.Glazier & R. R. Powell (Eds.), *Qualitative research in information management* (pp. 37–50). Westport, CT: Libraries Unlimited.

Davenport, T. H., & Prusak, L. (1993). *Working knowledge: How organizations manage what they know.* Boston: Harvard Business School Press.

Dixon, N. (2000). *Common knowledge.* Boston: Harvard Business School Press.

Djelic, M-L. (1998). Exporting the American model. Oxford: Oxford University Press.

Djelic, M-L. & Ainamo, A. (1999). The co-evolution of new organizational forms in the fashion industry: A historical and comparative study of France, Italy, and the United States. *Organization Science, 10*(5), 622–637.

Djelic, M-L., & Quack, S. (Eds.). (2003). *Globalization and institution: Redefining the rules of the economic game.* Cheltenham, UK: Edward Elgar.

Eerola, A. (1997). *Expert knowledge.* Helsinki: Acta Academiensis Helsingiensis, Helsinki School of Economics.

Eskola, J., & Suoranta, J. (1999). *Johdatus laadulliseen tutkimukseen.* Vastapaino: Tampere.

Fiol, C. M. (1996). Squeezing harder doesn't always work: Continuing the search for consistency in innovation research. *Academy of Management Review, 21*(4), 1012–1021.

Fligstein, N. (1990). *Transformation of management control.* Cambridge, MA: Harvard University Press.

Galbraith, J. (1977). *Organization design.* Reading, MA: Addison-Wesley.

Gersick, C. (1991). Revolutionary change theories: A multilevel exploration of the punctuated equilibrium paradigm. *Academy of Management Review, 16*(1), 10–36.

Godfrey-Smith, P. (1998). A modern history of function. In C. Allen, M. Bekoff, & G. Lauder (Eds.), *Nature's purposes: Analyses of function and design in biology* (pp. 453–477). Cambridge, MA: MIT Press.

Greiner, L. E. (1972). Evolution and revolution as organizations grow. *Harvard Business Review, 50*(4), 37–46.

Haapala, P. (1989). *Sosiaalihistoria: Johdatus tutkimukseen.* Helsinki: SHS.

Hammer, M., & Champy, J. (1993). *Reengineering the corporation: A manifesto for business revolution.* New York: HarperCollins.

Hargadon, A. (1998). Firms as knowledge brokers: Lessons in pursuing continuous innovation. *California Management Review, 40*(3), 209–227.

Hargadon, A. (2002). *How breakthroughs happen.* Boston: Harvard Business School Press.

Hargadon, A., & Douglas, Y. (2000). When innovation and institutions: Edison and the electric light. *Administrative Science Quarterly, 46*(3), 476–501.

Hargadon, A., & Fanelli, A. (2002). Action and Possibility: Reconciling Dual Perspectives of Knowledge in Organization. *Organization Science, 13*(3), 290–302.

Hargadon, A., & Sutton, R. (1997). Technology brokering and innovation in a product development firm. *Administrative Science Quarterly, 42*, 716–749.

Hass, L. (1978). Jaakko Poyry's years of phenomenal growth. *Pulp and Paper International, 20*(9), 45–48.

Heinonen, V. (1994). *Ihminen arkielämän rakenteisiin uponneena: Fernand Braudel kulutuksen tutkijana.* Helsinki: Kuluttajatutkimuskeskus.

Hirsjärvi, S., & Hurme, H. (2001). *Tutkimushaastattelu: Teemahaastattelun teoria ja käytäntö.* Helsinki: Yliopistopaino.

Hjerppe, R. (1989). *The Finnish economy 1860–1985: Growth and structural change.* Helsinki: Bank of Finland/Government Printing Centre.

Hobsbawm, E. (1994). *The age of extremes: The short 20th century, 1914–1991.* London: Michael Joseph.

Hobsbawm, E. (1971). From social theory to the history of society. *Daedalus, 100*, 20–45.

Hutton, P. H. (1981). The history of mentalities: The new map of cultural history. *History and Theory, 20*(3), 237–259.

Jaakko Pöyry Group. (2002). *The story behind.* Vantaa: Author.

Jakobson, M. (1984). *Finland: Myth and reality.* Helsinki: Otava.

Kaelble, H. (1981). *Historical research on social mobility: Western Europe and the USA in the nineteenth and twentieth centuries.* New York: Columbia University Press.

Kim, D. H. (1993). The link between individual and organizational learning. *Sloan Management Review, 35*(1), 37–50.

Kipping, M., & Bjarnar, O. (Eds.). (1998). *The Americanization of European business: The Marshall Plan and the transfer of US management models.* London: Routledge.

Kipping, M., & Engwall, L. (Eds.) (2002). *Management consulting: An emerging knowledge industry.* Oxford: Oxford University Press.

Kukko, M., & Ainamo, A. (2004). Tietämyksenhallinta Kasvuyrityksessä. *Hallinnon Tutkimus, 50*(1), 50–63.

Laurila, J., & Lilja, K. (2002). The dominance of firm-level competitive pressures over functional-level institutional pressures: The case of the Finnish-based forest industry firms. *Organization Studies, 23(4)*, 573–599.

Levinthal, D. A. & March, J. G. (1993). Myopia of learning. *Strategic Management Journal, 14*, 95–112.

Levitt, B., & March, J.G. (1988). Organizational learning. *American Journal of Sociology, 14*, 319–340.

Lewin, A., & Volberda, H. (1999). Prolegomena on co-evolution: A framework for research on strategy and new organizational forms. *Organization Science, 10*(5), 519–534.

Lewin, A. Y., & Volberda, H. (2003). Co-evolutionary dynamics within and between firms: From evolution to co-evolution. *Journal of Management Studies, 40*(8), 2111–2136.

Lloyd, C. (1986). *Explanation in social history.* London: Blackwell.

Maister, D. H. (1997). *Managing the professional service firm.* New York: The Free Press.

March, J. G. (1991). Exploration and exploitation in organizational learning. *Organization Science, 2*(1), 71–87.

Marchak, M.P. (1995). *Logging the globe.* Montreal: McGill-Queens University Press.

Mayer, E. (2001): *What evolution is.* New York: Basic Books.

McCraw, T. (Ed.). (1995). *Creating modern capitalism.* Cambridge, MA: Harvard University Press.

McKenna, C. (forthcoming). *The world's newest profession.* Cambridge, UK: Cambridge University Press.

Näsi, J., Lamberg, J-A., Ojala, J., & Sajasalo, P. (2001). *Metsäyritysten strategiset kehityspolut: Kilpailu, keskittyminen ja kasvu pitkällä aikavälillät.* Helsinki: Tekes.

Nonaka, I., & Takeuchi, H. (1995). *The knowledge-creating company.* New York: Oxford University Press.

Normann, R. (1979). *Management for growth.* London: John Wiley.

Normann, R. (1971). Organizational innovativeness: Product variation and reorientation. *Administrative Science Quarterly, 16*, 203–215.

North, D. (1981). *Structure and change in economic history.* New York: Norton.

Peltonen, M. (1988). *Viinapäästä kolerakauhuun: Kirjoituksia sosiaalihistoriasta.* Helsinki: Hanki ja Jää.

Pfeffer, J., & Salancik, G. (1978). *The external control of organizations: A resource dependence perspective.* New York: Harper & Row.

Pfeffer, J., & Sutton, R. (2000). *The knowing-doing gap: How smart companies turn knowing into action.* Boston: Harvard Business School Press.

Rennel, J. (1984). *The future of the paper in the telematic world.* Helsinki: Jaakko Pöyry Review.

Sarvary, M. (1999). Knowledge management and competition in the consulting industry. *California Management Review, 41*(2), 95–107.

Shapiro, C., & Varian, H. (1999). *Information rules: A strategic guide to the network economy.* Boston: Harvard Business School Press.

Skaates, M. A., Tikkanen, H., & Alajoutsijärvi, K. (2002). Social and cultural capital in project marketing service firms: Danish architectural firms on the German market. *Scandinavian Journal or Management, 18*(4), 589-609

SKOL visio. (2001). 10 suunnittelun edistäjää palkittiin elokuussa: Jaakko Pöyry: Kansainvälistyminen on ainoa tie kasvuun. *Skol Visio*, Elokuu, s. 5.

Sonnenfeld, D. (1999). Vikings and tigers: Finland, Sweden, and adoption of environmental technologies in Southeast Asia's pulp and paper industries. *Journal of World Systems Research, 5*(1), 26–47.

Steinmetz, L. L. (1969). Critical stages in small business growth. *Business Horizons, 12*(1), 29–36.

Stone, L. (1979). The revival of the narrative. *Past & Present, 85*, 3–24.

Sutton, R., & Hargadon, A. (1996). Brainstorming groups in context: Effectiveness in a product design firm. *Administrative Science Quarterly, 41*, 685–718.

Tuomi, I. (2001). *Networks of innovation*. Oxford: Oxford University Press.

Thompson, J. (1967). *Organizations in action*. New York: McGraw-Hill.

Thompson, P. (1978). *The voice of the past: Oral history*. Oxford: Oxford University Press.

Trevelyan, G. M. (1942). *The English social history*. London: Longman.

Van Maanen, J. (1988). *Tales from the field: On writing ethnography*. Chicago: University of Chicago Press.

Weeks, J., & Galunic, C. (2003). A theory of the cultural evolution of the firm: The intra-organizational ecology of memes. *Organization Studies, 24*(8), 1309–1352.

Yin, R. K. (1989). *Case study research: Design and methods*. Newbury Park, CA: Sage.

PART II

DYNAMICS OF KNOWLEDGE SHARING AND DISSEMINATION

CHAPTER 6

A DISPERSED REPERTOIRE

Exploring Struggles to Knowledge
Dissemination within Consultancies

Stefan Heusinkveld and Jos Benders

This chapter further explores the elements that shape knowledge codification and transfer within management consulting firms. The generation and dissemination of knowledge is seen as a consultancy's key capability (Hansen, Nohria, & Tienery, 1999). The work at client organizations can be regarded as an important source of knowledge creation. Consultancies are regarded as important suppliers of management knowledge involved in "productivizing" the knowledge into packaged and commercially viable commodities (Fincham, 1995; Suddaby & Greenwood, 2001). Therefore, it is argued that the development of such knowledge systems may enhance the impression of consultancies as innovative knowledge providers and support them in gaining competitive advantage (Sarvay, 1999).

To enhance their reputation as progressive knowledge brokers, consultants seek to develop a knowledge repertoire that supports the commercialization and implementation of a new commodity (Heusinkveld &

Challenges and Issues in Knowledge Management, 133–154
Copyright © 2005 by Information Age Publishing

Benders, 2002, 2005; Visscher, 2001). The resulting codification of such a repertoire into methods plays an important role in reducing uncertainty—both for the client and the consultant (Visscher, 2001; Werr, Stjernberg, & Doucherty, 1997). The availability of a codified knowledge repertoire influences expectations of service quality and eventually the choice(s) of the clients.

Theorists have argued that within consultancies knowledge is codified and included in large knowledge systems (Hansen et al., 1999; Morris & Empson, 1998; Olivera, 2000; Sarvay, 1999). Current accounts focus on the large array of different possibilities for knowledge transfer within consulting firms (Werr, 2002; Werr et al., 1997; Werr & Stjernberg, 2003). It is assumed that the codified knowledge will be intermingled with more tacit items and automatically used in daily consulting praxis without further complications. However, this conceptualization neglects some key limitations to the dissemination of knowledge (Szulanski, 1996). Specifically, there is a lack of attention to significant barriers in realizing possibilities of knowledge transfer and utilization. The dissemination of management knowledge within consultancies is not simply constructing a useful method that is automatically included in a consultancy's knowledge system. The process also involves generating and channeling the interests of the consultants. In praxis, efforts to disseminate a knowledge repertoire within a consultancy are often accompanied by considerable struggles.

The chapter seeks to further our understanding about the supply side of the management knowledge market by exploring those elements that impede and support the dissemination of knowledge repertoires within consultancies. In the next section, we argue that consultancies are generally presented as important knowledge suppliers, using a knowledge repertoire to sell and support their services. The discussion then draws on the literature related to *organizational knowing* because this provides important insights into the barriers to knowledge transfer within a firm. After discussing the research approach, the chapter empirically illustrates our main argument by showing the difficulties involved in knowledge dissemination within consultancy firms. Specifically, the analysis reveals that consultants experience significant struggles in the development, transfer, and utilization of a new knowledge repertoire. These struggles have their sources in (1) a persistent fear of losing ownership and (2) a reluctance to accept knowledge from peers. This implies that the presence of various codified knowledge items does not guarantee that consultants will not "reinvent wheels." The chapter concludes with our reflections on the implications of this work for our thinking about consultancies and their knowledge systems.

A SUPPLY OF MANAGEMENT KNOWLEDGE

Consultants are regarded as important producers and propagators of knowledge commodities on the management knowledge market (Benders, van den Berg, & van Bijsterveld, 1998; Clark & Fincham, 2002; Faust, 2002; Huczynski, 1993; Kieser, 2002; Suddaby & Greenwood, 2001). The literature mainly emphasizes the specific consultants' strategies in the marketing of knowledge commodities, thereby stressing notable difficulties in selling their services. The inherent ambiguity of consultants' knowledge products and the difficulties in evaluating the quality of their services create an important base of uncertainty to clients. In addition, while consumers may be highly susceptible to new ideas, they typically remain critical as to whether it serves their own interests (Guillén, 1994; Wright, 2002).

Given the specific difficulties of enhancing demand for consultancy services, theorists have particularly emphasized the importance of managing client relationships (Fincham, 1999; Glückler & Armbrüster, 2003; Sturdy, 1997) and convincing knowledge consumers of the value of one's skills (Clark, 1995). In addition, Pettigrew (1975) argued that consultants should make use of the politically loaded environment in client organizations to promote their ideas. Therefore, the consultancy process is not only seen as a matter of expert knowledge but is indissolubly linked with games of representation (Alvesson, 1993; Bloomfield & Danieli, 1995). This means that consultancy services cannot be separated from the attempt to manage impressions (Clark, 1995; Pettigrew, 1975) aimed at persuading clients of the value of their knowledge.

A key element in selling and delivering consultancy products is the development and utilization of a knowledge repertoire (Visscher, 2001). While consultants are easily regarded as opportunistic merchants of management ideas, providing a useful consulting service requires more than referring to a fashionable management idea. As Visscher (2001) noted, consultants have to put forward structured plans for clients while they often know little about the specific problem situation within a specific organization. To enhance a reputation as an innovative knowledge provider, firms must show that they are capable of collectively generating experiences and converting them into useful services for their clients (Hansen et al., 1999; Sarvay, 1999). This requires the development of a specific knowledge repertoire that supports the commercialization and implementation of a commodity (Heusinkveld & Benders, 2002, 2005; Visscher, 2001). This process of commodification starts with sensing and selecting promising ideas and results in the introduction of a knowledge product via a range of different media (Abrahamson, 1996). In this, the ideas become codified into a repertoire (Suddaby & Greenwood, 2001), not only to enhance their ability to flow in a population of knowledge consumers (Røvik, 2002) but also to claim ownership as a key supplier of a particular topic (Fincham, 1995; Morris, 2001).

Our premise is that consultants seek to translate their experiences into a recognizable knowledge repertoire. In this light, Werr (1999) refers to methods as explicit and relatively stable consulting procedures in relation to a specific goal or organizational change process. These consulting methods may take shape as a set of phase models, tools, and techniques that are articulated by a particular terminology (Werr, 1999, p. 18). Both Visscher (2001) and Werr (1999) further stress the role these methods play in reducing uncertainty for both client and consultant. For a client organization, a consulting method may increase understanding and enhance justification of the expected advice trajectory. For consultants, a method is regarded as a means to enhance communication with a client organization and offers cognitive support in the advice process. Yet, while a structured repertoire may provide guidance during assignments, consultants do not necessarily follow it strictly. Visscher shows that the way such a repertoire is applied in praxis is related to the specific design strategy deployed by a consultant.

The consultant's repertoire not only plays a role in client interaction and problem solving but also in the consultancy's internal knowledge system (Werr, 1999). Here codification is often referred to as the translation of expertise into an explicit form (Morris, 2001; Suddaby & Greenwood, 2001). A codified repertoire serves as a common denominator for both the storage and exchange of experiences within a consultancy. The ongoing interaction between articulated knowledge elements and tacit knowledge (in the form of experiences of consultants) constitute the basis of a repertoire on a certain topic in a consultancy (Werr & Stjernberg, 2002). As we have seen in the above, the translation of a general concept into various knowledge elements allows consultants to demonstrate their expertise toward clients (Fincham & Evans, 1999; Morris, 2001). However, consultancies are not uniform in the way they shape a repertoire. Rather, the specific method-making strategy determines whether these knowledge elements are stored in a structured or loose manner.

A centralized, technique-oriented strategy is intended to produce a coherent arrangement of well-elaborated techniques surrounding a leading knowledge model (Visscher, 2001). This implies that some consultancies may invest considerable effort in writing down ideas and experiences associated with a commodity, thereby generating a significant collection of codified traces. This may result in the development and structuring of knowledge elements that are embodied by written methods, tools, and case descriptions, which are then incorporated into a consultancy's formal knowledge system. In many instances, these items are stored in different carriers, such as manuals and database applications (Morris & Empson, 1998; Olivera, 2000). So-called product managers and central departments act as internal "gatekeepers" for these techniques (Morris, 2001, p. 830). Such actors have a central role in the generation, codification, and dissemination of a concept's repertoire and provide support in its application. This role may also include translating experiences generated in assignments into central methods and providing internal courses to the population of consultants.

In contrast, a diversified, anticipation-oriented strategy is likely to put less emphasis on formalized methods (Visscher, 2001). In this case, a consultancy builds up a collection of different, loosely coupled general approaches that allow for greater flexibility—and support for dealing with a large range of different organizational problems. This perspective implies that some consultancies do not extensively and formally codify elements of a concept into an internal knowledge system. It also means that experiences obtained during the application of a commodity become very heavily concentrated in the heads of certain individuals. As a result, knowledge items are easily highly dispersed throughout the consultancy. Approaches that are incorporated into a repertoire become more application oriented rather than equipped with elaborate techniques.

A SOURCE OF MANAGEMENT PROBLEMS

As suggested above, the current literature presents consultancies as important knowledge suppliers. The emphasis in this work is on the external struggles of these knowledge suppliers in marketing their "products"—while leaving the impression that the internal knowledge generation and dissemination process is largely uncomplicated. Consultancies, of course, may pursue different knowledge management strategies (Hansen et al., 1999), but their realization is considered as a fairly straightforward effort. This would mean that a newly developed repertoire is readily incorporated in a consultancy's daily routines. Theorists of organizational knowing, however, have persistently emphasized that the transfer of knowledge *within* organizations is unavoidably a source of problems. It is stressed that various barriers increase the inertia of knowledge. The dissemination of new ideas in organizations is often highly contested and generally encounters substantial resistance. As a result, developing a successful knowledge repertoire is not restricted to simply translating a new idea into a consulting method, but particularly involves managing the distribution of a repertoire within the firm. The underlying process involves such challenges as generating attention to new ideas and routinizing them into the daily practices of consultants.

Knowledge Transfer

Theorists of organizational knowledge emphasize the important role of the interplay between organizational members' experiences and codified knowledge systems (Nonaka & Takeuchi, 1995; Roberts, 2001). The experiences acquired in the course of past practices and within previous situations can be made explicit, thereby enhancing the possibilities for their storage and transfer. In line with this view, the organization's members and codified manifestations of their experiences can be regarded as main carriers of the organization's knowledge. However, organizations tend to be distributed knowledge systems (Tsoukas, 1996). This view suggests that knowledge in organizations cannot be seen as a single coherent entity, but instead be considered as highly dispersed and largely unrealized.

The presence of knowledge items prima facie suggests that organizations readily use all prior experiences as a foundation for their current practices. These knowledge items, however, are not automatically known or even utilized within organizations. As theorists of organizational knowledge have stressed, continuity of accumulated expertise is not predetermined but an ongoing achievement (Orlikowski, 2002; Tsoukas, 1996). In line with this notion, we emphasize that knowledge in organizations cannot be regarded as stable and enduring manifestations. Rather, a firm's knowledge constitutes the product of *how organizational members enact it*. Such a view implies that a knowledge product's traces can only survive when they become an inherent part of organizational practice and are thereby constantly shaped and reshaped in the daily activities of organizational members (Nelson & Winter, 1982; Starbuck, 1992).

Unless organizational knowledge is actually used in daily practice, it can readily become a "dead letter." There may be a significant gap to what is known in an organization and what is actually utilized. This means that to become established throughout an organization, knowledge constantly has to move beyond its initiator. However, as Szulanski (1996) stressed, expertise cannot be easily replicated within a firm as there are important barriers to the transfer of knowledge. Various factors, such as those related to the source and recipient unit, influence the stickiness or inertness of organizational knowledge. For instance, a source may lack motivation to share experiences and facilitate access to it. Such a reluctance to share knowledge can have its origin in the *fear of losing ownership*. Also a recipient unit within an organization may have *little stimuli to accept knowledge* from an external source, even if this source resides within the same organization. This reluctance may also be shaped by an inability to recognize and absorb new knowledge because of limitations of the existing stock of knowledge (Cohen & Levinthal, 1990) or because of little basis for entrenchment (Zeitz, Mittal, & McAulay, 1999). As stressed before, to be maintained, knowledge has to become an enduring part of the organizational members' cognitive base and be incorporated in organizational routines (Nelson & Winter, 1982). Therefore, knowledge in organizations has to continuously survive organizational barriers by which its viability may be threatened.

Struggling Consultancies

The concept of organizational knowing suggests that the transfer of knowledge within organizations provides a fertile breeding ground for dissention and struggle. We believe that this view of knowledge transfer has significant implications for the process of knowledge dissemination within consultancies. Instead of simply a matter of developing a repertoire and making it available through various knowledge carriers, our premise is that the knowledge dissemination process is a fundamentally contested enterprise. A repertoire's development process is not without tensions or resistance (Heusinkveld & Benders, 2002, 2005), and neither is the process of its internal dissemination. The ambiguity characterizing a consultant's ideational "products" (Alvesson, 1993; Benders & van Veen, 2001; Starbuck, 1992) will likely be reflected in the specific shape of the distribution process and the struggles associated with it. This would imply that knowledge dissemination goes well beyond the construction of knowledge manifestations, and involves drawing on persuasive skills to establish a new repertoire within a consultancy. As Alvesson (1993, p. 1013, emphasis added) argues: "Ambiguity calls for a well-articulated and persuasive language in order to convince *outsiders*, as well as *insiders* that the [knowledge-intensive firm] has something to offer worth paying money for and attributing authority to."

STRUGGLES TO KNOWLEDGE DISSEMINATION

The chapter now turns to an empirical exploration of the dissemination of a knowledge repertoire within consultancies. The analysis draws on the relevant literature on organizational knowing and primary data from interviews with 40 management consultants focused on the development of new knowledge commodities within 24 different consultancies. The consultant informants were closely involved with new concept development in their firms and were asked to describe their experiences during the entire process. In the analysis, we followed an inductive approach in which we compared relevant theory and interview data (Glaser & Strauss, 1967; Wester, 1995). We focused particularly on the organizational struggles during the dissemination process as experienced by the consultants and categorized these struggles in light of the relevant literature. The constant comparison and interplay between data and theory (Glaser & Strauss, 1967; Wester, 1995) resulted in further specification of different clusters of struggles related to knowledge transfer in consultancies.

Our key proposition is that the dissemination of a new knowledge repertoire within consultancies constitutes an intricate process as it is not without significant struggles. Rather, this process is shaped by the actions of relevant groups within a consultancy that principally follow their own interests. The analysis stresses the interactive nature of the internal development process that pioneering innovators have to "orchestrate" (Alvesson, 2001, p. 874).

This portion of the chapter illustrates knowledge transfer as a contested enterprise by discussing two typical struggles in which conflicting interests about the dissemination of a new repertoire in a consultancy are resolved. Within this context, our analysis points to two additional insights into the specific organizational problems that occur during knowledge transfer within important management knowledge suppliers. First, we distinguish struggles related to the fear of losing ownership of a new repertoire. Second, we reveal important impediments to the distribution of a repertoire among colleague consultants who are also able to sell and apply it. Each of these struggles typifies a coherent constellation of tactics that plays an important role in the dissemination of a new knowledge repertoire in a consultancy.

Dispersed Development

Although consultants may be working in the same firm and share similar professional interests, this does not automatically guarantee cooperation in the development and transfer of a new knowledge repertoire. The problems related to proprietary aspects of management knowledge do not only appear on the market (Fincham, 1995; Morris, 2001) but are particularly apparent within a knowledge supplier. This could mean that development efforts are highly dispersed across a consultancy and may easily compete with each other. Distinct clusters of consultants within a consultancy involved in developing a new repertoire tend to define and protect their own territory, thereby seeking to gain ownership. Thus, rather than being accompanied by knowledge sharing and cooperation, the development of a repertoire may easily generate competition within the consulting firm. This internal competition may significantly impede the internal transfer of knowledge and generate complications in the market toward clients since it may lead to fundamentally different interpretations of a knowledge product by distinct consultants from the same firm. One important way of controlling a repertoire is gaining ownership, thereby fueling reluctance to knowledge sharing.

Competition

Presenting appealing service offerings requires consultancies to both sense and shape market needs, as consultants seek to take advantage of the attention for a new commodity (Benders et al., 1998). This means that consultancies must be constantly aware of the central issues in the market and what their clients are dealing with. Creating appealing services to clients and conveying the impression that these services reflect the state of the art involve using the right terms and positioning. When a commodity is perceived as becoming popular, consultants seek to contribute to the managerial discourse (Faust, 2002) to mark their presence on the market. As one of the respondents in the study noted, "When the success is big enough, many consultants want to present themselves as *the* vendor of such a concept" (*Consultancy T*).

When a commodity becomes appealing in the market, there is a tendency for many consultants to become associated with the new management idea. New commodities offer a potential entrance to clients and enable consultants to sell their services. In addition, being associated with a successful new management idea provides an opportunity to build up a reputation as an expert in the field and enhances a consultant's career within a firm. As Prasad and Rubenstein (1994) argue, when an innovative idea is regarded as important or profitable, many members want to be associated with it or control its destiny within a firm. As a respondent in *Consultancy C* noted, "What generally happens is that the specific moment when there is an interesting subject, a number of people likely dive after it. Sometimes this even happens at different locations in the bureau."

In realizing a new knowledge repertoire, different organizational units tend to adapt the initial ideas to their own demands. As van de Ven (1986, p. 597) puts it, "When a single innovative idea is expressed to others, it proliferates into multiple ideas because people have diverse frames of reference." Although it is in the interest of a consultancy to develop a uniform commodity, its inherent interpretative viability (Benders & Van Veen, 2001) allows for the possibility that different consultants will translate it in different ways (Benders et al., 1998; Czarniawska & Sévon, 1996). A member of *Consultancy C*, for example, pointed out that, "Clearly different clones of the BPR [business process reengineering] concept emerged within the consultancy." This interpretative viability also offers the opportunity for different consultants to claim ownership of a new commodity, thereby "grafting" their own repertoire on a specific knowledge product. As a result, different versions of a new repertoire begin to crop up (Brunsson, 1997) and crystallize at several distinct places in a consultancy: "The presence of those 15 different BPR methods had everything to do with the fragmented structure of the consultancy" (*Consultancy P*).

Such differentiation could easily mean that development efforts are dispersed throughout the firm and may compete with each other. When distinct clusters of consultants develop a repertoire underlying a new commodity, they tend to create their own territory (Morris, 2001). Thus, parallel to a repertoire's construction process, a form of competition emerges of people who work together and those who deliberately avoid each other and develop it independently. This dynamic makes the internal cooperation within a firm sometimes rather troublesome and hampers clarity toward the market. As an example, one of the consultants noted, "Within [*Consultancy P*] a situation emerged in which we had five different BPR approaches. Only we found that out at the moment we provided different offers to the same client."

In addition, if a group of consultants around a specific repertoire seeks to protect their own ideas, they often feel the need to include certain competencies within their own borders. The effect of this may be that every unit tends to become a duplication of the entire consulting firm. Also, when a unit within a consultancy develops a successful consulting repertoire, others easily tend to "lay their hands on it" and quickly present it to the market. Unsurprisingly, this results in substantial frictions within consultancies because others are perceived as trying to take advantage of the investments in expertise and reputation of the pioneering consultants. As illustrated by the comments of one of the respondents from *Consultancy Q*, as a way of attempting to prevent the loss of knowledge to another unit— even in the same firm—consultants extensively seek to protect their own knowledge repertoire: "These concepts flow to other units, but this process runs automatically because there is obviously a lot of thievery.... So there is a big wall between the knowledge that is kept within [one unit] and what is available to other units."

As this discussion suggests, a lack of coordination between different functions constitutes a major source of problems, a reality that easily generates conflicts in achieving internal product consistency (Clark & Fujimoto, 1991). At the same time, allocating the ownership of a project to an individual person or team leader will likely be an issue that constitutes a base for significant struggle. As a result, the allocation of a new repertoire's leadership within a consultancy relates to ability of the consultants to compete for ownership of the repertoire. In essence, within consulting firms various individuals or groups contest the privilege to develop and exploit a new repertoire. The lack of a material component both enables and complicates attempts to define the ownership of the new knowledge repertoire (Fincham, 1995; Morris, 2001).

Obtaining Ownership

The development of an internally coherent knowledge repertoire requires cross-functional coordination and centralized decision making. This would imply that achieving internal integrity of a knowledge repertoire is related to obtaining its ownership. Obtaining a repertoire's ownership enables consultants to internally control its development and exploitation, thereby increasing the possibility for knowledge transfer. This means that everything associated with a new repertoire—from intakes, offers, and further development efforts, to external marketing— becomes coordinated by a dominant cluster within a consultancy that has been able to gain the most experience and power.

Gaining ownership, of course, does not occur automatically. Rather, it may even take shape in the confiscation of a repertoire by a more powerful unit within a consultancy. Such a "hostile takeover," for example, could occur when a particular unit has been able to successfully exploit a concept in the marketplace. As a consequence, the pioneering unit's expertise and reputation becomes very attractive for other parts of the consultancy. When these units are powerful enough, they might consider bringing the concept within their own borders. This means that the methods, approaches, and people associated with the concept are deliberately transferred from one unit to another, so that these individuals can further develop—and perhaps even customize—the original repertoire for a new unit. Such movements, however, are likely to encounter considerable opposition because they are easily seen as simply giving away valuable knowledge. As a respondent from *Consultancy P* noted,

> the daughter company managed to yield an outstanding turnover, had large margins, and did large projects at important clients with BPR, while under the [*Consultancy P*] label nothing was achieved. In this situation, it was considered to remove someone from [the daughter] to set up BPR at [*P*]. At that moment, I was partner at [the daughter] and my senior partner was not able to block this idea.... What I did at [*P*] was obviously considered in [the daughter company] as just giving away the silverware. I told the current chairman that he had to realize that this just would cost [daughter company] turnover.

A consulting unit covering a particular part of the consultancy market may feel considerably threatened when another group gains a reputation on overlapping business by developing a new repertoire. When different units are unable to monopolize a new repertoire, defining its ownership may result in conflicts about its labeling. The resulting tensions often trigger the different powerful units to negotiate the vocabulary of the new concept. The outcome of this game determines which terminology becomes acceptable to the different parties involved. While the intense struggles may result in a situation in which different labels are coupled with similar repertoires, this allows the different units to develop and control their own versions of a repertoire. In this instance, the "territory" of the other unit is protected, and the probability of intrafirm cannibalization is reduced. A respondent in *Consultancy Q*, for example, pointed out that "the tensions between [mother company] and [daughter company] appeared to be so large that it was decided that both would develop it [a new concept] in their own way and under their own label." Such efforts at turf protection, however, suggest reduced cooperation between different units in the development of a repertoire, which readily hampers the transfer of knowledge within a consultancy.

In some instances, the ownership of a repertoire will settle at the unit that has been able to gain the most experience or power. This allows people to monopolize the repertoire throughout the consultancy. However, while this dynamic may increase the repertoire's coherence and internal consistency, it can still hamper the application of the underlying repertoire at other units. As illustrated by the comments from a member of *Consultancy C*, a monopolizing unit may restrict others in the development and application of a knowledge repertoire: "The label BPR is still in use within [consultancy], only this concept belongs to the territory of another group. Not surprisingly, such a situation can generate certain frictions…"

Dispersed Reception

A consultancy may not only experience a reluctance to share knowledge internally, but the firm can also encounter significant difficulties at the receiving end. Szulanski (1996) recognized that a recipient's motivation and its absorptive capacity are important barriers for the transfer of knowledge in an organization. The development and application of a knowledge repertoire are typically allocated to different, specialized units that are spatially separated and characterized by incongruent orientations and structures (Tidd, Bessant, & Pavitt, 1997). As a result, new repertoires are not automatically used at the "production" site. In practice, the internal reception of new repertoires by consultants is much more problematic and easily obstructed.

A general characteristic of consultancy services is that knowledge "production" occurs in the interaction process with clients (Clark, 1995). A new repertoire, therefore, has to be introduced in such a way that consultants within a firm are willing and able to make use of it in their daily practice with their clients. To enhance the application of a new knowledge repertoire on a wider scale throughout a consultancy, pioneering consultants have to catch the attention of their peers and persuade them to adopt the repertoire. So consultants do not only have to advertise their commodities in the marketplace but also propagate the underlying repertoire within their own firm. However, this is not without further complications as there are important barriers to the dissemination of knowledge within the firm.

Dissemination Barriers

Unlike what would be expected within a consultancy, the dissemination of a new repertoire is often an intricate process. The codification of a knowledge repertoire does not automatically mean utilization in daily consulting practice. As a member of *Consultancy T* noted, "It is 2 minutes' work to put a method into a database, but it is much more difficult to get it into people's heads." As this quote suggests, consultancies may not only face a fear of losing ownership in their efforts to develop a useful repertoire in the external marketplace, but are also confronted with colleagues who are unable or unwilling to adopt the knowledge repertoire in their own practices. A lack of application by knowledge users clearly obstructs the long-term viability of a repertoire. A deficiency in continuous usage easily leads to an inability of application (Nelson & Winter, 1982). Ultimately, the applicability of knowledge is determined by whether it is kept alive by different people in a consultancy. As reflected by the comments from a member of *Consultancy N*, a lack of enthusiasm will likely result in a repertoire becoming a "dead letter" rather than a viable slice of knowledge: "Large consultancies hold a considerable amount of knowledge on their intranet, but it is not likely that it will be applied if people do not feel any enthusiasm about it."

The codification of knowledge into a new consulting repertoire does not necessarily mean that consultants are able and willing to apply it in practice during their assignments. Rather, within consultancies attempts to transfer new knowledge repertoires from "development" to "production" may run aground in problems of understanding, creating critical barriers in the repertoire's dissemination. In spite of commercial success, dissemination efforts do not necessarily result in wider usage of a repertoire within a consulting firm when there is an inability of the receiving consultants to fully understand it. So while a repertoire may be commercially attractive, it may not necessarily be comprehended by its possible users. Reflecting on this problem, a *Consultancy N* member noted,

> So I was given some time to develop that manual, give courses, write and
> distribute leaflets.... I was allowed to hire people for this, but it wasn't easy

to find good BPR consultants. Learning the theory is not the same as applying it, that's a completely different story…. consultants trying to learn from a manual hardly ever succeeds. That also happened with BPR. Every time these consultants did not want to learn something, but wanted to contemplate it and be the "cock of the walk," it resulted in endless discussions. So it was very difficult for the consultants to learn these things.

Even if consultants are able to understand a new repertoire, it does not necessarily become part of their services for clients. The dissemination of a new repertoire within a consulting firm is associated with different actors following their own interests, a given that likely creates important barriers in its reception. When a new repertoire is seen as not contributing to perceived personal gains, consultants are less interested in using it. A consultant in *Consultancy C*, for example, argued, "When you force consultants too much into a standardized straightjacket [that fits] the market's taste by sending them all to a CRM course so they are able to tell clients they have to implement CRM, a number of people quickly drop out and will go to another firm." Obviously, a lack of interest on the "receiving side" hampers the knowledge transfer process (Szulanski, 1996).

It is clearly in the interest of a consulting firm to deploy a disciplined, company-wide effort to develop a clear and recognizable repertoire. Such efforts support introducing a clear-cut proposition to the market. It also decreases the probability that the "wheel" will be invented and reinvented at different places within the firm. However, efforts to distribute a new repertoire as a medium for increased standardization across a consultancy may easily cause internal dissentions and objections. After all, many people within a firm hold the idea that they constantly have to come up with something new themselves to enhance their career. As illustrated by the comments of a member of *Consultancy B*, individual consultants are often highly self-willed and tend to develop and apply their own approaches: "Simply following a manual is not so exciting for a consultant, but if you repeatedly develop things from scratch clients will not accept it and at a certain moment will hire people that already have an elaborate idea." The enthusiasm of consultants for a new knowledge repertoire will likely fade when it is imposed on them from a higher managerial level with little room for their own interpretations. Moreover, autonomous units are not likely to abandon their own ideas in favor of a repertoire that has been developed elsewhere. As one of the consultants (*Consultancy T*) commented, "the dissemination of the concept became a time-consuming process in which consultants in other countries showed lots of interest in what we had developed here, but they did not adopt it. They did not consider it as applicable in their situation." As a result of such dynamics, the internal dissemination of a concept within a consultancy should be viewed as a highly demanding task.

Temptation: Going Beyond In-house Training

The way consultancy services are produced is essential in the success of a new repertoire. As has been stressed earlier, in the consultancy industry, the "product" cannot be separated from the specific consultant who is producing it (Clark, 1995). This would mean that the successful transfer of knowledge (about a new repertoire) between "development" and "production" is essential to facilitate sufficient understanding among colleagues so they will be able to apply it in practice. In-house training programs thus not only increase knowledge about a new repertoire but can also enhance its acceptance. Dissemination efforts within a consultancy have to aim not only at making a repertoire available to peers, but also educating colleagues and supporting them in applying the repertoire:

> If clients come to us and want to use [a particular] method, it becomes important that more people are actually able to do it. Currently we are working on developing an internal course to educate our colleagues in the method so that they are able to apply it. (*Consultancy B*)

The dissemination of a new repertoire throughout a consulting firm requires that the pioneering consultants also develop internal courses that both fascinate and educate colleagues, helping them to apply the knowledge associated with the consulting repertoire. As illustrated by the comments of a respondent from *Consultancy A*, consultants often develop "internal marketing efforts to inform and train [their own] people." In many instances, firms produce flyers and manuals on a new repertoire and organize workshops for *internal* use. In some cases, consultants use an intranet environment to transform a repertoire into a living mechanism, instead of simply disseminating a static manual. As the comments from *Consultancy F* indicate, however, formal training situations still appear to be the most effective way of transferring a knowledge repertoire within a company: "Our courses are the most important carrier of the method and are the most important way to disseminate the ideas."

Merely educating consultants in a new repertoire, however, is not sufficient to ensure widespread use in assignments. Consultants also have to be persuaded to integrate a new repertoire's knowledge into their current approaches. As a consultant from *Consultancy P* noted, "In any case, knowledge management in consultancies is not about writing down a method, but making people understand references, standards, and approaches." To increase such understanding, innovation theorists point to the importance of integrated activities in both the initial development process and subsequent standardization in product components (Vermeulen, 2001). These efforts may entail the development of a common standardized language (Werr, 1999), while also realizing the involvement of other consultants in the development process. Standardization can be realized by developing a general framework and common language in which the repertoire becomes embedded (Visscher, 2001; Werr, 1999), especially if it is strongly maintained throughout the firm:

> Those frameworks are built by the [development] team and constitute a theoretical basis for the way we see work related to process development. You have to establish the nomenclature and vocabulary for the organization. It is particularly clumsy if people in England talk about it in a different way than the people in the Netherlands. (*Consultancy F*)

If consultants want to distribute a new repertoire, they need to convince other consultants that it does not make sense for them to develop their own methods and tools. Specifically, it is essential to generate attention for a new repertoire, to show that it has already been developed and to motivate other consultants to use it. Reflecting on this challenge, one of the respondents from *Consultancy T* observed,

> The question is how to sell a new concept to your own people.... We present the [consultancy] method to the consultants and tell them that they may use it or develop their own method, but we clearly indicate that the latter is particularly clumsy. If they adopt the [consultancy] method, we allow them to give it their own interpretation because every client is different and you cannot apply the same method across different industries.... We put it on our internal websites and databases.... Thus in the internal dissemination of concepts, we elaborately use the technical means, but that is not the most important factor. By using these technological systems, you show what you want to sell on the market as a consultancy, but you also let people look for themselves, to see how they can use it ... and this works.

If a concept "works" in praxis and becomes widely accepted, then other consultants may not be inclined to develop their own repertoire.

Involving consultants during development of the repertoire allows them to partly construct their own version of the standardized repertoire, providing space to include their own ideas. Offering the possibility for co-development allows adopting consultants to give the new concept a personal interpretation under the veil of tailoring their services to an individual client's requirements (Clark, 1995). Such temptation mainly involves emphasizing the advantages of an elaborately developed repertoire, while allowing for the possibility of context-specific adaptations by the consultants who will ultimately use it. Adopting consultants thus feel that the repertoire includes their own work and not something that is simply handed down from the firm.   A related advantage is that clients get the impression that they are getting a concept specifically constructed for their industry rather than a general, "cookie-cutter" solution from the consultancy. Finally, it also allows the director of the consultancy to sell standardized services on a large scale, with the potential of generating additional business (and enhancing his or her career).

A disadvantage of this approach, however, is that it can unavoidably result in a large number of variations on each repertoire, legitimated by the argument that each client is unique. While it is in the interest of a consultancy to homogenize its approaches, when disseminating a knowledge repertoire throughout the firm it is important to remember that individual consultants are likely to give it their own, highly personal interpretation. The challenge is to manage a balance between consultant freedom to adapt a concept to the needs of a specific client and firm-wide restrictions that interventions have to conform to certain guidelines. As a managing consultant who developed a new knowledge repertoire in *Consultancy T* argued, "Regarding E-business, consultants clearly had to comply with the main lines in the phasing... and they got an angry phone call from me if they did not do that." Obviously, when consultants initially conform to the main script in a repertoire, it is more difficult to deviate from the intended repertoire because the application is more or less "filling in."

CONCLUSIONS

The chapter sought to further our understanding of knowledge transfer processes within management consultancies by analyzing some basic struggles to and tensions in the internal dissemination of knowledge repertoires. Consultancies are generally regarded as important suppliers of management knowledge and, given the knowledge-intensive character of their services (Clark, 1995), developing and utilizing new knowledge repertoires are crucial to maintain and enhance their position in the marketplace. At the same time, theorists of organizational knowing argue that the transfer of knowledge within organizations can be a highly problematic activity. This chapter showed that these insights have some notable implications for the development and dissemination of new knowledge repertoires in consultancies. By drawing on this literature and our interview data, the chapter provides a critical perspective on the process of internal knowledge transfer. Unlike current conceptualizations, which portray knowledge development and transfer within consulting firms as largely unproblematic, we argue that such processes constitute an intricate enterprise.

While the consultancy literature mainly stresses the external struggles to promote their knowledge products on the market, there is still little attention placed on the internal repertoire development processes. Consultancies are mainly presented as systems of persuasion that continuously seek to impress and convince clients of the value of their prescriptions. By solely regarding consultants as (external) marketers of knowledge commodities, however, we lose sight of the relevant activities that must occur during the pre-dissemination phase. Various theorists emphasize the importance of internal knowledge systems and highlight the technical means by which they become accessible to preserve knowledge in a consultancy (Werr & Stjernberg, 2003). In addition, these systems also become a sales argument when they support the impression of consultants' knowledge ability (Alvesson, 1993). However, as suggested in this chapter, these accounts tend to neglect the intricate process of *internal* dissemination. Our emphasis can be seen in light of an emerging literature studying "backstage processes" (Clark, 2001, 2004a, 2004b; Heusinkveld & Benders, 2005) that concentrates on understanding how knowledge suppliers seek to develop and exploit commercially viable ideas.

The current literature on consultancy methods considers the process of management knowledge dissemination as if it is largely unproblematic (Werr, 2002; Werr & Stjernberg, 2003). These accounts mainly focus on the large possibilities for knowledge transfer within consultancies. However, as the growing literature on organizational knowledge indicates, this dissemination process is often fraught with significant struggles within consultancies. The chapter indicates that the development of a new repertoire goes well beyond the challenge of constructing a coherent "method." Rather, a more fundamental problem lies in establishing the new repertoire in the consultancy. Our analysis reveals that the viability of knowledge items is not a matter of building a collection of techniques, but is particularly about their propagation within consulting firms. The data support the belief that while knowledge may already be widely dispersed, it is still difficult to render it viable. In essence, the presence of various codified and cognitive items does not guarantee that management consultants will actually use them in their daily practice. Rather, the accumulation of knowledge (Lammers, 1988) requires extensive and persistent dissemination efforts within a consultancy. The knowledge-intensive character of consultancies and their ideational "products" (Alvesson, 1993) implies that the establishment of new concepts within the firm entails drawing on political and persuasive skills, not only in claiming its ownership but also in its internal dissemination. A knowledge repertoire has to be continuously and extensively marketed internally to inform, train, and convince consultants of its usefulness.

The study also indicated that consultancies are increasingly collecting and codifying knowledge associated with new repertoires into large databases and intranet applications. The emergence of such computer-based information technologies has induced debates on their perceived effectiveness in consulting organizations (Hansen et al., 1999; Morris & Empson, 1998; Olivera, 2000). Our data suggest that most of a concept's traces remain largely fluid, hard to catch, and highly dependent on the particular interest of individuals. As these knowledge bases grow, over time it becomes more and more difficult to acquire a well-informed overview, and retrieval becomes a time-consuming matter. Therefore, although knowledge on a concept may be codified, without the professional and pragmatic interest of individual consultants it is not likely to become viable and applied in daily practice. As Starbuck (1992) observed, the storage of knowledge in such firms only brings short-term continuity.

In the long run, the viability of a knowledge repertoire is shaped by perceived market opportunities, personal interest in present-day issues, and the grouping of different people within a firm. These elements interact and become a major incentive for recognizing and vitalizing codified knowledge items, as well as building experiences around a specific issue. Given the dynamics and pressures associated with within-firm knowledge transfer, however, the mere presence of these factors is no guarantee that consultants will not continue to "reinvent wheels."

ACKNOWLEDGMENTS

An earlier version of this paper was presented as part of the Management Consulting Division (MCD) program at the 2004 Academy of Management conference in New Orleans. The authors would like to thank the session participants and the MCD reviewers for their valuable comments.

REFERENCES

Abrahamson, E. (1996). Management fashion. *Academy of Management Review*, *21*(1), 254–285.

Alvesson, M. (1993). Organizations as rhetoric: Knowledge-intensive firms and the struggle with ambiguity. *Journal of Management Studies*, *30*(6), 997–1015.

Alvesson, M. (2001). Knowledge work: Ambiguity, image and identity. *Human Relations*, *54*(7), 863–886.

Benders, J., van den Berg, R.-J., & van Bijsterveld, M. (1998). Hitch-hiking on a hype: Dutch consultants engineering re-engineering. *Journal of Organizational Change Management*, *11*(3), 201–215.

Benders, J., & van Veen, K. (2001). What's in a fashion? Interpretative viability and management fashion. *Organization*, *8*(1), 33–53.

Bloomfield, B., & Danieli, A. (1995). The role of management consultants in the development of information technology: The indissoluble nature of socio-political and technical skills. *Journal of Management Studies, 32*(1), 23–46.

Brunsson, N. (1997). The standardization of organizational forms as a cropping-up process. *Scandinavian Journal of Management, 13*(3), 307–320.

Clark, T. (1995). *Managing consultants: Consultants as the management of impressions.* Buckingham, UK: Open University Press.

Clark, T. (2001). Management research on fashion: A review and evaluation. *Human Relations, 54*(12), 1650–1662.

Clark, T. (2004a). The fashion of management fashion: A surge too far? *Organization, 11*(2), 297–306.

Clark, T. (2004b). Management fashion as collective action: The production of management best-sellers. In A. F. Buono (Ed.), *Creative consulting: Innovative perspectives on management consulting* (pp. 1–28). Greenwich, CT: Information Age.

Clark, T., & Fincham, R. (2002). *Critical consulting: New perspectives on the management advice industry.* Oxford: Blackwell.

Clark, K., & Fujimoto, T. (1991). *Product development performance.* Boston: Harvard Business School Press.

Cohen, W., & Levinthal, D. (1990). Absorptive capacity: A new perspective on learning and innovation. *Administrative Science Quarterly, 35*(1): 128-152.

Czarniawska, B., & Sévon, G. (1996). *Translating organizational change.* Berlin: Walter de Gruyter.

Faust, M. (2002). Consultancies as actors in knowledge arenas: Evidence from Germany. In M. Kipping & L. Engwall (Eds.), *Management consulting* (pp. 146–163). Oxford: Oxford University Press.

Fincham, R. (1995). Business process reengineering and the commodification of management knowledge. *Journal of Marketing Management, 11*(7), 707–719.

Fincham, R. (1999). The consultant–client relationship: Critical perspectives on the management of organizational change. *Journal of Management Studies, 36*(3), 335–351.

Fincham, R., & Evans, M. (1999). The consultants' offensive: Reengineering—From fad to technique. *New Technology Work and Employment, 14*(1), 32-34.

Glaser, B., & Strauss, A. (1967). *The discovery of grounded theory.* Chicago: Aldine.

Glückler, J., & Armbrüster, T. (2003). Bridging uncertainty in management consulting: The mechanisms of trust and networked reputation. *Organization Studies, 24*(2), 269–297.

Guillén, M. (1994). *Models of management: Work, authority and organization in a comparative perspective.* Chicago: University of Chicago Press.

Hansen, M., Nohria, N., & Tienery, T. (1999). What's your strategy for managing knowledge? *Harvard Business Review, 77*(2), 106–116.

Heusinkveld, S., & Benders, J. (2002). Between professional dedication and corporate design: Exploring forms of new concept development in consultancies. *International Studies of Management and Organization, 32*(4), 104–122.

Heusinkveld, S., & Benders, J. (2005). Contested commodification: Consultancies and their struggle with new concept development. *Human Relations, 58*(3), 283-310.

Huczynski, A. (1993). *Management gurus: What makes them and how to become one.* London: Routledge.

Kieser, A. (2002). Managers as marionettes? Using fashion theories to explain the success of consultancies. In M. Kipping & L. Engwall (Eds.), *Management consulting* (pp. 167–183). Oxford: Oxford University Press.

Lammers, C. (1988). Transience and persistence of ideal types in organization theory. In N. DiTomaso & Bacharach, S. (Eds.), *Research in the sociology of organizations* (pp. 203–224). Greenwich, CT: JAI Press.

Morris, T. (2001). Asserting property rights: Knowledge codification in the professional service firm. *Human Relations, 54*(7), 819–838.

Morris, T., & Empson, L. (1998). Organization and expertise: An exploration of knowledge bases and the management of accounting and consulting firms. *Accounting, Organization and Society, 23*(5/6), 609–624.

Nelson, R., & Winter, S. (1982). *An evolutionary theory of economic change.* Cambridge, MA: Belknap Press.

Nonaka, I., & Takeuchi, H. (1995). *The knowledge-creating company.* New York: Oxford University Press.

Olivera, F. (2000). Memory systems in organizations: An empirical investigation of mechanisms for knowledge collection storage and access. *Journal of Management Studies, 36*(6), 811–832.

Orlikowski, W. (2002). Knowing in practice: Enacting a collective capacity in distributed organizing. *Organization Science, 13*(3), 249–273.

Pettigrew, A. (1975). Towards a political theory of organizational intervention. *Human Relations, 28*(3), 191–208.

Prasad, L., & Rubenstein, A. (1994). Power and organizational politics during new product development: A conceptual framework. *Journal of Scientific and Industrial Research, 53*(6), 397–407.

Roberts, J. (2001). The drive to codify: Implications for the knowledge-based economy. *Prometheus, 19*(2), 99–116.

Røvik, K-A. (2002). The secrets of the winners: Management ideas that flow. In K. Sahlin-Andersson & L. Engwall (Eds.), *The expansion of management knowledge: Carriers, flows and sources* (pp. 113–144). Stanford, CA: Stanford University Press.

Sarvay, M. (1999). Knowledge management and competition in the consulting industry. *California Management Review, 41*(2), 95–107.

Starbuck, W. (1992). Learning by knowledge-intensive firms. *Journal of Management Studies, 29*(6), 713–740.

Sturdy, A. (1997). The consultancy process—An insecure business? *Journal of Management Studies, 34*(3), 389–413.

Suddaby, R., & Greenwood, R. (2001). Colonizing knowledge: Commodification as a dynamic of jurisdictional expansion in professional service firms. *Human Relations, 54*(7), 933–953.

Szulanski, G. (1996). Exploring internal stickiness: Impediments to the transfer of best practices within the firm. *Strategic Management Journal, 17*(4), 27–43.

Tidd, J., Bessant, J., & Pavitt, K. (1997). *Managing innovation: Integrating technological, market and organizational change.* Chichester, UK: Wiley.

Tsoukas, H. (1996). The firm as a distributed knowledge system: A constructionist approach. *Strategic Management Journal, 17*(4), 11–25.

van de Ven, A. (1986). Central problems in the management of innovation. *Management Science, 32*(5), 590–607.

Vermeulen, P. (2001). *Organizing product innovation in financial services: How banks and insurance companies organize their innovation processes.* Nijmegen: Nijmegen University Press.

Visscher, K. (2001). *Design methodology in management consulting.* Enschede: University of Twente.

Werr, A. (1999). *The language of change: The roles of methods in the work of management consultants.* Stockholm: Stockholm School of Economics.

Werr, A. (2002). The internal creation of consulting knowledge: A question of structuring experience. In M. Kipping & L. Engwall (Eds.), *Management consulting* (pp. 91–108). Oxford: Oxford University Press.

Werr, A., & Stjernberg, T. (2003). Exploring management consulting firms as knowledge systems. *Organization Studies, 24*(6), 881–908.

Werr, A., Stjernberg, T., & Doucherty, P. (1997). The functions of methods of change in management consulting. *Journal of Organizational Change Management, 10*(4), 288–307.

Wester, F. (1995). *Strategieën voor kwalitatief onderzoek.* Bussum: Coutinho.

Wright, C. (2002). Promoting demand, gaining legitimacy and broadening expertise: The evolution of consultancy-client relationships in Australia. In M. Kipping & L. Engwall (Eds.), *Management consulting: Emergence and dynamics of a knowledge industry* (pp. 184–202). Oxford: Oxford University Press.

Zeitz, G., Mittal, V., & McAulay, B. (1999). Distinguishing adoption and entrenchment of management practices: A framework for analysis. *Organization Studies, 20*(5), 741–776.

CHAPTER 7

IN SEARCH OF KNOWLEDGE SHARING IN PRACTICE

Lotte Henriksen

Knowledge management is turning up in more and more companies. Interest in knowledge and the processes that create and manifest knowledge has grown throughout the last several decades. As Drucker (1995, p. 31) suggests, "Knowledge has become *the* resource rather than a resource." For the knowledge-intensive firm in particular (Starbuck, 1992), knowledge is the most important factor in competitive advantage, which is why related management challenges have been receiving steadily increasing attention. Companies are changing and are no longer characterized as hierarchical structures that simply channel the commands of management. In the knowledge-intensive firm, the employees themselves must know what needs to be done and the subsequent shaping and forming of this knowledge places new demands of the firm's formal leadership. In order to internalize knowledge and develop their competencies, these employees must have opportunities to be creative, to experiment, and to challenge their assigned tasks.

In knowledge-intensive firms, the product emerges directly from employee knowledge. In order to maintain its competitiveness, the knowledge-intensive firm is forced to combine modern technology with effective use of the employees' knowledge and qualifications. Product

Challenges and Issues in Knowledge Management, 155–178
Copyright © 2005 by Information Age Publishing

development is about creating new knowledge and enhancing personal competencies and qualifications. Accordingly, it becomes increasingly important to understand how knowledge can be managed—"how knowledge assets are grounded in the experience and expertise of individuals, how firms provide the physical, social and resource allocation structure so that knowledge can be shared into competences" (Teece, 1999, p. 62).

Companies are being forced to discover new ways to work—in part in order to keep up with the competition and in part in order to set themselves apart from it (Porter, 1996). These new conditions are a result of the emergence of a post-industrial or knowledge society, which situates companies in new and more loosely coupled systems (Christensen & Kreiner, 1991). The challenges should also be viewed in light of the enormous amount of information that companies have access to, affording them much more knowledge about each other.

The basic idea in the contemporary management literature is that knowledge management (KM) ensures that the right knowledge reaches the right person at the right time. Companies typically apply a series of IT support systems, including intranets, in an effort to get knowledge sharing to work. Many KM theorists, including Davenport and Prusak (1998), however, do not believe that technology is the only solution to the problems of managing knowledge. The greatest challenge for the firm is increasingly that of developing an appropriate organizational culture and infrastructure that encourages organizational members to develop and exchange knowledge (O'Dell & Grayson, 1998). Yet, the very broad interpretation of knowledge management that is employed in the literature raises unavoidable questions about what actually needs to be developed and communicated when a company attempts to put knowledge management into practice.

Many KM theorists (including Nonaka & Takeuchi, 1995, and Krogh, Roos, & Kleine, 1998) take as their common point of departure the fact that knowledge becomes a visible organizational resource in production (explicit knowledge) primarily through IT systems. They lack a treatment, however, of what is needed to make space for the development and exchange of the knowledge that is stored in the individual (tacit knowledge), that is, a treatment of knowledge sharing *in practice*. It is this lacuna that this chapter takes as its point of departure. The analysis is based on a case study of an accounting and consulting firm, referred to as ServCo. It is an empirical study of knowledge management that focuses on knowledge sharing in particular.[1]

The aim of the chapter is to map out some of the essential organizational challenges that are crucial for true knowledge sharing. The chapter attempts to contribute to our understanding of the practice of knowledge sharing in the knowledge-intensive firm, elaborating on the essence of the firm in relation to its knowledge. Emphasis is placed on how ServCo understands its own cognitive situation and how we might come to understand the changes that transpire in the firm and its members. The chapter concludes with a brief discussion of where this company stands today in its relation to KM-related initiatives.

KNOWLEDGE SHARING AT SERVCO

ServCo is a knowledge-intensive firm—one that has always lived with, survived, and succeeded based on what it "knows." Knowledge sharing is therefore a major part of the way the company executes its tasks. This section will share insights into the ways that trust, relationships, management, and culture influence knowledge-sharing practices at the company.

Inquiry and Communication

The basic fact that accountants convert information to knowledge, which is stored and exchanged through a series of electronic ledgers, does not automatically mean that there is knowledge or knowledge sharing at ServCo. It simply illustrates that managers and employees at ServCo experience knowledge sharing as a basis for success without necessarily knowing what form of knowledge is to be shared. Put differently, the knowledge that emerges and is talked about is the explicit knowledge that our attention concentrates on when we think about knowledge sharing. This emphasis can be devoid of nuance, and it is important to probe into the specific forms of knowledge that have the potential to create value for firms like ServCo. What is of interest here is that both information and knowledge are context-specific notions, which are created and transferred through social interaction or on-the-job training.

Within ServCo, the search for information at the beginning of an audit is conducted mainly through the ledgers used in the prior year's audit and updates that pass between the partner and the supervisor or manager in charge of the account.[2] Support software contains checklists, ledgers, and documentation, and is used throughout the process, from startup, through the audit itself, to completion. In the course of the audit, the team can face problems that require the application of other tools, such as the Accountant's Library (current standards for how different tasks are to be executed and problems are to be solved) or the company intranet. Startup meetings, in which the team is informed about the audit, are rare. Such meetings, in which team members are assigned their portfolios, happen only in the case of certain large customers and depend on how the manager or supervisor wants to run the audit.

The other major source of information during the audit process is informal communication between colleagues. The accountants at ServCo develop highly specialized knowledge over time that pertains to particular types of customers, trades, and industries. Cooperation with colleagues is therefore seen as valuable and edifying. New accountants are introduced to the firm and given on-the-job training, which implies a focus on professional interaction. By this means, the transfer of skills and abilities through informal learning processes becomes an important part of cooperation at the team level. Knowledge is often attached to the specific auditing task, especially within the context of customer-specific knowledge. The ensuing dialogue that emerges as different tasks are being executed is one of the most important tools of knowledge sharing because the accountants can relate to the concrete task being carried out on site. Although the accountants initially attempt to solve problems by themselves, they turn to colleagues as needed.

In the late 1990s, ServCo developed a company intranet referred to as KnowSource, a repository for data, information, and knowledge and a medium that provided employees and partners with an open site for discussion. This tool was intended to support the development and exchange of knowledge, both within and across the service centers (local accounting units) and business units. The initial goal was to create more flexibility and efficiency in ServCo's auditing and consulting services. Its longer-term objective was to foster a deeper understanding of the importance of knowledge and the need to develop relevant ways to share it, enriching communication across the country.

As is the case in many companies, the intranet was the first formally structured initiative in knowledge sharing. It would soon become apparent, however, that the mere availability of KnowSource did not foster knowledge sharing. Organizational members expressed concerns that the system's "knowledge" was not necessarily useful to others just because it was accessible. They pointed out that a model or document always needed to be accompanied by comments and qualifications in order to reach the level of detail and anonymity that is required if it was to be applied by a colleague. Such documentation, of course, is time consuming and is considered "indirect time" (i.e., time that the customer is not billed for), which raises the question of who will pay for the work.

Time Pressures

Time plays a significant role in the accountant's working day and the enormous time pressures that accountants work under means that the experience a team develops during an audit is rarely followed up on.

Knowledge that could be valuable to others in the firm often remains within the team or with the individual accountant. Unfortunately, there is typically no debriefing session at the end of the audit, in part because the employees are already engaged in new tasks. As one of the accountants noted, "There is a need for a debriefing, but if you ask whether there is time to have one, the answer is no."

Each audit must take the time that has been negotiated, that is, the time that ServCo is paid for by the customer, and no more. As customers have become better at carrying out many of the tasks themselves, the fee has become smaller and employees are expected to conduct the audit within a shorter time period. This has also created a risk of *underabsorption*, the use of more hours on a given task than was originally calculated. The supervising accountant must also complete an evaluation[3] for each team member, which provides feedback on how well the employee functioned during the audit. A comprehensive internal evaluation and debriefing of the whole process, which can be very time consuming, is simply not part of the auditing methodology. Thus, the risk of underabsorption, reduced fees, and pressures created by the evaluation process all contribute to a lack of time to reflect on prior audits. Any time that cannot be billed directly to the customer is considered an expense for ServCo.

In general, accountants' work is characterized by a high degree of autonomy. They have opportunities to act independently, albeit within a given framework. Accountants find this flexibility motivating and it allows them to seek new challenges. They are apt to seek independent and challenging tasks, preferably tasks that afford an opportunity to influence the evolution of the firm. While generally positive, such autonomy can also be time consuming, since the accountants often try to solve problems themselves before seeking help from colleagues and specialists. The same discoveries are thus made independently in various locations across the firm and its various office locations. As one of the accountants pointed out, "If we find a good way to execute a task, it isn't passed on, for example, through KnowSource. We assume that a similar model already exists somewhere and we're pressed for time, rushing around."

While employees and partners at all levels agree that it is important to share knowledge, they also admit that it is a difficult process. People generally like to receive knowledge but are reluctant to contribute—often because they do not believe that they have an ingenious contribution to make. As the comments by one of the firm's members suggest, this must also be viewed in light of the lack of an incentive structure to foster commitment: "I'd like to contribute to knowledge sharing if it resulted in a bonus when my yearly salary is reviewed. But it doesn't." As another colleague noted, "I am assessed in terms of the amount of direct hours and the amount of overtime I put in. The more overtime the better. I've sometimes received a bottle of champagne at the successful completion of a task or if a deadline has been honored."

Organizational members at ServCo do not necessarily demand financial rewards (although the younger employees are more prone to this), but rather seek recognition of the importance of knowledge sharing and a clear signal to proceed in this direction. Such recognition is important to legitimize the time spent sharing knowledge with others, especially since accountants typically prioritize time spent with customers over internal projects or helping colleagues.

Knowledge sharing at the team level works well because of the strong cooperation *within* the team, which fosters the exchange of what each member knows with the other members. Yet, while individual teams might develop a model for the solution of a specific class of problems, this knowledge remains within the team.

Relationships and Social Interaction

Although knowledge sharing often occurred inside teams at ServCo, on occasion it also moved beyond individual teams, albeit most often within the same business unit. There are great differences, however, between departments within a given business unit (there are typically three to four departments in a business unit). In one unit, people might express the view that cooperation across departments is minimal, while members of another unit have consciously established cooperative ventures across departments. It appears that a driving force is partner behavior—if a partner takes the lead and cooperates across departments, his or her employees tend to do the same.

At ServCo, interdepartmental networks are formed in primarily two ways. First, they emerge from a strong informal network. As one of the respondents noted,

> I talk to my neighbor, or go elsewhere in the unit. My first thought about knowledge sharing is that we have a lot of it already. If I run into a problem I haven't seen before, I consult a colleague who has had a similar problem. The hard part is knowing whether or not the colleague has had a similar problem. This can sometimes be a bit tricky, so you've typically got a group of regulars that you almost always talk things over with.

The second way networks form emerges from the formal structure and reflects hierarchical interactions—managers interact with partners; the supervisor interacts with the manager—often through the work in the team. Since it is the partner's responsibility to create incentive structures, different demands for feedback are made depending on the position the employee occupies in the hierarchy. Younger employees, for example, typically demand praise and encouragement, while more senior employees demand professional "sparring," looking for opportunities to take on "good" clients and get "good" tasks assigned to them.

ServCo has also been well known for its internal educational efforts, and it is often in these educational contexts that the informal networks that cut across business units are established. The members of each "graduating class" pass through the firm's educational system together. As one of these individuals described,

> You get to know your whole graduating class and information flows [through these people]. Why, I know someone everywhere! I draw on this when I have a question about an audit, for example. Then I just call someone at my level in another auditing department. Otherwise we use each other in the department.

Each graduating class meets year after year and spreads the knowledge its members have gathered at subsequent courses across various company boundaries. People who have gone through these classes together often maintain their network throughout their career and draw upon it whenever problems have to be solved. These informal networks are used increasingly as individual accountants rise through the ranks. Thus, accountants typically first seek knowledge vertically and thereafter horizontally, drawing on the networks they have created over the years.

Culture, Geographical Distance, Rewards, and Interpersonal Relationships

ServCo's partnership structure, time pressure, and system for registering hours mean that organizational members, first and foremost, are interested in their own results. As a result, internal competition between partners can emerge, and ServCo can be viewed as several companies in one. As one of the respondents argued, "We are a pile of organizations in one organization, ... we are chiefs and Indians." All units are measured by their profitability, which means that partners often pursue their own interests before those of the firm—especially since the annual profit depends on who has been able to earn the most money. The resulting competition is reflected in the expression that partners do not feel compelled to help each other more than "10 hours a week" without getting something in return. In fact, partners who help each other with a particular customer typically ask for the case number so that a portion of the earnings can be accrued to their account. Accordingly, partners are motivated to try to find the relevant competency in their own unit in order to ensure that the earnings accrue to their "account" instead of giving the task to another department.

Within this context, culture is a central topic, both geographically and professionally. The senior assistants experience ServCo as a place of hard and sometimes hectic work, though there is "always room for a bit of fun." The professional environment is of great importance, and pride is taken in appropriating as much knowledge as possible. There is an underlying attitude that ServCo accountants can complete any task.

The supervisors focus largely on the cultural differences between units and geographical distance is often used as an argument for the lack of interdepartmental cooperation. They all have a sense of enormous distance between the units around the country and the main office. As one of these individuals noted, "It's a long way from the local office to the main office; we can't put faces to the names of top management."

Looking at the cooperation that goes on between units and the main office, however, it became apparent that geographical distance was not the main barrier. The problem, rather, lies in the interpersonal, face-to-face communication that is the basis of interdepartmental cooperation. Geographical distance by itself does not necessarily mean a low level of knowledge sharing. Knowledge sharing across geographical boundaries is about the formation of trust, and trust is created when people meet. When reflecting on knowledge sharing, for example, many of the respondents noted the importance of social interaction with their colleagues.

It appears that the way in which people experience the firm is a crucial factor. Some individuals, for example, suggest that "There's no hierarchy here, it's a matter of teamwork," while others argued that ServCo is definitely structured as a hierarchy:

> The hierarchy and the pecking order are built around knowledge, which is to say, if you have reached a level of experience and knowledge that is just slightly higher than someone else, then you will be his superior. It doesn't have anything to do with whether you are a good or a bad manager ... the one who is the smartest decides.

These statements also reflect the range of cultures and management styles in ServCo. It is an expression of the power of knowledge in the firm, as the more knowledge an individual acquires the higher his or her position will be in the hierarchy.

Boundaries and Barriers

ServCo consists of a number of business units beyond the auditing units. Many business units are located at the main office, which creates a geographical barrier for the units that are dispersed around the country. Yet, even the units within the main office experience "distance" in their interactions, suggesting that the barriers are just as much personal and professional as they are geographical. Employees working in the audit units, for example, emphasize that beyond the tax and quality assurance departments they do not know what the other business units are occupied with. The taxation and audit units are closely tied to each other due to the need for cooperation in order to ensure service and quality. The accountants complain, however, that they "don't know the faces of the consultants" in the departments devoted to special services. As one of these individuals observed, "You are much more willing to latch onto someone if you know that he's a jolly, reasonable guy and not just some 'bloody [city dweller].' He might have grown up in the country, which means he might actually be of use to us." While there is obviously a humorous undertone in this statement, it underscores the importance of face-to-face contact as a basis for fostering trust and a comfort level between the professional units.

Reflecting on what it would take for the consultants to make better use of the specialists, one of the respondents noted,

> We have to be more open when we are on site with customers, where there might be [the possibility of] advisory tasks. We have to pick up on these and establish an informal contact with the customer and ask whether they see a task in it. It would be strange if that weren't possible. But that isn't the primary concern when we're working with customers.

In order for such interaction to occur, the business units must be visible throughout the organization, but this does not necessarily mean that a subject-matter expert must be physically present at all locations.

Trust and Incentive Systems

As reflected in the following comments, the formation of trust is of central importance to several aspects of knowledge sharing:

> It's about a sense of security. Those who believe that they can do it on their own don't have to protect their knowledge.... For that reason alone they get some advantages. People who are unsure of themselves believe that their knowledge is what makes them worth something.

You have to feel secure before you can show openness and vulnerability. Most of the partners, however, expressed a need to be constantly on guard against their colleagues. As one of these individuals revealed, "We don't dare open up to each other. The bonus system encourages us to keep an eye on the bottom line."

As noted earlier, the partners are judged in terms of their earnings. An individual partner's reward is assessed within the partner group, according to the unit's total earnings, relative efficiency, and the size of the customer portfolio. Individual partners are also judged in terms of the earnings that the partner's customers have brought in elsewhere in the organization. This system, however, does not benefit the unit's partners, which creates an organizational dilemma. While individual partners receive recognition for productivity elsewhere in the organization, if the task is assigned outside the unit then that unit's earnings are reduced. Moreover, accountants also have enormous self-confidence and they prefer to solve problems themselves rather than applying solutions that already exist. In a culture that is characterized by control systems, they prefer to keep what they know to themselves rather than share it with the firm.

Knowledge sharing, therefore, must be about transforming an error-seeking culture into one where mistakes are accepted—as long as the mistake does not reach the customer. A knowledge culture in which it is legitimate to share knowledge and apply the knowledge of others is required. Yet, the fact that accountants primarily receive feedback when they make mistakes slows knowledge-sharing initiatives. Yet, while the accountants believe that their work should be error-free, they seem to lack confidence when it comes to sharing their work with others. Humility with regard to one's own work is especially pronounced in relation to sharing with others.

It takes trust and professional respect for the colleagues whose knowledge one is to apply. This is especially the case when the knowledge comes from KnowSource, or when one has to use a colleague's knowledge from one of the specialized departments. It appears that even in knowledge-intensive firms, knowledge sharing is limited to one's closest colleagues and people who are trusted.

MANAGERIAL AND ORGANIZATIONAL CHALLENGES

Knowledge-intensive firms typically start by establishing a technological platform to provide structural support for knowledge sharing. In ServCo, for example, KnowSource was its first initiative. Yet, as suggested by ServCo's experience, even though the technology can make explicit knowledge accessible, it does not necessarily lead to increased knowledge sharing. The employees did not use KnowSource as much as management had expected, and both employees and partners preferred informal communication.

At the team level, networks and relationships play an important role in what individuals know and where they seek the knowledge they need to perform their work. Since the various levels in the hierarchy place different demands on these networks and relationships, it is useful to explore the dynamics associated with the different forms of knowledge that exist in ServCo. This analysis can provide us with an understanding of who shares knowledge with whom and which channels of communication are useful to support the different forms of knowledge.

The team structure creates a good foundation for the sharing of knowledge, since (1) trust plays an important role and (2) knowledge sharing is an entirely natural part of the audit process. A consequence of ServCo's error-seeking culture, however, is that it can be difficult to establish relations of trust because the accountants do not feel secure in revealing their ignorance.

Time is money in a culture where the accountants are judged in terms of the amount of hours that can be billed directly to the customers. As a result, while the accountants may see knowledge sharing as important, they feel that they do not have time for it. Knowledge sharing takes time—time that the firm is not willing to pay for. As a consequence, knowledge sharing is seen as unproductive time as short-term economic returns have higher priority than longer-term internal development. For knowledge sharing to be embraced at the firm level, such short-sighted economic justification must be balanced with a more far-sighted justification for organizational development.

ServCo's structure, however, has a built-in tendency to foster internal competition, which can result in suboptimized knowledge sharing. Such internal competition, of course, can also create opportunities for initiative, dynamism, and sales. The democratic partnership structure also suggests that there is room for everyone and that decision-making power is lodged in the community. In essence, a partnership means that there could be as many management styles as there are partners, and just as many firm subcultures as there are units and business areas. There will, therefore, always be major differences between how knowledge sharing unfolds and how much support it receives across different units.

In order to understand the challenges of management and organization that are connected with the practice of knowledge sharing at ServCo, the discussion now turns to five crucial management challenges in the practice of knowledge sharing. The need for: (1) management to do what it says it is going to do; (2) coherence among different forms of knowledge, channels of communication, and employment structures/professional units; (3) opportunities provided by firm to be put to use; (4)

management to create a framework for knowledge sharing; and (5) knowledge sharing to be viewed as a process rather than as a concept.

Management Has to Do What It Says It Is Going to Do

The primary aim of KnowSource was to create a tool that could support the development and exchange of knowledge across the units in the firm. Despite the fact that management did not explicitly call this a knowledge project, the idea from the very beginning was to foster an understanding of the importance of knowledge and the need to develop relevant means of sharing knowledge throughout ServCo.

An early decision was made to centralize the company's intranet, and organizational members were encouraged to make contributions—but on their own initiative. Before it was distributed through KnowSource, however, all entries had to be approved by one of its editors. These editors were also responsible for keeping KnowSource dynamic by providing new and updated data. The technological platform was relatively easily established, and an outcome was that information was now gathered in one place and accessible to the whole firm. As part of the intranet, a "news service" was also provided as a source of information about current developments in the company.

The news service placed new demands on both the accountants and the partners, who were now expected to be active inquirers. However, even though they were no longer given information and news on paper, it took a long time before even half the employees consulted the intranet on a daily basis in order to stay abreast of what was happening. Yet, even when organizational members did use the new service, it seemed that a high degree of interaction through KnowSource was missing. Although the new medium created more visibility in the communication of news, it also demanded a more frequent replacement of news. In the past, each professional group published news bulletins only a few times a year. The concept of "news" took on an entirely new meaning with KnowSource, however, as some employees and partners began to push for "fresh" news every day—and people began to express frustration due to a lack of "news." A reaction, which quickly spread through ServCo, was that "KnowSource doesn't work" because the news on the start page was the same from one day to the next. Although the intention was to increase a sense of dynamism through KnowSource, the rare replacement of news items made KnowSource insufficiently interactive.

ServCo experienced the implementation of the intranet as being in perfect accord with the company's "one-firm" philosophy (Maister, 1993)—instead of having each unit act locally, the expectation was that the company would act nationally, as a "single whole." The platform was expected to create a common language and a common framework for the communication of information and news across the units across the entire country.

The strategic point of departure for establishing the knowledge project was founded in the fact that customers were increasingly demanding consultancy services. Since ServCo did not have a standard way of dealing with this opportunity, the company wanted to focus on knowledge sharing within the consultancy area for purely knowledge-strategic reasons. ServCo's objectives were to enhance customer service and increase and cross-fertilize its sales base through knowledge sharing by gathering and applying the knowledge that existed in the firm. In this sense, ServCo did not distinguish itself from many other companies on this score, namely, building on "intimacy" with the customer as a central concern (O'Dell & Grayson, 1998). Yet, because ServCo did not have any specific standards or methods for consultancy, any related knowledge sharing placed significant demands on the ability of people to draw on, communicate, and share their experiences. Some tasks can be shared through IT (such as documented analyses), but knowledge that is based more on personal experience cannot be easily codified because it is appropriated through actions and activities.

ServCo's formal knowledge strategy can primarily be characterized by what Hansen, Nohria, and Tierney (1999) call the *strategy of personification* because there is a demand for a "person-to-person relation" in order to share the knowledge that is associated with consultancy. The company's actual strategic action plan, however, was more of a *strategy of codification*, which is primarily about the documentation of knowledge (Hansen et al., 1999) and more of a "person-to-computer relation." In essence, there was a gap between ServCo's strategic desire to share knowledge about consultancy while simultaneously documenting what its members know. An underlying explanation for this conflict between strategy and practice was that the initial project itself did not consider the nature of knowledge and the various forms of knowledge that existed in ServCo. The basic assumption was that both tacit and explicit knowledge could be captured and shared through the KnowSource system.

Coherence Is Needed

The analysis of the development of knowledge activities showed that there was little clarity about which knowledge should shared with whom and what kinds of communication channels were best suited to sharing these different forms of knowledge. In fact, questions about the kinds of knowledge that existed in ServCo were not even raised. This is a problem because it has a direct influence on the interaction of strategy and knowledge activities, and as a result, on how knowledge sharing was constituted at the firm. The aim of identifying knowledge forms is to enhance the organization's capability to develop knowledge activities in relation to the knowledge that is to be shared. It is not sufficient to simply understand the difference between data, information, and knowledge. It is also necessary to identify the different forms of knowledge that the firm possesses, and who (or what) possesses that knowledge in order to tie the need for knowledge sharing to people and appropriate media.

ServCo had a range of different knowledge forms, including craft-based, experience-based, theoretical, special, social, and concrete knowledge. As illustrated in Figure 7.1, when knowledge is to be shared it is important to see connections between positions in the hierarchy, forms of knowledge, and channels of communication. The KnowSource system, which was directed at all levels of the firm and all forms of knowledge,

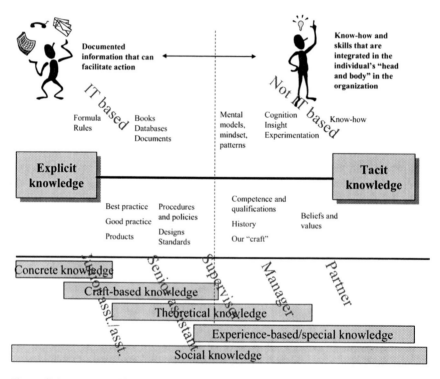

Figure 7.1.   Forms of knowledge, channels of communication, and hierarchical position.

became a source of complication and frustration because different forms of knowledge make different demands to the channels of communication.

It is important to understand the knowledge that is intended to be shared, which employees or positions should make use of it, and which tools they will use in their work. For example, the software support package and Accountant's Library that were discussed earlier are well suited to a series of activities that facilitate knowledge sharing, including providing information about who knows what, customer needs and expectations, storing standards and rules, the availability of craft skills, and keeping track of an audit as it proceeds. IT-based systems, however, are less suited for organizing tacit knowledge. Since different kinds of knowledge place different demands on the channels of communication, Figure 7.1 also indicates the different kinds of communication channels that are directed at the various employment levels in the organization. For example, a manager who might typically have a lot of experience-based knowledge that is difficult to explicate would probably have a difficult time using KnowSource to share that knowledge. Information technology alone cannot communicate experience-based knowledge, because this form of knowledge is stored in the individual.

Socializing channels of communication, such as dialogue, observation, participatory observation, historical narratives, and imitation, are better suited for sharing tacit knowledge. In essence, the utility of IT-based knowledge-sharing systems decreases the higher up the hierarchy the employee advances. Information technology is therefore only really applicable to particular levels at ServCo—and the knowledge needs of the accountants change as their level of education, their position in the hierarchy, and their tasks change. Managers and partners have the greatest need to share their experiences, but this form of knowledge is best shared through dialogue. The primary users of IT systems such as KnowSource are found among people in positions under that of partner/manager and/ or among those organizational members who possess relevant theoretical and craft knowledge. These latter forms of knowledge are where knowledge sharing through IT-based systems are most promising.

It is thus important to look at the connection between strategy, forms of knowledge, channels of communication, and who (or what) contains the various forms of knowledge in the development of knowledge activities. In this way, one begins to attain a sufficient connection between strategy and action that will ensure that knowledge activities and channels of communication fit the forms of knowledge the firm wants to share. This observation, of course, might seem overly rational because even when it is possible to identify types of knowledge in a firm, different professional groups, layers of the organization, and geographical units each have a different sense of what knowledge is and how one should work with it. The challenge is to develop the ability to work with dynamic kinds of knowledge across the organization, as different kinds of knowledge place different demands on communication channels.

Using the Opportunities

Establishing the "right" culture for knowledge sharing is a critical factor, and ServCo's culture is in many ways suited to knowledge sharing. The analysis identified three primary factors that influence the culture at Servco: social space, professional identity, and time.

ServCo's social space created an environment for knowledge sharing. As noted earlier, ServCo can be conceptualized as many companies in one, and as a result social space is situated around individual teams and individual units. The team structure, the coaching system, and the formation of trust define the framework for knowledge sharing that emerges during task execution. Knowledge sharing is a natural part of the audit process, and networks and relationships emerge from the team and the unit as the work is accomplished. Networks are also created across the units, largely through the prior schooling of accountants and the internal courses they take as part of their career development. Interdepartmental relations are based on interpersonal relationships, and the ability to "put a face" to a colleague's name was decisive in the pursuit of future opportunities to collaborate. Accountants begin to trust each other when they meet and communicate face to face. Especially in ServCo's environment, trust and security are necessary before an accountant is willing to reveal that there is something he or she does not know.

While the social space created by the accountants is an important dimension of the willingness to share knowledge, most organizational members believe that their direct hours and overtime are what "count." This belief reflects ServCo's values, which are built on granting first priority to customers and to professionalism. Yet, while there does appear to be a common set of values underlying ServCo's strategy, only a few people within the firm appear to fully know and understand them. As a result, it is difficult for a more formalized approach to knowledge to emerge as a central part of ServCo's shared values.

To a large extent, customer service and professionalism are also shaped by time pressures. A basic lack of time means that individual auditing tasks are not debriefed and important knowledge is often lost. For employees, it is all about putting in as many direct hours as possible, and the system that is used to register hours inhibits knowledge sharing because it does not honor the time spent at this task. Knowledge sharing is thereby situated outside the individual and the system becomes a barrier. Auditing, however, is seasonal work and less busy periods are often exploited for knowledge sharing. During slack periods, there is more time for documenting problem-solving models, good practices, and new ideas, which does contribute to the development of KnowSource.

In general, the culture at ServCo means that knowledge sharing is constituted through rules, norms, and routines, in essence through factors that are a significant part of the way tasks are executed. But in a culture that is at one and the same time social and professional, knowledge is shared through the individual's social and professional network, making dialogue and coaching a natural part of the execution of tasks, which further promotes knowledge sharing.

Managerial Roles, Tensions, and Knowledge Sharing

As a partner-owned firm, ServCo operates as a professional bureaucracy. This context is different from many other knowledge-intensive companies in which employees, owing to their expertise, are often more knowledgeable than their managers. ServCo's audit division, for example, is overseen by a circle of partners, all of whom are well trained and current in their knowledge. This makes them capable of executing the relevant tasks on par with lower-level organizational members. The partners are formally managers, and they set the agenda for how the firm is to be run and how the tasks are to be executed.

The partners consider it an asset to have power and influence over how the firm is managed. Such positioning, however, creates a number of management problems that affect knowledge sharing. For example, ServCo has approximately 120 partners, which means that there are 120 owners of the firm providing input into both strategic and day-to-day operational decisions. The power in many other companies is distributed to those who have management responsibility, but in ServCo power rests with the individual partners.

The partners often find it difficult to combine the management role with the role of being responsible to the customer. This is due to the fact that partners, who take their management role upon themselves, are typically not recognized for the personnel responsibilities that this role implies. Second, a basic tenet in the firm is that the customer always has first priority. As some partners note, this can result in organized anarchy. One example is when the partners make a decision collectively, by means of a democratic vote to which they express commitment, but then return to their units and act as they always have. It is therefore important that the partner is able to distinguish between the role of partner and the role of manager, because it can have consequences for employees if there is a lack of guidelines. It becomes difficult to set common goals for the firm and thereby to foster affinity among the employees. When a partner refers to the circle of partners, it is the partner group in the unit that is being referred to—and the partners feel a sense of duty toward the partner group, largely because their total earnings are at stake when the profit is distributed.

A related problem is that responsibility is related to education and technical expertise rather than managerial skills. The most able accountants, therefore, become partners and managers, while employees who have management skills are not necessarily considered for such positions. Within the circle of partners, however, there is a lack of recognition of those individuals who take on management responsibilities, to the point where those partners who do accept such responsibilities do not want to relinquish their responsibilities for the customers. As a result, knowledge sharing is limited by the intermittent tensions between seeking collaboration within the circle of partners and personal responsibility for the collective decisions. The fact that the tendency is not to be bound by strategic decisions suggests that the partners do not see themselves as role models for the employees. Knowledge sharing therefore becomes something for others to deal with. Despite the fact that knowledge sharing is a lynchpin in the strategy, not all partners are committed to this collective strategic foundation.

A third tension point is the balance between autonomy and control. Although professional competence is at the core of ServCo's practices, the company distinguishes itself from the traditional knowledge-intensive firm. The lengthy education and need for certification displaces employees as the primary knowledge carriers since partners are in possession of this knowledge to an equal extent. This contributes to a combination of a rule-oriented form of management (e.g., the auditing process itself is built on rules, norms, and error-seeking processes) with a high degree of autonomy in the work itself. The depth and extent of the partners' knowledge means that they need to involve themselves in knowledge sharing just as much as lower-level employees.

The bonus system—the system for registering hours worked and determining what counts as valuable work—is determined by a hard and fast set of rules. As long as knowledge sharing is not defined as a value-creating activity in the various systems, it is difficult for the partners to pay attention to knowledge sharing. This can be seen in the fact that while the partners like to work out conceptions of knowledge sharing and participate in the debate about the importance of knowledge sharing, they are not willing to commit themselves to any knowledge strategy. As a result, there is a conflict between strategy, action, and understanding.

Knowledge Sharing as a Concept and a Process

In conceptualizing knowledge sharing, the ServCo experience indicates that it develops differently across individual units. A certain degree of knowledge sharing is possible through IT-based systems and explicit rules. At ServCo such sharing is largely done on a volunteer basis. Not all employees, however, are accustomed or willing to take on this responsibility, and at ServCo the individual units have different points of departure. The nature of management and culture in the individual unit determines the degree of focus that the unit places on knowledge-sharing processes.

The literature on knowledge sharing suggests that success stories are often found in traditional knowledge-intensive firms, marked by a flat organizational structure, continuous challenges, and few standardized tasks (Sveiby, 1992). The ServCo case illustrates that a certain degree of knowledge sharing can also happen in environments characterized by rule-oriented management, where the work is marked by standard tasks, control, and rules. Thus, knowledge sharing is possible in professional bureaucracies and companies where the organizational structure is more hierarchical in nature. In fact, units that have a rule-oriented form of management seem to focus on knowledge sharing as a ready-made concept, and measured in concrete terms such as the number of hits in Know-Source or the number of submitted practices.

A focus on documenting knowledge, however, also initiates an ability to create a process that can shape values in which knowledge activities can become a norm for the way tasks are executed. As Nygaard (1999, p. 31) suggests, "Many norms ... are so widely accepted that they become a deeply integrated part of the personal orientations of most individuals. Thus if a norm is generally accepted, most people do not even notice the possibilities for violation." Norms can be institutionalized in the systems so that knowledge sharing becomes a natural part of the execution of tasks.

A basic set of knowledge-sharing activities can be made available to an entire organization, but it appears that it is the individual unit's point of departure that determines where the focus will lie in relation to knowledge sharing. The question will therefore be one of how management can create framework for a knowledge-sharing environment, for example, by influencing culture, management, structure, and technology. The challenge is to conceptualize and operationalize new and dynamic ways of working with knowledge sharing.

IN SERACH OF KNOWLEDGE SHARING IN PRACTICE

ServCo's strategic focus is shifting from auditing to consultancy. This transition demands both specialization and collaboration across geographical and professional units. The new focus on consultancy also places demands on knowledge sharing and business orientation. By closely comparing the opportunities and limitations that are embedded in ServCo's culture, infrastructure, and technology, there is a clear opportunity to exploit what the firm is good at—the cultural realm and socialization within the work units. In terms of its infrastructure and technology, in contrast, there appear to be limitations on the possibility of sharing knowledge across geographical locations and professional units. The ServCo case suggests that you have to combine the use of existing systems and forms of work (exploitation) and develop new ways to do things (exploration) to create truly useful frameworks for knowledge sharing. As March (1994, p. 2) argues, it is critical for a firm to establish an appropriate balance between such exploitation and exploration:

> Understanding the relation between efficiency (exploitation) and adaptiveness (exploration) is fundamental to understanding how intelligently ordinary individuals and ordinary organizations deal with the dilemmas and difficulties posed by efforts to be simultaneously efficient and adaptive.

By combining exploitation and exploration, it is possible to observe and encourage knowledge sharing in its context. As part of this process, it is important to remember that managing knowledge sharing is not a ready-made concept—it should be viewed as an opportunity to both incorporate and challenge current frameworks and existing systems.

Based on the ServCo experience, a number of implications for knowledge sharing in practice can be raised. First, knowledge-sharing places demands on management While debates continue as to whether knowledge can be managed, from a managerial perspective emphasis must be placed on establishing frameworks within which knowledge can be developed, shared, integrated, and applied. The practice of knowledge sharing becomes increasingly about establishing such frameworks for dealing effectively with knowledge in the firm. Within this context, management can be seen as a matter of coordination rather than control, as knowledge sharing and knowledge management come to be about managing knowledge processes within the firm. As a result, it is important to look at how knowledge is stored in the individual employee's experience and expertise and how management can establish physical, social, and resource structures in ways that facilitate knowledge sharing. It is not enough to suggest that knowledge strategies should be an integral part of the business strategy. Knowledge strategy must become management practice in both word and deed. Consistency must be established between strategy and action, and this happens through management.

Second, a related dimension concerns demand for knowledge sharing through IT-based systems. Many companies establish databases, discussion forums, and so forth in the hope of enhancing knowledge sharing. Virtually all experience the same problem, namely, the difficulty of getting members of the organization to contribute voluntarily and use the system. In this chapter, we have seen that there can be a variety of reasons for this, which point to a number of factors that companies should be aware of if they want to use IT-based systems to share knowledge, including the need to:

- define roles and rules for how members should respond to each other and procedures to resolve conflicts;
- take the time to inform the members about what it means to be a member of a virtual universe and allow for time to build trust among members;
- exchange personal data (e.g., resumes, and carry out a physical meeting if possible before virtual collaboration is initiated);
- establish a system of rewards and incentives for the members; and
- celebrate each success.

A third aspect concerns the importance of appropriate physical space for knowledge sharing. The physical environment has an enormous impact on how knowledge sharing is constituted, not just on how members of an organization are situated, but also on how the physical environment is used to emphasize a firm's processes. The exploitation of physical space as a source of information ensures that employees receive professional knowledge about what other departments are working with, which is especially important in a culture that expects them to be seekers of knowledge and information. This emphasis can be made through pictures or posters that illustrate what the firm does. It can also happen by creating meeting places in the "departmental divide" so that informal conversations can arise between departments and business units.

Increasing the visibility of what happens throughout the firm can serve both an internal and an external function. Internally, it means that information becomes accessible to the employees in other ways so that they can easily command a view of what is happening elsewhere in the company. It can also foster conversations as members interact on a casual basis. The informal conversations that can arise in the spaces can strengthen and enhance network relationships (Cohen & Pruzak, 2001). Externally,

ServCo used the physical environment to advertise itself during customer visits, affording greater visibility of what the company has to offer the customer. The physical space can also support knowledge sharing and communication across units in an activity-based environment.

A final aspect, which is by no means the least important, concerns the measurement of knowledge sharing. Measurement of knowledge sharing is at once both a theoretical and practical challenge. How can management make the utility of knowledge sharing manifest and how can it be measured? This is a recurrent theoretical challenge for knowledge management. How does the firm get from knowledge sharing to some assurance that the management of knowledge leads to satisfactory results? And how can this be measured? As Drucker (1995) notes, firms must be aware that new forms of measurement are called for but this cannot be allowed to limit the development of less measurable areas. It is a theoretical and practical challenge to identify points and methods of measurement for the value created by knowledge sharing so that it is not just seen as a matter of counting "hits" on the company intranet or other databases. Unfortunately, as noted by Fahey and Prusak (1998), "Regrettably, it seems that an increasing number of organizations seek to measure knowledge directly rather than by its outcomes, activities, and consequences."

The management challenges that are associated with the practice of knowledge sharing are manifold and not always obvious. Elements that both inhibit and make knowledge sharing possible must be put into play in the practice of knowledge sharing. But these are important challenges to address in order to get a good start and determine what sort of knowledge is to be introduced. It is in the interaction between knowledge strategy and forms of knowledge that "correct" knowledge activities can be developed. The real participants in the knowledge society are those companies that understand how to deal with these challenges and that true knowledge sharing goes well beyond IT-related databases.

The challenge for companies like ServCo is to target those elements that lead to the use of relevant technologies. Because organizational knowledge is primarily stored in individuals, firms need to design social structures that support an internal sharing of that experience. ServCo's capacity to convert individual knowledge to organizational knowledge will continue to depend on those factors that affect the development and exchange of knowledge—in essence, cultural change. Knowledge activities must be adjusted to local conditions within the framework of the firm's overall knowledge strategy. Knowledge activities must focus on behavior and the creation of cultural, managerial, and structural spaces for knowledge sharing.

NOTES

1. As Silverman (1993, p. 52) argues, we should "focus on what is observable, like behaviour and avoid that which is not observable like motivations and attitudes." The chapter focuses on those variables that are observable in the empirical field. By working as a participant-observer, it has been possible to combine observation and communication through interviews and active participation in the current knowledge project.

2. The participative aspect of the method is influenced by action research (see Argyris, Putnam, & Smith 1985; Denzin & Lincoln 1994), focusing on how we can spur an organization to cooperate and reflect on its actions and the results that have emerged from empirical analyses. This is done through interviews that have been conducted and the experience of working with knowledge sharing itself. Through active participation and observation of ServCo, I have tried to gain access to its implicit processes and thereby to understand the way people and the firm *really* act.

3. Knowledge sharing is itself a continuous process and this study is in many ways submitted to the field on the field's own premises. The processes have undergone constant change as personal changes have forced running revisions in the knowledge project and the strategies that pertain to it. The study is influenced in many ways by its immersion in this dynamic and changeable context in an attempt to study events as they happen. The analyses can tell us something about the organizational factors that affect knowledge sharing in the firm. This means selecting those factors that establish the frameworks that make knowledge sharing possible as the object of analysis.

4. The team assigned to a medium-sized customer includes a supervisor or manager and a number of accountants depending on the size of the customer (which may include assistants, junior assistants, and/or senior assistants). The accountant responsible for the team plans the audit and distributes the tasks among the team members. Partners are rarely involved in the production itself, but typically participate in financial meetings. ServCo is a partner-owned firm, with two types of partners: the partners who own the firm (120) and the partners who are functionary employees. ServCo does not distinguish between these partners in daily life at the firm.

5. The intention behind the evaluation/assessment is to evaluate the individual employee in relation to the accountant's educational, career, and task level. The assessment is a supplement to continuous oral evaluation and is referred to at the annual employee development interview. The assessment evaluates the accountant on the management of the task (in the case of the accountant responsible for it), the professional execution of tasks, the completion of ledgers, and utilization of IT tools. The assessment is to be completed by the accountant responsible for the team upon the completion of all tasks of a week's duration or longer. The evaluation is part of concluding an audit, which is why it must be completed before the audit can be officially closed. This is the partner's responsibility; "as a minimum requirement, the partner must complete an assessment of the manager's contribution and ensure that an assessment of the rest of the audit team has also been completed" (AuditFocus, 1995, 70).

REFERENCES

Argyris, C., Putnam, R., & Smith, D. M. (1985). *Action science: Concept, methods and skills for research and intervention*. San Francisco: Jossey-Bass.

AuditFocus. (1995). *Statsautoriseret Revisionsaktieselskab*. Denmark: Author.

Christensen, S., & Kreiner, K. (1991). *Projektledelse i løst koblede systemer*. Jurist- og Økonomforbundets Forlag.

Cohen, D., & Prusak, L. (2001). *In good firm: How social capital makes organizations work*. Cambridge, MA: Harvard Business School Press.

Davenport, T. H., & Prusak, L. (1998). *Working knowledge: How organizations manage what they know*. Cambridge, MA: Harvard Business School Press.

Denzin, N. K., & Lincoln, Y. S. (Eds.). (1994). *Handbook of qualitative research*. Thousand Oaks, CA: Sage.

Drucker, P. F. (1995). *Managing in a time of great change*. Oxford: Butterworth Heinemann.

Fahey, L., & Prusak, L. (1998). The eleven deadliest sins of knowledge management. *California Management Review, 40*(3), 265–276.

Hansen, M.T., Nohria, N., & Tierney, T. (1999). What's your strategy for managing knowledge? *Harvard Business Review, 2*, 106–116.

Krogh, G., Roos, J., & Kleine, D.(1998). *Knowing in firms: Understanding, managing and measuring knowledge*. London: Sage.

Maister, D. (1993). *Managing the professional service firm*. New York: Free Press.

March, J.G. (1994). *Three lectures on efficiency and adaptiveness in organizations*. Helsingfors: University of Helsinki.

Nonaka, I., & Takeuchi, H. (1995). *The knowledge-creating company*. New York: Oxford University Press.

Nygaard, C. (1999). *The efffect of embeddedness on strategic action*. Copenhagen: Samfundslitteratur.

O'Dell, C., & Grayson, J. (1998). *If only we knew what we know: The transfer of internal knowledge and best practice*. New York: The Free Press.

Porter, M. E. (1996). What is strategy? *Harvard Business Review, 74*(6), 61–78.

Reason, P. (1994). *Participation in human inquiry*. London: Sage.

Silverman, D. (1993). *Interpreting qualitative data: Methods for analysing talk, text and interaction*. London: Sage.

Starbuck, W. H. (1992). Learning by knowledge intensive firms. *Journal of Management Studies, 29*, 713–740.

Sveiby, K. E. (1992). The knowhow company: Strategy formulation in knowledge-intensive industries. *International Review of Strategic Management, 3*, 167–186.

Teece, D. J., & Glenn, R. (1999). *Firms, markets and hierarchies: The transaction cost economics perspective*. London: Oxford University Press.

CHAPTER 8

MERGING KNOWLEDGE

A Study of Knowledge Management in a Consulting Firm Merger

Markus Ejenäs and Andreas Werr

Global management consulting companies are commonly discussed as the archetype of knowledge-intensive firms (Alvesson, 1993, 1995; Starbuck, 1992). Consulting companies are also well-used examples in the literature on knowledge management (cf. Empson, 2001; Hansen, 1999; Morris, 2001; Sarvary, 1999), and they are increasingly discussed as important actors in creating and disseminating management knowledge by acting as knowledge brokers between their client organizations (Bessant & Rush, 1995; Hargadon, 1998; Sahlin-Andersson, 1996).

Since the end of the 1990s, the consulting industry has experienced substantial structural change—and an important feature of this change has been a wave of mergers and acquisitions. Smaller local companies have been bought by larger, multinational firms (e.g., the U.S.-based Concourse Group bought Swedish Cepro), former "Big Fives" have merged (e.g., Deloitte & Touche's purchase of Arthur Andersen), and, the empirical focus of this chapter, information technology (IT)-focused consultan-

Challenges and Issues in Knowledge Management, 179–207
Copyright © 2005 by Information Age Publishing
All rights of reproduction in any form reserved.

cies have merged with more traditional management consultancies (e.g., IBM's purchase of PriceWaterhouseCoopers).

An important driving force behind these mergers in the consulting industry is a belief in value creation through the combination of knowledge assets. However, the realization of these knowledge synergies is not without problems. Previous studies, for example, indicate that the integration process in consulting organizations is highly vulnerable (Löwstedt, Schilling, Tomicic, & Werr, 2003) as well as time-consuming and difficult to direct (Empson, 2000). Integration tasks include the need to align both the companies' and ultimately individual consultants' knowledge structures. As such, it appears that mergers in the management consulting industry pose a set of very specific knowledge management (KM) problems, which have not been studied to any large extent. Studies of knowledge management have largely focused on the management of knowledge in relatively stable situations, where focus has been on learning from experience, thus assuming a rather evolutionary development of the knowledge base.

Mergers, however, represent a disruptive situation in which two knowledge systems are confronted with each other. The alignment of two diverse KM systems has only received limited attention in the literature thus far. Therefore, this chapter has an exploratory character. In general, we focus on the KM challenges emerging from the disruptive event of a merger and how these issues may be handled in order to realize sought-after knowledge synergies. More specifically, two questions are explored in relation to mergers between IT and management consulting companies:

- How does the process of integrating knowledge systems unfold over time and which actions help to integrate the knowledge systems of the merging organizations?
- What challenges are encountered in the process of integrating these knowledge systems?

The chapter begins with a review of the literature on knowledge management in consulting organizations and proposes a model for conceptualizing the knowledge system in consultancies. The discussion then turns to the challenges involved in merging professional service firms (PSFs), with a specific focus on unfolding KM activities in a merger between an IT and a management consulting organization. The chapter concludes with a discussion of the challenges in merging KM systems and the implications for the field of management consulting.

KNOWLEDGE MANAGEMENT IN MANAGEMENT CONSULTING COMPANIES

The central resource in management consulting organizations is knowledge. It is the consultants' individual and collective expertise that provides the basis for value creation in the management consulting industry (Løwendahl, Revang, & Fostenlökken, 2001; Sarvary, 1999), and accumulated knowledge is often viewed as a defining feature of this industry (Dunford, 2000; see also Chard, 1997; Davenport & Hansen, 1998; March, 1997; Martiny, 1998).

A unique feature of knowledge in management consulting organizations is that, to a large extent, it emerges from the ongoing practice of the consultants. Learning takes place in individual consulting projects and is through various processes of "knowledge management" leveraged and made available to the rest of the organization (Morris, 2001). Management consultants thus lack a well-defined professional knowledge base like that of lawyers or accountants (Alvesson, 1993; Kyrö, 1995). Knowledge in the consulting industry is consequently more organization-specific and internally generated compared to knowledge in other types of professional services firms (Løwendahl et al., 2001; Sarvary, 1999).

The importance of practice in the accumulation of management consulting firms' knowledge base contributes to a logic of increasing returns linked to knowledge. The more knowledge on a certain issue or industry a consultancy possesses, the better its reputation will be, which in turn yields more assignments in that specific area, creating more experience and consequentially adding to existing knowledge (Cabrera & Cabrera, 2002; Sarvary, 1999). The character and content of the consulting organization's knowledge base thus to a large extent defines the strategic options of the organization. Entering new markets both implies the building of a new knowledge base as well as a market reputation that will create the kind of assignments that enable the development of the new knowledge base (Løwendahl et al., 2001). In this potentially paradoxical situation, mergers or acquisitions may be an attractive way to speed up the building of new services or entering of new markets. However, as will be explored in the chapter, this strategy has its challenges.

Knowledge management in the sense of activities related to capturing and making collectively available the learnings and innovations of individual consultants in consulting projects is a key activity for management consulting organizations. Especially in the global consultancies, significant resources are invested in these kinds of activities in terms of time and personnel resources as well as in IT-based KM systems. The latter have traditionally been a central aspect of KM activities (Ruggles, 1998).

Given the centrality of KM activities in consulting organizations, they are related to both operative and management systems. Morris and Empson (1998) view the management of knowledge in PSFs as a central activity connecting the market for the professional workforce with the market for the firm's services. Knowledge management is thus central to the PSF's value creation and has effects on the firm's structure and economic performance as well (see also Hansen, Nohria, & Tierney, 1999; Sarvary, 1999). Løwendahl and colleagues (2001) further argue for understanding the process of knowledge management as interplay between organizational and individual knowledge.

Two different models for this interplay in knowledge management in the consulting industry are identified. These frameworks differ in terms of whether they focus on explicit or tacit knowledge. Hansen and colleagues (1999), for example, distinguish between codification and personalization strategies, Zack (1999) between integrative and interactive strategies, and Sarvary (1999) between centralized and decentralized strategies. Despite the different labels, the different authors describe similar strategies. *Codification* (integrative, centralized) strategies focus on making individuals' expertise explicit in order to make it organizationally available in large knowledge repositories containing documents of different forms such as methods, models, procedures, cases, and so forth. *Personalization* (interactive, decentralized) strategies, in contrast, focus on knowledge sharing through interpersonal interaction, thus focusing more on tacit kinds of knowledge. Knowledge management in this context is about creating networks and structures that facilitate the identification and contact of individuals with specific expertise.

Despite these models' foci on *either* explicit *or* tacit knowledge, it is mostly acknowledged that a combination of these kinds of knowledge is essential for value creation. "Knowledge in action" (Schön, 1983) has both explicit and tacit aspects, and all knowledge has a tacit dimension that may not be formalized (Morris, 2001; Morris & Empson, 1998). Skillful action in practice always requires a certain amount of improvisation in the specific situation, requiring a tacit kind of knowledge (Morris, 2001; Schön, 1983).

Werr (1999) and Werr and Stjernberg (2003) provide a conceptualization of the interplay between tacit and explicit knowledge elements in the knowledge system of management consulting organizations. They argue that the knowledge system of management consulting firms may be understood as consisting of three knowledge elements: (1) individual consultants' experience, (2) methods and tools, and (3) cases. Whereas *experience* represents tacit and situated knowledge, *methods and tools* and *cases* represent explicit knowledge that is easily transferable, for example, through an IT-based KM system. As illustrated in Figure 8.1, these three

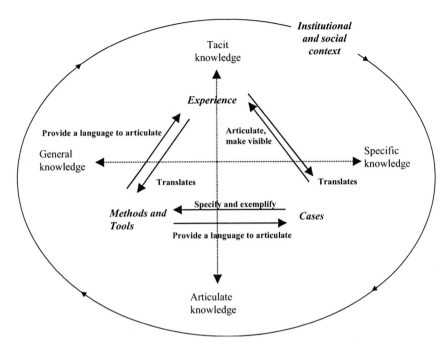

Figure 8.1.   Three basic elements of the knowledge system and their interrelations.

knowledge elements are viewed as tightly interlinked and embedded in an institutional and social context that may support or hinder the interplay between the elements.

The mainly tacit *experience* of the individual consultants within the consulting firm plays a vital role in translating or adapting the general methods and tools as well as the specific cases to the current specific situation at hand. The consultants' experience is thus a vital element for a successful application of the general methods and tools that are fairly common in large consulting organizations.

Methods and tools include the consultancies' explicit roadmaps and templates, providing information on how to carry out different kinds of consulting processes—in part or in their entirety. The central role of this element in the overall knowledge system is providing a common language for the interpersonal exchange of experiences as well as the documentation of cases. The methodology provides a common vocabulary, structure, and overall perspective on the consulting process, and thereby facilitates the face-to-face exchange of experience between consultants. The structure provided by the method is also applied in the documentation of cases, which makes these easily accessible and understandable for those sharing the method.

Finally, the *cases* fill the role of specifying and exemplifying the use of the general methods and tools in a specific situation. Cases are thus carriers of the central and mainly tacit knowledge involved in adapting the general methods to a specific situation (e.g., a specific industry, management culture). Within this context, the cases also have an important role in articulating the tacit experience of consultants (see Brown & Duguid, 1991).

The accumulation of knowledge in management consultancies against this background may be viewed as an ongoing refinement of these knowledge elements. The set of individual consultants' experiences is continuously updated through new experiences made in new projects, as well as through the sharing of experiences between individuals. Methods and tools are updated based on experiences made in their application, and new projects continuously update the set of cases available.

This process of developing the knowledge system—either by articulating made experiences or by spreading them through interpersonal contacts—however, is not unproblematic, as ensuring consultants' contribution to and use of the collective knowledge resources (both explicit and tacit) is not automatic (Dunford, 2000). Rather, it is to a large extent dependent on the *social and institutional context* in which the knowledge system is embedded. The sharing of knowledge in organizations is often presented as a public good dilemma (Cabrera & Cabrera, 2002; Ruta, 2004), as the payoff function for the individual user of a KM system does not encourage contribution. Contribution of knowledge to the system helps all but the contributor who already has the knowledge.

While the main focus of organizational KM activities has been the technological aspects of KM systems, organizations find that the greatest challenges are related to personal and structural issues, such as mapping knowledge resources, establishing networks for knowledge workers, and creating specific roles for knowledge workers. According to managers themselves, the largest impediment to knowledge sharing is organizational culture (Ruggles, 1998).

A main challenge, therefore, is to create incentives for individual consultants to engage in KM activities. Cabrera and Cabrera (2002) discuss three principal ways of doing this by (1) restructuring the payoff function of contributions, (2) increasing the efficacy perceptions of contribution, and (3) working with group identity and personal responsibility as a way of fostering contributions to the collectivity. The consultants' *payoff function* contains costs and benefits of contributions on an individual and collective level. The individual is affected by access and usability of IT systems, direct rewards connected to knowledge-sharing behavior, and the connection between knowledge management and career development.

The *efficacy perceptions of contribution* is about the consultant's feeling that contributions to KM systems make a difference for someone else in the organization. This perspective is dependent on the feedback to the contributors. A critical mass, however, is also necessary, otherwise the probability for a contribution to reach an interested receiver is small. At the same time, large systems might also be problematic due to redundancy and search difficulties. Therefore, it is important that the system is well organized and sufficient search functions are developed. Training can also affect the perceived efficacy of KM activities.

Finally, *group identity and personal responsibility* can be promoted through encouraged communication, and the creation of groups around certain knowledge areas. This last factor—the social pressures created by a group identity—was found to be essential for fostering knowledge sharing in Ruta's (2004) comparative study of CapGemini Ernst & Young and IBM. Ruta (2004, p. 31) found that the most important predictor of knowledge sharing was group pressure and collective behavior: "People decide to contribute in terms of quantity, based on the actions of others around them. Knowledge sharing is seen as an institutional factor, and individuals feel the need to contribute knowledge because other colleagues are doing so." Morris and Empson (1998) and Cabrera and Cabrera (2002) also underscore the importance of values, expected behavior, and the social environment in encouraging knowledge sharing.

POST-MERGER INTEGRATION OF KNOWLEDGE SYSTEMS IN PROFESSIONAL SERVICES FIRMS

Mergers between consulting organizations are often motivated by knowledge-based arguments. The expressed purpose is either to expand the service range to new geographical or functional areas, or to enhance capabilities within existing service areas. In any case, the realization of these benefits requires the alignment of two different knowledge systems. The degree of alignment, however, may vary depending on the level of overlap between the knowledge systems. In some cases, such as a merger between two management consulting firms with similar service offerings, knowledge systems may overlap to a large degree, thus requiring extensive integration of the different knowledge elements. In other situations, for instance a merger between a management consulting company and an IT consultancy, overlap would be more limited. Integration in this case would basically mean the creation of a common interface between the services of the two companies, with an emphasis on enabling communication and interaction.

Given the above conceptualization of knowledge systems as consisting of both tacit and explicit knowledge elements anchored in the consulting practice, the integration of knowledge systems appears far from trivial. Even though the integration of the explicit knowledge elements may seem straightforward—for instance migrating the contents of one database into another—the interrelation between explicit and tacit knowledge elements makes it difficult for consultants from one company to benefit from the cases, methods, and tools of the merger partner. In essence, organizational members lack the specific experience needed to interpret and effectively apply the methods and cases in practice (Empson, 2001). These same conditions also make it difficult to simply abandon one set of methods or cases in favor of the other firm's resources. Consequently, the development of a common set of experiences emerges as central to the building of a common knowledge system. Based on these experiences, common methods and tools may be created and a set of common cases accumulated. We would thus expect the integration of knowledge systems in consultancies to be a long-term process in which the development of a common practice (through interaction) among the consultants from the different organizations is of central importance.

In the relatively few studies on post-merger integration processes in professional service firms, interaction between professionals is repeatedly noted as the main integrating mechanism (Empson, 2000, 2001; Greenwood, Hinings, & Brown, 1994). This interaction is described as determined by the professionals themselves, who thus to a large extent set the pace of the integration process (Empson, 2000). Yet, while managers may create the context for integration, they cannot control the evolving process. Empson (2000) introduces the metaphor of the "high school dance" to describe the process through which consultants from merging firms gradually start interacting with each other, as they attempt to align their practices and create a common knowledge base.

Opportunities for joint action are thus a central prerequisite for the development of a joint practice and thereby a joint knowledge system. As observed by Greenwood and colleagues (1994), in a merger between two accounting firms, however, the nature of work practices could be a barrier in this context. The conventional practice of audit in the studied organizations did not demand joint working across the firms. Furthermore, staff was frequently working at their clients' sites rather than in the local office, limiting the opportunity for interaction within the office and prolonging the period of integration, which ultimately created problems in the merger.

While important, the mere opportunity for interaction is no guarantee of the development of a joint practice, as this also requires a willingness by organization members to cooperate. In the above-mentioned studies, this was rather problematic, as the limited cooperation that did take place initially led to the discovery of differences in values and procedures, which created reluctance to collaboration (Greenwood et al., 1994; Löwstedt et al., 2003). In the merger between the IT and the management consulting company, once the consultants started working with each other, the initially positive attitude toward each other was replaced by rather negative and pejorative views. These negative attitudes also created unwillingness among the consultants to share knowledge with each other (Löwstedt et al., 2003).

The potential unwillingness of consultants to share knowledge with new colleagues in a merger is further explored by Empson (2001). In a study of six accounting and consulting firms, she found that professionals resisted knowledge transfer when they perceived that the merging firms differed fundamentally in terms of the quality of their external image and the form of their knowledge base. She claims that organizational and knowledge-based impediments to knowledge transfer can only be understood by reference to individuals. Fears of exploitation and contamination are identified as main barriers to knowledge exchange. *Fears of exploitation* emerge from different perceptions of the values of each others' knowledge, creating a feeling among the consultants that they contribute more than their new colleagues. *Fears of contamination* relate to worries that consultants from the other organization may spoil the relationship with their clients (e.g., due to differences in fee rates, the way the client is perceived and treated).

Study Design and Methodology

The chapter's empirical foundation is a study of the integration process between the Swedish branches of a multinational management consulting organization, hereafter referred to as ManCon, and an international IT consultancy, referred to as ITCon. The merger of ManCon and ITCon was realized in 2000, and involved approximately 40,000 employees worldwide and 3,000 employees in Sweden.

The post-merger integration process of the Swedish branches of ITCon and ManCon was studied in a longitudinal design. A first round of interviews with nine managers and consultants was carried out between the end of 2001 and the beginning of 2002, roughly one year after the announcement of the merger. A second round of 20 interviews took place between September 2003 and June 2004. The respondents were managers, consultants with a special responsibility for knowledge management, and regular consultants from both merging organizations. The interviews were semi-structured and each one lasted approximately one hour. All interviews were taped and transcribed. Based on the interviews, a detailed chronological case study of the post-merger integration process was produced, and the pre-merger KM processes and activities in ITCon and ManCon were reconstructed. The case study was then analyzed in order to identify the specific challenges faced in the integration of KM activities, processes, and structures.

The ManCon–ITCon Merger

ManCon was a partner-owned management consulting firm that was part of a Big Five auditing firm, referred to as AudiCon. ITCon was a listed IT consulting firm. One of the strategic plans for the merger was to create integrated IT and management consulting services, a motive common to several other mergers in the Swedish consulting industry at that time. Such integrated services were perceived to be increasingly important, largely due to the current boom in IT consulting and the increasing number of new competitors offering combined IT and management consultancy services.

ManCon

ManCon's primary focus was delivering strategic advisory and organizational change consulting services. The firm had also created a small group of IT consultants working with the implementation of standard business systems like SAP.

Individual Consultants' Experiences

Senior consultants' experience was a central knowledge element within ManCon. Being a partner-owned firm, with a large base of junior consultants recruited directly from university and a few partners, the average age was relatively low. Consequently, the senior consultants, based on their expertise and experience, played a central role in designing and executing client projects. The junior consultants represented a hard-working resource, but were dependent on the senior consultants and the firm's formal methods and tools for guidance[1]—at least initially. Through practice, however, these individuals became increasingly independent.

Besides participating in client projects, it was also common that newly hired junior consultants spent a period of time working on one of the analysis teams, doing research and analysis and producing reports of different kinds, before participating as a full member on a project team. Thus, the consultants' learning, to a large extent, took place in their day-to-day work in client-related activities. This made staffing a central aspect of managing the development of ManCon's knowledge base. Staffing of projects, however, was done on an informal basis, possible due to the relatively small size of ManCon:

> We had at ManCon what we playfully called the "coffee machine principle." You went for a cup of coffee and said, "Hello, what are you doing now?"— "Well, I don't currently have a project."—"But I have a project!" And so on. Playfully, but if one group sold a project, that group manager checked for available resources. So there was no central function, it was managed within the group. (Knowledge manager, former ManCon employee)

The individual consultants' experience was also central in the sales activities at ManCon. Sales of consulting services were an integrated part of the senior consultants' work and generally based on established relations between the consultant and the buying manager. Acquiring new assignments was considered part of the delivery of client projects, and the personal relationships between senior consultants and clients were an important part of value creation. ManCon's clients were generally CEOs or business area managers.

Cases, Methods, and Tools

ManCon's KM activities, focusing on the more explicit knowledge elements (cases, methods, and tools), were often referred to as "best practice." ManCon had been referred to as a pioneer and role model for knowledge management in a KM journal, its strategy for knowledge management had been the base for a teaching case at a prominent American business school, and it had been awarded for its KM by a large private research company. The high standard of knowledge management within ManCon was also acknowledged by its merger partner—ITCon:

> I think you could put it like this: On a ten-graded scale, ManCon was as close to God as you could possibly get concerning knowledge management … and ITCon had managed to reach a four, in comparison. (Member of global integration team for knowledge management, former ITCon employee)

The main purpose of ManCon's elaborated KM strategy was to reuse knowledge generated by its consultants in projects in order to avoid continuously "reinventing the wheel." The formalization of knowledge into methods and tools and making the documentation from earlier cases available to others in the firm was also viewed as an important source of support for junior consultants, helping them to become independent faster.

In addition, central to the management of the more explicit knowledge elements were a number of databases on a global and local level. The databases contained deliverables from previous projects, such as offerings, presentations, and reports as well as consulting tools and methods. The firm's methods and tools were developed and constantly refined, on both international as well as national levels. In Sweden, for example, both an international method for business process reengineering (BPR) as well as a Nordic one was available.

The knowledge databases were based on Lotus Notes technology, accessed through a Web-based interface called "K-base." The interface with the KM system was also used to access the common mail server, which made employees interact with the system on a daily basis. A powerful full-text search engine made searches in the system easy and possible to carry out on a global basis. For example, if working with business process reengineering, consultants could find documents from that kind of project from ManCon locations all over the world. Another strength within the system was replication in Lotus Notes, which made it possible to have local replicates of databases on national servers and personal computers. As high bandwidth and even network connections were rather scarce when the system was introduced, this was an important factor for usability.

Institutional Context

Knowledge management activity, both in terms of exploiting others' knowledge and contributing to the collective knowledge stock at the company, was high in ManCon. A number of structural and cultural factors contributed to this. First, on a structural level, each project team had to assign one member responsible for knowledge management. Project teams also routinely searched the system for material that might be valuable for a new project (e.g., previous cases) during the startup phase. After finishing a project, the team was also responsible for submitting project deliverables from the client case to the system. This data was reviewed by a local knowledge manager who ensured the quality of the content in different subject areas before it was made available to all users.

Second, the use of the system was supported by its simplicity and perceived value:

> The knowledge system we had, the recycling system, worked pretty well, because it was global and open to everybody, fairly easy to search. So my experience is that people did that [used the system] to a fairly large extent. (knowledge manager, former Manon employee)

Third, individual incentives for using the KM system—both in terms of using the material and making contributions to it—were embedded in the performance review process:

> One of the primary reasons it was so much used was that it was in our personnel development, the dialogues, we had built in knowledge management. (knowledge manager, former ManCon employee)

ITCon

ITCon delivered implementation and integration of IT systems, programming services, and outsourcing of IT operations. ITCon also had a group of management consultants, but their profile differed vastly from ManCon's consultants. These people were experienced managers who had opted for a career in consulting later in life—their average age was higher, and their knowledge was more tightly connected to a specific industry or even a specific client company.

Individual Consultants' Experiences

While ManCon was structured as a pyramid, with few experienced consultants at the top and a bulk of rather inexperienced consultants providing the basics, ITCon had a different profile. Consultants in ITCon were older and, in general, had more external experience. ITCon's consultants, to a large extent, relied on their personal experience, rather than that of more experienced colleagues and company-based formalized methods and tools.

Interchange of individual experiences largely took place in international knowledge networks (see, e.g., Teigland, 2003). These networks spanned all geographical divisions and consisted of people working on the same type of tasks or technologies, but in different parts of the organization. They interacted with each other, both physically and electronically (through e-mails and video conferences), exchanging advice concerning their work, often focusing on highly technical matters. In reflecting on ITCon, a member of ManCon noted:

> ITCon worked a lot with ... [and] gained from their communities [of practice].... They were focused on specific services and products. They had communities of programmers who exchanged information with each other, and they were their own islands. These islands existed everywhere [in the organization]. (knowledge manager, former ManCon employee)

The technical nature of the products ITCon worked with provided a central structure for knowledge, one that facilitated the identification and exchange of expertise. For example, one of the company's communities of practice concerned Microsoft-related products. Programmers in different regions working with Microsoft Information Server were connected to each other in this network.

While client relations were a central aspect of the consultants' experience in ManCon, especially as part of the sales process, these were of less importance in ITCon. In ITCon, the acquisition of new projects was managed by a separate sales organization:

> The first thing I noticed when I started working here was that we had a sales organization. I did not have to sell my own projects, they seemed to just show up suddenly. (team manager, former ITCon employee)

The buying counterpart in the client organization was also at a different level for ITCon. Most often ITCon consultants interacted with the chief information officer (CIO) or chief technology officer (CTO) in the information systems department instead of the CEO or business area manager, as in the case of ManCon.

Cases, Methods, and Tools

The formal parts of ITCon's KM system were not as fully developed as in ManCon, though during the latter half of the 1990s ITCon did undertake a serious effort to establish a central, IT-based KM system. The system, called Knowledge Space, was similar to ManCon's system and contained project deliverables, methods, and tools. However, routines and structures supporting the system were not as well developed as in ManCon, creating some confusion in its use. One former ITCon consultant, with experience from launching Knowledge Space, describes the encountered problems this way:

> First, it [the system] demands that everyone who puts something into the system will know where to put it. That is the fundamentally hard thing to begin with, that all users must know the whole system. And that was not the case. So at that point it fell. Besides that, everybody could put in whatever they wanted to—this meant that the first 6 months we had a flood of content coming in, unstructured, everywhere, at the same time. Someone thought that my content fits in there, although it should be over there. And it resulted in a structure that was impossible to maintain. There was no one with time to oversee the system, there was no budget for maintenance, and fairly soon the utility was lost. So it was a nice try, but they had not thought about the process. (member of global integration team for knowledge management, former ITCon employee)

ITCon's KM work was also more decentralized, run by the strategic business areas, which corresponded to the company's geographical areas.

Nordic countries, for example, had their own KM program. This reflected the general organizational structure of ITCon, which traditionally had a decentralized character and used geography as a principle for dividing work.

With respect to methods and tools, however, ITCon had a strong position. To begin with, development and implementation of IT systems concerns large and complex projects—which demand a structured way to work. ITCon was known to deliver projects on time and on budget, which could be explained partly by its strong methodology. Furthermore, methodologies for implementation are supplied by software producers like SAP. Finally, ITCon's development in Sweden was the result of a number of acquisitions, and the acquired companies were also known to be good with methods and tools.

Institutional Context

The more decentralized KM structure and the more individually oriented way of working created a different pattern of knowledge sharing in ITCon as compared to ManCon. Whereas the development of a more formal IT-based knowledge management system seemed to be hindered by a lack of centralization, and well-defined roles, procedures, and structures, the observed institutional context seemed to support a more interpersonal knowledge exchange within virtual "communities" structured around software products (e.g., SAP and Microsoft products). As one of the respondents noted,

> What is common for our consultants is that they are firmly rooted in an application. Our task within the technology division is to implement an application, a solution, based on a standard system, SAP for example. (manager, former ITCon employee)

An interesting point to note is that for ITCon common language and procedures are, to a large extent, provided by the product itself and the education/training that was supplied with it. ITCon's methodology for implementation of SAP systems, for example, was based on a development of SAP's own methodology package. The external software thus provided a structure for network building outside of formal organizational boundaries.

Integrating Knowledge in ITManCon

The integration of ManCon's and ITCon's knowledge systems was perceived as strategic and central to the success of the merger. Accordingly, shortly after the announcement of the merger, a global project team was set up to handle knowledge management in the integration process. The five-person team consisted of representatives from both ManCon and ITCon. The activities toward the integration of the system involved the creation of a structure of responsibility related to knowledge management, the integration of existing IT systems for knowledge management, and creation of KM processes. Activities began with the creation of a common structure of responsibility for KM issues, followed by the integration of KM databases, which for the first 2 years following the merger were run separately.

Integrating Experiences

The KM integration team was not directly concerned with the informal aspects of knowledge—in essence, the individual consultants' experiences. Yet, fairly early on in the merger, the individual consultants were confronted with each other due to a general integration strategy oriented to "integrate toward the market" (i.e., to sell client projects with a mix of management and IT consultants). Client projects, embodying the vision of integrated IT and management consulting, were thus envisioned as a prime integration vehicle in the merger. The underlying rationale, however, was to avoid losing pace in the marketplace rather than for any explicit KM purpose. As one of the respondents noted:

> That was the basics, let's call it the first merger strategy. It went under the name "quick-wins." Rather than focusing on what the structure will be in 4 years, the idea was to focus on how we could gain something from this now, so that we not lose pace. And that is what I have been talking about—how we gain key customers, how we staff projects, start cross-staffing projects. But without structures in place, nothing was changed. We started working together, but it was to increase sales, to increase utilization. That was the first part. (integration manager, former ITCon employee)

To some extent, this approach was supported with a new organization structure. ITManCon created a matrix structure with geographical regions on one axis and functional divisions on the other. The new structure had a unit of salesmen who were fully dedicated to selling, which led to some mixing of former IT and ManCon consultants. For the most part, however, the organizational groups from pre-merger times were kept intact in the new structure.

Through collaboration on projects, the consultants from the merger partners were able to gradually get to know each other, creating a basic understanding for each others' tasks and approaches. Respondents also reported that learning took place in these shared projects, from the perspective of both IT and management consultants. The management consultants learned more about the specifics of different IT systems, becoming more realistic in their expectations of what IT solutions could offer an organization. The IT consultants learned more about the logic of business, and the fact that IT systems serve economical and organizational purposes of different kinds. As one of the respondents noted:

> An important thing here is exchange effects. We can get some business thinking, process thinking for our [IT] consultants. Equally, the management consultants get some training and learn about what IT and its applications are, what you can achieve, and what you can realize. This [understanding] decreases the risk of creating desktop products that don't do what is promised—perfect models are hard to put to practice. You deliver a pre-study or an analysis, and then the customer has no ability to realize it [the suggested changes]. (manager, former ITCon employee)

While generally positive, the close interaction between ManCon and ITCon consultants also revealed some fundamental differences between their experiences and approaches. As a former ManCon consultant pointed out:

> [There were] huge differences in culture, huge differences in reward systems—in how you are raised, in how you sell projects. We experienced large differences all the way down to the choice of words. If somebody says "risk" I see one thing and others see another—something fundamentally different. And if we don't understand that early on, which I don't think we have, it's easy to think everything is all right—that we understand each other. But we don't. (team manager)

These differences reflected other aspects of the knowledge-seeking behavior of the consultants. For instance, in ITCon, consultants typically relied on personal networks for advice and access to formalized knowledge. In ManCon, consultants relied more heavily on their KM IT system.

Consultants from the different organizations also had very different perceptions of what it took to become an experienced consultant. Within ManCon, consultants with 5 years of consulting were regarded as experienced. Given the complex project management tasks in IT-related consulting projects, consultants with the same amount of experience in ITCon were regarded as "rookies." These differences in status and the valuation of experience were a common source of irritation in the early integration period. As a manager from ManCon noted:

> [Compared to ITCon], ManCon built from the bottom and up, maybe not as much as Accenture or McKinsey, but the company recruited new graduates and built on them. If you are 29, you may have worked here for 5 years and be a rather experienced manager, and run projects with a whole bunch of consultants. If you are 29 in ITCon, you are still sort of a rookie. (former ManCon employee)

In spite of the initial high hopes that were placed on consulting projects as an integrating mechanism, such projects proved more difficult to acquire than expected. Only a few projects that provided real opportunities for interaction between the IT and management consultants were initially sold. There appeared to be two reasons for this shortfall: (1) the limited demand for integrated IT and management consulting services and the general downturn of the consulting market at the time of the integration process; and (2) the reorganization in the merged company that placed the IT and management consultants in different divisions with different profit and loss responsibilities. In essence, the incentives for cross-staffing projects were decreased.

Integrating methods, Tools, and Cases

The KM integration team established a common organizational structure for knowledge management and led the integration of the knowledge databases into one single database, including the design of a new technical infrastructure. The organization of KM responsibilities was the first operational issue dealt with and a formal KM structure was launched shortly after the merger. KM teams were installed for all domains of the company (industry, service offerings, geography). The teams were led by chief knowledge officers (CKOs), which in turn formed a global KM Council. The operative KM work was done by knowledge managers at different hierarchical levels—for instance, regional (Nordic), national (Swedish), and group (strategy). An elaborate hierarchy of knowledge-related positions was thereby installed.

The integration of the firms' existing databases included both the design of a common technical infrastructure and the integration of the content in the databases. Initially, the KM integration team perceived large differences between the two businesses and their need for documented knowledge. As a member of ITCon noted with a laugh, "The businesses were very disparate, that's for sure." Similarly, as a subgroup knowledge manager in ManCon argued, "Soon it was realized that the businesses that merged had very different views on and need for knowledge management tools."

As a first solution, it was decided that ManCon's existing system would coexist with ITCon's systems. The initial changes were limited to a common interface in the form of a Web portal, through which all employees could access ITCon's as well as ManCon's old systems. IT resources for the former ManCon KM system were at this time still leased from ManCon's former owner. Until they were told otherwise, the consultants were supposed to keep using their existing systems—as they did before the merger.

Initially the employees' perceptions of the KM integration process could be described as tentatively positive. At first, however, relatively little was known about what would change and what the merger partner had to offer in terms of knowledge management. Insecurity quickly began to grow as people began to speculate about what might happen.

> And then they started to look at if they were going to integrate these [systems] ... and then a year-long discussion begun concerning whether we would keep Lotus Notes, and there were different answers all the time. (Subgroup knowledge manager for ManCon)

With several existing systems and an expensive agreement with ManCon's former owner concerning ManCon's part of the system, it seemed inescapable that some kind of consolidation would occur. Therefore, several local initiatives were taken to create interim systems. For example, the strategy consultants from ManCon created their own KM system to ensure access to and sharing of their existing knowledge databases. The increasing uncertainty concerning the future of the systems was a strong threat against the day-to-day use and maintenance of the KM system. Consultants to a large extent stopped using and updating the system. As a subgroup manager from ManCon lamented:

> It was to and from, the frustration just grew. You did not know where to input anything anymore, if it was in the new or the old [system], or if there was anything new whatsoever. Not even those of us who worked with this could give any answers. We just said do as you have always done. People were frustrated that only old stuff [information] was put in.

Within 12 months, the anticipated consolidation of systems was initiated. The market for consulting services had begun to turn downward and the costs for the KM infrastructure were too high, a tension that accelerated the decision to create the joint KM system. However, the downturn also implied that the available resources for the KM team would be drastically reduced, and the team had to design the new system with a very limited budget. As one of its members pointed out:

> But in 2001, the market just collapsed. We really didn't have a lot of money. So we realized that the only way for us [the group responsible for KM] to build something was to invent the solution during our allocated meeting time, which was once a month. We couldn't commission a large investigation that cost a lot of money and send in our expensive management consultants to investigate what we should have. (member of global integration team for knowledge management, former ITCon employee)

Material in the new system was organized according to three globally common dimensions: markets, disciplines, and general areas. Markets were the specific industries focused on by ITManCon. Disciplines referred to organizational domiciles, and general areas were the different functions within ITManCon. Thus, the organization of content in the new system, to a large extent, followed the organizational structure. Knowledge managers on different levels migrated the contents of the former databases with the help of these categories. Efforts were also made to go through the two KM systems and sort out usable material. The new system, referred to as "K-new," was fully operative approximately 2 years after the formal merger.

Regarding the use of each others' documents, the consultants soon realized that ManCon and ITCon projects generated different kinds of information, and the documentation produced for the databases satisfied different needs. For a management consulting project, documented cases could consist of written reports and PowerPoint presentations and would serve as a basis for making business decisions or as a way to mobilize organizational change. The documentation of an IT project, in contrast, could be the configuration specifications of the system, test run protocols, and education material for end users. The purpose of these documents was to make it possible for the customer to understand, maintain, change, or extend the system. Thus, through a time-consuming but fairly simple process, it was possible to integrate the formal part of both firms' knowledge systems. However, the content of the documentation was practice-specific and hard to interpret and use for an outsider. Based on this experience, it appears that the integration of the formal part is not sufficient to create an integrated practice.

Making KM Work: The Challenge of Creating a Supportive Context

From having been an integrated part of the consulting process (especially within ManCon), in the wake of the merger KM activities rapidly deteriorated. The many shifts and turns regarding the KM systems, as well as the nonexistence of organizational support structures, heavily impacted the consultants' knowledge-sharing behavior. Demand for existing information as well as supply of new information to the system decreased. Consultants had a harder time finding relevant databases, and it was perceived as meaningless to contribute when the systems had been changed several times. The results from a KM survey during this period found that the consultants were unaware of existing tools but they still felt there were too many tools, KM organizational structures were unclear and a common search engine was missing, and, in general, use of the KM system was low.

Furthermore, the value of sharing knowledge was perceived as both of limited value and at times even risky. The consultants soon realized that even similar types of documents were hard to understand and use for employees from the other firm, although they were migrated into the same system. ManCon consultants had also become rather reluctant to share information with ITCon consultants, as they feared abuse of this material. During the early phases of the integration process, for example, documents that were to be treated as confidential, with information about customers, had been used by ITCon consultants in sales pitches, thus breaking a strong code of client confidentiality within ManCon. This created suspicions among ManCon consultants, and created a loss of trust in how the information entered into the KM system would be used:

> If it said strictly confidential, you [as a management consultant] knew what it meant. We had three steps—codification steps—so you knew when you could or couldn't use the information. And they had this at ITCon as well, but they did not create any understanding for how that material should be used. So therefore many were terrified for putting something in K-new because they did not now how it would be used. That was also a factor that kept people from using the new [system]. And I still don't think that confidence exists for K-new because many of our consultants have had some bad experiences. (knowledge manager, former ManCon employee)

In connection with the launching of K-new, efforts were made to revitalize the merged firm's KM activities. New tools were introduced, a KM contact network was established, and KM activities were aligned with other activities in the organization, such as sales, delivery, employee development reviews, and quality systems. Efforts were also made to align KM initiatives with economic incentives, for instance, including knowledge insights as part of the economic reporting after finishing a project.

A new KM survey the following year showed increased awareness and use of the KM system. That spring, a change program was started with the purpose of increasing awareness of the importance of KM for ITManCon, informing and educating employees about the new knowledge management system and its tools, and increasing knowledge sharing and use of knowledge in the organization. The program was first launched in the Management Consulting Division, which was the part of ITManCon that mostly consisted of former ManCon people.

Three years after the merger, however, the integration of the formal part of the merging firms' knowledge systems was still limited. The change program had only been launched in the management consulting area and the consultants still used different KM methods and tools. The sharing of knowledge between ITCon and ManCon consultants was impeded by problems of understanding caused by the use of different methods and frameworks, and an underlying fear of misuse of shared knowledge due to differences in business logic and culture.

THE CHALLENGE FOR KNOWLEDGE MANAGEMENT SYSTEMS

The chapter's depiction of the KM efforts in this merger indicates that knowledge integration in such interfirm combinations is a complex and difficult process. In spite of high ambitions and large initial investments in integration activities, the actual integration of knowledge bases in this case has been limited. The envisioned organizational integration of knowledge bases has not only lagged behind expectations, but the merger also seems to have negatively impacted KM behavior on an individual level. Based on these insights, our discussion now turns to the challenge of integrating knowledge systems and the impact of a merger on the individual activities that keep existing as well as new knowledge systems running.

Tensions in Integrating Knowledge Systems

The KM integration team was, to a large extent, focused on the firm's IT-based support systems and their integration and the creation of a structure of KM officials. In terms of the approach to knowledge systems in the case discussed in this chapter, integration activities mainly focused on explicit knowledge elements—"methods and tools" and "cases."

Although the integration of the formerly two knowledge systems into one database made all knowledge accessible to all consultants, this measure was not sufficient to enable and facilitate knowledge transfer. Consultants had little use for documents and cases from the other organization, even though they had access to them. They lacked a more fundamental understanding of the other consultants' projects and frameworks and how they were intended to be used, which is exemplified by the fact that ManCon consultants felt that their documents were often used in inappropriate ways. In this case, the former ITCon consultants appeared to lack the experience with which to interpret and understand the methods and the common language of the merged firm's shared methodology.

These observations underscore the systemic nature of the knowledge system in consultancies, especially the situated character of knowledge in management consulting. Experiences, methods and tools, and cases are tightly integrated in a mutually interdependent system, as shared experiences become the basis for the creation and use of methods/tools and cases. These, in turn, represent articulations of experience but also facilitate the transfer of experience between consultants by providing common frameworks for communication and knowledge sharing. Integrating knowledge systems thus has to simultaneously take into account both explicit knowledge elements and the more tacit knowledge elements necessary for the interpretation of the former. Creating a new knowledge system in which the combinations of the formerly separate companies' knowledge is leveraged requires the creation of a shared framework of the consulting process, building on shared experiences across the merger partners. Without such a shared framework and experience, knowledge transfer is difficult (Cohen & Levinthal, 1990)

The integration of experiences is thus a central task for knowledge integration in merger processes, as these provide a platform for interpreting each others' explicit knowledge. However, in the ITManCon case, the KM integration strategy was heavily focused on IT systems, which mostly involved methods, tools, and cases. Yet to be truly effective, the creation of a joint knowledge base requires much more than shared databases, moving toward shared experiences and models through which to understand and interpret the content of the databases. Joint action is thus an important aspect of integrating knowledge management. Technical concerns have, however, been the focus of most KM practice (Ruggles, 1998).

The integration of experiences and frameworks thus proves to be a central challenge for knowledge integration in mergers. One way of accomplishing such integration may be through joint practice and collaboration in, for example, client projects. As pointed out by Empson (2001), this may go well beyond a question of mere opportunity, and involves the need to overcome the participants' individual resistance toward interacting with their counterparts from the other company.

Even though cultural clashes were initially experienced in the Man-Con–ITCon merger, it is difficult to argue that this was the primary reason for limited collaboration in client projects. Instead, structural factors and broader industry conditions seem to hold a large part of the explanation. The consulting industry experienced a downturn at the time of the merger, and the demand for combined IT and management consulting had been overestimated when the merger plans were made. Furthermore, ManCon and ITCon consultants were organized in different business areas. These business areas were responsible for their own profit and, as the market turned, securing the utilization of one's own consultants became the number one priority of the business area managers. Often, managers first tried to staff projects with persons from within their own business area. Only when this was impossible (e.g., due to capacity or competence reasons), any involvement from other business units was sought. The organization structure in combination with the market situation thus created strong structural forces against interaction, the creation of shared experiences, and ultimately the integration of knowledge within ITManCon.

This study thus corroborates the finding by Empson (2001) that knowledge sharing in mergers requires high levels of interaction, but that such interaction may be difficult to accomplish. In explaining these difficulties, Empson focuses on differences in the consultants' judgment of each others' knowledge, which create fears of exploitation, and differences in their perceived images, which create fears of contamination. The present study, in contrast, points to economic and structural conditions as the main impediments toward the necessary interaction. While members of ITCon and ManCon at least initially viewed each other as contributors to the realization of a new and promising type of service (integrated IT and management consulting), the general downturn in the consulting business together with split profit and loss responsibility hindered interaction and, subsequently, the establishment of a shared knowledge base (see also Greenwood et al., 1994).

The Vulnerable Nature of KM Processes

The case illustrates that while the integration of the *content* in knowledge systems was problematic, the merger also created threats to ongoing KM activities. In the integration period following the formal merger, KM activities deteriorated, and both the maintenance and use of the existing KM systems decreased. In spite of the initial decision to run the two merger partners' knowledge systems in parallel during the transition period, the merger created uncertainties as to the future of the systems, which negatively impacted the use of the old systems and the willingness to contribute to the new system. It also resulted in the creation of local, ad hoc systems in some parts of the organization.

The ITManCon experience points to the importance of stable organizational systems that support KM activities. Knowledge management in professional service firms is constantly under threat by individuals' unwillingness to share their knowledge (Morris 2001), which is often compounded by the time pressures associated with company activities (Dunford, 2000). Knowledge management activities thus need to be continuously reinforced by structural and cultural arrangements. Uncertainties as to the system's and the supporting arrangements' future, which typically emerge in merger situations, appear to be quite detrimental to the carrying out of KM activities. Even well-established practices could rapidly deteriorate, as merger-related uncertainties in the supporting structures reduced individual incentive to engage in knowledge-sharing and KM activities.

Based on the present case, it appears that mergers threaten the three core factors (as identified by Carbrera & Cabrera, 2001) that increase propensity of organizational members to participate in KM activities. The first important factor is the *perceived payoff function* from KM efforts. The merger between ITCon and ManCon increased the perceived individual costs associated with the use of the KM systems. The new systems required learning new structures and new routines to use and update the system. Furthermore, the benefits of engaging in KM activities during the integration period become less clear, as these activities partly lost their relevance in personal development reviews and as routines for these assessments were changed as well. In essence, the focus shifted from personnel reviews to dealing with merger issues.

The second factor is the *perceived efficacy of engaging* in KM activities. Such engagement efficacy was threatened by the ManCon–ITCon merger on two levels. First, the consultants were aware of the limited usability of their material for the "other" consultants, largely due to problems of interpretation. Second, the consultants also perceived a negative utility in their sharing information, as such information had occasionally been used in unintended and unauthorized ways. However, the new system also included the *potential* for an increased perception of efficacy, as it provided global reach, a clear structure to facilitate knowledge input, and a strong search engine—factors that further support the use of information once entered into the system.

Finally, *group identity* and *personal responsibility* are important motivators for KM activities. In this respect, the merger raised questions about the companies' strong existing communities and norms of knowledge sharing. The existing loyalty to one's organization and colleagues that drove KM activities in both IT and ManCon before the merger was now being questioned, as a new company and new set of colleagues were being created. Existing loyalties to the legacy companies had to be replaced by new loyalties to the joint company. Merger-related tensions, however, created an atmosphere in which loyalty and group identity to the legacy companies required knowledge hoarding rather than knowledge sharing. Existing constellations remained the basis for knowledge sharing, with the strategy consultants building their own KM system.

This case further indicates a paradox in professional service firm (PSF) mergers. While Empson (2000) points to the difficulties that managers face in directing PSF merger processes, largely due to the risk of losing knowledge workers in the process, the ITManCon case underscores the risk of keeping existing systems and delaying the creation of new organizational solutions. It is important to have clear and shared structures that support KM activities. Knowledge management processes cannot be considered as an isolated part of the integration process, but must be connected to other parts of the combined organization. In the ITManCon merger, a slow and careful integration strategy was employed granting the two companies' initial autonomy when it came to KM activities and databases. While this approach may have temporarily placated organizational members, it also contributed to the deterioration of knowledge management in the merged company—to the extent that a "KM awareness program" was needed to reinvigorate a previously well-functioning process.

CONCLUSIONS

One important motive in many mergers between professional service firms is the creation of knowledge synergies. By combining the knowledge of two companies, it is envisioned that more attractive and lucrative services can be created. This goal requires the integration—or at least linking—of the different knowledge bases of the merger partners. The few studies of PSF mergers, however, suggest that this is not an easy task. As Empson's (2000) work illustrates, fears of exploitation and contamination can readily hinder knowledge sharing between professionals from different companies in a merger situation.

While earlier studies have focused on integration and the building of a common knowledge base as a question of interaction between professionals, this study has focused on the role of the more formal parts of the merging companies' KM systems—the knowledge databases, document repositories and formalized methods and frameworks, and their interplay with the more tacit elements of the knowledge system. Our study indicates that the integration of the formal elements of the KM system is a delicate process that entails much more than moving data from two databases into a single, unified database. Knowledge management systems and procedures are deeply integrated with organizational values, routines, and practices. When these become challenged in a merger, there is a direct, powerful, and typically dysfunctional impact on KM activities. The integration of formal knowledge systems is deeply integrated with the emergence of an integrated practice and experience base within the organization. As such, an integrated knowledge repository goes hand in hand with the creation of shared experiences through which the content and utility of the knowledge databases can be interpreted.

The use and maintenance of formal KM systems seems highly vulnerable to uncertainty, as illustrated by this study. Uncertainty around the future of systems and KM routines easily disrupts KM activities. The interplay between the explicit knowledge in knowledge repositories and the tacit, experience-based knowledge of individual consultants is crucial for success. The proper use of the formal parts of a knowledge system requires sufficient tacit knowledge about how the information should be interpreted and how it could be used. As seen in the ITManCon merger, a lack of such knowledge and insight makes it difficult to fully understand the explicit knowledge and contributes to the potential misuse of the other party's knowledge. This void created suspicion and bad will in the relationship between consultants in the merger partners, temporarily blocking interaction and limiting the creation of shared experiences, which further undermines the development of the necessary tacit knowledge.

The integration of knowledge bases in a PSF merger involves a unique set of challenges and dilemmas. As illustrated in the ITManCon combination, there was a need for a simultaneous and reciprocal integration of three key knowledge elements—experiences, methods and tools, and cases—*and* the social and economic environment supporting (or hindering) the interplay and development of these knowledge elements. True integration of the knowledge system thus implies an integration of consulting practice, as this is the basis for the different knowledge elements. Achieving this goal goes far beyond the integration of IT systems and includes issues of managing different business logics and organizational structures in a way that encourages and enables the emergence of a shared consulting practice.

NOTE

1. For a detailed study of the interplay between individual and formal knowledge in the ManCon organization, see Werr (1999).

REFERENCES

Alvesson, M. (1993). Organizations as rhetoric: Knowledge-intensive firms and the struggle with ambiguity. *Journal of Management Studies*, *30*(6), 997–1015.

Alvesson, M. (1995). *Management of knowledge intensive companies* (D. Canter, Trans.). Berlin: Walter de Gruyter.

Bessant, J., & Rush, H. (1995). Building bridges for innovation: The role of consultants in technology transfer. *Research Policy*, *24*, 97–114.

Brown, J. S., & Duguid, P. (1991). Organizational learning and communities-of-practice: Toward a unified view of working, learning and innovation. *Organization Science*, *2*(1), 40–57.

Cabrera, Á., & Cabrera, E. F. (2002). Knowledge sharing dilemmas. *Organization Studies*, *23*(5), 687–710.

Chard, M. (1997). *Knowledge management at Ernst and Young* (Case S-M-291). Stanford, CA: Graduate School of Business, Stanford University.

Cohen, W. M., & Levinthal, D.A. (1990). Absorptive capacity: A new perspective on learning and innovation. *Administrative Science Quarterly, 35*(1), 128–152.

Davenport, T. H., & Hansen, M. T. (1998). *Knowledge management at Andersen Consulting* (Case 9-499-032). Boston: Harvard Business School Press.

Dunford, R. (2000). Key challenges in the search for the effective management of knowledge in management consulting firms. *Journal of Knowledge Management, 4*(4), 295–302.

Empson, L. (2001). Fear of exploitation and fear of contamination: Impediments to knowledge transfer in mergers between professional service firms. *Human Relations, 54*(7), 839–862.

Empson, L. (2000). Mergers between professional services firms: Exploring and undirected process of integration. *Advances in Mergers and Acquisitions, 1*, 205–237.

Greenwood, R., Hinings, C. R., & Brown, J. (1994). Merging professional service firms. *Organization Science, 5*(2), 239–257.

Hansen, M. T. (1999). The search-transfer problem: The role of weak ties in sharing knowledge across organization subunits. *Administrative Science Quarterly, 44*, 82–111.

Hansen, M. T., Nohria, N., & Tierney, T. (1999). What's your strategy for managing knowledge? *Harvard Business Review, 77*(2), 106–116.

Hargadon, A. B. (1998). Firms as knowledge brokers: Lessons in pursuing continuous innovation. *California Management Review, 40*(3), 209–227.

Kyrö, P. (1995). *The management consulting Industry described by using the concept of "profession."* Unpublished doctoral thesis, University of Helsinki, Faculty of Education.

Løwendahl, B. R., Revang, Ø., & Fosstenløkken, S. M. (2001). Knowledge and value creation in professional service firms: A framework for analysis. *Human Relations, 54*(7), 911–931.

Løwendahl, J., Schilling, A., Tomicic, M., & Werr, A. (2003). Managing differences in post-merger integration: The case of a professional service firm. *Nordiske OrganisasjonsStudier, 5*(1), 11–36.

March, A. (1997). *A note on knowledge management.* Boston: Harvard Business School Press.

Martiny, M. (1998). Knowledge management at HP consulting. *Organizational Dynamics, 27*(2), 71–77.

Morris, T. (2001). Asserting property rights: Knowledge codification in the professional service firm. *Human Relations, 54*(7), 819–838.

Morris, T., & Empson, L. (1998). Organization and expertise: An exploration of knowledge bases and the management of accounting and consulting firms. *Accounting, Organizations and Society, 23*(5/6), 609–624.

Ruggles, R. (1998). The state of the notion: Knowledge management in practice. *California Management Review, 40*(3), 80–89.

Ruta, D. (2004). *Knowledge sharing and communication technologies in consulting firms: A motivational analysis.* Paper presented at the annual meeting of the Academy of Management, New Orleans, LA.

Sahlin-Andersson, K. (1996). Imitating by editing success: The construction of organizational fields. In B. Czarniawska & G. Sevón (Eds.), *Translating organizational change* (pp. 69–92). Berlin: Walter de Gruyter.

Sarvary, M. (1999). Knowledge management and competition in the consulting industry. *California Management Review, 41*(2), 95–107.

Schön, D. (1983). *The reflective practitioner: How professionals think in action.* Aldershot, UK: Avebury.

Starbuck, W. H. (1992). Learning by knowledge-intensive firms. *Journal of Management Studies, 26*(6), 713–740.

Teigland, R. (2003). *Knowledge networking—Structure and performance in networks of practice.* Unpublished doctoral thesis, Institute for International Business (IIB), Stockholm School of Economics, Stockholm.

Werr, A. (1999). *The language of change: The roles of methods in the work of management consultants.* Unpublished doctoral thesis, Stockholm School of Economics, Stockholm.

Werr, A., & Stjernberg, T. (2003). Exploring management consulting firms as knowledge systems. *Organization Studies, 24*(6), 881–908.

Zack, M. H. (1999). Managing codified knowledge. *Sloan Management Review, 40*(4), 45–57.

CHAPTER 9

KNOWLEDGE-SHARING BEHAVIOR AND POST-ACQUISITION INTEGRATION FAILURE

Kenneth Husted, Jens Gammelgaard, and Snejina Michailova

Existing research on mergers and acquisitions (M&A) has suggested several theoretical frameworks and perspectives for studying the reasons for acquisition failure. Most studies have focused on the integration process following the acquisition and in particular on integration barriers (e.g., Haspeslagh & Jemison, 1991). The emphasis has primarily been on cultural clashes (Buono, Bowditch, & Lewis, 1985; Nahavandi & Malekzadeh, 1988), communication difficulties (Schweiger & DeNisi, 1991), employee perceptions and reactions (Risberg, 2001), and conflict resolution (Blake & Mouton, 1985). These studies have focused on single issues and, therefore, have been largely fragmented (Chatterjee, Lubatkin, Schweiger, & Weber, 1992), producing mixed and sometimes conflicting results (Seth, 1990). Notable exceptions are the work by Larsson and Finkelstein (1999) and Buono (2003). Larsson and Finkelstein suggest a broader, process-oriented model on acquisitions, integrating theoretical perspectives from economics, finance, strategy, organization theory, and

Challenges and Issues in Knowledge Management, 209–226
Copyright © 2005 by Information Age Publishing

human resources management. Following a similar vein, Buono proposes a socioeconomic approach to post-merger integration strategies.

During the 1990s, a series of takeovers took place where the knowledge possessed by the target firm was emphasized as a strategic acquisition motive (Bower, 2001; Chakrabarti, Hauschildt, & Süverkrüp, 1994). Some of the post-acquisition literature points out that efficient knowledge sharing following an acquisition is imperative to capturing the value potential of knowledge synergies between the acquiring and the acquired company (Bresman, Birkinshaw, & Nobel, 1999; Capron & Mitchell, 1998; Haspeslagh & Jemison, 1991).

The present chapter offers an approach to acquisition failures that has not been systematically explored in the post-integration literature. We argue that by borrowing insights from the knowledge-sharing literature, especially regarding individual knowledge-sharing behavior, and applying them in an acquisition context, additional explanations can be found for why knowledge synergies in the post-acquisition process are often not realized.

In order to analyze this issue, the chapter initially explores the notion of synergy, its specific features in post-acquisition integration, and the main reasons why acquisitions often fail to capture positive synergy effects. The concept of individual knowledge-sharing behavior is then introduced and used in a model that presents a framework for linking individual knowledge-sharing behavior with knowledge processes underlying the synergy benefits in the post-acquisition integration. Finally, the implications for business and management consultants are explored and discussed.

SYNERGIES IN POST-ACQUISITION INTEGRATION

Capturing positive synergy effects is often claimed to be an explicit aim in post-acquisition integration. For the purposes of this chapter, the synergy effect is meant to describe the cooperative action between two or more agencies whose combined effect is greater than the (1) sum of their separate efforts and (2) subsequent value-creation effect of combining the formerly independent entities. The underlying assumption is that sharing of resources leads to improved performance of the newly formed entity as compared to the aggregated performance of the acquiring and the acquired firms if they remained independent. This argument builds on the resource-based view of the firm, where sustained competitiveness, in the case of an acquisition, is a product of resource combinations of the two firms (Ahuja & Katilla, 2001; Karim & Mitchell, 2000; Wernerfelt, 1984).

In general, there are two ways to reveal synergy. One is to utilize the differences in efficiency between the two firms and improve the "weak" firm through transfers of resources from the acquiring firm to the acquired firm in the form of managers, management systems, knowledge, capital, and so forth. The purpose is to replace or renew the consolidated practices of the target firm (Nooteboom, 1999; Weston, Chung, & Hoag, 1990), which sometimes requires the replacement of management (Manne, 1965) or heavy rationalizations in the nonefficient target firm (e.g., case of takeovers of Eastern European enterprises during the 1990s). This differential efficiency approach is sometimes considered to be the opening of bottlenecks by redeploying the target firm's resources (Capron & Mitchell, 1998) or emphasizing the full utilization of intangible resources, such as specialists or high-tech equipment in the target firm (Itami, 1987).

Second, the aforementioned opportunities for resource combinations give both firms an opportunity to tap into knowledge areas located outside their normal organizational and cultural contexts (Zander, 1999). The two firms' knowledge bases will be broadened through intensive in- and outflows of knowledge in both firms (Gupta & Govindarajan, 2000). One example could be a promising product design, owned by a relatively small firm, being acquired by an experienced, older firm, with the needed capital, process technologies, and distribution channels (Bower, 2001; Teece, 1987). The sharing of intangible assets between more equal partners, like R&D engineers from two firms forming project groups subsequent to an acquisition, is another engine for synergy (Capron & Mitchell, 1998; Markides & Oyon, 1998; Morck & Yeung, 1992). The access to specific valuable resources of the target firm is in these cases emphasized as a key motive for acquisition (Chakrabarti et al., 1994), which puts a further request for proper integration and knowledge-sharing strategies.

Some of the acquisition literature points out that efficient knowledge sharing following acquisitions is imperative to capturing the value potential of synergies in acquisitions (Bresman et al., 1999; Capron & Mitchell, 1998; Haspeslagh & Jemison, 1991). Assumed this is true, an obvious managerial implication is that synergy effects following an acquisition are only achievable through successful integration of the two firms, not only at the operational and procedural level, but also at the human level (Buono, 2005; Birkinshaw, Bresman, & Håkanson, 2000; Grant, 1996; Shrivastava, 1986). This includes, among others, creating a friendly atmosphere for knowledge sharing (Haspeslagh & Jemison, 1991). Within this context, synergy can be seen as an outcome of knowledge integration rather than knowledge itself (Grant, 1996). Therefore, as Ranft and Lord (2002, p. 422) emphasize, "It is not enough for an acquirer to simply 'buy' a technology or capability and keep it in stasis; to create value, it must be nurtured and integrated throughout the process of acquisition implementation, long after the deal is done."

Synergy is created through learning effects, since the combination gives both firms an opportunity to tap into knowledge areas located outside their own organizational and cultural contexts (Zander, 1999). It has been emphasized that in post-acquisition integration, the two firms' knowledge bases will therefore be broadened through intensive in- and outflows of knowledge in both firms (Gupta & Govindarajan, 2000). The strategic fit (i.e., the fact that resources of the two firms are complementary) is seen as the fundamental for reaching synergy (Hagedoorn & Duysters, 2002; Harrison, Hitt, Hoskisson, & Ireland, 1991; Healy, Palepu, & Ruback, 1997; Hitt, Harrison, & Ireland, 2001; Hopkins, 1999; Larsson & Finkelstein, 1999; Markides & Oyon, 1998). The disparity between the two firms' resources can be interpreted as a potential value gap. If the acquired resources are very similar to the acquiring firm, the opportunities for creating synergy-based value from the amalgamation of resources are only marginal (Ahuja & Katila, 2001).

Cooperation is emphasized in this symbiotic approach, where both organizations adapt and learn from the best practices of the other (Haspeslagh & Jemison, 1991). One example of a company oriented toward integration-based acquisitions is Cisco. Cisco acquires firms with specific R&D capabilities within the Internet server and communication equipment fields. The company manages much of the post-acquisition tension extremely well, since it is part of its culture to acknowledge the superiority of the target firm (Bower, 2001). Cisco ensures that the top people of the acquired firm maintain or get key positions in the new organization, and in general the target firm is quickly integrated into the organization, normally within about 3 months.

Strategic fit needs to be combined with organizational and cultural fit before synergy can be achieved (Larsson & Finkelstein, 1999). Utilizing a strategic fit opportunity requires simultaneous integration of operational procedures and people (Birkinshaw et al., 2000). The writings oriented toward the human side of acquisitions suggest a number of relatively broad explanations as to why acquisitions fail to deliver the expected benefits. These accounts can be clustered in reasons related to cultural clashes, size differences, and a destructive asymmetry of power, which can result in opportunistic behavior and goal conflicts (Buckley & Carter, 1999).

Minimizing cultural clashes and revealing synergies are naturally connected through integration practices. A preservation strategy, with a minimum of changes in the acquired firm, is proposed in cases where the target possesses unique knowledge embedded in persons or organizational routines and there is a risk of key employees leaving the firm. However, over time, a symbiotic approach, a kind of merger of best practices, is emphasized to facilitate knowledge sharing and resource combination. Here, a dilemma is foreseeable: since integration may ultimately lead to improved performance due to the obtained synergy effect, it may also lead to internal resistance in the acquired company. The effect of integration in relation to acquisition is therefore unclear. The study by Datta (1991) provides an example. It concludes that failure was an outcome of differences in management style between the two firms rather than an outcome of integration efforts. Therefore, a high degree of integration did not lead to success in the case of lack of organizational fit. A low degree of integration and an assumable high level of autonomy of the acquired firm were only successful in diversified acquisitions. However, integration takes time, often years, and time is needed to reveal synergies. The time elapsed since acquisition speaks for positive performance effects (Calori, Lubatkin, & Very, 1994; Very, Lubatkin, Calori, & Veiga, 1997).

The above-mentioned causes of acquisition failure, which resulted from cultural differences, differences in size, and power allocation, can all negatively influence the effectiveness with which members of the acquired and the acquiring organization share knowledge. In addition to these relatively broad explanations of acquisition failure in the M&A literature, we propose that insights from the knowledge-sharing literature can offer more specific and detailed explanations of the failure phenomenon. Brush (1996) highlights the importance of knowledge sharing for acquisition performance and a recent survey by Schoenberg (2001) of 121 British acquisitions into continental Europe reveals that knowledge sharing played an essential role in achieving operational synergy, especially within the area of marketing and distribution. At the same time, a thorough analysis of knowledge sharing on the individual level is lacking in this post-acquisition discussion. Thus, whether the tendency for employees to either hoard or reject knowledge is a barrier to obtaining post-acquisition synergies has remained a lacuna in our understanding of M&A failure.

INDIVIDUAL KNOWLEDGE-SHARING BEHAVIOR: THE LESS EXPLORED CAUSE FOR POST-ACQUISITION FAILURE

When organizational members share the relevant personal knowledge they possess, they make knowledge available to those who need to solve a certain problem without being dependent on where knowledge has been obtained or stored originally in the organization. In this way, the organization avoids redundancy in knowledge production, secures diffusion of best practice, and enables efficient problem solving. Moreover, knowledge sharing contributes to knowledge creation. The latter is a social process involving sharing tacit knowledge and converting part of the tacit knowledge into explicit knowledge (Nonaka & Takeuchi, 1995). Knowledge is created by individuals, but is also expressed in rules by which members cooperate in a social community. According to Kogut and Zander (1992, p. 383), what firms do better than markets is sharing knowledge of the individuals and groups within the organization. These issues become even more crucial in multinational corporations (MNCs). It is widely accepted that the major reason why MNCs exist is their ability to transfer and exploit knowledge more efficiently in the intracorporate context than through the market (Gupta & Govindarajan, 2000).

However, although it may sound simple, sharing knowledge in and across organizations is far from being a smooth and self-propelled process. Knowledge sharing is flawed by ineffectiveness and often depends purely on chance. Knowledge sharing is costly, and should therefore be restricted to sharing relevant knowledge with those who need it. At the same time, the uncertainty regarding what specific piece of idiosyncratic knowledge is to be shared with whom in order to create benefits for the organization is relatively high (Jensen & Meckling, 1996). Potential receivers/users are often not aware of the existence of the knowledge they need, and likewise, the potential sources are not aware that there may be a need for their knowledge somewhere else in the organization. In other words, unawareness at both the end of the transmitter and the receiver is a major barrier to knowledge sharing (Szulanski, 1996). The problems caused by this lack of transparency are further reinforced by people's tendency merely to seek the missing answers in the local environment (Davenport & Prusak, 1998). These obstacles, we claim, are perpetuated in an acquisition context since the two organizational entities are usually independent of and/or possibly unknown to each other prior to the acquisition.

Another well-described barrier for efficient knowledge sharing is related to the differences between tacit and explicit knowledge (Kogut & Zander, 1993; Nonaka & Takeuchi, 1995). At one end of the spectrum, knowledge is almost completely tacit—it is stored semiconsciously and unconsciously in people's brains and neural systems and it is uniquely personal and complex (Leonard & Sensiper, 1998). At the other end of the spectrum, knowledge is predominantly explicit and codified and thus more easily accessible to other people (e.g., blueprints, description of best practice, manuals). Tacit knowledge is more "sticky" (Szulanski, 1996) and difficult to share than articulated knowledge (Winter, 1994). Between the two poles, knowledge is seen as partly explicit (or articulated) and partly tacit, and applying explicit knowledge requires mastery of the associated tacit knowledge (Leonard & Sensiper, 1998).

Acknowledging that epistemological differences and difficulties in identifying the exact location of relevant knowledge are important for studying knowledge-sharing processes, we turn our attention to individual knowledge-sharing behavior. Ideally, systematic knowledge sharing relies on individuals' autonomous and constructive behavior. Barriers to knowledge sharing, however, reflect difficulties in interpersonal communication, and problems with such sharing can only be fully understood by reference to the individual level (Empson, 2001). Additionally, knowledge sharing is largely dependent on the willingness of individuals to (a) signal what knowledge they possess and (b) share (or hoard) when a particular piece of knowledge is requested (Nonaka, 1994). This dynamic is especially true in terms of sharing valuable tacit knowledge that, to a large extent, is stored semiconsciously in people's neural systems.

From an organizational perspective, successful knowledge sharing also implies that the shared knowledge is actually reused by somebody in the organization. Again, reusing knowledge is most of the time also an individual decision. It is the individual who is confronted with a specific situation or a particular need; he or she has to decide whether his or her own knowledge base is sufficient to solve a particular problem. It is also the individual who decides to trust (or not) the knowledge received from somebody else and whether to apply it. In this respect, Bresman and colleagues (1999) point out that the lack of knowledge sharing after a takeover is mainly caused by a lack of personal relationships among individuals in the acquiring and the acquired firm.

Individual Knowledge-Sharing Behavior in the Post-Acquisition Stage

Much of the knowledge-sharing literature implicitly assumes that individuals are essentially positive toward knowledge sharing (Nonaka & Takeuchi, 1995; Szulanski, 1996) as long as they are given the right incentives (Davenport & Prusak, 1998). Contrary to this position, we argue, in line with Husted and Michailova (2002), that people have a deeply rooted resistance not only to sharing the knowledge they possess, but also to reusing knowledge from others. This concept of knowledge-sharing hostility offers important insights into barriers toward knowledge sharing at the level of individual organizational members.

While the value of knowledge sharing is typically obvious to the firm, knowledge sharing from an individual perspective is time- and resource-consuming, and may even offset potential individual benefits (Cabrera & Cabrera, 2002). The reality is that most organizational members are to some extent hostile to knowledge sharing. This is partly because of the deeply anchored belief that they need to keep knowledge secret in order to maintain their competitive advantages. The model of knowledge sharing hostility suggested by Husted and Michailova (2002) distinguishes between three parameters: (1) the behavior of the knowledge transmitter (i.e., the person who possesses knowledge that someone else in the organization demands); (2) the behavior of the knowledge receiver (i.e., the person who needs knowledge input from someone else in the organization); and (3) the individual behavior related to the substance of the knowledge. The model suggests that knowledge-sharing hostility on the transmitter side is related to *knowledge hoarding*, whereas knowledge-sharing hostility on the receiver side is associated with *knowledge rejecting*. The authors link the substance-related behavior with the attitudes toward sharing knowledge about mistakes and failures.

In this chapter, we utilize the distinction of barriers as related to the knowledge transmitter's and the knowledge receiver's individual behavior. Additionally, we propose a differentiation of obstacles to knowledge sharing as experienced in the acquired and the acquiring firm. We insert a link between individual knowledge-sharing behavior in the two formerly independent organizational entities and the synergies in post-acquisition integration.

In the rest of the chapter, we focus on the differentiation of obstacles to knowledge sharing as related to the individual behavior of knowledge transmitters and knowledge receivers. We follow a similar logic in both exploring knowledge-hoarding and knowledge-rejecting behavior. First, we analyze different reasons for this behavior in general. We then outline a number of specificities of knowledge-sharing behavior in the post-acquisition integration context. In so doing, we link the specificities of knowledge sharing at the individual level in the acquiring and the acquired organizations with the processes of capturing post-acquisition synergies.

Knowledge-Hoarding Behavior

According to Chow, Deng, and Ho (2000), both the propensity to hoard knowledge and the motivational factors behind such behavior depend on the nature of the knowledge to be shared, the employees' national culture, the relationships among employees, and the culture of the workplace. Knowledge-hoarding behavior is also embedded in perceived psychological safety. If people equal an acquisition with workforce reduction, the tendency will be to hoard knowledge to protect, as best one can, their position within the company. Merchant, Chow, and Wu (1995) have pointed out that senior managers' education and experience, the company's stage of development, and the company's type of business are also important factors when analyzing knowledge-hoarding behavior. Industry specifics and functional areas should also be seriously considered when discussing the use of different channels and forms of knowledge sharing.

In line with the defined level of analysis in this chapter, we argue that although the factors mentioned above are relevant, the decision to share or to hoard knowledge is largely individual. The decision to hoard knowledge may be destructive from an organizational point of view, however, it is often rational and well justified from an individual perspective. Organizational philosophies, norms, and values, by which people are evaluated according to what they know and do individually, naturally invite knowledge hoarding and perpetuate a behavior of "playing one's cards close to one's chest." Sometimes knowledge hoarding is mainly an instrument supporting individual economic concerns, whereas in other cases, involvement in power games becomes decisive and often dominant in justifying knowledge-hoarding individual behavior (Husted & Michailova, 2002).

Individual economic concerns are related to the fact that individuals, and especially knowledge workers, associate their own market value and bargaining power with the quality and value of the knowledge they possess. They therefore fear that they may lose their bargaining position by sharing their relevant knowledge (Szulanski, 1995). Consequently, they resist the organization's attempts to establish property rights over their knowledge (Empson, 2001). In this sense, knowledge hoarding is a natural mechanism for protecting individual competitive advantages. Organizational structures and incentives, too, may tend to promote a tendency by individuals to optimize their own accomplishments and, as a consequence, conceal knowledge from other individuals. This is often linked with organizational cultures (De Long & Fahey, 2000) where it is accepted and even valued that people are "territorial" (i.e., that they hoard their knowledge in order to protect themselves and secure their own position). Particularly in environments that are characterized by a lack of trust, individuals are uncertain whether sharing knowledge would be appropriate (Empson, 2001).

Reluctance toward spending time on knowledge sharing is another economic concern that contributes to knowledge hoarding. Knowledge sharing is a costly process demanding a great deal of resources, either to articulate knowledge or to share it in tacit form, or both. The time spent sharing knowledge with others could be invested in what may appear to the individual to be more productive priorities.

A third economic motive is the fear of hosting "knowledge parasites" (Husted & Michailova, 2002). The main reason why a person possesses knowledge that could be attractive to others is that the knowledge possessor has invested additional effort into acquiring this knowledge. Consequently, he or she as a potential knowledge transmitter may be unwilling to share the return on this investment with someone who has put less or no effort into his or her own development. In other words, a request for knowledge sharing can also mask a lack of effort and/or talent on the side of the individual making the request for knowledge sharing.

The potential loss of value and bargaining power is relevant to understanding individual knowledge-hoarding behavior in acquisitions. Being subordinated to the dominant culture of the acquiring firm automatically lowers the organizational status of the acquired employees. Empson (2001) points out that knowledge hoarding in relation to loss of power increases after an acquisition and that this is a natural outcome of protecting what remains of one's position. At the same time, knowledge sharing may prove to be the only way to be recognized by the headquarters, which delegates resources, decides on career developments, and upgrades some organizational positions while downgrading others. The acquired personnel can, for that reason and from the viewpoint of purely individual economic concerns, be initially positive toward sharing knowledge with their new colleagues.

Acquired personnel typically experience work overload immediately after an acquisition, since they need to follow new orders while simultaneously carrying out their old duties. This work overload can reinforce the inclination of individuals to hoard their knowledge because of economic concerns. The fear of hosting "knowledge parasites" is also relevant here, especially when the motive for the acquisition is to utilize the acquired firm's knowledge. In these cases it is natural for acquired personnel to resist sharing the knowledge they possess in the absence of clear incentives for doing so.

In organizations that are very hostile to knowledge sharing, knowledge hoarding is driven by an individual urge to extend influence and/or control *power games* (Husted & Michailova, 2002). An important factor to consider in this context is the uncertainty that relates to how the receiver uses the shared knowledge and for what purposes, and consequently whether the shared knowledge can damage the sharer's self-interests.

Avoidance of exposure is another feature that tends to be typical in respect to power games related to knowledge hoarding. Avoidance of exposure is associated with the fact that not all knowledge is robust or a good solution to a problem. By hoarding knowledge, individuals protect themselves against external assessment of the quality of their knowledge. High respect for hierarchy and formal power may also potentially lead to knowledge-hoarding behavior. Especially in organizations embedded in high power-distance national contexts (Hofstede, 2001), subordinates may intentionally hoard their knowledge, knowing that their superiors would dislike subordinates who appear to be more knowledgeable than they are. Additionally, managers may deliberately hoard their knowledge to maintain power—for them knowledge could be a source of greater power rather than a basis for making optimal managerial decisions. Difficulties in knowledge sharing between superiors and subordinates can also be detected in terms of barriers to knowledge sharing between old and new staff in an organization.

The obstacles to the process of signaling that one possess the knowledge needed somewhere else in the organization are even greater in acquisitions because of organizational cultural differences, asymmetrically distributed power, and the relatively low levels of psychological safety perceived by organizational members. When the new company experiences high ambiguity and the primary concern of the acquired personnel is to secure their jobs, one can expect a limited desire on the part of organizational members to share the knowledge they possess. Additionally, individuals who have invested resources in building up a specific competence may not be willing to share this knowledge with others unless they are given the right incentives for doing so. At the same time, however, knowledge creation in firms today is highly dependent on relationships outside the firm. Pre-acquisition relationships often exist where firms have already established certain communication patterns prior to an acquisition, which may make the entire post-acquisition processes less troublesome.

Knowledge-Rejecting Behavior

Knowledge-rejecting behavior is captured in the notion of the "not-invented-here" syndrome. Katz and Allen (1982) define this syndrome as the tendency of a project group of stable composition to believe it possesses a monopoly of knowledge in its field, which leads it to reject new ideas from outsiders to the likely detriment of its performance. According to Szulanski (1995), a potential knowledge receiver can choose among a number of behavioral strategies for avoiding external knowledge, including procrastination, passivity, feigned acceptance, sabotage, or outright rejection in the implementation and use of new knowledge.

Doubt about the validity and reliability of external knowledge and the preference for developing in-house solutions are usually associated with organizational members' *professional pride*. External knowledge in such cases is often rejected because it is more prestigious to create new knowledge. Another reason may be that knowledge receivers often doubt the quality of the shared knowledge, possibly because they do not find the source trustworthy (Szulanski, 1995). In this case, they will prefer to develop the specific knowledge themselves rather than going through a process of validation of the external knowledge. At the same time, knowledge receivers do not always possess the necessary knowledge for assessing the quality of external knowledge. In those situations, they will be even more inclined to develop their own knowledge.

Acquired firms placed in a dominating culture may find a need to manifest themselves through autonomous knowledge-creating programs. From the acquired firm's perspective, the fact that the firm has lived its own independent life—for decades or even longer—creates an initial preference for its own knowledge compared to that of the acquiring organization. Similar behavior is described by Empson (2001) in the example of a merger of two professional consulting firms. In this case, knowledge resistance was due to certain interpretations of the partner's image. This negatively influenced the way they perceived the value and reliability of their new colleagues' knowledge. This ethnocentric interpretation was expressed by evaluating the partner firm's knowledge stock as simplistic and unsophisticated on the one hand, and insubstantial and unreal at the other. As a result, no efficient knowledge sharing took place.

Maintaining the status quo is an even greater obstacle to knowledge sharing. This sometimes occurs explicitly, but more often behind a veil of minor, unimportant changes. Strong group affiliation may also be a substantial inhibitor to knowledge sharing outside the boundaries of the group. In older companies with low employee turnover, there are usually long-standing relationships among organizational members. The longer a group of people has been together, the higher the likely degree of ethnocentric behavior (Katz & Allen, 1982). As a consequence, organizational members tend to resist new external knowledge, since it might fracture not only the stability and familiarity of the particular group, but also the continuity of the overall development of the organization. In a well-defined group, a common set of values and beliefs among individuals creates a governance system in which the risk of opportunistic behavior is low. Therefore, knowledge sharing will take place *within* the group, but only to a limited extent *across* different groups (Kogut & Zander, 1995).

In an acquisition context, acquired personnel often considers their old culture highly valuable (Berry, 1980), and they will seek to protect their positions and identities (Buono & Bowditch, 1989). The lack of alignment between different subcultures leads to conflict and often to collision (Buono et al., 1985). The degree of acceptance of the counterpart's culture therefore depends on the acquired employees' wish to preserve their own culture and how attractive they find the acquiring firm's culture (Nahavandi & Malakzadeh, 1988).

Knowledge-rejecting behavior might also take the shape of groupthink, where a stable group (e.g., a project group or management team) believes that it possesses a monopoly of knowledge in its field and therefore rejects new ideas from outsiders. Under the motto "Why change a winner?," it is often perceived as unnecessary or even disruptive to allocate resources to changing the way of doing things based on new external knowledge. Especially in an acquisition, this tendency is further reinforced by winner–loser dynamics. Since the acquiring firm usually "wins," the dominant view is that their approach (knowledge) is superior. If not, the target firm would have acquired them.

KNOWLEDGE SHARING VERSUS KNOWLEDGE HOARDING AND REJECTING: IMPLICATIONS FOR MANAGEMENT CONSULTING

The chapter has explicitly integrated notions drawn from the post-M&A and knowledge-sharing literatures in order to offer explanations for acquisition failure, which have been underestimated in previous research. In line with the argument that individuals have a deeply rooted resistance toward both sharing the knowledge they possess and reusing external knowledge, we have outlined the specificities of knowledge-sharing behavior in a post-acquisition integration context. Capturing synergies from knowledge sharing in post-acquisition integration is a multifaceted and complex process, which often turns out to be problematic. We suggest that an important reason for this is individual knowledge-sharing behavior. Hoarding and rejecting knowledge is justified rational behavior anchored in a number of factors, although it is usually counterproductive from an organizational point of view.

Knowledge management has in general been a stepping-stone for the development of a wide range of consulting products and services. The consultancy business has not only stepped into the game, but has contributed much to the establishment of the "knowledge management" concept as such. For example, the first conference in the United States that focused on knowledge[1]—beyond the theories of artificial intelligence—was entitled "Managing the Knowledge Asset into the 21st Century" and was convened by Digital Equipment Corporation and the Technology Transfer Society at Purdue University in 1987. The second forum was on "Knowledge Productivity" and was coordinated by Steelcase North America and EDS in April 1992. McKinsey and Company initiated their knowledge management practice during the same timeframe.

Beyond the development of new insights into knowledge management, the application of these concepts in post-acquisition processes and strategies also offers a range of opportunities for management consulting products and services:

Developing diagnostic tools. Although this chapter is primarily concerned with post- acquisition integration, it is important to recognize that management consultants can add to securing the synergy in the early planning process of the M&A by including knowledge- sharing behavior as a dimension of due diligence. This emphasis could reveal potential knowledge-sharing behavior-related obstacles, and suggests possible solutions of how to address those obstacles.

Putting knowledge sharing on the management agenda. It is well known that managerial attention toward operational aspects of the integration process during the post- acquisition stage is crucial for capturing expected synergies. In this stage, a number of issues compete for resources and managerial attention. Management consultants can assist by raising the visibility of the knowledge-sharing dilemma, attempting to ensure that managers realize its importance to acquisition success.

Mediating the process. As argued in the chapter, both potential knowledge sources and receivers believe they are in a vulnerable situation. These two entities often also have conflicting interests. A management consultant, as a neutral party, can facilitate the process of verifying knowledge, connecting sources and users, and translating and helping to apply shared knowledge.

Designing appropriate motivation and reward mechanisms. It is important for organizations to develop supportive systems to encourage sharing and reusing relevant and valuable knowledge in the post-acquisition stage. Dealing with knowledge-sharing obstacles is tricky, vulnerable, and dependent on a high level of sensitivity toward individual knowledge-sharing behavior—on both the acquirer and acquired side. Firms that only occasionally acquire another organization particularly need professional support and guidance in this process, not only about the financial aspect but also about the knowledge-sharing behaviors and reactions of the staff influenced by the acquisition.

Management consultants can assist first-timer and occasional acquirers in gaining advantage from the actions of more frequent acquires. By drawing on experiences and learnings from past acquisitions, firms can begin to create a stronger foundation for knowledge sharing and acquisition success (see Hitt et al., 2001; Markides & Oyon, 1998). At the same time, heavy reliance on prior success may lead to inertia in adapting new ideas (Finkelstein & Haleblian, 2002), and integrating two previously autonomous organizations is an exceedingly complex and idiosyncratic process (Buono, 2005). As such, the dynamics associated with knowledge sharing, knowledge hoarding, and knowledge rejecting provide a useful perspective through which management consultants can assist firms in framing and capturing crucial knowledge-based synergies in the post-acquisition stage.

NOTE

1. See www.entovation.com/momentum/momentum.htm for additional information on the momentum of knowledge management.

REFERENCES

Ahuja, G., & Katila, R. (2001). Technological acquisitions and the innovation performance of acquiring firms: a longitudinal study. *Strategic Management Journal, 22*, 197–220.

Berry, J. (1980). Acculturation as varieties of adaptation. In A. Padilla (Ed.), *Acculturation: Theory, models and some new findings* (pp. 9–25). Boulder, CO: Westview Press.

Birkinshaw, J., Bresman, H., & Håkanson, L. (2000). Managing the post-acquisition integration process: How the human integration and task integration processes interact to foster value creation. *Journal of Management Studies 37*(3), 395–425.

Blake, R., & Mouton, J. (1985). How to achieve integration on the human side of the merger. *Organizational Dynamics, 13*(3), 41–56.

Bower, J. (2001). Not all M&As are alike—and that matters. *Harvard Business Review, 79*(3), 93–101.

Bresman, H., Birkinshaw, J., & Nobel, R. (1999). Knowledge transfer in international acquisitions. *Journal of International Business Studies, 30*(3), 439–462.

Brush, T. (1996). Predicted change in operational synergy and post-acquisition performance of acquired businesses. *Strategic Management Journal, 17*, 1–24.

Buckley, P., & Carter, M. (1999). Managing cross-border complementary knowledge: Conceptual developments in the business process approach to knowledge management in multinational firms. *International Studies of Management and Organization, 29*(1), 80–104.

Buono, A. F. (2005). Consulting to integrate mergers and acquisitions. In L. Greiner & F. Poulfelt (Eds.), *The contemporary consultant: Insights from world experts* (pp. 229–249). Cincinnati, OH: Thomson/South-Western.

Buono, A. F. (2003). SEAM-less post-merger integration strategies: A cause of concern. *Journal of Organizational Change Management, 16*(1), 90–98.

Buono, A. F., & Bowditch, J. L. (1989). *The human side of mergers and acquisitions: Managing collisions between people, cultures and organizations.* San Francisco: Jossey-Bass.

Buono, A. F, Bowditch, J. L., & Lewis, J. W. (1985). When cultures collide: The anatomy of a merger. *Human Relations, 38*(5), 477–500.

Cabrera, Á., & Cabrera, E. (2002). Knowledge-sharing dilemmas. *Organization Studies, 23*(5), 687–710.

Calori, R., Lubatkin, M., & Very, P. (1994). Control mechanisms in cross-border acquisitions: an international comparison. *Organization Studies, 15*(3), 361–379.

Capron, L., & Mitchell, W. (1998). Bilateral resource redeployment and capabilities improvement following horizontal acquisitions. *Industrial and Corporate Change, 7*(3), 453–484.

Chakrabarti, A., Hauschildt, J., & Süverkrüp, C. (1994). Does it pay to acquire technological firms? *R&D Management, 24*(1), 47–56.

Chatterjee, S., Lubatkin, M., Schweiger, D., & Weber, Y. (1992). Cultural differences and shareholder value: Linking equity and human capital. *Strategic Management Journal, 13*, 319–334.

Chow, C., Deng, J., & Ho, J. (2000). The openness of knowledge sharing within organizations: A comparative study of the United States and the People's Republic of China. *Journal of Management Accounting Research, 12*, 65–95.

Datta, D. (1991). Organizational fit and acquisition performance: Effects of post-acquisition integration. *Strategic Management Journal, 12*, 281–297.

Davenport, T., & Prusak, L. (1998). *Working knowledge.* Cambridge, MA: Harvard Business School Press.

De Long, D., & Fahey, L. (2000). Diagnosing cultural barriers to knowledge management. *Academy of Management Executive, 14*(4), 113–127.

Empson, L. (2001). Fear of exploitation and fear of contamination: Impediments to knowledge transfer in mergers between professional service firms. *Human Relations, 54*(7), 839–862.

Finkelstein, S., & Haleblian, J. (2002). Understanding acquisition performance: The role of transfer effects. *Organization Science, 13*(1), 36–47.

Grant, R. (1996, Winter). Toward a knowledge-based theory of the firm. *Strategic Management Journal, 17*, 109–122.

Gupta, A., & Govindarajan, V. (2000). Knowledge flows within multinational corporations. *Strategic Management Journal, 21*(4), 473–496.

Hagedoorn, J., & Duysters, G. (2002). The effect of mergers and acquisitions on the technological performance of companies in a high-tech environment. *Technology Analysis & Strategic Management, 14*(1), 67–85.

Harrison, J., Hitt, M., Hoskisson, R., & Ireland, R. D. (1991). Synergies and post-acquisition performance: Differences versus similarities in resource allocations. *Journal of Management, 17*(1), 173–190.

Haspeslagh, P., & Jemison, D. (1991). *Managing acquisitions: Creating value through corporate renewal.* Oxford: The Free Press.

Healy, P., Palepu, K., & Ruback, R. (1997). Which takeovers are profitable? Strategic or Financial? *Sloan Management Review, 38*(4), 45–57.

Hitt, M., Harrison, J., & Ireland, R. D. (2001). *Mergers and acquisitions: A guide to creating value for stakeholders.* Oxford: Oxford University Press.

Hofstede, G. (2001). *Culture's consequences: Comparing values, behaviors, institutions, and organizations across nations.* Thousand Oaks, CA: Sage.

Hopkins, D. (1999). Cross-border mergers and acquisitions: Global and regional perspectives. *Journal of International Management, 5*, 207–239.

Husted, K., & Michailova, S. (2002). Diagnosing and fighting knowledge sharing hostility. *Organizational Dynamics, 31*(1), 60–73.

Itami, H. (1987). *Mobilizing invisible assets.* Cambridge, MA: Harvard University Press.

Jensen, M., & Meckling, W. (1996). Specific and general knowledge and organizational structure. In P. Myers (Ed.), *Knowledge management and organizational design* (pp. 17–38). Boston: Butterworth-Heinemann.

Karim, S., & Mitchell, W. (2000). Path-dependent and path-breaking change: Reconfiguration business resources following acquisitions in the U.S. medical sector, 1978–1995. *Strategic Management Journal, 21,* 1061–1081.

Katz, R., & Allen, T. (1982). Investigating the not invented here (NIH) syndrome: a look at the performance, tenure, and communication patterns of 50 R&D project groups. *R & D Management, 12*(1), 7–19.

Kogut, B., & Zander, U. (1992). Knowledge of the firm, combinative capabilities, and the replication of technology. *Organization Science, 3,* 383–397.

Kogut, B., & Zander, U. (1993). Knowledge of the firm and the evolutionary theory of the multinational corporation. *Journal of International Business Studies, 24*(4), 625–646.

Kogut, B., & Zander, U. (1995). Knowledge and the speed of the transfer and imitation of organizational capabilities: An empirical test. *Organization Science, 6*(1), 76–91.

Larsson, R., & Finkelstein, S. (1999). Integrating strategic, organizational, and human resource perspectives on mergers and acquisitions: a case survey of synergy realization. *Organization Science, 10*(1), 1–26.

Leonard, D., & Sensiper, S. (1998). The role of tacit knowledge in group innovation. *California Management Review, 40*(3), 112–130.

Manne, H. G. (1965). Mergers and the market for corporate control. *Journal of Political Economy, 73*(2), 110–120.

Markides, C., & Oyon, D. (1998). International acquisitions: Do they create value for shareholders? *European Management Journal, 16*(2), 125–135.

Merchant, K., Chow, C., & Wu, A. (1995). Measurement, evaluation and reward of profit center managers: A cross-cultural field study. *Accounting, Organizations and Society, 20*(7-8), 619–638.

Morck, R., & Yeung, B. (1992). Internalization: An event study test. *Journal of International Economics, 33,* 41–56.

Nahavandi, A., & Malekzadeh, A. (1988). Acculturation in mergers and acquisitions. *Academy of Management Review, 13*(1), 79–90.

Nonaka I. (1994). A dynamic theory of organizational knowledge creation. *Organization Science, 5*(1), 14–37.

Nonaka, I., & Takeuchi, H. (1995). *The knowledge-creating company.* New York: Oxford University Press.

Nooteboom, B. (1999). Innovation, Learning and Industrial Organisation. *Cambridge Journal of Economics, 23,* 127–150.

Ranft, A., & Lord, M (2000). Acquiring new knowledge: the role of retaining human capital in acquisitions of high-tech firms. *The Journal of High Technology Management Research, 11*(2), 295–319.

Risberg, A. (2001). Executives perceptions in foreign and domestic acquisitions: An analysis of foreign ownership and its effect on executive fate. *Journal of World Business, 36*(1), 58–84.

Schoenberg, R. (2001). Knowledge transfer and resource sharing as value creation mechanisms in inbound continental European acquisitions. *Journal of Euromarketing, 10*(1), 99–114.

Schweiger, D., & Denisi, A. (1991). Communication with employees following a merger: A longitudinal field experiment. *Academy of Management Journal, 34*(1), 110–135.

Seth, A. (1990). Value creation in acquisitions: A re-examination of performance issues'. *Strategic Management Journal, 11*, 99–115.

Shrivastava, P. (1986). Postmerger integration. *Journal of Business Strategy, 7*(1), 65–76.

Szulanski, G. (1995). Unpacking stickiness: An empirical investigation of the barriers to transfer best practice inside the firm. *Academy of Management Journal* [Special issue], 437–441.

Szulanski, G. (1996). Exploring internal stickiness: Impediments to the transfer of best practice within the firm. *Strategic Management Journal, 17*, 27–43.

Teece, D. (1987). Profiting from Technological Innovation: Implication for Integration, Collaboration, Licensing and Public Policy. In D. Teece (Ed.), *The competitive challenge—Strategies for industrial innovation and renewal* (pp. 185–219). Cambridge, MA: Ballinger.

Very, P., Lubatkin, M., Calori, R., & Veiga, J. (1997). Relative standing and the performance of recently acquired European firms. *Strategic Management Journal, 18*(8), 593–614.

Wernerfelt, B. (1984). A resource-based view of the firm. *Strategic Management Journal, 5*, 171–180.

Weston J. F., Chung, K., & Hoag, S. (1990). *Mergers, restructuring, and corporate control*. Englewood Cliffs, NJ: Prentice-Hall.

Winter, S. (1994). Organizing for Continuous Improvement: Evolutionary Theory Meets the Quality Revolution. In J. A. C. Baum & J. V. Singh (Eds.), *Evolutionary dynamics of organizations* (pp. 90–108). New York: Oxford University Press.

Zander, I. (1999). How do you mean 'global'?: An empirical investigation of innovation networks in the multinational corporation. *Research Policy, 28*(2-3), 195–213.

PART III

METHODOLOGICAL APPROACHES TO STUDYING KNOWLEDGE IN ORGANIZATIONS

CHAPTER 10

ORGANIZATIONAL PHOTOGRAPHY

A "Snapshot" Approach to Understanding Knowledge Sharing[1]

Nicoline Jacoby Petersen and Sille Østergaard

The use of photography as a research methodology is relatively new within management consulting. Photography, however, has been used in the social sciences for almost a century, usually under such headings as visual sociology, visual ethnography, or visual anthropology (cf. Banks, 2001; Collier & Collier, 1986; Harper, 1988). The approach has been used in many different ways to portray, describe, and analyze social phenomena and culture.

Analyses of complex issues in organizations, from assessments of culture to change-related dynamics, are typically guided by semantic exchanges and questions and answers in interviews and surveys. Responses to such questions, however, even when open-ended, are likely to fall within the framework of the researcher or the boundaries imposed by the question. Organizational photography, in contrast, introduces a visual element that allows researchers to pose questions in a way that

Challenges and Issues in Knowledge Management, 229–248
Copyright © 2005 by Information Age Publishing
All rights of reproduction in any form reserved.

prompts organizational members to talk about themselves and their everyday working life in a different way. The process often results in useful data that is difficult to get otherwise and, in the best cases, enriches the research with new ways of perceiving the topic under investigation.

The basic objective of the chapter is to frame the concept of organizational photography, distinguishing between using photos as research data per se (i.e., when the photos *are* the data) and using photos *as a means* to collect additional data (i.e., interviews based on the photos, where transcribed interviews are the data). The first approach to using photos in research has been more widespread than the latter, with myriad publications on how to interpret and analyze photos for research purposes (cf. Prosser, 1998; Rose, 2001; Van Leeuwen & Jewitt, 2001). The use of photography as a data collection device, in contrast, is far more limited (see Buchanan, 2001). Thus, the chapter explores how photos can be used as a *vehicle* for encouraging respondents to reflect on and discuss research questions within the context of their own experience. The discussion draws from our field experiences with knowledge sharing among engineers and management consultants in the consulting industry.

The concept of knowledge sharing is ambiguous and can be viewed and interpreted in a variety of ways. An underlying problem is that researchers and respondents may not always be referring to the same things when discussing knowledge sharing in a particular organization— a reality that has become quite clear to us in our field work (see, e.g., Petersen & Poulfelt, 2001). In essence, our experience suggests that the key to understanding barriers to knowledge sharing in an organization lies in the way(s) organizational members think about knowledge sharing. If employees are never provided with the opportunity to explain what *they conceive* as knowledge sharing—typically constrained by questions posed within the boundaries of a researcher's understanding of knowledge sharing—an important source of information to identify exactly what encourages and impedes knowledge sharing in that particular organization is lost. Accordingly, we have found that organizational photography is useful in developing a fuller understanding of what knowledge sharing constitutes in practice, especially in terms of what organizational members are thinking about when talking about knowledge sharing in their companies.

Introducing visuals in the research process changes the entire way people reflect on and talk about things—for a variety of reasons. First, the visuals function as a "third party," and third parties always alter interaction patterns. Second, having something "material" to refer to, point at, and center the discussion on also changes the conversation style. Finally, the simple fact that visuals are another way of conveying meaning

Table 10.1. Different Approaches to Organizational Photography

	Role of the Researcher	
Status of the Photos	Photos are Taken by the Researcher	Photos are Taken by the Respondents
Photos as Data per se —*photo analysis*	I The researcher takes the photos, analyzes them, and reaches conclusions on the basis of the photo material	II The researcher lets the respondents take the photos, but analyzes them on his or her own
Photos as Elicitation —*photo views*	III The researcher takes the photos and discusses them with the respondents	IV The researcher lets the respondents take the photos and discusses them with the respondents

(beyond words per se) changes the way one "talks" about the presented phenomena.

CHARACTERIZING ORGANIZATIONAL PHOTOGRAPHY

Our initial attempt to use photos in organizational research is a modest one and, as such, the chapter poses as many questions as it tries to answer about the use of photography in organizational research. Based on our experience, there are four main ways in which photography can be used in organizational research.

As illustrated in Table 10.1, there are two basic issues involved in organizational photography: (1) *who* takes the photos (the researcher or respondent), and (2) *how* the photos are used in the research (as the final data that can be analyzed as any given "text" or as a means to "create" new data). Analytically, these two dimensions produce four different categories. While there are likely to be many variations within each category (and possibly even new categories that can be created), the key for our discussion is that each approach has a number of underlying assumptions that have consequences for the type of interaction the researcher has with the respondents, the research process itself, and the research results.

Category I

When the photos are taken by the researcher and used as data per se, the researcher analyzes the photos "for what they are." Depending on the theoretical background and orientation of the researcher, the photos can be analyzed based on a range of different principles, from semiotics and discourse analysis to psychoanalysis and content analysis (see Rose, 2001). In some cases, photos are merely used as a photographic record of the research process to supplement other kinds of data, a technique often referred to as *photo-documentation* (Buchanan, 2001).

Jorgensen (1991), for example, has used photo analysis as part of a larger cross-disciplinary research project to illustrate service production in public organizations and organization–customer relationships. Her research material mainly consisted of photos of (management) meetings, physical surroundings in the organizations, and service production with an emphasis on social interaction—both internally and in relation to customers. Jorgensen took roughly 900 pictures in each of the five organizations involved in her study, and the photos were used to supplement the findings of other researchers using more traditional quantitative and qualitative methods.

Category I pictures can also be a useful tool in cases where it is difficult to get sufficiently close to the respondents, either because the researcher doesn't speak the same "language" or because the research question involves "tacit knowledge," like skills and processes tied to bodily action. In these instances, photographs are often capable of capturing what is otherwise difficult to express in words.

Category II

In Category II approaches to organizational photography, the respondents are actively involved in the research process *as they* take the photos, which are subsequently analyzed by the researcher. Staunaes (1999) has worked with this technique during a research project where she gave 11 children in a refugee center, who were waiting for their families' asylum applications to be processed, each a disposable camera and asked them to take pictures of their everyday life.[2] By letting the children take the pictures without her being present, Staunaes got access to the various dynamics inside the center and the children's perception of themselves without the potentially biasing influence of her presence.

As Staunaes (1999) points out, by letting the respondents take their own photos, they are no longer just being observed and examined but in fact become *co-researchers*. This way the data, to a larger extent, consist of what Staunaes refers to as the respondents' *self-representation* rather than representations made by the researcher. However, she also warns against going to the opposite extreme, letting the respondents' stories stand alone as self-representations that are true in themselves. As Staunaes suggests, "Blind angles are also a problem in respondent's stories. What is *not* said can be just as important—or even more important—than what is said explicitly. Silence can be very expressive" (p. 46, our translation). In this respect, it is important to pose questions to the respondents about the photographing process (e.g., the context in which they were taken, the motives for taking certain pictures and not others) so misinterpretation is avoided or at least minimized.

As already hinted, the basic difference between Category I and Category II approaches relates to the underlying theory of science and the researcher's view of reality. In Category I, the researcher alone decides what to photograph and what to deduce from the content, leaving those who are being examined as objects of the research process. It also shows that the researcher views reality as a fact that is common to all participants and can be discovered by outsiders. The image of the researcher thus becomes that of a kind of "reporter" who is able to tell the story (based on the content of the photos) to others (the audience of the research).

By involving the respondents directly in the data gathering (Category II), the perspective changes from viewing them as mere objects of the research process to become active subjects whose action and reflection are an important part of data creation. In essence, the researcher views reality as culturally and socially distributed, best known and described by its members (see Staunaes, 1999). By letting the respondents become active participants, the role of the researcher is no longer to depict the objective world, but to be a critical and analyzing intermediary of the subjective narratives that the respondents choose to "tell" through their photos.

Category III

As in Category II, the researcher involves the respondents actively in the research process but in the opposite way: the researcher takes the photos him- or herself and the respondents are invited to "interpret" them during subsequent discussions. As opposed to the two previous categories, the photos are not the primary data material. Instead, emphasis is placed on the *dialogue* that viewing the photos provokes. Collier and Collier (1913/1986) are among the first to describe the use of images as guides and stimulation in interviews,[3] which has since been referred to as photo-interviewing and photographic interviewing (Heisley & Levy, 1991; Pink, 2001), projective photo interviewing (Carlsson, 2001), and, most commonly, *photo-elicitation* (Harper, 1988). Within this context, "elicitation" refers to drawing out what is latent—bringing out, extracting, or evoking a response from a person.

The point with photo-elicitation is that the photos are used to bring out the respondents' associations and reflections connected to the pictures. In other words, it is not the content of the pictures that is of interest to the researcher, but rather the respondents' explanations and interpretations of them (Carlsson, 2001). In essence, the research analysis is built on the way the respondents think about their reality, and Harper (1988) also refers to this particular approach to data collecting as the "reflexive mode." In connection with exploration of consumption behavior, Heisley and Levy (1991) refer to this methodological approach as *auto-driving*, as respondents drive the feedback based on stimuli taken directly from their own lives.

When using the photos as a means to elicit statements from respondents, it is no longer the researcher who is deciding and posing the questions (at least not directly) but a third party, namely the pictures themselves. Even though the photos are subjective and, as will be discussed, representative of the photographer's view of the world, this intersubjectivity opens up the possibility of *negotiation* between researcher and respondent about the research topic. Thus the research becomes a matter of creating *our* story rather than "my" story and "your" story.

There are several ways that this version of organizational photography can be conducted. For example, prior to an interview one could walk around the organization on a random day, taking photos or following and observing an employee during the course of a day, taking digital photos (which can be printed immediately) of selected situations that would be discussed with the employee at the end of the day. A variant that we have tried on several occasions is the *group photo view*, using a group of people to discuss photos that have been taken by the researcher and arranged in a number of photo-series. The group discusses each topic introduced by the researcher that is associated with a photo-series, without having the researcher moderate the discussion in any way. The discussion is tape-recorded and then transcribed, much like in formal interviews. The Category III approach is sufficiently flexible that researchers are only limited by their imagination and creativity.

Category IV

In the final variant, respondents take the photos themselves and they are subsequently used as the basis for interviews with the same respondents. Since this approach has the least control by the researcher and allows the highest degree of self-representation, it has both advantages and disadvantages. By talking about the photos with the respondent, the researcher not only gains insight into what issues the respondent finds relevant, but also into the underlying drivers of these particular choices and the thoughts attached to them. At the same time, this approach is possibly the most difficult to handle for the researcher. A large part of the research depends on other peoples' ability to understand what they are supposed to do (and why) and furthermore to actually carry out the task in practice.

It is crucial, therefore, that respondents are able to produce data material that can be of use to the researcher. In Category II, where the respondents take the photos but the researcher analyses them on his or her own, it is important that the photos are of sufficient quality. At a minimum, for example, one needs to be able to see what is going on. In Category IV, this is not as crucial as long as the respondents are able to reflect on the motives and reasons for taking the particular photo. But when respondents are asked to take photos and given free reign for the assignment (it is pointless to ask respondents to take photos if they are given highly detailed instructions regarding the theme), the task can also be perceived as being too vaguely defined, thus rendering the results useless. As an example, people might take photos of friends or colleagues simply because they like them, or because they have to take photos of something. Concrete activities (like meetings or events) are also easier to photograph than more abstract concepts like knowledge sharing or time.

The strength of this approach is that it facilitates our understanding of what preoccupies the respondent in relation to a research topic, rather than defining these themes beforehand, which increases the level of respondent self-representation. As respondent self-representation increases, however, the relation between the researcher and the respondent becomes less asymmetric. Normally the researcher has the power to define what is relevant to investigate, which themes are relevant to touch upon when dealing with a specific research topic, and how the results should be analyzed. When using organizational photography—and the techniques in Category IV in particular—such control becomes less predominant (Carlsson, 2201; Holliday, 2000).

Summing up on the four categories, photos have a different status in each category. In Category I and II, the photos are viewed as *representations of knowledge* that can be interpreted and analyzed. In Category III and IV, the photos are merely *illustrations* intended to prompt reflection and discussion, which in return can be interpreted and analyzed. In the first version, the photos are the goal in themselves, whereas in the second version the photos are only a means to an end.

PHOTOS AND THE RESEARCH PROCESS

Human beings are exposed daily to an enormous amount of visual images, which we process more or less consciously. Whenever we see something, it is in our nature to investigate and try to construct a "story" based on what we see in order to comprehend it (Carlsson, 2001). Within this context, photographs represent a very direct form of visual stimulus. Our attention toward them is perhaps more immediate than most stimuli and might therefore explain our spontaneous desire to explain their content. As Hesily and Levy (1991, p. 269) suggest, "A photograph motivates people to provide a perspective of action, to explain what lies behind the pictures, and to relate to how the frozen moment relates to the reality as they see it."

The use of photos in the research process can be thought of as an attempt to introduce the visual into an otherwise semantically oriented (research) world that is highly preoccupied with words and numbers. There is considerable disagreement among researchers and photographers, however, about the relative power of photos. Proponents argue that photos can literally say more than a thousand words: "Photos and films can say things that not only would require pages and pages of words to describe, but in the end could not be adequately described with words" (Carlsson, 2001, p. 127).

Compared to a mere phrase or quote, which is inevitably "caught" in the language (due to the predominantly fixed and collectively decided meaning of words), a photograph contains a variety of meanings. And as opposed to semantics, visuals like photos, drawings, or even comics are capable of capturing and presenting very complex situations (Carlsson, 2001) in ways that most people can relate to and therefore respond to.

Critics, however, contend that photos only show a particular extract of a particular reality, captured by the subjective eye of the photographer. Buchanan (2001, p. 162), for example, suggests that "The resultant images may reveal more about the photographer than the photographed." From this perspective, photos can be as limited as language in framing a story or presenting a limited version of "what really happened" or "what really is." In other words, photos can include as well as exclude stories and thereby manipulate the viewer.

A third perspective is that photos are neither of the above. In essence, photos are "numb" and the viewer creates the stories that evolve from the photos. Hence, photos will be interpreted differently by different individuals depending on their cultural background and beliefs (Elling Magnus, 2004)

Our position is that photos reflect all three perspectives. Photos can frame a particular meaning, but photos can also be ambiguous. Photos may be a subjective snapshot of a given frame in time, but they can also present complexity in a way that words cannot. And even in those instances where photos are deliberately biased, they still can be very useful. Schwartz, for example, undertook a photographic survey of the North American Waucoma farming community. Schwartz (reported in Pink,

2001, p. 58) saw her photos as representing her "point of view" and uses this idea to "study the range of meaning they [the photographs] held for different members of the community." As Pink (2001, p. 58) points out, Schwartz "made the idea that visual meanings are arbitrary, a key element of her research method." As will be explored later in the chapter, photographs can provoke and stimulate a discussion, which can be very useful when you want respondents to tell you what they think.

The "Good" Research Photo

What actually constitutes a "good research photo," however, is still open to debate. Is it an ambiguous photo that contains a variety of meanings and can be interpreted in numerous ways or is it a framed and subjective photo that clearly demonstrates a certain point of view but can provoke discussion? Ironically, we have only come to discuss this question explicitly after our empirical surveys were finished. The issue does not appear in the research literature and it remains to be explored in depth.

From our perspective, the issue of whether photos represent multiple meanings in themselves or it is the interpreters who create stories ("meanings") around the photos is less important in our approach to organizational photography. Our point is that the *combination* of taking photos *and* asking respondents for their reactions *opens up* the discussion. When trying to understand a cultural or social phenomenon in practice, it is important to find ways of posing questions that *broadens* rather than limits *the range of possible answers*. As mentioned earlier, answers to semantic questions are likely to fall within the framework of the researcher or the boundaries imposed by the question. Respondents rarely say: "I don't think that question is relevant. Instead, why don't you ask me…" When using photos, a visual element is introduced and the way questions are posed is changed, thus opening the opportunity to elicit new insights and ways of seeing the topic under investigation.

Taking Photos

Organizational analysis often benefits from anthropological investigation, where the researcher observes and participates in the daily life of an organization over a certain period of time. Such access, however, is not always possible, and organizations are often resistant to the idea of a researcher observing their everyday life for long periods. There are also times when a researcher might want to include several organizations and the ideal of being present for long periods of time becomes unrealistic.

Consequently, the researcher is often left with such questions as: "Do I know enough about the organization to pose the "right" questions? Are the respondents telling me what there is to know about the topic I'm investigating? Am I missing something? How can I be sure that they actually do what they say they do?" Our own personal experience is that these questions come to mind when you have a superficial relationship with the organization, prompting the feeling that you haven't "seen and heard enough" to make an informed analysis.

Organizational photography can—to some extent—help overcome this feeling, because it provides the researcher with the opportunity to get "under the skin" of the organization. As one walks around taking photos, the researcher also has the chance to talk informally with organizational members. When talking informally to employees or participating in social gatherings, researchers are able to "pick up" things that can supplement or exemplify other kinds of data. This interaction enables researchers to develop their own impression of the organization and its culture instead of just being told by an employee what it is like.

Several researchers point to this fact. Collier and Collier (1986), for example, refer to the camera as a "can opener," and Jorgensen (1991) points to the fact that moving around in the organization taking photographs is an intimate way of collecting data because you move around the organization in a different way: "When taking photographs, a variety of other legitimate ways to have contact with the people being researched become possible compared to using traditional research methods" (p. 72, our translation). This way the camera is not only being used to take pictures, but the photographing process has a double function: (1) to get material that can be of use during later focus group interviews, and (2) to get richer insight into the organization itself, especially in terms of such dynamics as how culture is expressed or how knowledge is shared.

Practical Considerations

Neither of us are expert photographers and we used a small pocket camera with a 120mm zoom. Yet, even when using a relatively simple camera it is important to be familiar with its features and functionality (e.g., light and cutting) and that its physical appearance doesn't make you stand out. Hirshman (in Heisley & Levy, 1991), for example, warns against the potential risk of the camera's appearance that might bring unnecessary attention to the presence of the researcher, which could alter the behavior of the subjects. Heisley and Levy (1991) therefore suggest that one should use as discrete and easily handled equipment as possible. But they also claim that the presence of the camera becomes less intrusive over time, as long as subjects are engaged in their normal surroundings and are able to conduct their activities without constant interaction with the person observing them.

Before we took any photographs in the organizations we studied, we made sure that the employees had received an e-mail informing them about our presence, who we were, what we were doing, and why and how the photos were going to be used. In cases where we didn't have access to the mailing system, we asked our contact person to do it. The idea of informing organizational members stems from Jorgensen (1991), as a way of creating awareness and trust. This is important advice, and our experience indicates that employees who did not receive such notification were far more skeptic and suspicious than those who did.

What "Is" and What "Is Not"

We took roughly 100 photos in each organization, including general photos (e.g., an office landscape) and more detailed photos showing only parts of the larger organization (e.g., photos of a single desk or shelves with documents). When forming the photo series, we found it useful to have several variants of the same motive to choose from, including both general and more detailed and specific pictures. We not only took photos of situations showing knowledge sharing directly (like a meeting, or two employees in a discussion in an office), but also photos where it seemed absent (like an empty hall or walls filled with art). Thus, the photos not only show what is present and therefore evident, but also try to include "what is not." With a digital camera you can easily shoot many more than we did and cut them according to needs.

The issue of "what is not" is also addressed by other researchers in the field. When analyzing video diaries of respondents, Holliday (2000, p. 516) notes that, "Equally important here is not just what is performed, but also what is not performed." Staunaes (1999) even takes the point a step further by arguing that what is not expressed or shown is perhaps even more important than what is. She gives an example of the fact that the children she asked to photograph their daily lives in a refugee camp never photographed adults. Staunaes wondered about this and thought that maybe adults weren't important in their lives, but the contrary was the case—the adults simply didn't want to be photographed.

Organizational Photography and Group-Level Analysis

While organizational photography works very well with individual respondents, as described briefly above, it can also be used to elicit *group photo views*. We have undertaken this approach in four different organizations. This is obviously not sufficient experience to ground the method as a valid and useful research tool. The aim of this chapter, however, is not to convince the reader that we have *the* answer, but rather to explore ways of using photos in organizational research and share our experiences in a way that might make other researchers and practitioners feel inclined to do experiments of their own. Our hope is that others will share their experiences so that a more substantial body of experience and evidence can be built.

In one of our studies, a group of employees was asked to discuss conditions of knowledge sharing in their company based on a series of company photos that were taken by the researchers. We walked around the organization for an entire day, taking photos that we thought were related to knowledge sharing. We took approximately 100 photos in each of the four organizations. We then selected key photos and arranged them into six to eight photo series with four to five photos in each series. While the process used in the selection of motifs will be discussed later, it is important to note that the photo series were not decided beforehand but instead "grew" out of the experience. A group of employees (approximately four in each focus group) were then asked to discuss the topic investigated, drawing from the photo series. This process is accomplished by exposing the focus group to a new series of pictures every 12 minutes, with the researcher remaining silent during the 1½-hour session. Hence, the photos "pose the questions" instead of using a moderator who normally guides a focus group discussion.

The Issue of Subjectivity and Control in Group-Level Analysis

When undertaking group photo views, since there is no interaction between the researcher and the respondents when they discuss and interpret the photos, the process requires photos that are visually strong and poignant. As noted earlier, respondents cannot ask for clarifications of the motifs chosen—and the researcher cannot offer them. Thus, as Buchanan (2001, p. 162) cautions, when selecting photos for such presentations there is a danger that "visually interesting and photogenic images [might be] privileged in favor of less glamorous or less dramatic shots of otherwise significant aspects" of the organization. In our experience, we often chose to include photographs that were visually strong (i.e., clear and interpretable) in favor of photos that did not appear to show as much (but could have still held an interesting point).

As touched upon earlier, the selection of the motifs in the organization and the later selection of the photos that are finally shown can become just as framing and controlling as semantic questions in normal interviews. Hence, the photographing process is a continuing balance between taking photos that are visually strong, photos that pose "open-ended questions," and photos that can "control" the discussion to a certain degree. Such balance, of course, is not easy to achieve, and we do not claim that we have managed this perfectly.

Since photos often show events and artifacts (e.g., meetings, physical surroundings in an organization) rather than processes and concepts (e.g., chatting on the Internet, knowledge sharing in general), the group photo view discussion often runs the risk of remaining at the descriptive, artifact level. Respondents might simply offer casual observations—for instance, "This looks like a nice office, it is very cozy" or "That coffee machine is terrible, I hate the coffee so I never go there"—and leave it at that. In order to avoid this, one should make sure that the photo material also contains motifs that are metonyms that will promote richer discussion (e.g., a picture of a computer screen as a metonym for electronic knowledge systems within the organization).

Although many people are curious about photos and have an urge to "explain them," it is also clear that some people are more easily stimulated by visuals than others and are better at making associations. Some respondents will easily move away from the artifact/denotative level and turn to what the photo(s) represent on a higher level, while others might appear unable to do so. While this tendency might reflect a "personality issue," it could also be that the content of the photos are not sufficiently representative of the daily life of some of the respondents that they are simply *too unfamiliar* with the situation to provide any real insights.

There are also dangers that the researcher might read things into a situation that might be uncalled for. In one of the organizations we studied, for example, we were struck by its long, hideous-looking office corridors that seemed vacuumed from any kind of dynamic. While we initially thought that these photographs reflected an absence of knowledge sharing, when looking at the photos some of the respondents simply replied, "Is this our hallway? Does it really look like that? This must be angled in a strange way ... I often meet colleagues out there."

Despite these problems—photos are subjective and can "manipulate" the situation—they are also excellent vehicles for generating interesting data, as respondents are provoked to tell "the truth" as they see it. At the same time, photographs can help researchers confront their own hypotheses in a very direct way. Because researchers always have more or less explicit hypotheses about the world around them, photographing this world and thereby visualizing what *is seen* (or not seen), such assumptions become more explicit. And when things are explicit, they are much easier to detect and discuss.

Conducting Group Interviews

Besides the photographing process, a core strength of the group photo view is the group discussion. Instead of doing single interviews, the idea behind the group discussion is the same as the purpose of focus groups. As Morgan (1988, p. 9) points out,

> focus groups are basically group interviews, although not in the sense of an alternation between the researcher's questions and the research partici- pants' responses. Instead, the reliance is on interaction within the group, based on topics that are supplied by the researcher, who typically takes the role of the moderator.

When the dialogue takes place between several people, a concurrent exchange of ideas takes place that further stimulates the discussion. Oth- ers' views about the photos prompt alternative interpretations and create a dynamic that can be difficult to create in a single interview. Also, as noted by Morgan (1988), the possibility of observing the interaction *within* the group provides useful information.

Our experience suggests that bringing a group of employees together can create "inside talk" about the organization because the respondents know each other—and the organization. In traditional interviews, respon- dents sometimes "neglect" to tell things because internal affairs seem too complex or too detailed to explain to a "stranger." In the focus group dis- cussion, where employees know each other, this barrier is omitted. The kind of inside talk that the focus group produces is very valuable, espe- cially when investigating knowledge management issues, since you tend to get more information about the organization and you get a richer feel- ing for the internal relations between departments or employee groups that are otherwise difficult or time-consuming to grasp.

The Missing "Why"

While there are obvious advantages to using this type of group-level analysis, there are problems as well. One of the disadvantages of this type of group interview is that the discussion often fails to reveal *why* associa- tions, meanings, and beliefs differ. When respondents use "I think ..." or "I feel that ..." in traditional interviews, the researcher can use prompts (e.g., "Why is that?"; "Why do you feel this way?") to pursue the underly- ing reasons. Since the researcher remains silent in the group photo view discussion, the use of such prompts are not possible—the point is to let the photos "do the talking." While one can hope that the fellow partici- pants pose such questions and challenge each other, a useful option is to urge the discussants to do so before the session begins.

This dilemma is a consequence of the (seemingly) low mediator control in group photo views. There is always a potential risk of the discussion moving away from the research topic on to general issues that are of cur- rent interest to the members of the organization—and that the respon- dents feel an urge to discuss now that they are given the opportunity. The discussion can prove to be very interesting and relevant, but can also prove to be completely irrelevant to the topic under investigation and thus a waste of time.

A related problem is that since photos are open to interpretation some respondents focus on trying to figure out why the researcher is showing a particular photo, in essence trying to "guess" the underlying point of showing the photo. Some respondents may even express their own insecurity, literally asking the researcher what he or she would like them to say.

Finally, it is often presumed that good interview questions will stir the respondent and provoke (new) reflections (Fog, 1998). Photographs, even "good" photos, may not necessarily "pose" sufficiently "disturbing" questions to prompt such reflection and the respondent will only "reply" to the "questions" they feel the pictures pose. This is, of course, also one of the points of using this kind of methodology, but it is important to be aware of what might be "left out," and the realization that questions the respondent does not feel comfortable answering will not be addressed.

Methodological Triangulation

As summarized in Table 10.2, organizational photography has significant potential, but there are some underlying problems with respect to both individual discussions and the group photo view. These problems—including the "missing why" and the "what is not" concerns—lead us to suggest that, while useful, group photo views should never be used exclusively. Rather, this approach should be considered a fruitful supplement to other kinds of data gathering.

In the present study, the interviews were tape-recorded and transcribed, indicating who said what (much like in a movie script) and codes were inserted referring to the photos mentioned in the discussion. The transcriptions from these group interviews were not analyzed in their own right, but used as a part of the total research data comprised of individuals' interviews, notes from management meetings, field notes, organizational publications, and so forth. Also, as a way of compensating for the silence that can occur during photo-session discussion, we found it fruitful to get an idea of how the participants experienced the session and if they felt that the topic discussed had been sufficiently covered (to the best of the participants' knowledge, of course). We therefore posed follow-up questions like:

- What was it like to talk about knowledge sharing this way?
- Did the photos represent knowledge sharing in your company?
- Would you have taken other photos? Like what?
- Do we know by now what there is to know about knowledge sharing in your company?

**Table 10.2. Overview of the Problems and
Potential Involved in Organizational Photography**

	Potential	*Problems*
The Photographing Process	• Facilitates getting "underneath the skin" of the organization • Gives the chance to talk informally with employees • Makes it possible to form your own impression of the organization and its culture • Legitimizes and demystifies the presence of the researcher	• Company security • Raises the issue of confidentiality • The observation guide might lead to "blindness" • The camera's and researchers' presence might alter the behavior of the respondents
The Photo Material	• Contains a multiplicity of meanings • Poses no direct questions, thus increasing the range of possible answers • Makes the familiar unfamiliar • Makes the respondents *tell* rather than *answer* • Can capture and present complex situations • Not only shows what is present and therefore evident, but also makes explicit "what is not"	• The subjective selection of motifs, thus representing the researchers view of reality • Visually interesting and photogenic images are privileged in favor of less glamorous or less dramatic shots of otherwise significant aspects • Photos can be "seducing" or too concrete, leaving limited space for open interpretation • Photos can be too unfamiliar
The Focus Group	• Respondents change from being objects of research to become active *subjects* • The traditional power relation between the researcher and the respondent becomes less asymmetric • The inter-subjectivity facilitates a negotiation between researcher and respondent about the research topic • Provides an "inside talk" between employees that share the same language • The open discussion leaves room for multiple perspectives	• Photos of artifacts lead to discussions of artifacts • Respondents become impatient and answers redundant when the session is too long • Some respondents are better at associating from visual stimuli than others • People respond to questions they think or want the photos to pose-- some are more willing to let their preconceived beliefs be disturbed than others. • The potential risk of the discussion moving away from the research topic • Risk of not getting answers to the "*why's*"

We have had success using group photo views as a way to better comprehend knowledge-sharing processes in specific organizations, using this insight as a stepping-stone to pose more qualified and meaningful questions when interviewing other employees. In other words, to ensure the validity and variation of the data, the use of photography should be part of a larger body of different research methods. Hence we suggest that any of the techniques under the heading organizational photography should be embodied in what Donaldson (2001) refers to as a *multiple-method research strategy* (2001) and Denzin (1970) refers to as *method triangulation*.

The point in triangulating several methods is that the research topic is being analyzed from different angles and thereby generating a more qualified "picture" than when using a single approach. As Denzin (1970, p. 13) argues,

> Concepts and methods open new realms of observation, but concomitantly close others. Ttpwo important consequences follow: if each method leads to different features of empirical reality, then no single method can ever completely capture all the relevant features of that reality; consequently, sociologists must learn to employ multiple methods in the analysis of the same empirical events.

By viewing the same topic through different lenses (from a quantitative as well as a qualitative perspective), researchers are provided with more varied data and reciprocal verification of the different techniques chosen. If one part of the research results stands out remarkably from the other results, it can of course be an empirical curiosity but the contradiction could also be due to methodological weakness. This would be difficult to detect if the research was only based on one particular method.

For example, in one of the four organizations we studied, our data—stemming from a group photo view, several semi-structured interviews, and informal conversations—suggested that the employees were under the impression that knowledge sharing within their own department was very successful while knowledge sharing across departments was poor. But when this finding was questioned and employees were asked to note their daily contacts in a "who speaks to whom and how" scheme, it actually turned out that they had slightly more contacts with people in other departments than in their own. The results of this quantitative survey came as a surprise to the respondents themselves and it gave us an opportunity to start a discussion with them of why the results turned out the way they did.

ORGANIZATIONAL PHOTOGRAPHY IN PERSPECTIVE

The chapter has attempted to illustrate how photographs can be used to stimulate dialogue about knowledge-sharing processes. As part of this process, photos and pictures can also be a way of *materializing the intangible*. Visualizing something as intangible as knowledge is perhaps not something that knowledge-intensive organizations think about, but we propose that it could enhance knowledge sharing as the visual elements function as vehicles for communication. In one of the companies in our study, for example, a participant noted,

> In connection with [a KM project], I had a large colored poster on our door and a lot of our colleagues knocked on the door asking what it meant— "What is it you have here? It sure looks interesting. Can we help, or would you tell us about it?" The effect it had was huge.

In this instance, the visual depiction (picture poster) was helpful in involving other organizational members, facilitating knowledge sharing across a wider group of people.

Manufacturing companies always have showcases or exhibitions of products in public arenas, but in knowledge-intensive companies, where the production is more intangible, this dimension is often neglected. This is unfortunate as material objects do play a part in shaping corporate identity—employees become aware of what goes on in the other departments and it can also be good public relations, providing greater visibility when clients visit the firm.

Hence, photos can be a way to facilitate organizational development and—as Buchanan (2001) explains—help to improve organizational processes. When preparing a slideshow of the patient trail in a hospital and showing it to a group of employees, Buchanan (2001) realized that the slideshow captured the different employee groups dealing with different aspect of the patient trail. Such visualization helped them to realize and better understand what their colleagues in other departments were actually doing. Also, the slideshow made it possible to directly include organizational members in the discussion of both the consequences of the research results and how they might improve the quality and effectiveness of the patient trail process.

Clearly, organizational photography has significant potential as a research technique, but there are a number of methodological issues still to be investigated, ranging from practical issues in the carrying out of the method to more general concerns associated with using visuals in research in general. As suggested in this chapter, photos taken by a researcher should not be viewed as representations of the respondents' world, but rather representations of their world that we, *as researchers*, see it. While letting respondents photograph themselves increases their self-representation, presenting visuals (photos) to respondents also helps them visualize their surroundings and processes. This can also make explicit the presumptions and hypotheses that we, as researchers, inevitably form. Using pictures as part of the research process can facilitate a rich negotiation with respondents about their reality as they see it—a valuable step forward for research in general and knowledge management in particular.

NOTES

1. An earlier version of this chapter was presented as part of the Research Methods Division program at the 2003 Academy of Management meeting in Seattle, Washington.

2. While there are several classic anthropological studies using this method, we haven't found any records of this method in an organizational setting. We have thus chosen to illustrate the category by describing Staunaes's (1999) exciting study of the everyday life of children in a Danish refugee camp.

3. This way of prompting people to talk about themselves and the issue being researched can be traced to psychology, in which visual objects are used as helping devices to make people talk (e.g., the Rorschach test and other kinds of projective testing). In this case, the psychologist has not taken photos him- or herself but uses general photos/fictive images that represent different themes. Some attempts to employ fictive images in organizational research have already been made, for example by Holtham, Ward, and Rosander (2001).

REFERENCES

Banks, M. (2001). *Visual methods in social research*. Beverly Hills, CA: Sage.

Buchanan, D. (2001). The role of photography in organization research: A reengineering case illustration. *Journal of Management Inquiry, 10*(2), 151–164.

Carlsson, B. (2001). Depicting experiences. *Scandinavian Journal of Educational Research, 45*(2), 125–143.

Collier, J., & Collier, M. (1986). *Visual anthropology: Photography as a research method*. Albuquerque: University of New Mexico Press. (Original work published 1913)

Denzin, N. K. (1970). *The research act in sociology*. London: Butterworth.

Donaldson, P. J. (2001). Using photographs to strengthen family planning research. *Family Planning Perspectives, 33*(4), 176–179.

Elling Magnus, I. (2004, May 19–27). Spor (Interview with photographer Joachim Koester). *Weekendavisen*, p. 9.

Fog, J. (1998). *Med samtalen som udgangspunkt*. København: Akademisk Forlag.

Harper, D. (1988). Visual sociology: Expanding sociological vision. *American Sociologist, 19*(1), 54–70.

Heisley, D. D., & Levy, S. J. (1991). Autodriving: A photoelicitation technique. *Journal of Consumer Research, 18*(3), 257–272.

Holliday, R. (2000). We've been framed: Visualising methodology. *Sociological Review, 48*(4), 503–521.

Holtham, C., Ward, V., & Rosander, C. (2001). *Designing spaces for knowledge work: Can the use of fiction help construct new realities?* Paper presented at the Managing Knowledge, Conversations and Critiques Conference, Leicester University, Leicester, UK.

Jorgensen, J. B. (1991). *Organisationsfotografering: Erfaringer, problemer og anvendelsesmuligheder* (COS Forskningsrapport 5/1991). Copenhagen: Copenhagen Business School.

Morgan, D. L. (1988). *Focus groups as qualitative research*. Berkeley, CA: Sage University Paper Series on Qualitative Research.

Petersen, N. J., & Poulfelt, F. (2002). Knowledge management in action: A study of knowledge management in management consultancies. In A. F. Buono (Ed.), *Developing knowledge and value in management consulting* (pp. 33–60). Greenwich: Information Age.

Pink, S. (2001). *Doing visual ethnography*. Beverly Hills, CA: Sage.

Prosser, J. (Ed.). (1998). *Image-based research: A sourcebook for qualitative researchers*. Falmer Press.

Rose, G. (2001). *Visual methodologies: An introduction to the interpretation of visual objects*. Beverly Hills, CA: Sage.

Staunæs, D. (1999). *Transitliv: Andre perspektiver på unge flygtninge*. København: Forlaget Politisk Revy.

Van Leeuwen, T., & Jewitt, C. (2001). *Handbook of visual analysis*. Beverly Hills, CA: Sage.

CHAPTER 11

VIDEO VIEWS OF KNOWING IN ACTION

Analytical Views In Situ in an IT Firm's Development Department[1]

Sisse Siggaard Jensen

This chapter is based on an explorative analysis of a series of *video-views*—in essence, digital video data—in an effort to increase both the awareness of video analysis as a research method (cf. Alrø & Dirckinck-Holmfeld, 1997; Banks, 2001; Christiansen, Jensen, Nielsen, & Orngreen, 2001; Eriksen, 1998; Grimshaw, 2001; Henderson & Jordan, 1994; Jensen, 2001a; Jensen, Olsen, & Mønsted, 2004; Pink, 2001; Suchmann & Trigg, 1991) and the knowledge of reflective practices (Argyris & Schön, 1987, 1996; Brown & Duguid, 2000; Cook & Brown, 1997; Dewey, 1899/1966, 1933, 1938; Schön, 1987; Wenger, 1998) or knowing in action (Goffman, 1986; Gourlay, 2001a, 2001b; Jensen et al., 2004; Latour, 1987, 1991, 1998; Latour & Wolgar, 1979; Pan & Scarbrough, 1994; Stacey, 2001; Tsoukas, 2000; Tsoukas & Hatch, 2001; Tsoukas & Vladimirou, 2001). The term "video-view" is used to generate an association with qualitative interviews rather than video observation, which is the method most com-

Challenges and Issues in Knowledge Management, 249–269

monly associated with video analysis. The main difference is that video observation has objective registration as its ideal, an ideal that, like all ideals, is unreachable. Video-views constitute a qualitative method that acknowledges the close relationship between observation and the observed, and between the recording and the recorded. The relationship between these phenomena is sufficiently "close" that the joint acts—concrete as well as symbolic—constantly interact, as is the case with conversation. The form thus takes on the quality of an open, in-depth research interview.

The chapter describes video-analytical practice in sufficiently concrete terms to exemplify the analytical practice while at the same time forging an initial path "through" the video material. Seen in this light, the explorative analysis is a process in which the purpose of the analysis, its theoretical references, and the empirical material work form an interpretation of knowing and reflective practices. The actual video-views thus constitute empirical data procured for analytical purposes with the aim of describing and understanding reflective practices and knowing in action.

VIDEO-VIEWS ANALYSIS: PREPARING THE CASE STUDY

The case (field of practice) illustrated in this chapter takes place in the development department of a Danish IT company within the e-learning and multimedia businesses. The analysis is focused on questions about the "what and how" of dynamic knowledge processes as they develop as intermediaries between reflection and action (Latour, 1998), between different forms of knowledge (cf. Depres & Chauvel, 2000; Dierkes, Antal, Child, & Nonaka, 2001; Gourlay, 2000, 2001a, 2002; Nonaka & Takeuchi, 1991, 1995; Polanyi, 1958, 1966, 1969; Polanyi & Harry, 1975; Tsoukas, 2001), and between knowledge and learning (Stacey, 2001; Wenger, 1998). These dynamic processes and interplay take place both in time and in the live images of video data. Time plays a key role in these dynamics (Adam, 1990, 1996; Jensen, 2001b) and the researcher's analytical interest is directed toward projection and comprehension of the relationship between knowledge creation and time as it unfolds in practice.

The Setting: The Study Site

The Danish company focused on in this research is located in an area noted for its knowledge-intensive firms, including market research institutes, consulting firms, and nongovernment organizations. As a visual image of the company, it is located on the second and third floors of an office building, with the entrance on the second floor and an internal stairway leading to the third floor. The reception area is at the end of a long corridor, with two well-equipped, glass-walled meeting rooms on the left and four private offices on the right. The sales department is halfway down the corridor, located in an open office with an internal staircase leading up to the production department. The development department, which is where the video-views analysis takes place, is at the end of the corridor. The production department comprises most of the third floor, sharing the space with manuscript writers and the company's IT support. In essence, the company's "face" to the outside world is reflected in the reception area and meeting rooms, while the development department—the company's "brain"—is "out of the way," at the end of the corridor.

The series of video-views in the Danish IT firm started out with test recordings and practical arrangements made in the company's development department (D-department). Since it can be difficult to capture useful video-views, it is important to initially inspect the location of the planned recordings. An underlying capability here might be thought of as the "artist's eye," determining the workstations that will be involved in the recordings, how they will be placed vis-à-vis each other, the possible angles that would provide coverage of the entire department, and so forth. The goal is to obtain a close view of work methods, interactions, and workstations of the individual developers—with attention to such technical factors as light and sound. These two factors have proved to be extremely critical in my video-view work, and they are at the top of my internal checklist used to determine the angle, radius, and movements of the recording. In essence, they "color" the first view of the situation, framing the initial, rough outline of the premises.

Preparing the Case Study: Space and Angle

The video-views process begins by constructing a rough outline of the location, drawing out the space and angles in the area to be recorded. In this case study, the developer group worked in a large common room, lit by eight large windows. Together, the walls and windows constituted "one angle" of the room. The developers had 10 workstations that were spread out along the walls and windows, forming the basic structure of the room. A large table was in the middle of the room, and it was used for group meetings where the individual employees could simply turn their chairs around and "roll" to the meeting.

Angles, radius, and movements are almost predetermined with this layout. In this instance, the video camera could remain stationary in the middle of the room at the meeting desk, where general views of all workstations could be obtained—with the ability to zoom in on the individual developers. While it is relatively easy to move the microphone around so the sound direction can be weighted as needed, as with most settings, the room also allowed for hand-held recordings. Two low book-cases, which subdivided the workstations, served as "support" when close-up work with a hand-held camera[2] was required. An initial glimpse of the location shows excellent conditions for making video-views (see Figure 11.1).

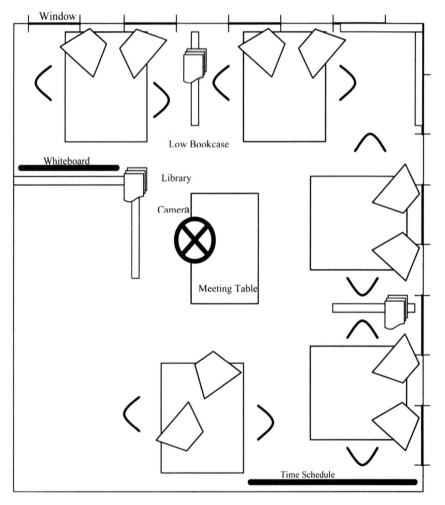

Figure 11.1.   A visual depiction of D-department (based on "Space and Angel" inscriptions).

Preparing the Case List: Actants and Parts

The next step is to prepare a list of the actants that are going to be part of the video-views—including both human and nonhuman actants (Jensen, 2001a; Jensen et al., 2004; Latour, 1991, 1998)—that becomes a "cast list." In this case, the first actants noted on the cast list are the 10 workstations and the employees, including their numerous artifacts. On the surface, there does not appear to be any obvious differences between these items. The 10 workstations, for example, are more or less the same in terms of hardware, equipment, facilities, capacity, and furniture. Similarly, a quick glance at the chairs, desks, or computers does not reveal anything about the department's principal players and parts. Based on observations of interaction patterns, however, it gradually becomes clear that the project manager ("Simon"[3]) sits at one end of the room and Paul, the informal head of the department, is at the other end. A timetable hangs on the wall above the project manager and serves as the unifying medium, capturing the entire project in a synoptic glance. The two principal players are placed at opposite ends of the room, with a full view of the entire room that supports and communicates the joint work processes involved in the project.

Further observation reveals layers beyond the distinction between managers and employees. Gradually, the cast list expands to include "newcomers," "green ones," "the experienced," those who "belong," and those who "just sit there." The newcomers sit at the two darker workstations, away from the windows. One of them "belongs," and although he is new, he is a highly experienced programmer. The second newcomer is from another firm with which the company had just merged. He is now based in the same department, but, at the present time, doesn't belong and is one of those who "just sits" in the department. The other six developers are distributed evenly between "green" and "experienced" developers. The green developers are still studying for medium-length degrees (such as computer science), while the experienced developers have already completed relevant master's-level degrees.

Little by little, the cast list takes shape and literally imposes itself on the room by shaping the researcher's vision and, therefore, the camera's focus. Close observation can also reveal roles beyond those dictated by workplace interactions (e.g., manager–nonmanager, experienced–green). In this case, for example, smoker and non-smoker distinctions were also important to include, especially since smoking took place outside the work area, on the staircase by the emergency exit. Separated from the rest of the department, during smoke breaks a lot of tips, experiences, and references were exchanged—but only among the smokers.

The cast list is largely determined by the interactions between and ways in which the human actors observe and look at each other. Nonhuman elements, however, also enter into the "picture." The D-department, for example, differs significantly from the "upstairs" production floor. The D-department has light, windows, room, comfortable chairs and desks, and excellent facilities for group meetings. These amenities are in short supply in the production department, and it quickly becomes clear that the developers relish this distinction and consider themselves to be the principal players in the company (see Goffman, 1959, 1986; Latour, 1987; Latour & Wolgar, 1979).

The meeting table also plays a leading part in the D-department and is therefore recorded at the same level as the individual workstations. Less prominent but nevertheless important parts are also played by the library, which consists of books and CD-ROMs on the bookcase in the middle of the room next to the meeting table. In this space, the developers share literature of common interest and their programming "bibles." Since this space is where the shared project documentation is found, it also serves as an actant, with a key part to play in the knowledge creation process.

There are two additional principal parts in the story—which are invisible and only emerge after careful observation, discussion, and documentation—time and reflective practices. These parts and their influence differ widely. Time plays an important role for everybody as it impacts everything that goes on in the project and in the company. Deadlines are everywhere and everyone is expected to respond to them. Reflective practices, in contrast, appear to have a different effect as they are only mentioned by a few of the actors. As will be illustrated, however, they still constitute a powerful force in the D-department's knowledge-based practices.

Processing the Data: The Utility of a Registration Card

As a way of adding structure to many hours of video-views, a "registration card" can be useful. This approach summarizes sequences (i.e., recordings that are framed by technical starts and endings) and analytical views (i.e., a beginning and ending of a specific exchange or situation). Using this structured summary, a picture of the widely differing practices in the D-department begins to emerge (see Table 11.1) across pictures where the rhythm of the camera changes between panning and zoom-in, and where the camera is alternately hand-held and placed in a stationary position.

Analyzing the Video-views

While the reflective practices in D-department, as captured in the video-views, take on many different forms, they emphasize analysis as the dominant form of practice. A picture begins to emerge of a literal bee hive of activity. Thorough studies are undertaken among piles of thick

Table 11.1.   Illustrative Summary of Video-recordings based on "Registration Cards" from each of the Recorded Views and Sessions

Friday Morning

Session 1/ Individual Practice/ Analysis
1. Stationary view of 'studies' in corner 1 and 'coding, keyboard, and thought' in corner 2. Tape 1.
2. Hand-held zoom-in and interview with Niklas (D2) about 'work methods.' Tape 1/ Tape 2

Session 2/ Sparring/ Analysis
3. Hand-held zoom-in on 'sparring in the form of joint research and evaluation' between Simon (D3) and John (D9). Tape 2
4. Hand-held panning in the entire D-department. Tape 2.
5. Stationary view of 'coding, keyboard, and thought' in corner 2 and especially Theis (D4). Tape 2
6. Stationary panning on 'studies' in corner 1 and 'coding, keyboard, and thought' in corner 2. Tape 2
7. Hand-held zoom-in on 'sparring in the form of joint research and evaluation' between Simon (D3) and John (D9) in corner 4 at the whiteboard. Tape 2.

Lunch
8. Stationary panning on 'lunch with the screen.' Tape 3

Afternoon

Session 3/ Individual Practice and Sparring / Analysis
9. Stationary view of 'sparring' in the form of neighbor training in corner 2,especially between Theis (D4), Sam (D8), and Simon (3). Tape 3
10. Brief stationary zoom-in on 'individual practice in the form of navigation' with Søren (D7) and 'individual practice in the form of coding' with Thomas (D6). Tape 3
11. Stationary view of 'sparring and neighbor training' in corner 2 with 'the three' from point 9 in focus. Tape 3
12. Brief stationary view of 'individual practice' in corner 3. Tape 3
13. Stationary view of 'individual practice in co-operation' in corner 2 - again 'the three' from point 9 and with brief visits to corner 3 and 1. Tape 3/ Tape 4

Friday Summary
Data include a view of the situation as a whole in the D-department; a view of individual practice in the form of studies and coding where the voice of the keyboard blends in with the thought processes of problem solution; and close up in two hand-held zoom-in situations: (1) an interview with Niklas about his work practices and methods, and (2) cooperation and sparring in the form of joint research and evaluation between Simon and John; a stationary view of individual practice that takes place in close cooperation between 'the three': Simon, Sam. and Theis.

Monday Morning
Session 4/ Monday Meeting and Debriefing / Analysis
NOTE: The server is down. There is hectic activity to solve the problem. Tape 4
14. Stationary view of 'Monday meeting with status and debriefing' and agreements to 'run code in critical review'—interrupted by the staff meeting. Tape 4.
15. Hand-held zoom-in on 'status and debriefing' between Theis (D4), Paul (D10), and Simon (D3). Tape 4 and Tape 5.

(Table continues)

Table 11.1.   Continued

Lunch

Afternoon

Session 5/ Cooperation and Sparring/Analysis

16. Stationary view of 'critical reviews' in corner 4 with Niklas (D2), John (D9), and Thomas (D6). John is running the code. Tape 5/ Tape 6.
17. Stationary view of 'sparring in the form of joint problem solving' between Søren (D7) and Hans (D5). Tape 5/ Tape 6.
18. Stationary view of 'sparring in the form of neighbor training' in corner 3 with Sam (D8) and Simon (D3). Tape 5/ Tape 6.
19. Stationary view of 'briefing' between Hans (D5), Søren (D7), and Theis (D4) across low bookcase. Tape 6.
20. Stationary zoom-in on the project timetable, which shows 'the relationship between time, tasks, people, and thereby competences.' Tape 6.
21. Stationary view of 'sparring in the form of joint research and evaluation' in corner 1 between Niklas (D2) and Thomas (D6). Tape 6.
22. Stationary zoom-in on 'fire-fighting' in corner 2 and 3 with Sam (D8), Søren (D7), and Simon (U3). Tape 6.

Summary:

Data include a view of the 'meeting culture' and the 'male culture' in the D-department; close up in a hand-held zoom-in on 'status and debriefing' between Theis, Paul, the head of the D-department, and Simon, in which Theis explains his coding, which is vital; a view of several different forms of sparring (1) critical reviews between Niklas, John, and Thomas, (2) joint problem solving between Søren and Hans, (3) neighbor training between Simon and Sam, (4) joint research and evaluation between Niklas and Thomas, (5) fire-fighting between Simon and Sam, and 6) a view of briefing between Hans and Theis across the low bookcases. In addition, a view of "time" hanging on the wall, presented in a timetable.

books. Competitors' codes are broken and checked in a search for "short cuts," with all that this entails in terms of the creation of "intelligent methods" (see Dewey, 1933, 1938). Codes are carefully scrutinized, "run" and checked with colleagues. Inexperienced colleagues are closely supervised as they sit next to an experienced colleague who keeps an eye on the screens the "greens" are working on. The developers think aloud, while media simulate computer screen and user interface. Inexperienced colleagues run codes next to experienced colleagues. Codes are run together with experienced colleagues who act as critical reviewers, looking for gaps and problems with the code. Knowledge is constantly shared both between experienced colleagues and across levels so that inexperienced developers can learn from their more experienced colleagues. The screen and the computer are also actants, which participate all the time and everywhere as vehicles for these continuous processes. In essence, a picture begins to emerge of knowledge in action, from when it is created, used, and revised to when it is shared.

The video-views must be studied more than once, as the eye continually searches for high-quality views, both technically (i.e., views where one can hear what is being said and see what is being shown) and analytically (i.e., the content reveals different types of reflective practices). In this subsequent stage, the individual views are examined in the context of different "story boards," a practice referred to as *reversed storyboarding*. As part of the analysis, individual video frames, which are of primary importance to the story being told, are selected through a process of *grabbing frames* (see Jensen, 2001a; Jensen et al., 2004). The storyboards and frames are then integrated to tell stories that capture the exchange and activity—the meaning—of the knowledge base in the organization. Some stories, for example, deal with knowledge-sharing *situations* (Andersen, 1990; Suchmann, 1991). In the process of identifying such situations, the researcher's analytical focus is directed toward several simultaneous *patterns of interaction* (e.g., "beginnings and endings of situations," "temporal organization," the "framing of situations") (Goffman, 1986), the "spatial organization of activity" (e.g., artifacts, media, work stations, architecture), "turntaking," participation structures, and "trouble and repair activity" (see Henderson & Jordan, 1994).

A VIDEO-ODYSSEY IN KNOWING AND THINKING

The cast list in D-department involves several central characters. Theis is a developer and a master of the computer keyboard. You can hear him "think" as his fingers dance across the keyboard and he talks to himself and the screen. He talks expressively, but without coherent language. He appears in agony when problems cannot be immediately solved, or when others have to assist him. Kurt and Niklas, who sit next to Theis, are also lost in their work, but their work consists more of studying and pouring through books. They are absorbed in the books, papers, and folders that surround them, and if you didn't know better, you would think they were students preparing for an exam. Kurt is a "green" newcomer and he reads constantly. He is expected to acquire a lot of knowledge in a relatively short period of time and, thus far, he is only given minor tasks to solve. He is young and his voice is full of admiration and envy when he talks about Theis. As he reflected, "I know maybe 20% of this stuff, so it is overwhelming to sit here and listen to Theis typing away on his keyboard." Theis's command of the keyboard is obviously not music to his ears, rather more of a constant reminder of the gap between his current status and desired goal. Although new, Kurt likes to show that he is not completely green and inexperienced. He advises an employee from "upstairs" (production) who would like tips on how to get started with development and code writing. To illustrate his experience, he shares a code he has written and his pride during the display is quite clear.

Niklas is also new to the department, but he is an older employee who describes himself as the company's "Nestor," an experienced programmer who has been part of the game since the "early days." In contrast to Theis, he is not typing but instead juggling paper, pen, and books. One would almost think that he is a math teacher busy correcting homework, but closer inspection reveals he is a developer busy breaking a competitor's code. In between, Kurt and Niklas exchange a few words, but otherwise the only sound accompanying the concentrated work comes from Theis's keyboard. The room is buzzing and people are working in a highly concentrated manner.

Within this setting and context, the discussion will focus on three central stories gleaned from the video-views. These stories reveal the knowledge creation and sharing processes that exist in the department. As the stories unfold, a picture begins to emerge about the multitude of approaches utilized—from highly intuitive, individualistic approaches to team-based sharing and discussion-oriented interactions.

When the Code Is Broken, It Has to Be Checked[4]

Many different kinds of knowledge come into play in the process of "breaking" a code. Some knowledge is "at hand" in that it is readily available and the programmers can literally "reach out" to the books and guides at their disposal (knowledge as product). Other knowledge, in contrast, has to be created (knowledge as process flow). With respect to breaking codes, the line between knowledge as a product and knowledge as process flow is a dynamic one. From a programmer's perspective, someone else's code is knowledge that exists, but not immediately available. It has to be explored and revealed, in ways that require significant experience in how to "go behind the code" and "work it backward."

Capturing this process with video-views, however, is a challenge. As the camera zooms in on Niklas's papers and his work, for example, he stops his efforts and talks about the need to keep the video data confidential. Although it is obvious that checking a competitor's code is a fairly common practice, it is just as clear that the programmers—for a range of reasons—do not want this process documented.

Niklas works backward, starting with the code as a given, something that exists, and then going behind the code by imagining what it could be "based on," exploring the algorithms and mathematical configurations the competitor utilized. In general, this is an imaginative process, based partly on concrete, explicit, and publicly available knowledge, and partly on personal experience, which comes to light as intuitive knowledge or the "programmer's nose." To a large extent, breaking a code involves a fair amount of guesswork—"What could the competitor possibly have been thinking?" Guesswork, ideas, "suspicions," and working backward are factors that play an interactive part in code breaking—when knowledge has to be found but is not at hand.

The understanding of what the competitor was thinking—how they worked, the general mathematical principles they drew on—is formed in continuous interplay between existing knowledge and the way in which it is used. Ideas are constantly evaluated in light of experience and "nose" in order to allow the many different forms of uncertainty (e.g., guesswork, suspicion) to "coax" the code and create an opportunity for new knowledge to be created. The dynamic oscillation between certainty and uncertainty, between knowledge as a product and a process, between knowledge as something that exists and something to be created, is a permanent feature of the code-breaking dynamic. The desired end result is finding the solid and stable foundation of knowledge that exists "underneath the code."

Observing Niklas at work on the code suggests a combination of intellectual pleasure and aesthetic enjoyment. Preparation, analysis, and detailed design, which are all required before a code can be written, oscillate between code breaking and code checking. Drawing on explicit knowledge in the form of textbooks, referred to as "bibles," is part of the process. On a prominent space on Niklas's desk, for example, is a big, thick book on computer game programming. With roughly 20 years of experience in programming computer games, Niklas proudly notes that this book is among "the best." Watching him, it becomes obvious that using the book as a reference is a "pleasure." His esthetical enjoyment provides insight into how a true code artist can "create" complex chains of events, movements, figures, and environments—captured in the action and fantasy in a computer game—through his or her code. The joy of seeing a simple code solve complex problems is almost like the experience a reader gets when life's complexity is distilled by a poet, especially when relatively little expresses an endless amount. This is the essence of Niklas's challenge—to express as much as possible in a code that is as simple as possible. The video-views capture the pure joy and pride experienced by the programmers when they are able to tell the project manager and other developers that "there won't be much to the code."

To get to something that is simple and reliable is a complex process. It requires many different approaches, detours, secret paths, experience, and a "feeling of certainty'" about one's own knowledge together with the will to venture into uncertainty by guessing, sensing, following suspicions, and, in general, coaxing one's way through sets of uncertain ideas, presumptions, and guesswork. Handling a work practice as complex as this requires well-developed systems and explicit methods blended through dynamic oscillation between situations where there is access to knowledge and information and situations where there is no such access. In these latter situations, where there is no direct access to knowledge and new information, the challenge is one of "digging," delving deeply into what is available. Niklas's system is based on such a process, as the video-views capture both his access to knowledge and information and his being cut off from this access. At work, the focus is on gathering as much "input" as possible, to obtain the knowledge resources and codes that require further scrutiny. At home, in clouds of cigarette smoke, which is not allowed in the department, he shifts to literally digging into what others might have thought, exploring differences and similarities, deducing abstract figures of thought "behind" concrete manifestations, and, in general, following his "nose" for "what appears to have been done in this code."

Thinking the Code Aloud, Together

In another part of the room, Simon (the project manager) and John are consulting each other in front of John's screen. They are sitting together, with their heads "deep into the code" as they attempt to "tackle it together," trying to think through its various components. Yet, they don't converse in the usual sense of the word. Instead, they "think aloud" with each other, using a whiteboard, which represents a type of third party. In their interactions, they express themselves through typing and coding, continually creating a new medium of exchange that "wipes the board clean," forcing their thoughts to come out as conversation as much as code. As part of their exchange, the whiteboard "becomes" part of the computer, as Simon uses it to create a focus for their thoughts and a basis for their conversation.

Simon begins by feeling his way. He tries to find his way into the thoughts behind the codes John has made, asking probing questions that force John to explain his own thoughts. John has to rethink the thoughts he had when he made the codes, and he has to make them explicit. It is quite difficult to remember one's own thoughts in this way. Without perceiving it as such, programmers often "think" through action, "making" a code. Now these ideas, which were not "thought" as much as "made," have to be translated into spoken language. A number of translations and transformations come into play in such an "exercise." While it appears to be relatively simple on the surface, an underlying question is the extent to which it is possible to think the same thoughts twice. The mere fact that they have been thought creates new conditions for the thoughts that are being rethought. In this instance, for example, John's rethinking of his codes creates many more questions than answers. The exercise is nevertheless a prerequisite for thinking through the logic of the code, and the initial conversation quickly progresses to a joint evaluation of the possible consequences of different approaches.

Two particular modes of thinking are involved in the exchange between Simon and John. While these two modes typically blur in practice, it is useful to examine them separately, as each momentarily dominates from time to time. The first appears as a *thought process* where each developer in turn tries to understand the other's thoughts. One thought follows the other; they proceed side by side until a given moment when a certain thought causes the developers to bring the thought and its consequences out in the open. At this point, they both stop and "honor" the direction of their thoughts. It may be an idea that appears to solve a problem, or the discovery that an imagined procedure doesn't work after all. In this case, the knowledge odyssey in the thoughts of Simon and John takes the shape of a "what if" game. Simon tries to follow John's examples of codes and the thoughts behind them. He then points out a problem that John didn't see or know how to resolve, but toward the end of the exchange we see glimpses of a conceptual breakthrough in both developers.

At first Simon tries to follow John's thought processes and understand his examples. When they reach an impasse, however, they turn to more of a dialogue in which they shift between "translating'" each other's thoughts to "thinking through" each other's thoughts together—and in this particular example, rejecting their initial train of thought as the consequences of their thinking are revealed. In this mode, Simon and John begin to *think aloud together.* John starts a thought process, which Simon follows and John continues. The conceptual breakthrough doesn't take place, however, until their thinking takes a new turn and new ideas are "born." It is as if the thoughts suddenly materialize, literally staring both of them in the face as the code "appears" on the whiteboard. Simon constantly draws the thoughts and thought processes on the board, drawing the path taken by their thoughts and their contexts and consequences. The diagrammatic flow, which serves as a key part of their communication, creates a common direction for the developers' thoughts. In essence, they have created a shared view of the situation.

By continuing to follow the two developers, we get a closer look at how their thought processes generate ideas and conclusions in each other's minds. At first they progress side by side, but as one of them "accelerates" to a solution the other tries to dismantle it. They seem to take turns pushing and simultaneously trying to help the other. It is amazing how easily they follow each other's thoughts. It is as if they share a world where everything is implied, and in most instances, these exchanges lead to agreement and resolution.

Debriefing the Code

A key point in the knowledge creation process is when the code is presented and "debriefed." Several people are typically present when a code is debriefed, a lesson the company learned through an earlier experience when an important code was "stuck in the head of a top developer" and his knowledge was not shared with the rest of the department. Since a code is highly personal, implicit, and silent, and it is only "expressed" when it is running, difficulties can quickly arise if the code doesn't work as intended—especially if others in the department do not understand how the code was constructed. As the company's experience suggests, unless these debriefings are held, it becomes impossible to plan and estimate work load, time demands, and personnel requirements. From a knowledge-sharing perspective, the thought processes behind the code have to be thought through as a group, which allows the other programmers to follow, understand, and challenge the process as needed.

In debriefing the code, the code's creator (Paul), top developer (Theis), and project manager (Simon) all have a role to play. The code has to be brought to light, and as Paul explains the code, Simon, on the sideline, challenges the code through the eyes of a user. Paul continues to explain the code with obvious pride and joy; he listens and appears to be open-minded through the exchange. Each player seems to trust his own understanding of the debriefing and the only thing made explicit is when the code is amended.

This knowledge sharing and recreating process requires experience and insight to understand the code and how it was created, especially if the group will be able to see the possibilities for optimizing the code, making it simpler and more elegant and discovering its pitfalls. Paul, Theis, and Simon sit together, three strong in front of the code, in an effort to better understand its thought processes and discovery. The code is the obvious center of the debriefing and the computer screen flickers while Theis points and explains how the thought processes behind the data model and structure the code.

As evidenced by the video-views, the explanations of the code are very expressive. The code is visualized using body language, which constantly gives shape and direction to the account. The language of the body becomes an integrated part of the expression of thought, almost as if the developers' hands shape their thoughts and the code serves as a stage for the visualization process. Theis's comments are accompanied by acknowledgments from Paul, who nods and says yes as Simon listens attentively. Several times the code is confirmed when Paul finishes off Theis's sentences. He thinks together with and across Theis's account and its underlying thoughts and coding. Theis does the same when Paul comments on his code. He then thinks Paul's thoughts through. In that way, the two developers constantly create and recreate each other's thoughts, leading to mutual understanding. Simon also participates actively in the debriefing process, especially in the way that he "sees" the code through the eyes of the user.

The debriefing is interrupted halfway through because Simon (the project manager) has to deal with other issues. His departure changes the form of the debriefing, as Paul shifts the conversation toward system facilities and upcoming coding. When Simon returns, the focus also returns to debriefing the code, but now with an even greater emphasis on challenging the code. In this process, the analysis shifts between the code, potential problems, and possible solutions as the developers work as a group. Theis takes notes only once during the entire debriefing process, when a new user problem is discovered. Otherwise, he appears to keep all the consequences of the debriefing in his head. A few times he mentions his doubts and concerns, but they are not followed up. In one case, Theis asks Paul if they can code together, and while Paul is obliging, he vaguely responds, "In a few weeks." It appears that Paul would rather code alone, only meeting when it is necessary to debrief the other key developers.

CONCLUSION

For the developers on the D-team, there is no doubt that knowledge is seen as being able to "code." This knowledge implies not only knowing examples of good codes, but also the ability to make the code "come alive" to create a multitude of possible actions and meanings in software-based functionality and experiences. In isolation, the ability to code, in and of itself, is not of much use. The developers' knowledge only becomes truly useful in the context of the project at hand. In the D-department, the ultimate proof of knowledge has a concrete expression—the code either works or it doesn't work. The code thus becomes both a symbolic construction of creativity and imagination and an action item in that the code "can be run," providing proof of its functionality.

The D-department's knowledge is tied to practice through the creative processes of coding. This knowledge base exists in many forms: explicit knowledge in the form of books, "bibles," and documentation of the code, and tacit knowledge in the form of the thoughts and thought processes underlying the code. The ability to "quote"' examples of codes (explicit knowledge), without the ability to turn those codes into practice (tacit knowledge), is obviously of limited relevance. At the same time, a potentially less obvious implication is that the ability to code without knowing why and how (tacit knowledge) is of limited organizational use without the ability to explain and document the code (explicit knowledge). If the code only exists as personal and silent ability, organizations are vulnerable in the sense that others lack the understanding of the code and its thought processes. This problem becomes increasingly serious with increasing complexity, when the code becomes difficult to handle without being made explicit in shared practice. As the D-department's early experience revealed, such realization and the resulting sharing of this knowledge must be built into professional practice.

Knowledge exists both inside and outside of its context. As illustrated by the knowledge-creating and -sharing processes in D-department, explicit knowledge goes hand in hand with intuitive knowledge—in essence, certain knowledge with uncertain knowledge. In other words, the many different forms of knowledge continuously merge in dynamic processes; they unfold as variations of simple themes as knowledge constantly undergoes transformations and translations. Knowledge that comes from the *outside* in the shape of existing code must still be transformed and translated to knowledge that is *inside*. Knowledge that exists *out of context* in "bibles" and documents must be brought *into context* and given life through shared experiences and programmer "nose" and intuition. In the video-views of D-department, the observer's eye gets close to these various forms of knowledge, as they unfold and merge in practice. Through video-views, the observer's eye is able to focus on dynamic knowledge processes in practice. This approach helps to identify and understand the chains or spirals of translations and combinations that constantly arise between knowledge that exists and knowledge that is being created, when knowing is in action. The resulting analysis, which is focused on knowledge as dynamic processes, also reveals the different relationships between time and place on which these dynamics depend.

The D-department "runs code" every Monday so that abstract knowledge and practical ability can merge in varying movements, translations, and combinations. This is the time when they take stock of each developer's coding and of the department as a whole. As captured by the video-views, the practices of the department are reflected in the contours of various *knowledge zones*. These knowledge zones are part of a social universe much more than they are part of any action plan or job description. They are not "written into"' the equipment and facilities of the room, but rather emerge from and are created in the reciprocal glances of the developers through their mutual observation. The ways they look at each other create, shape, and reshape the contours of these knowledge zones and play a major role in practice. The video-views reveal these zones through observations that the code is run differently *in* the different zones and *between* the zones. In this way, they form the basis of learning and knowledge sharing in the D-department's practice community.

Organizational members operate at various levels of these knowledge zones, from central participants to literally existing on the periphery. Kurt, who is one of the D-department's members, for example, does not participate in running the code. He sits in the outer periphery of the department, absorbing its style, atmosphere, and tone while studying to become a developer. His eye is purposefully focused inward, toward the center of the department and its inner circles. He is not part of the knowledge creation and sharing process, at least at this point in his career. Other members, such as Sam, run the code, but typically do so next to one of the experienced developers, such as Theis or Paul, so that he can help if the problems become insurmountable. Supervision and support are needed, and in this way Sam and Theis participate in a kind of neighbor training. As described in the previous vignette, Niklas works intensely on researching, explaining, and documenting the code. He is part of the innermost circle, but not in the center of the knowledge zone.

Top developers, such as Paul and Theis, and the project manager (Simon) are at the knowledge zone's center. They appear to enjoy undisputed authority in the department based on their expertise, hard-earned experience, and "nose." The creative talent and tacit knowledge for making a simple and systematical code place Paul and Theis in the inner center of the knowledge zones. As project manager, Simon is faced with the challenge of getting the code "out of their heads and bodies," translating it into explicit knowledge for the organization. The ability to document a code and think it through with others, making it an explicit part of the shared knowledge in the D-team, is at the center of the knowledge zones. While the D-department was originally based on the ideal of the developer's "natural gift," through reflective practices it attempts to systematically capture that tacit knowledge.

There appears, however, to be walls separating the D-department's complex systems of knowledge zones and reflective practices from the rest of the company. The coding goes hand in hand with the expertise of the specialist—the artist, the musician with refined techniques—and "intelligent" work methods and reflective strategies. At the organizational level, however, projects, with their timetables, deadlines, and budgets, seem to operate very differently. The video-views suggest that D-department's reflective practices are only found within its knowledge zones, especially in contrast to those situations where the D-department operates as part of the company as a whole. In this way, the D-department's system of knowledge zones is "closed" unto itself, rather than an integrative knowledge strategy that applies to the company as a whole.

Studying knowledge sharing through video-views enables the researcher to capture phenomena and interplay otherwise easily overlooked, such as the mutual *reverberating of thoughts* in the living moments of activity and the social universes created in the *reciprocal glances* of the developers through their mutual observation and interactions in the department's knowledge zones. Furthermore, the researcher can "see" how the process of coding is loaded with *feelings* of pride and joy, and the key role played by *intuition* in the developer's otherwise systematic and explicit working methods becomes obvious. Finally, as illustrated by the video-views in this case study, this approach can make substantial contributions to the visualization of the micro-moments of *change and variation* in knowledge sharing. Even in situations where the developers present and review existing codes, the video-views show that knowledge sharing is not a process of mutual "transfer" or "copying" of knowledge. Rather, knowledge sharing is part of a dynamic process in which new knowledge (e.g., coding) is created, even if only in small variations.

Time also plays a key role in these dynamics, and video-views enable the researcher to capture the dynamics of the temporal organization and the rhythms of knowledge sharing. In this way, researchers can combine visual documentation with temporal organization to get a rich picture and multifaceted understanding of the complexities of knowledge sharing. The video-views method holds great promise in helping us better understand knowing in action, providing researchers with insights into the knowledge creation and sharing process that will have utility for both theory and practice.

NOTES

1. This chapter is based on a LOK Working Paper (8) at the Copenhagen Business School.
2. Placement of the microphone and where sounds take place can limit how close you can get with a stationary camera. For hand-held recordings, I typically use the camera's built-in microphone.
3. Pseudonyms are used for all the participants (actors) in the case.
4. A useful way to document video-views stories is to note the time codes when the material was taped. This story, for example, was recorded on Tape_1 time code [00.12.49 to 00:20:29] and Tape_2 time code [00:00:00 to 00:16:14].

REFERENCES

Adam, B. (1990). *Time and social theory*. Cambridge, UK: Polity Press.

Adam, B. (1996). *Time in social context*. Cambridge, UK: Polity Press.

Alrø, H., & Dirckinck-Holmfeld, L. (Eds.). (1997). *Videoobservation*. Aalborg: Aalborg Universitetsforlag.

Andersen, P. B. (1990). *A theory of computer semiotics* (Cambridge Series on Human–Computer Interaction). Cambridge, UK: Cambridge University Press.

Argyris, C., & Schön, D. A. (1987). *Theory in practice: Increasing professional effectiveness*. San Francisco: Jossey-Bass.

Argyris, C., & Schön, D. A. (1996). *Organizational learning II: Theory, method and practice*. Reading, MA: Addison-Wesley.

Banks, M. (2001). *Visual methods in social research*. London: Sage.

Brown, J. S., & Duguid, P. (2000). Mysteries of the region: Knowledge dynamics in Silicon Valley. In C. M. Lee, W. F. Miller, M. G. Hancock, & H. S. Rowen (Eds.), *The Silicon Valley edge: A habitat for innovation and entrepreneurship* (pp. 16–39). Stanford, CA: Stanford University Press.

Christiansen, E., Jensen, S. S., Nielsen, J., & Orngreen. R. (2001). Learning happens: Rethinking video analysis. In L. Dirckinck-Holmfeld (Ed.), *Learning in virtual environments* (pp. 310–339). Frederiksberg: Samfundslitteratur.

Cook, S. D. N., & Brown, J. S. (1997, August). *Bridging epistemologies: The generative dance between organizational knowledge and organizational Knowing*. Paper presented at the Conference on Path Creation and Path Dependency. Copenhagen, Denmark.

Depres, C., & Chauvel, D. (Eds.). (2000). *Knowledge horizons*. Oxford: Butterworth-Heinemann.

Dewey, J. (1933). *How we think: A restatement of the relation of reflective thinking to the educative process*. Boston: D.C. Heath and Company.

Dewey, J. (1938). *Experience and education*. New York: Kappa Lecture Series, Collier Books.

Dewey, J. (1966). *Lectures in the philosophy of education*. New York: Random House. (Original work published 1899)

Dierkes, M., Antal, A., Child, J., & Nonaka, I. (Eds.). (2001). *Handbook of organizational learning and knowledge*. Oxford: Oxford University Press.

Eriksen, S. (1998). *Knowing and the art of IT management: An inquiry into work practice in one-stop shops*. Unpublished doctoral dissertation, Ronneby Högskola, Ronneby, Sweden.

Goffman, E. (1959). *The presentation of self in everyday Life*. New York: Anchor.

Goffman, E. (1986). *Frame analysis: An essay on the organization of experience*. Boston: Northeastern University Press.

Gourlay, S. (2000, September). *On some cracks in the "engine" of knowledge-creation: A conceptual critique of Nonaka & Takeuchi's (1995) model*. Paper presented at the British Academy of Management Conference, Edinburgh.

Gourlay, S. (2001a, July). *Getting from A to B: On the question of knowledge transfer.* Paper presented at the European Group for Organizational Studies, Lyon.

Gourlay, S. (2001b, October). *Situated cognition and knowledge: A contribution towards conceptual clarity for knowledge management*. Paper presented at the eighth International Symposium on the Management of Corporate and Industrial Knowledge, Compiégne, France.

Gourlay, S. (2002). *Tacit knowledge, tacit knowing or behaving?* Unpublished paper.

Grimshaw, A. (2001). *The ethnographer's eye: Ways of seeing in anthropology*. Cambridge, UK: Cambridge University Press.

Henderson, A., & Jordan, B. (1994). *Interaction analysis: Foundations and practice*. Unpublished working paper from Xerox Palo Alto Research Institute & Institute for Research on Learning.

Jensen, S. S. (2001a). *De digitale delegater: Tekst og tanke i netuddannelse—en afhandling om hyperlinks i refleksiv praksis, der er face-to-interface. (Digital delegates: Text and thought in networked learning—a dissertation on hyperlinks in reflective practices when learning is face-to-interface)*. København: Multivers.

Jensen, S. S. (2001b, November). *Kairic rhythmicity in the Turing-Galaxy*. Paper presented at the International Conference on Timing and Spacing: Rethinking Globalization and Standardization, Palermo.

Jensen, S. S., Olsen, S. F., & Mønsted, M. (2004). *Viden, ledelse og kommunikation. (Knowledge, management and communication)*. Frederiksberg: Samfundslitteratur.

Latour, B. (1987). *Science in action: How to follow scientists and engineers through society*. Cambridge, MA: Harvard University Press.

Latour, B. (1991). Technology is society made durable. In J. Law (Ed.), *A sociology of monsters: Essays on power, technology and domination* (Sociological Review Monograph, no. 38). London: Routledge.

Latour, B. (1998). *Artefaktens återkomst: Ett möte mellan organisationsteori och tingens sociologi*. Studier i företagsekonomi 5. Nerenius & Santérus Förlag.

Latour, B., & Wolgar, S. (1979). *Laboratory life: The social construction of scientific facts*. Los Angeles: Sage.

Nonaka, I. (1991). The knowledge creating company. *Harvard Business Review*, pp. 91–104.

Nonaka, I., & Takeuchi, H. (1995). *The knowledge creating company: How Japanese companies create the dynamics of innovation*. Oxford: Oxford University press.

Pan, S. L., & Scarbrough, H. (1998). A socio-technical view of knowledge-sharing at Buckman Laboratories. *Journal of Knowledge Management, 2*(1), 55–66.

Pink, S. (2001). *Doing visual ethnography*. London. Sage.

Polanyi, M. (1958). *Personal knowledge: Towards a post-critical philosophy*. Chicago: University of Chicago Press.

Polanyi, M. (1966). *The tacit dimension*. Garden City, NY: Doubleday.

Polanyi, M. (1969). *Knowing and being: Essays* (M. Grene, Ed.). Chicago: University of Chicago Press.

Polanyi, M., & Harry P. (1975). *Meaning*. Chicago: University of Chicago Press.

Schön, D. (1987). *Educating the reflective practitioner*. San Francisco: Jossey-Bass.

Stacey, R. (2001). *Complex responsive processes in organizations: Learning and knowledge creation*. New York: Routledge.

Suchmann, L. (1991). *Plans and situated actions—the problem of human–machine communication*. Cambridge, UK: Cambridge University Press.

Suchmann, L., & Trigg, R. (1991). Understanding practice: Video as a medium for reflection and design. In J. Greenbaum & M. Kyng (Eds.), *Design at work: Cooperative design of computer systems* (pp. 65–91). Hillsdale, NJ: Erlbaum.

Tsoukas, H. (2000). Knowledge as action, organization as theory. Reflections on organizational knowledge. *Emergence, 2*(4), 104–112.

Tsoukas, H. (2001). The firm as a distributed knowledge system: A constructionist approach. *Strategic Management Journal, 17*(9), 11–25.

Tsoukas, H., & Hatch, M. J. (2001). Complex thinking, complex practice: The case for a narrative approach to organizational complexity. *Human Relations, 54*(8), 979–1013.

Tsoukas, H., & Vladimirou, E. (2001). What is organizational knowledge? *Journal of Management Studies, 38*(7), 973–993.

Wenger, E. (1998). *Communities of practice: Learning in doing. Social, cognitive and computational perspectives.* Cambridge, UK: Cambridge University Press.

CHAPTER 12

COMPLEX PROJECT MANAGEMENT IN SMALL HIGH-TECHNOLOGY FIRMS

Small Firms as Learning Models?

Mette Mønsted

The perspective of the chapter is to illustrate the complexity of project management by exploring levels of interactive dependency and interrelational knowledge in small high-technology firms. The problems handled by managers in these firms can also provide insight into the difficulties faced by units within larger companies, such as different profit centers, that have many features similar to smaller firms. While the management of complexity and resources outside formal control is an integral feature of small firms, it is increasingly characteristic of the challenge faced by many managers in larger firms as well.

Programmed project management tools are, in many ways, based on complex, modular large systems (Langlois & Robertson, 1992), where the individual functions are well known. They are often analyzed in terms of a well-defined Tayloristic division of labor, with clear-cut separated tasks and independent modules to be combined afterward (Simon, 1962). As a

Challenges and Issues in Knowledge Management, 271–289

way of exploring the complexities involved in project management activities, therefore, the chapter goes beyond such programmed contexts, focusing on projects in information technology (IT) and research and development–based (R&D) organizations, where the whole is difficult to reduce to such a clear-cut division of labor. The interdependency in these firms adds to the complexity of subdividing tasks, and regular communication becomes essential, especially since knowledge workers are typically loosely coupled (Orton & Weick, 1990; Weick, 1979).

Some of these processes may be difficult to capture in large firms as they are often "hidden" within the organization (Mønsted, 2004). The premise of this chapter is that complexity in small firms, especially in chaotic circumstances, is increasingly characteristic of the challenges in larger firms due to their increasing complexity and mutual dependency of work tasks.

Small high-tech firms do not usually have the chance to plan in detail or implement in a linear project-management style. They have to survive and thrive on chaos and complexity, as they do not control the context, the customer, or technological developments. A larger number of externalities have to be handled by the manager than is the case in more specialized functions in large firms. In small IT firms, for example, the ability to persuade customers about expertise, to create credibility, and sell ideas is fundamental for their survival. The value of the solution is seen only if it works afterward in the application, a dominant feature of service-related production (Normann, 2000). Yet, since developers in these smaller firms rarely have the requisite skills to persuade customers, a challenge is to capture these skills from other staff of the company to help explain the solution's applicability.

Knowledge workers are viewed as highly educated professionals (see Alvesson, 2001, p. 863; Davenport & Prusak, 1998; Newell, Robertson, Scarborough, & Swan, 2002). Knowledge workers in nonstandard settings, who are asked to innovate, analyze, and reflect on their own—literally independent from colleagues—constitute a special group, with an emphasis on autonomy and authority of their expert skills. Those knowledge professionals with more routinized work may act on the basis of existing knowledge, as would be the case with lawyers, some engineers, and architects. As professionals, knowledge workers in these fields must also draw on their expertise, insights, and skills as needed, but the group of knowledge workers who independently exploit and explore new knowledge are faced with more demanding challenges. For example, knowledge workers in IT development face challenges in handling the embedded uncertainty and unpredictability in innovation. As a result, this requires the capacity to create meaning in dialogue—in essence, creating knowledge through the learning in dialogue (Stacey, 2001), embracing entrepreneurship, and renewing processes. These skills also include the capacity to evaluate relevance and the potential of knowledge. The ambitions of managers and knowledge workers may not be the same, however, as R&D or consultancy projects may "slide away" and expand to "interesting related issues" in an entrepreneurial fashion. While this may serve as motivation for knowledge workers, it takes more time and resources than initially planned by managers.

A related problem is that skill requirements and specific needed competencies in many knowledge firms are hard to define in terms of educational competence (as with consultancy and IT programmers), and experienced-based learning plays an important role. The autonomy of knowledge workers makes it difficult for managers to define what is relevant, interesting, and necessary, and it is hard to control and judge individuals who are outside the manager's profession or community of practice. Moreover, since these skills may be quite difficult to evaluate, knowledge-intensive firms are seen as systems of persuasion (Alvesson, 2001), where knowledge workers have to legitimize their skills and competence through problem solving and accomplishing tasks, and persuading other, related experts. The role of persuasion becomes even more important across different fields of expertise, as signals to experts within the same field are relatively easy to communicate. Across complementary fields of expertise, it is more difficult to evaluate the signs and level of expertise at the interfaces, especially in a loosely coupled system. The system perspective here is close to the perception of creating a system of organizational knowledge, the "capability of members of an organization to draw distinctions in process of carrying out their work by enacting sets of generalizations" (Tsoukas & Vladimirou, 2001, p. 973).

The two cases presented in this chapter—a small IT firm examined through interviews and video analysis[1] and a R&D engineering company in the energy sector—are intended to illustrate a number of problems and dilemmas. The cases are used to analyze extreme forms of uncertainty and complexity, which create management challenges in knowledge-based firms, and the concomitant ramifications for project management initiatives. While a limitation is that the cases could be seen as covering extreme entrepreneurial situations, they are intended as models for illuminating problems in larger firms. Within this context, project management is viewed as a balanced negotiation between partners and their colleagues, a perspective that illuminates new challenges for managers in complex knowledge-based organizations. The focus is on communication and knowledge sharing, as well as different forms of negotiated management with self-managed knowledge workers.

COMPLEXITY, INTERDEPENDENCY, AND MODULARITY

System complexity has been a long-term concern for both organization theorists and natural scientists. As systems become more complex, concomitant demands for and pressures on organization and their management emerge. In identifying such systems, Simon (2003 [1962], p. 16) noted that:

> by a complex system I mean one made up of a large number of parts that interact in a non-simple way. In such systems the whole is more than the sum of the parts in the weak, not in an ultimate, metaphysical sense, but in the important pragmatic sense that, given the properties of the parts and laws of their interaction, it is not a trivial matter to infer the properties of the whole.

The initial focus on complexity was its architecture—its structure and how that structure could be created—though concern was also placed on definitions and classifications related to process descriptions. The concept was further developed by Weick (1979, 1995), with an emphasis on loosely coupled systems that change the basic premises of a simple division of labor.

The issues of complexity and decision making have been further examined by Garud, Nayyar, and Shapira (1997) in their volume on technological foresight, looking at high levels of uncertainty when the knowledge necessary for evaluating technology is not available. Similarly, Garud and Kumaraswamy (2003) explore management demands in modular production and the creation of "decomposability" to increase flexibility and limit interdependency, which is directly related to the need for communication and coordination.

Knowledge-based organizations faced with innovation and development problems have to cope with many different strategies of exchanging knowledge and creating meaning before it becomes knowledge. Small firms dealing with R&D have to handle internal complexity and communicate with specialized staff, both inside and outside the firm, customers, and partners in other firms. They have to develop an entrepreneurial leadership and communication style in order to survive. Analyses of small firms handling these types of project management activities under high levels of uncertainty and rapidly changing conditions can help us to understand some of the challenges in larger knowledge-based firms. They also challenge the theory of linear and modular project management (Brunsson, 2002; Christensen & Kreiner, 1991).

These challenges become quite obvious, especially when many projects are dependent on expert knowledge from different disciplines and people have to create a common platform of communication. The underlying dynamics, however, are not always clear. As Stacey suggests, while the "plans never [seem to] work, ... the problems are solved anyway."[2] The question, of course, is how are these issues resolved? What influences people to "make it anyway"? How do people transition from set plans to communication-led mutual adjustment? Stacy's (2001) work focuses on the larger context and action possibilities necessary to adapt to external change, and changes the focus from classical plans and structures *for* people to action and communication *between* engaged people.

An Entrepreneurial IT Firm: Complexity and Project Management

Managing developers and scientists requires the recognition of individual creative knowledge workers, and observing how managers at different levels try to understand what individual developers actually do and how their efforts can be best utilized in joint projects points to a number of concerns. An underlying problem is that attempts at a planned division of labor presupposes that the work task is known, that it can be delimitated and specified for all involved, and that the individual parts are not creatively changed. In innovation and most IT projects in their early stages, however, a lack of apparent inertia challenges management as coordination efforts on the boundary of knowledge often fall short of what is needed.

The asymmetric knowledge vis-à-vis managers demands sufficient learning-spaces to communicate the content of the work, in an effort to coordinate the consequences for other organizational members. While the process of debriefing existing staff may take a lot of time, it is the foundation for transferring both information and sufficient knowledge to enable organizational members to act and work along with their colleagues (e.g., other programmers).

Observing interactions in the IT firm (Jensen & Mønsted, 2001a, 2001b), for example, it becomes apparent that, even in situations without immediate crisis, the project manager has to make an ongoing effort at regular intervals to debrief the developers:

A video-scene shows the project manager, who tries to find out what the programmer has been doing. They start talking, leaning over a piece of paper. Then the project manager goes to the whiteboard and starts explaining how he interprets what the programmer is saying (mumbling). The project manager questions and interprets the answers. After a while they begin to "think together" on possible solutions and interpretations.

The scene illustrates some of the problems of communication and translating codes by the programmer, who cannot formulate in words what he is doing or the rationale underlying his decisions. The whiteboard serves as a "boundary object" (Star, 1989), a means to communicate and translate the part of tacit knowledge that is routine and self-evident (to the programmer) in a way that the project manager can understand it. The project manager uses the drawings and codes to create a dialogue for understanding. The insight and understanding—the knowledge—of the knowledge worker are thus not in a form that can easily be explained, as also seen in tacit knowledge in other scientific work (Collins, 2001).

Insights into what is necessary to communicate to create understanding and to make explicit what is evident for the programmer suggest a highly complex debriefing process. The project manager needs the information, not only to give feedback to the programmer, but also to coordinate with other staff working on other parts of the program. Managing this type of division of labor demands that either the manager or the team knows the task well enough to be able to create overlapping knowledge to handle boundaries between the different parts of the program. The complexity of the tasks makes simple knowledge management impossible and may require a lot of valuable time in an efficiency production perspective. Knowledge is tied to the people and the actions involved, as well as to the communication process (see also Stacey, 2001).

An observation of another debriefing process points to similar problems. In this instance, one of the "talented" young programmers is having difficulty talking about what he does. In addition to the project manager, the debriefing effort also involves a senior programmer, who is one of the owners. In this scene, the young "prima donna" cannot formulate into words what he is doing in a way that is understandable for the senior project manager, who has strong programming skills. The other "star" has to participate in the debriefing to help translate, and follows up with supplementary questions to create a shared interpretation of the codes and consequences and the decisions underlying the program. By being creative in developing solutions to the segment of codes, the young programmer is, in effect, also making decisions for other segments of the program. The project manager has to stress implementation considerations and the consequences of choices for applicability, rather than the aesthetic codes per se.

In both scenes, the ability of the programmers to put into words what the codes mean and how they link to other parts of the program and application work is rather limited. In this case, it involves a totally different language and culture, and the translation to explain meanings and interpretations becomes important as a part of the joint development in creating organizational knowledge. "Beautiful codes" are not the purpose of the firm. Codes have to be used, and the young talent often has to be reminded about end users. Ultimately, the young "prima donna" puts a Post-it note on his computer screen—*"Remember user."* The manager's dilemma is captured between the programmers' need to "play" at the forefront of their craft and the need to only do what is necessary to make price-competitive products. Entrepreneurial and innovative processes have to be related to applications, rather than serve as inventions for their own purpose.

These scenes also illustrate some of the fundamental problems involved between *what a firm knows* and *who knows what* in a firm. Although this case is based on a very small firm, the boundaries between the groups of people are very similar to the boundaries between communities of practice. The problem is tied to individual learning and the way(s) in which it can become organizational knowledge (Tsoukas & Vladimirou, 2001). It is tempting, of course, to go into a discussion of transforming tacit to explicit knowledge (Nonaka & Takeuchi, 1995), or translating one form of explicit knowledge in the form of codes to another form of explicit knowledge in the form of an explanation of what is achieved and the purpose of the codes. Such translation, however, is not based on the same perception of tacit knowledge as in Nonaka and Takeuchi's (1995) framework, but refers to a more fluid process, focusing on communication and learning across communities of practice or structural holes in networks to create complementary knowledge (Burt, 1992; Mønsted, 2003).

The debriefing in this case was seen as a communication of personal knowledge across cultural and professional barriers. The perception of knowledge is not just a translation, but is closer to Stacey's (2001) perception of *creating knowledge*, not only as an individual mental map, but also as a social communication (and sharing) process. The debriefing is not only an effort to get knowledge as a ready formulated "thing" out of the head of the programmers, but an effort to create a learning space to place the codes into a perspective of creating knowledge about codes, drawing out the purpose and consequences for other parts of the system. Managers have to constitute meaning in the fragments of information, and this is a highly social, communication process (Weick, 1995).

In terms of project management in such IT projects, the turbulence and time pressures are extreme, and often changing and tightening during the project's lifecycle. While uncertainty related to the technology clearly has to be dealt with, questions are raised about the needed overlap between programmer skills and the technical insight of the managers. Such uncertainty is tied to technology, the time perspective for new development, and to customer relations, where customers often change projects and conditions, especially during a project's early stages, when they do not yet know what is possible.

Project management, however, is often based on linear thinking and very concrete work or production tasks, the types of activities that are easily planned with a traditional differentiation strategy (Riis & Mikkelsen, 1992). As project-related crises become more and more prevalent, to the point of being perceived as "normal," a number of basic project management tools are becoming obsolete. While this situation may be viewed as an extreme position—in essence, everything is crisis management—it raises questions with respect to how knowledge workers handle their responsibilities of coordinating work at many levels. It also raises questions about the type of management needed to cope with seemingly impossible and highly entrepreneurial situations. Before the dot.com bubble burst, a number of firms created projects with very high and unrealistic levels of ambition, but were unable to fulfill those ambitions and objectives in practice. Such ambitions and ideas, however, inspired project management experts (e.g., Christensen & Kreiner, 1991), and created a special motivation to "do the impossible."

A third scene in the IT firm illustrates this dynamic. In this instance, a newly recruited project manager was managing a large project focused on creating a PC-based learning system. It was the largest project the small firm had undertaken, and the sales manager had promised the client "too much." The firm's developers and programmers, however, decided that they could create the system, even if they had to develop their own approach rather than draw on existing tools and frameworks. It appeared to be a totally impossible task.

The new project manager started building up a unit of the production team by creating text and drawings. Although they were knowledge workers, most of the firm's employees did not have a high degree of formal education and they relied heavily on on-the-job training. The project manager, who took her tools from informatics and her business school background, created a large GANTT scheme in an attempt to provide an overview of the project's complexity. While useful, the chart only captured the application side of the project, as the tool development process was dependent on the developers. The effort to mobilize, motivate, and energize the staff quickly became a major aspect of the job.

The complexity of the project was increased by the parallel development of tools and applications. In this instance, the project manager was "the helmet man" balancing between Scylla and Charybdis (Hampden-Turner, 1990). She was faced with the prospect of managing a project that was dependent on a tool (A) that was not yet developed. As illustrated in Figure 12.1, usually the "producer tool" would be developed first and the application for learning (B) would follow. As the timeline "folds" as a parallel process, there is a need for ongoing communication and coordination between the tool developers (A) and the application (B). The

Work flow in a linear process, with the xml-tool (A) being developed to enable its application (B):

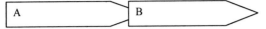

Parallel work flows when there is no time to wait for the xml-tool (A) to be finished; the application (B) is placed parallel to (A):

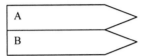

Source: Based on Jensen and Mønsted (2001).

Figure 12.1.   Linear and parallel development processes.

application (B) is still highly dependent on the tool (A), but the resulting interaction is not simply manifold complexity as in Serres and Latour's (1995) folded time, but rather a much more difficult simultaneous and parallel work effort. The need for communication and coordination increases not only at the project management level, but also at other levels of management. The means of control that are actually available for project managers, however, are meager.

During most of the project, one developer was making the xml-tool, but it became increasingly evident that more developers had to be recruited—both for tool development and its adjustment to the "learning" application. The clash between the original autodidact artist developer and the formally educated structured developers revealed a basic problem in the project. The two new developers demand a full briefing, insisting on a weeklong "time-out" or they would leave the project. The debriefing "time-out" was necessary because the new developers could not "read the mind" of the original developer. In essence, limitations in the ability to fully share and understand critical knowledge created a basic knowledge management problem in the project.

The complexity of the knowledge in such IT projects suggests that recruiting more people to join a project could increase the time needed to complete the program (see Brooks, 1995). The complexity of sharing knowledge within these projects makes it difficult to make explicit what the firm knows. In complex tasks, a lot of time is used on learning and exploring. The costs of introducing new staff can quickly become very high, as they need a long period of training and adaptation. Such staff additions, even when they are deemed necessary for a project, can make it extremely difficult to speed up the process, as it may demand more time to train and develop the new staff than actually add value to the process.

Any development based on experimentation and innovation takes a long time and, from an efficiency perspective, is time-consuming and inefficient. While an organization's focus is important here—for example, creativity and innovation versus efficient production—knowledge workers and managers do not always agree on the need for entrepreneurship and "new ideas" as opposed to rethinking and remodeling an existing module-based system. In relation to knowledge workers, opportunities for innovation are motivating, and thus difficult to eliminate if their commitment is to be maintained. From a commercial perspective, however, efficiency cannot be ignored.

In the IT firm, trying to accomplish this work in parallel (Figure 12.1) is extremely complex. The project manager is attempting to provide an overview through an enormous GANTT-scheme, recruiting and training new staff, while the tool development itself, for a long time, has been a "one-man-army." A picture begins to emerge of attempts to create a structured application process, with highly unstructured development processes with the xml-tool (A). The developer is literally developing during the daytime and correcting at night. Applications are developed as a separate process on the basis of the "black box." Such parallel processes require high levels of interaction and coordination, but errors are still to be expected due to B's dependency on A. Every interaction, however, takes time away from development. In this case, the IT firm managed to deliver the product, not on time as initially agreed, but still to the satisfaction of the customer.

Such entrepreneurial problem solving reflects an interesting and complex project management challenge—the need to orchestrate many voices, getting them to adapt to and communicate with each other, while focusing on production schedules and requirements. The lead developer (A) had to communicate with the applications group (B), but also felt the dilemmas of time. Communication was necessary, but at the same time it disturbed his creative thought processes and hindered his progress in programming the xml-tool.

While this case may represent an extreme example, it does illustrate the challenges involved in managing knowledge specialists and interdependent processes. The parallel development as described above is comparable to compressed product development processes in larger R&D firms, though not as transparent as it is in a small firm.

Entrepreneurial Project Management in an R&D Firm: The Role of Profit Centers

While small entrepreneurial firms and the complexities they face provide insights into knowledge management (KM) challenges, these complexities increase as firms get involved with a range of different technologies. In the second case, the R&D and consultancy firm focused on technology management in the energy sector, marine sector, off-shore installations, and the development of new materials to replace diamonds and steel as hard metal, and make new surface treatments as well as new measurement techniques. The firm was faced with two broad processes of change: (1) acquiring other companies in an effort to integrate them as new departments, while (2) placing more emphasis on entrepreneurship and individual project generation. The combination of these two strategic directions changed the roles at all levels of engineers and project and department managers.

The firm's strategy was to acquire a number of smaller firms to extend its technology portfolio and capabilities, but with each of the single units—most of which involved small, one-person projects—under pressure as profit centers to generate commercial contracts (see, e.g., Buono & Bowditch, 1989). The firm was in a transition stage, going from a focus on research and public contracts to the challenge of generating new and larger commercial projects mainly with foreign customers. As part of this change, it was increasingly necessary to draw on resources from other units, which required high levels of knowledge sharing and cross-unit insight into different work and methods, creating a type of broad-based community of practice.

The issue of cross-unit expertise is a special challenge in R&D sections. The specialists or experts "see" what could be defined as problems and their symptoms. The experts "catch the concepts and diagnosis of the problems," typically on the basis of a "first dialogue" with the customer. While the specialists have a broad knowledge base, their expertise is also very deep, enabling them to "see through a problem." New entrants into the organization soon realize that they have to learn a lot, and in many instances their education and experience do not allow them to fully grasp a diagnosis based on the "intuition" of the experienced specialists. Such "seeing" is very close to the type of expert-held tacit knowledge as described by Gourlay (2002) and Collins (2001). "Meaning" is created from new fragments of information based on the individual's deep insight. The challenge is to capture such insight and communicate its meaning to new staff, especially in those instances where such insight is necessary to recognize patterns.

Managing an organization of researchers is like anarchy-based project management, dealing with multidimensional artists in a loosely organizing perspective (Brunsson, 2002; Orton & Weick 1990). Some of the complex dimensions are tied to customer relations, and experts are often better positioned to understand customer problems than the customers themselves. Thus, customer dialogue is essential for both grasping the main problem(s) and persuading the customer of the value of the R&D firm's expertise. The "old experts" in this case, however, did not like to follow up and maintain communication with the customer. These requirements were perceived as "sales activities" and below their status as experts.

The problem was exacerbated as the salespeople had problems identifying customer problems and communicating with the technical staff. It took the firm roughly a full year to educate a salesperson with sufficient technical knowledge to enable them to communicate with customers, even for those individuals who had engineering-related experience. The salespeople also had to create legitimacy with the technical engineers in their own firm and the engineers in the client firm. If they were too marketing focused, they found it hard to be accepted within the broader community of practice among the engineers. While communities of practice typically handle learning and communication *within* the group with relative ease, the challenge lies in going beyond the community to "sell" their expertise and persuade customers abroad of their excellence, which is especially important in a firm with more than 60% of its turnover abroad, (i.e., outside Denmark). This demands persuasive skills in a diverse geographical and cultural setting.

In a Scandinavian unit outside Denmark, the firm generated a new market with a process-technology that could be used in other sectors and markets. The human resources in the "daughter company" were described as "a goldmine of good people," as they seemed to extend the organization's profile through complementary skills. The challenge was to effectively draw on these resources, getting the knowledge "into play" at the early stages of different projects. Such relational knowledge, however, takes time to develop. It challenges managers to get access to interorganizational resources while they are faced with the challenge of developing their own profit centers, which creates dilemmas between individual departments and the organization as a whole. The strategic portfolio at the top management level is much more difficult to activate across communities of practice (Buono & Bowditch, 1989; Wenger, 1998), where the research and method-based insights are not as easy to communicate.

In one of the R&D firm's mergers, the managers tried to work on these interorganizational relations by using focus groups with two to three people from each of the firms' themes, such as services, markets, methods, products, and competences. While only three of these groups survived past a relatively short introductory period, their interactions did provide personal knowledge of the competencies in the other departments, which was a definite step in the direction of being able to mobilize resources across departments.

Knowledge Sharing: Meetings versus Networking

Even within the same firms, the internal communication and methods for knowledge sharing both within and between departments differed widely. While some sections had department meetings once or twice a month to discuss projects or unfolding events, the actual knowledge-sharing activities were very different, sometimes taking place within defined "meetings," but also occurring as part of the practical collaboration and interaction that takes place in a project.

In one of the R&D departments, for example, the engineers working with complex technologies found that meetings were actually a barrier to effective communication. Although the different groups did hold meetings, the section manager felt that they resulted in a relatively poor exchange of knowledge. He pointed out that, "meetings could be the occasion for knowledge sharing or knowledge communication, but the perception of meetings is very negative." As the section manager noted, "we need networking, not meetings," stressing the problems associated with anything that resembled "meeting rhetoric." As he continued, "the informal network carries the projects and forms a skeleton of knowledge; the meetings do not provide that type of function." While the R&D department did hold regular brainstorming sessions on technological developments, these discussions were limited to four to five people at a time. The section manager felt that they were able to "get more serious about ideas and find new concepts" that could serve as a foundation to the technology they were developing.

While many of the projects were undertaken by teams, a number of them were one-person projects, a type of technically advanced consultancy, which moved the focus from research to commercial value. Responsibility for generating projects was highly decentralized, to the point where it was seen as a responsibility for everyone. This meant, however, that the focus was placed on individual efforts and personal projects to fulfill profit demands rather than sharing knowledge and disseminating new ideas.

Attempts at knowledge sharing on highly technical issues, such as the use of new materials or new methods in quality testing of tubes for energy and chemical production, was heavily dependent on coaching. Given that complex range of knowledge necessary for such issues was largely based on experience and generally not well covered in university education, the success of knowledge sharing was influenced by the mutual communication and respect between the senior expert and the younger staff. In the department, for example, true knowledge sharing and understanding only took place when the experienced coach and his younger staff created a supportive learning space and ability to collaborate on the project.

Although knowledge transfer, as a concept, was attempted in many of these departments, the underlying processes of communication and the creation of meaning and learning were very complex. In fact, the actual transfer of knowledge might be just as complex as the content of the personal knowledge held by the senior experts. It is always much easier to identify "the expert," the individual who can "see through" problems, than to specify the demanded skills to get this capacity.

POWER, COMPLEXITY, AND KNOWLEDGE SHARING

The challenge of capturing organizational knowledge and sharing that knowledge under entrepreneurial conditions raises questions about the role of power and leadership in dynamic, loosely coupled networks. Most project management tools are tied to well-defined organizations and relatively linear processes (Riis & Mikkelsen, 1992), where the tasks to be divided are also well defined. As illustrated in the cases in this chapter, however, when the level of complexity rises, the boundaries of the organizations are fluid, and projects involve simultaneous development efforts, a number of self-managed decision makers are involved in a complex set of reciprocal interactions (Jensen, Mønsted, & Olsen, 2004).

The leadership powerbase in this type of entrepreneurial context is based on relationships, and, within this context, power can be thought of as constituted in interpersonal relations and tied to knowledge. Haugaard (1997, 2003), for example, has elaborated on the constitution of power, focusing on its dynamic changes (based on Foucault [1980] and Barnes [1988]). Haugaard's emphasis is placed on both the constraints of the social structure *and* the facilitation of the creation of power through social order. Within this context, destructuring agents are seen as a social function (Haugaard, 2003), which raises an interesting perspective on the entrepreneurial constitution of power in relationships. Haugaard (2003, p. 92) continues his analysis of the power concept as closely tied to the "circles of validating knowledge," arguing that the leader is a leader "not only because he believes so, but because the others constitute a validating ring of reference for that belief." The power concept is important, therefore, not as power to steer and control, but rather power as constituted by the social relations around and in communication with the person in power.

The cases in this chapter point to three key issues about and insights into knowledge creation and knowledge sharing, entrepreneurial leadership, and the types of power necessary to build a true leadership role:

- **Power and forms of power.** Power is generated and constructed in social relations, and leaders must attempt to persuade project participants inside and outside of their departments of their legitimate leadership role.

- **Forms of control.** Formal authority and different informal persuasions constitute a set of social rules, creating a governance system of control and self-control, as a type of mutual obligation system. This dynamic is especially apparent in the networking activities of entrepreneurs.

- **Management as persuasion, communication, and negotiation.** Management and leadership are constituted in loosely coupled organizations and networks, and managers have to find ways of knowing what is on the agenda of their own staff in order to create the knowledge platform for external negotiations. *Negotiated management* of self-managed knowledge workers inside and outside the firm serves as a strong metaphor of the conditions for management in this environment.

These power-related issues have a number of implications for our thinking about knowledge sharing and communication. The idea of knowledge-based firms as systems of persuasion (Alvesson, 2001) leads to a perception of leadership as constituted power on the basis of negotiation. This is a kind of *entrepreneurial leadership*, as the ability to persuade others that they *can* be considered leaders. It moves leadership and power discussions beyond organizational positions, focusing more fully on the relationships between self-managed professionals and network-based leadership.

Knowledge sharing is tied to both the individual and to the internal relations in the firm as the network and contacts to other experts are important parts of the organization's intellectual capacity. Thus, the talent of developers is not only an individual-level phenomenon, but, as scientific and technological human capital, is dependent on the larger social context. As Bozeman, Dietz, and Gaughan (2001, p. 724) suggest:

> Much of this capital, especially that aspect that is interpersonal and social, is embedded in social and professional networks, technological communities or knowledge value collectives... none of these discounts the more traditional aspects of individual scientist's talent.... Our concept simply recognizes that in modern science being brilliant is only necessary, not sufficient.

Management in knowledge-intensive firms is less a position than an action, stressing the ability to facilitate and create the context and motivations necessary to create knowledge- intensive products. The role is much more similar to the network manager who is only a manager through the acceptance of his or her actions by the network partners (Mønsted, 2003). In this context, the position and control aspects of the manager's role are loosened considerably. Yukl (1989, p. 252) stresses the increasing need for more emphasis on shared leadership within leadership research. The profile of knowledge workers and their desire for autonomy creates a knowledge-sharing context, where leadership is tolerated—as long as the manager is credible both in actions and as a person, and does not set too many obstacles to the part of work that is interesting and fun. The platform for management has to be defined in this context, and the power base must be created rather than assigned through position. The power game is a dimension of management and leadership, but knowledge workers, who expect to be self-managed, do not accept positional power alone. To give "power," it has to be linked to personal power and credibility (see Haugaard, 1997; Yukl, 1989).

Entrepreneurship in Small Firms as a Role Model for Knowledge Leadership

The relationship between managers and expert knowledge staff in small, entrepreneurial, knowledge-intensive firms can help us to better understand the challenge of managing knowledge workers, especially as management is dependent on translators. Management roles are highly challenged in this type of firm, and managers have to literally fight for their legitimacy, creating new forms of dialogue and entrepreneurial leadership forms. The sharing of knowledge in research projects under a high level of complexity is fundamental for understanding the active creation of managerial roles and the importance of relationships with team members, both inside and outside the organization.

The asymmetry of knowledge in advanced IT firms and the problems of identifying knowledge that makes a difference among knowledge workers also raise a number of questions about management and communication. While communication directly within communities of practice (Wenger, 1998) is essential for understanding the creation of leadership relations, communication that is more indirect via boundary objects (Star, 1989) or quasi-objects (Serres, 1982) also serves as an important means to create translations of the technology-related insights.

The examples of problems of communicating across communities of practice point to different conditions of management communication in complex and entrepreneurial settings. The case illustrations also underscore the different types of tacit knowledge necessary for the actual use of knowledge in interaction with other communities within the organization.

Traditional project management approaches, with their assumptions of clear divisions of labor and linear processes, fall short of what is needed. Much more attention has to be placed on understanding exactly what is going on if knowledge is going to be "put into play" with knowledge workers and customers.

Our view of knowledge management is increasingly being shaped by leadership roles and challenges and platforms of power, as communication and motivation become inevitable variables to understand how leadership is constructed in social spaces. Management is a social construction, and managers must create legitimacy and relevance in their communication with self-managed knowledge workers. The ability to persuade "followers" is necessary to create a power base, not only as a fundamental perspective in entrepreneurship but also more and more in knowledge-based firms. Entrepreneurship can be seen as chaos handling and the ability to create meaning in complex innovative settings that involve different types of expertise and customers. The opportunity and challenge involve balancing exploitation and exploration, pushing the organization's ability to both create and share new knowledge. As larger firms are increasingly fragmented into profit centers as part of a short-term economic rationale, they also increasingly import many of the problems faced by entrepreneurs in smaller, knowledge-intensive firms—including the barriers to knowledge sharing and lack of concern for more complex communication and knowledge management processes. The subdivision in profit centers creates a demand for new project management strategies based on more flexible communication, and the legitimization of knowledge management as a social construction of leadership.

NOTES

1. The case draws from a joint research project financed by the Danish LOK-programme. Sisse Siggaard Jensen undertook the video analysis of the firm (Jensen et al., 2004); see Jensen, Chapter 11, in this volume.

2. Stacey's points were raised as part of a speech given at the LOK Conference in Kolding, Denmark, in November 2002.

REFERENCES

Alvesson, M. (2001). Knowledge work: Ambiguity, image and identity. *Human Relations*, *54*(7), 863–886

Barnes, B. (1988). *The nature of power*. Cambridge, UK: Polity Press.

Bozeman, B., Dietz, J. S., & Gaughan, M. (2001). Scientific and technical human capital: An alternative model for research evaluation. *International Journal of Technology Management*, *22*(7/8), 716–740.

Brooks, F.B. (1995). *The mythical man-month*. Boston: Addison-Wesley.

Brunsson, N. (2002). *The organization of hypocrisy: Talk, decisions and actions in organizations*. Copenhagen: Copenhagen Business School Press.

Buono, A. F., & Bowditch, J. L. (1989). *The human side of mergers and acquisitions*. San Francisco: Jossey-Bass.

Burt, R. (1992). *Structural holes: The social structure of competition*. Cambridge, MA: Harvard University Press.

Christensen, S., & Kreiner, F. (1991). *Projektledelse i løst koblede systemer: Ledelse og læring i en ufuldkommen verden*. København, Demark: Jurist- og Økonomforbundets Forlag.

Collins, H. M. (2001). Tacit knowledge, trust and the Q of the sapphire. *Social Studies of Science 31*(1), 71–85.

Davenport, T. H., & Prusak, L (1998). *Working knowledge: How organizations manage what they know*. Boston: Harvard Business School Press.

Foucault, M. (1980). *Power/knowledge: Selected interviews and other writings 1972–77* (C. Gordon, Ed.). Brighton, UK: Harvester Press

Garud, R., & Kumaraswany, A. (2003). Technological and organizational designs for realizing economies. In R. Garud, A. Kumaraswany, & R.N. Langlois (Eds.), *Managing in the modular age: Architectures, networks, and organizations* (pp. 45-77). Oxford: Blackwell.

Garud, R., Kumaraswany, A., & Langlois, R. N. (Eds.). (2003). *Managing in the modular age: Architectures, networks, and organizations*. Oxford: Blackwell.

Garud, R., Nayyar, P., & Shapira, Z. (Eds.). (1997). *Technological innovation: Oversights and Foresights*. Cambridge, UK: Cambridge University Press.

Gourlay, S. (2002). *Tacit knowledge: Tacit knowing or behaving?* Paper presented at the OKLC Conference, Athens, Greece.

Hampden-Turner, C. (1990). *Charting the corporate mind: From dilemma to strategy*. Oxford: Blackwell.

Haugaard, M. (2003). Reflections on seven ways of creating power. *European Journal of Social Theory, 6*(1), 87–113.

Haugaard, M. (1997). *The constitution of power: A theoretical analysis of power, knowledge and structure*. Manchester, UK: Manchester University Press.

Jensen, S. S., & Mønsted, M. (2001a). *Managing uncertainties in R&D processes in small IT firms*. Paper presented at the EGOS conference, Lyon, France.

Jensen, S. S., & Mønsted, M. (2001b). Tidsparadokser og ledelsesdilemmaer i IT projekter. In F. Poulfelt & M. Mønsted (Eds.), *Det er et spørgsmål om tid*. København: Samfundslitteratur CD-ROM.

Jensen, S. S., Mønsted, M., & Fejfer Olsen, S. (2004). *Viden, ledelse og kommunikation*. København: Samfundslitteratur.

Langlois, R. N., & Robertson, P. L. (1992). Networks and innovation in a modular system: Lessons from the microcomputer and stereo component industries. *Research Policy, 21*(4), 297–313.

Mønsted, M. (2003). *Strategic networking in small high-tech firms*. Copenhagen: Samfundslitteratur.

Mønsted, M. (2004). *Profit centres as barriers for knowledge sharing: From strategic networking to profit centres.* Paper presented at the EURAM Conference, St. Andrews, Scotland.

Newell, S., Robertson, M., Scarborough, H., & Jacky Swan, J. (2002). *Managing knowledge work.* New York: Palgrave.

Nonaka, I., & Takeuchi, H. (1995). *The knowledge creating company: How Japanese companies create the dynamics of innovation.* Oxford: Oxford University press.

Normann, R. (1984). *Service management: Strategy and leadership in service businesses.* New York: Wiley.

Orton, J. D., & Weick, K. E. (1990). Loosely coupled systems: A reconceptualization. *Academy of Management Review, 15*(2), 203–223.

Riis, J. O., & Mikkelsen, H. (1992). *Grundbog i projektledelse.* Rungsted: Promet.

Serres, M., & Latour, B. (1995). *Conversations on science, culture and time.* Ann Arbor: University of Michigan Press.

Serres, M. (1982). *The parasite.* Baltimore: John Hopkins.

Simon, H. (1962). The architecture of complexity. *Proceedings of the American Philosophical Society, 106,* 467–482.

Stacey, R. D. (2001). *Complex responsive processes in organizations: Learning and knowledge creation.* London: Routledge.

Star, S. L. (1989). The structure of ill-structured solutions: Boundary objects and heterogeneous distributed problem solving. In L. Gasser & M.N. Huhns (Eds.), *Distributed artificial intelligence, Vol. II* (pp. 37-54). London: Pitman.

Star, S. L. (1995). The politics of formal representations: Wizards, gurus and organizational complexity. In S. L. Star (Ed.), *Ecologies of knowledge: Work and politics in science and technology* (pp. 88-118). Albany: State University of New York Press.

Tsoukas, H. (1996). The firm as a distributed knowledge system: A constructionist approach. *Strategic Management Journal, 17*(9), 11–25.

Tsoukas, H., & Vladimirou, E. (2001). What is organizational knowledge? *Journal of Management Studies, 38*(7), 973–993.

Weick, K.E. (1979). *The social psychology of organizing.* Reading, MA: Addison-Wesley.

Weick, K.E. (1995). *Sensemaking in organizations.* Thousand Oaks, CA: Sage.

Wenger, E. (1998). *Communities of practice: Learning, meaning, and identity.* Cambridge, UK: Cambridge University Press.

Yukl, G. (1989). Managerial leadership: A review of theory and research. *Journal of Management, 15,* 251–289.

PART IV

REFLECTIONS OF KNOWLEDGE MANAGEMENT AND MANAGEMENT CONSULTING

CHAPTER 13

FLAWS IN THE "ENGINE" OF KNOWLEDGE CREATION

A Critique of Nonaka's Theory

Stephen Gourlay and Andrew Nurse

Nonaka's theory of organizational knowledge creation[1] has achieved paradigmatic status since its publication in the mid-1990s,[2] and has recently been described as "highly respected" (Easterby-Smith & Lyles, 2003b, p. 11). The theory rests on the assumption that knowledge is created through social interaction between tacit and explicit knowledge. Nonaka and his colleagues postulated four modes of knowledge conversion corresponding to different forms of such interaction (see Figure 13.1). According to their framework, knowledge creation begins with socialization (S), continues with externalization (E), combination (C), and internalization (I), before returning to socialization, but at a new level, hence the metaphor of a spiral of knowledge creation (cf. Nonaka, 1991a, 1994, 1995; Nonaka, Byosiere, Borucki, & Konno, 1994; Nonaka, Konno, & Toyama, 2001; Nonaka & Takeuchi, 1995).

These ideas, first published in 1991 (Nonaka, 1991a), drew on studies of information creation in innovating Japanese companies (Imai, Nonaka, & Takeuchi, 1985; Nonaka, 1988a, 1988b, 1990, 1991b; Nonaka &

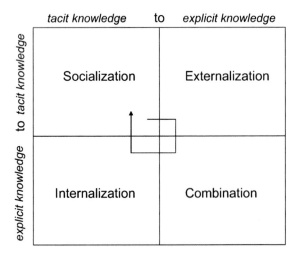

Figure 13.1. The "engine" of knowledge creation. Adapted from Nonaka and Takeuchi (1995, pp. 57, 62, 71).

Kenney, 1991; Nonaka & Yamanouchi, 1989). Subsequently, Nonaka (1994) published a more extensive theoretical paper and the results of a survey that validated the model (Nonaka et al., 1994). In 1995, the book-length exposition of the theory (Nonaka & Takeuchi, 1995) appeared where the SECI matrix (Figure 13.1) is described as the "engine" of knowledge creation. Other parts of the theory describing how new knowledge becomes organizational knowledge have since undergone considerable modification (see, e.g., Nonaka, Toyama, & Byosière, 2001; Nonaka, Toyama, & Konno, 2000), but the SECI "engine" remained intact.

Although several authors have highlighted important contingent factors, Nonaka's theory appears to have attracted little systematic criticism.[3] Becerra-Fernandez and Sabherwal (2001), for example, show that each of the SECI modes is dependent on the presence of appropriate task characteristics. Poell and van der Krogt (2003), treating the modes as forms of learning, also report that the type of work involved influences how workers learn. More generally, Doyle (1985) and Glisby and Holden (2003) argue that the model rests on Japanese management cultural practices, and is thus not transferable to other contexts.[4] Other empirical criticisms include Engestrom's (1999) discovery that problem finding is an important part of innovation missing from the SECI model, and Poell and van der Krogt's comment that Nonaka apparently assumes workers only learn within parameters set by managers. Their research points to the importance of self-organized learning, particularly in professional organizations.

Questions, however, have been raised about the theory itself. Adler (1995) suggested that Nonaka's discussion of externalization (e.g., Nonaka & Takeuchi, 1995, pp. 13, 64–67) may not be generalizable, and pointed out that although the other modes had been previously studied, Nonaka and his colleagues neglected that research. Jorna (1998) argued that Nonaka neglected learning theory, especially in his discussion of tacit and explicit knowledge. He also charged Nonaka and his colleagues with misreading important organizational writers, and suggested that better accounts of Western philosophy were available than those used. In addition, Jorna argued that "knowledge conversion" entails semiosis, but the model lacks a semiotic framework.

Nonaka's conceptualization of the relationship between tacit and explicit knowledge has also been criticized. While Nonaka treats tacit and explicit knowledge as separable, other theorists regard tacit knowledge as always necessary for explicit knowledge to be understood (cf. Adler, 1995; Stacey, 2001; Tsoukas, 2003). More generally, Griffin, Shaw, and Stacey (1999) suggested that Nonaka has subordinated Polanyi's (1969a, 1969b) concept of tacit knowledge to an objectivist strategic management theory, while Yolles (2000) argued that the SECI model employs a mixed ontology, trying to be both constructivist and positivist.

Recently Bereiter (2002) has identified four important shortcomings in Nonaka's approach. First, echoing Stacey (2001), he argues that Nonaka's theory cannot explain how minds produce (or fail to produce) ideas. Second, it overlooks the important question of understanding—in order to learn by doing, one has to know what to observe. Third, while the theory recognizes knowledge abstracted from context, it says little about how it can be managed. Finally, the view that knowledge originates in individual minds prevents Nonaka from conceptualizing knowledge that arises from collective actions, for example, as a product of teamwork. Overall, Bereiter argues that the theory is rooted in a folk epistemology that regards individual minds as full of unformed knowledge that must be projected into an external world, an approach that hinders any attempt to provide a theory of knowledge creation. As such, he suggests that Nonaka's theory fails both as a theory and as a practical tool for business.

These are serious issues that raise questions about the utility of the model as a guide to research and practice.[5] Yet, while Bereiter's (2002) remarks suggest the SECI model is ill-founded, he was only tangentially interested in Nonaka's theory and did not develop his critique. Similarly, other criticism remains largely piecemeal, and within organization and management studies circles the theory remains largely unchallenged. Having drawn the attention of this research community to these criticisms, we now turn to our main task. It is our view, however, that the "engine" of Nonaka's theory of organizational knowledge creation is fundamentally flawed on both empirical and theoretical grounds. As such, its utility—especially as a guide for organizational intervention and knowledge development—is questionable. As a basis for our critique, the chapter initially reviews the empirical evidence for the model, and then turns to key conceptual dimensions of the theory.

THE EMPIRICAL BASIS FOR THE SECI MODEL

In 1993, a convenience sample of 105 Japanese male middle managers was issued a self-completion questionnaire designed to test Nonaka's emerging theory of knowledge creation (Nonaka et al., 1994). The questionnaire comprised 185 items, 38 of which concerned "the content of organizational knowledge creation," as measured by the amount of time spent on specific activities (see Nonaka et al., 1994, pp. 342–343, 350). Hierarchical confirmatory factor analysis of the data confirmed the suggestion that knowledge creation comprised four modes of knowledge conversion, thus validating the SECI hypothesis (Nonaka et al., 1994; see also Nonaka & Takeuchi, 1995).[6]

Nonaka and his colleagues (1994) raised a number of cautions about this work: (1) this was the first time the questionnaire had been used, except for piloting; (2) the heterogeneity of the sample raised questions of internal validity; (3) the generalizability of the findings to other cultures was questionable; and (4) qualitative data would have enriched the study. There are, however, more fundamental issues involved than those noted by the researchers. First, the questionnaire focused on the *content* of organizational knowledge creation; *process* issues remained to be investigated. Yet, since the SECI model is a process model, the claim that the survey validated Nonaka's hypothesis cannot be accepted. Second, it is not clear how scales for measuring the knowledge conversion modes could have been constructed given the lack of previous research. Although we are told that externalization had only been studied in the context of research into semantic information creation (see Nonaka, 1991b; Nonaka et al., 1994), it appears that the only data available at that time was from such studies (see, e.g., Imai et al., 1985; Nonaka, 1988a, 1988b, 1990, 1991b; Nonaka & Kenney, 1991; Nonaka & Yamanouchi, 1989). Thus, we are forced to conclude that the measures of *knowledge* conversion mode content actually came from studies of semantic *information* creation. Insofar as Nonaka has made much of the difference between information and knowledge (e.g., Nonaka, 1991b, 1994; Nonaka & Takeuchi, 1995), this suggests that the 1993 survey actually focused on *semantic information* creation.[7]

Even if it were possible to set these difficulties aside, by arguing for example that semantic information and knowledge are equivalent,[8] another important difficulty remains. In confirmatory factor analysis, it is normal to accept a factor when at least 60–70% of the variance has been accounted for (e.g., Hair, Anderson, Tatham, & Black, 1998). While the percentage of variation explained for socialization (73%) and combination (64%) do fall within these limits, the figures for externalization (51%) and internalization (56%) fall below them. Thus, we cannot accept the claim that the survey "validated the existence" (Nonaka & Takeuchi, 1995, p. 91) of the four *knowledge* creation *processes*. At best, it provided support for two of four hypothesized modes of *semantic information* creation.

Turning to the case study evidence, as noted earlier, most if not all this data was originally collected for studies of innovation and information creation. It does not appear that studies of *knowledge* creation were carried out as part of the theory development process. While it might be quite acceptable to reinterpret data in light of a new theory, as we have just suggested, Nonaka has not justified treating semantic information as equivalent to knowledge. Moreover, much of this illustrative material is itself far from convincing.

Socialization

Nonaka proposed that knowledge conversion begins with socialization, the tacit acquisition of tacit knowledge by people who do not have it from people who do. Three examples are given: a brainstorming camp, the development of an automated bread-making machine, and interaction with customers (cf. Nonaka, 1991b, 1994; Nonaka, Konno, & Toyama, 2001; Nonaka & Takeuchi, 1995). Descriptions of both the brainstorming camp and customer interaction suggest these were arenas of intense discussion and exchange of ideas, but give no details of how or even whether tacit-to-tacit knowledge exchange occurred (Imai et al., 1985; Nonaka, 1988a, 1988b; Nonaka & Kenney, 1991; Nonaka & Takeuchi, 1995). Had these studies shown, for example, that participants' cognitive maps changed as a result of the discussions in ways that could not be attributed to anything that was explicitly said, Nonaka's case would be more convincing. Moreover, since dialogue is also central to externalization and combination (as we will explore below), it is difficult to understand why brainstorming and customer interaction exemplify "socialization" as distinct from the other modes.

The automatic bread-making machine case, which "shows how a tacit technical skill was socialized," is more extensively documented (Nonaka,

1991b, pp. 98–99; Nonaka & Takeuchi, 1995, pp. 63–64, 100–109), and, on the face of it, appears to provide better evidence of "socialization." A prototype machine produced a loaf with an overcooked crust that was raw inside. This machine did not produce "tasty bread," the problem the second phase of development sought to rectify (Nonaka & Takeuchi, 1995). While the issue of taste is emphasized in part of the account, we are also told that the second phase focused on how to knead bread dough properly. It is not clear whether there were two distinct objectives, or whether the team decided that attention to kneading would resolve the taste problem.

As a master chef could not "tell" them what they needed to know, a team member apprenticed herself to learn the appropriate skills. We are told that one day she "noticed the baker was not only stretching but also 'twisting' the dough, which turned out to be the secret for making tasty bread" (Nonaka & Takeuchi 1995, p. 64). We are not told why or how the team reached this conclusion, but only that they decided to replicate this "twist" by modifying the design. Eventually, the team "succeeded in developing a machine that could make tasty bread" and thus the baker's tacit knowledge (the "secret for making tasty bread") had been transferred (socialization) (Nonaka & Takeuchi 1995, pp. 64, 104–105).

One difficulty with this account is that kneading does not affect the taste of bread. Taste is influenced by the raw ingredients, the dough maturation process (which produces the complex chemicals that are further changed during baking), and by the baking process itself (see Barfield, 1947). Thus, we must conclude that the team solved the taste problem *accidentally* during the lengthy development process. Since they did not *understand* how to make tasty bread, it hardly makes sense to suggest that tacit knowledge about making tasty bread was transferred. Events like this are perhaps not unusual, as illustrated by scientists' accounts of their failure to fully understand how they had been able to complete an experiment (Collins, 1974, 2001a). Yet, unless we extend "knowing" to include such lack of understanding (which might better be called "ignorance"), we must conclude that no "knowledge" about making tasty bread whatsoever was transferred. Thus we have no evidence for tacit-to-tacit knowledge transfer.

If, on the other hand, the problem concerned the kneading process, then the following account seems reasonable. Each team member successfully learned how to knead bread dough, under the watchful eye of the master chef. The team members' primary concern was to identify aspects of the manual process that would help them improve the prototype, and discussion of this problem could be grounded in their common experience. One team member noticed what they called a "twist," and when they replicated this move the resulting machine produced tasty bread. Consequently, they concluded they had found the key to their problem.

While this account may be more coherent, it is still not clear that it exemplifies the tacit transfer of tacit knowledge. The team members learned a new skill by doing it, guided by an expert who could give instruction, demonstration, and feedback. That people regularly learn new skills without direct personal contact with an expert testifies to the centrality of learning-by-doing for acquiring skills. An expert can assist in this process, but there is no need to suggest that when they are present some indescribable kind of knowledge is "transferred" by an unknown process. Since the Nonaka account permits an alternative explanation, there is no unambiguous evidence for "socialization."

Externalization

Externalization, the next step in the knowledge conversion process, involves converting tacit into explicit knowledge, and holds the key to knowledge creation (Nonaka, 1994; Nonaka & Takeuchi, 1995). It is exemplified by stories of new product development, especially their best-documented Honda City case that describes how young designers produced a novel car design (Imai et al., 1985; Nonaka, 1988b, 1990, 1991a; Nonaka & Takeuchi, 1995; for the other cases, see Nonaka, 1988a; Nonaka & Kennedy, 1991; Nonaka & Yamanouchi, 1989). After several false starts, new ideas began flowing under the stimulus of the phrase "Automobile Evolution"—which resulted in a formal proposal or "concept."[9] The claim that this and similar cases provide evidence of externalization rests on the hypothesis that tacit knowledge is externalized through the use of metaphors and analogies (Nonaka, 1991b), a hypothesis that is *not* supported by evidence or theory. No evidence is given to substantiate the implicit claim that the design ideas somehow "tacitly" existed and were externalized by these techniques. All we have are anecdotes illustrating the use of creativity techniques and other Japanese management procedures that facilitated the development of novel products.

The bread-making case, however, does appear to provide better evidence. Attempts to describe the effects of exercising a physical skill, expressed within a group whose members could exercise that skill, facilitated production of descriptions of that skill in terms of engineering formulae and designs, and ultimately in machinery. Although this account is far from satisfactory, lacking details comparable to Collins's (1995, 2001a) studies of "tacit knowledge" in scientific work, it does suggest that a process akin to externalization took place. Collins's studies suggest a lot more talk, testing, and other activity went on than was reported by Nonaka and his colleagues. "Externalization" is probably the result of hard cooperative work.

Combination

Externalization is followed by combination—the process of "systematizing concepts into a knowledge system" (Nonaka & Takeuchi, 1995, p. 67). Combination occurs when someone writes a report synthesizing explicit knowledge (Nonaka, 1991b) and through meetings, conversations, and exchange of documents (Nonaka, 1994; Nonaka & Takeuchi, 1995). We are also told that an MBA education is "one of the best examples" of combination (Nonaka & Takeuchi, 1995, p. 67) and that "modern computer systems" (Nonaka, 1994, p. 19) and the "embodiment" of knowledge into products also exemplify combination (Nonaka, 1991b, p. 99; Nonaka et al., 1996, pp. 207–208). However, no details of any of these activities are given and it is impossible to understand how various forms of communication (using language, talking, listening, reading, or writing) can sensibly be treated as being characterized by explicit knowledge exchange.

Adler (1995, p. 111) suggested Nonaka's claim that an MBA involves "exchange" of explicit knowledge might be a "playful" remark, pointing out that the case study method was designed to help transmit managers' tacit knowledge. Some communication theories treat documents as channels along which messages pass to the reader, but this application of the mathematical theory of communication has long been criticized as inappropriate for human behavior (Cherry, 1966). Computer functioning and so-called knowledge "embodiment" processes might well be viable candidates for a distinct "combination" process, but as they have not been described, it is impossible to know what is intended. There is no empirical support for, nor even a clear description of, the notion of knowledge "combination."

Internalization

Internalization, the final step in the cycle, is also exemplified by a variety of activities: (1) it involves "embodying" explicit knowledge to become tacit knowledge; (2) it is "closely related" to the "traditional notion of learning" and "learning by doing" (Nonaka et al., 1994, pp. 340-41; Nonaka, 1994, p. 19; Nonaka & Takeuchi, 1995, p. 69); and (3) it is also "triggered" by learning-by-doing (Nonaka et al., 1996, p. 208). Furthermore, *documentation* (which can mean reading or writing) "helps individuals internalize what they experienced [and to] experience the experiences of others indirectly" (Nonaka & Takeuchi, 1995, pp. 69–70). Finally, internalization also involves, or is achieved through, the dissemination of explicit knowledge throughout an organization (Nonaka, 1991b; Nonaka et al., 2001b).

Learning by doing is exemplified by team members who enriched their tacit knowledge through the experience of creating a new product (Nonaka, 1991b), and employees who experienced working reduced annual hours by working at the new annual rate for a month (Nonaka & Takeuchi, 1995), which is suggested to show that workers gained a subjective understanding of working shorter hours. Insofar as tacit knowledge is personal and subjective, this seems to indicate that a process suggestive of the acquisition of tacit knowledge took place. It is difficult, however, to see how the knowledge of how many hours were to be worked, as distinct from the experience of working shorter hours, actually contributed to development of this subjective feeling. As for "the traditional notion of learning," it is far from clear what this means. "Embodying" is clearly a metaphor, and its meaning is also obscure. We are again forced to conclude that no clear evidence is offered for internalization in the sense of an explicit to tacit "conversion."

In summary, we have to conclude that there is no unambiguous evidence at all for any of the four modes, or for the hypothesis that knowledge is created by the "interaction" of tacit and explicit knowledge. The case study evidence only provides tentative support for externalization. Even if we overlook the likelihood that the survey actually concerns semantic information creation, it only provides support for socialization and combination. However, the latter mode appears extremely ambiguous as, like internalization, it comprises multiple forms of activity between which there is no obvious similarity.

Perhaps we should not be too surprised. Nonaka's data was drawn almost wholly from studies of semantic information creation and he and his colleagues categorically said that more research was needed, particularly to examine the relations between the four modes, the "spiral" sequence of knowledge creation, and the application of the model to other cultures (Nonaka et al., 1994). The empirical shortcomings highlighted here, however, concern the very validity of each of the modes and the key claim about knowledge creation, not just questions about the nature of relations between them. It is not unusual, of course, that a good theory may initially lack clear empirical support. Thus, to assess whether the SECI model is worth effort to substantiate it, we now turn to examine Nonaka's conceptual framework.

THE CONCEPTUAL FRAMEWORK

Bereiter's (2002) claim that Nonaka and his colleagues' epistemology hinders their enterprise deserves further consideration. While this discussion will doubtless inform forthcoming debates, it is not our intention to consider it further here. Should Bereiter's arguments be rejected, defenders of the theory might wish to fall back on details of Nonaka's ideas and it is on these that we focus here. In this section, we consider Nonaka's approach to tacit knowledge, the SECI process, and the implications of their particular definition of knowledge.

Tacit Knowledge

Nonaka took the notion of tacit knowledge from Polanyi (1969a, 1969b) and modified it in a "practical direction" by distinguishing technical tacit knowledge (concrete know-how and skills) from cognitive tacit knowledge (mental models of the world) (Nonaka, 1994, p. 16; Nonaka & Takeuchi, 1995, pp. 8, 60).[10] Tacit knowledge, we are informed, is a "rich, untapped source of new knowledge" and is the basis of organizational knowledge creation (Nonaka et al., 1994, p. 342; Nonaka & Takeuchi, 1995, pp. 72, 85). Such tacit knowledge is difficult to communicate or share because it has "a personal quality ... [and is] deeply rooted in action, commitment, and involvement in a specific context" (Nonaka, 1994, p. 16; Nonaka & Takeuchi, 1995, pp. 8, 59–60; Nonaka et al., 2001b, p. 15). Tacit knowledge is contrasted with explicit knowledge, and while they use the metaphor of an iceberg to refer to the relationship between these two forms of knowledge (Nonaka & Takeuchi, 1995, pp. 60–61), they more frequently treat them as separate entities. This tendency is reinforced by the "assumption" that their "social interaction" produces knowledge (Nonaka &Takeuchi, 1995, p. 62), a relationship that can be represented by a matrix.

It is difficult to see how the metaphor of an iceberg (a base-superstructure model) and of interaction can both be logically applied to the same relationship. More important perhaps is that treating tacit and explicit knowledge as opposites is a more radical modification of Polanyi than the one they acknowledge. On several occasions, Polanyi (1969a, p. 144; 1969b, p. 164) stressed that while "tacit knowledge can be possessed by itself, explicit knowledge must rely on being tacitly understood" (see also Adler, 1995; Tsoukas, 2003). Tacit knowledge is thus claimed to "underlie" all explicit knowledge—the iceberg metaphor is an apt one. Thus, it may not make sense to portray the relationship between tacit and explicit knowledge through a matrix, or even to describe it as an "interaction."

A further difficulty concerns their monolithic treatment of "tacit knowledge." There is a consensus that some tacit knowledge can be made explicit, while some is inherently tacit (Barbiero, 2002; Collins, 1974, 2001b; Janik, 1988, 1990). Janik (1988) suggested that tacit knowledge in the forms of trade secrets, craft knowledge and skill, and everyday presuppositions can be made explicit. On the other hand, there are "aspects of human experience which are *wholly* knowable self-reflectively" and thus "by their very nature ... [are] incapable of *precise* articulation" (Janik, 1988, pp. 54, 56). Such inherently tacit knowledge included sensuous experience or practice and rule-following. We "know" what coffee smells like or how a particular musical instrument sounds, knowledge that can only be acquired through experiencing the sensations. As regards rule-following, we cannot fully specify the rules for carrying out an action since any rules require additional rules concerning their application—and so on *ad infinitum*. Rule-following always rests on doing, practice, or activity, and therefore entails tacitly knowing what to do (Janik, 1988).

The omission of inherently tacit knowledge severely compromises Nonaka's theory. Even if it were useful to portray the tacit–explicit knowledge relationship in a matrix, several cells of a matrix including inherently tacit knowledge would be invalid. If we cannot use a matrix to categorize tacit–explicit knowledge relationships, perhaps the very notion of their "interaction" should be questioned—or at least treated as the metaphor that it evidently is, rather than as a statement of fact. This reinforces the claim that the tacit–explicit knowledge relationship might be more usefully conceptualized as a base–superstructure relationship than as an interaction between opposite poles.

Difficulties with the SECI Process

One problem with the SECI spiral concerns understanding what comes out of it. Of course the key "assumption" is that "knowledge" is created through the interaction of tacit and explicit knowledge involving the four modes of "knowledge conversion" (Nonaka & Takeuchi, 1995, p. 62). But we are also told that tacit knowledge is created through socialization[11] and internalization, and explicit knowledge by externalization. Elsewhere, however, we are told that externalization results in "conceptual knowledge," and that each of the other modes also produces a distinct type of knowledge (Nonaka & Takeuchi, 1995, p. 72). We thus end up with six types of "knowledge"—four created through the interaction of tacit and explicit—together with the grand product of this interaction: knowledge.

A further problem concerns understanding how one phase of activity relates to the next. The "spiral" metaphor draws attention to the idea of

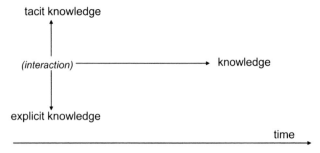

Figure 13.2.   The SECI process of knowledge conversion: A linear view.

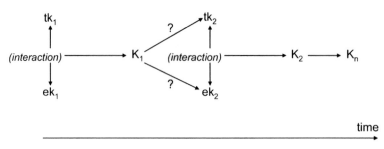

Figure 13.3.   Knowledge conversion over time.

knowledge conversion as a continual and progressive process. As illustrated in Figure 13.2, however, this metaphor obscures the fact that we are dealing with a linear process (see Griffin et al., 1999, for a similar argument).

The process is linear because it involves time. Figure 13.2 represents one phase of the SECI process operations—one or perhaps a number of spirals of interaction result in new knowledge. If we extend the time frame to include more than one phase of SECI processes, the question of the relationship between knowledge produced in former times and ongoing knowledge conversion becomes evident (see Figure 13.3).

It is not clear whether knowledge created in one phase of knowledge creation affects tacit knowledge, explicit knowledge, or both (or even neither) at the next phase of the process. Does knowledge subsequently *become* explicit knowledge? Perhaps some prior knowledge enters the next phase directly as tacit knowledge (internalization) while some enters as explicit knowledge, having been codified during phase one. These ambiguities suggest that much remains to be worked out if the "engine" of their theory of knowledge creation is to function as an adequate representation of real processes. Consideration of what Nonaka meant by "knowledge" answers some of these questions—but at the expense of the theory itself.

The argument that knowledge from one phase subsequently becomes explicit knowledge for a later phase runs as follows. Explicit knowledge is another name for *declarative knowledge* (Nonaka & Takeuchi, 1995, p. 61) and "knowledge of facts" (Alexander, Schallert, & Hare, 1991, p. 332), which, called propositional knowledge, is one of three types of knowledge recognized by epistemologists (see Klein, 1998). "Explicit," "declarative," and "propositional" are thus adjectives used by different groups of scholars to refer to the same type of knowledge. Furthermore, this is what Western epistemologists refer to as "justified true belief" (Klein, 1998; Nonaka & Takeuchi, 1995, p. 58).[12] Hence, knowledge produced by one phase of SECI processes could be regarded as the same as the explicit knowledge that enters subsequent phases. Nonaka and his colleagues would, however, reject this argument because they wish to differentiate the "knowledge" resulting from the SECI processes from knowledge as justified true belief.

Nonaka and his colleagues emphasize "the nature of knowledge as 'justified belief'" rather than justified true belief. This "critical" distinction is necessary, they claim, because "traditional epistemology emphasizes the absolute, static, and nonhuman nature of knowledge" against which they pose the idea of "knowledge as *a dynamic human process of justifying personal belief toward the 'truth'* ... " (Nonaka & Takeuchi, 1995, p. 58, original emphasis; see also Nonaka, 1994, p. 15; Nonaka et al., 2001b, pp. 14–15). There are actually two distinct notions here: knowledge ("justified belief") as the product of a process (justification) and knowledge itself as a "process." The latter idea does not appear to inform subsequent discussion,[13] but the claim that knowledge is "justified belief" remains central.

The full implications of their redefinition of knowledge as "justified belief" become clear in light of their discussion of "justification."[14] This is described as "the process of determining if the newly created concepts are truly worthwhile for the organization and society" (Nonaka & Takeuchi, 1995, p. 86). Thus the prototype bread-making machine failed to be "justified against the original product concept" because it did not make tasty bread. When the taste problem had been resolved, the "concept" still remained unjustified because it failed to meet cost criteria (Nonaka & Takeuchi, 1995, pp. 103–108). We have already seen that "concept" means ideas and plans for new products or processes. "Justification" clearly means the evaluation of "concepts" by managers in light of predefined performance or other criteria (Nonaka & Takeuchi, 1995, pp. 86, 103, 108–109; see also Nonaka, 1994, p. 26). In other words, "knowledge" as "justified belief" simply means ideas and plans that have been sanctioned by those in authority.

The SECI model is evidently a hypothesis about the generation of ideas for new products or processes that, when sanctioned by managers, acquire a special status, called "justified belief" by Nonaka and his colleagues. They are *justified* because they meet predefined criteria and presumably they are *beliefs* because managers believe them. The underlying problem with the SECI process that was described earlier can thus be resolved: the "interaction" of tacit and explicit knowledge results in managers' "justified beliefs," not "justified true belief" or even "explicit knowledge." Since these are not equivalent to knowledge in any more generally accepted sense of that ambiguous word, the SECI framework cannot be regarded as the "engine" of a theory of organizational *knowledge* creation.

Finally, Nonaka's claim that "justified belief" is preferable to "justified true belief" implies that "truth" is not particularly important to businesses and organizations. We have seen, however, that the bread-making team's "justified belief" that flavor is influenced by kneading was false. Should the team want to improve the process further, and acts on the basis of this belief, they would be likely to fail (or, at best, succeed once more by accident). The "truth" value of any claim to knowledge is surely important to businesses, depending as they do on "truths" rather than simply on "beliefs" about the material and other transformations on which their activities and their success depend.

CONCLUSIONS

Nonaka and his colleagues' "engine" of knowledge creation has been found wanting on both empirical and theoretical grounds. First, it appears that the data for the SECI modes of knowledge conversion came largely, if not entirely, from studies of semantic information creation. The necessary explanatory links between semantic information and knowledge are missing. Second, claim that a survey validated the SECI hypothesis cannot be accepted because it too draws wholly on the semantic information studies. The survey focused on content not process, and on the most generous interpretation only provides support for two of the four modes of conversion, one of which (combination) is also conceptually ambiguous. Third, examination of the case study evidence reveals ambiguity about the four modes, lack of detail or clarity about the processes, and an absence of convincing examples (with the possible exception of one instance of externalization). Furthermore, there is no persuasive evidence that "knowledge" is created by the interaction of tacit and explicit knowledge, the key assumption on which the whole model was based.

Turning to their concepts, they have used an unjustified monolithic notion of tacit knowledge, whereas other authorities argue for and provide illustrations of two types, one that can and one that cannot be made explicit. Nonaka and his colleagues only recognize the former, and their matrix cannot be modified to accommodate the latter. There are also important ambiguities about the SECI processes, in particular the relation between the different types of knowledge alleged to be involved. These problems can be resolved when it is appreciated that "knowledge" as "justified belief" actually means *managers' beliefs* that product or process ideas appear to meet preestablished criteria. Thus the SECI process should be described as a hypothesis concerning the production of managers' "justified beliefs." Making "knowledge" a matter of authority harks back to premodern practices in Europe. While this may reflect the way employees' ideas are treated by managers, had authority been the judge of knowledge we would probably still think the earth was the center of the universe. Such a radical redefinition of the word "knowledge" hinders communication and thus development of understanding about whether and how knowledge might be managed.

Finally, since the SECI matrix is the "engine" of Nonaka and his colleagues' theory of organizational knowledge creation, and that engine has now been shown to be empirically unsupported and conceptually flawed, we have to question whether the rest of the theory can be sustained. The SECI model and related ideas have undoubtedly been of heuristic value and, like the erroneous conclusion about making tasty bread, may have generated insights that will turn out to be more than someone's justified beliefs. Its value, however, has now been exhausted, and we need to begin afresh, if at a higher level than before.

Implications for Knowledge Management Theory and Practice

Two avenues may prove fruitful—and indeed much work has already been done or is under way. First, we need to work to develop useful theory. If knowledge management is to progress and provide useful advice (even to provide clear evidence on whether or not "knowledge" is manageable, and if so in what sense) we need common working definitions of the concept. Establishing these will not be an easy task. Dewey and Bentley (1949, p. 48) concluded that "the word 'knowledge' ... is a loose name ... for which it is impossible to give a precise definitive account." Bentley noted that at least all the meanings they considered concerned living things (see Ratner & Altman, 1964, p. 459), but knowledge management authors have extended "knowledge" to cover something "embedded" (or "embodied") in "technology" (e.g., Teece 2001, pp. 126–130; see also Nonaka & Takeuchi, 1995, pp. 223). A review of knowledge-related concepts in the field of learning and literacy (Alexander et al., 1991) reveals a further lack of agreement and Bereiter (2002) has recently offered a new way of thinking about knowledge specifically directed at educational issues. While researchers in artificial intelligence did have a clear definition, that too has been criticized and new approaches are emerging (e.g., Clancey, 1997).

This is not to suggest that we can do no useful work unless or until we agree on a definition of knowledge. Students of knowledge management might benefit by drawing on previous work in cognitive science, education, biology, psychology, and other empirical disciplines rather than, on the whole, ignoring such work, and trying to literally invent a "new wheel." In the absence of consensus on a working operationalizable definition of knowledge, knowledge management researchers could at least be more explicit about which definition they are using so that the effects of using different perspectives can be discussed, and consensus can emerge on which approach seems more useful than others. Unless we recognize this confusion and develop and share as clear and unambiguous a meaning (or meanings) of what we mean by "knowledge," we are unlikely to make any progress, or even to discover whether what we now call "knowledge" was previously called something else (e.g., "information").

A second potentially useful avenue of research would be to conduct systematic reviews of existing research in knowledge management with a view to determining the extent to which something new is being studied, and if so, what the dimensions and characteristics of that new object are. This implicitly bottom-up approach to establishing what the field of knowledge management is concerned with is a necessary task complementary to that of theory-building and synthesis. All these kinds of work are already taking place—witness two recent knowledge management handbooks (Dierkes, Antal, Child, & Nonaka, 2001; Easterby-Smith & Lyles, 2003a)—and our remarks are intended to underscore the importance of such work.

As regards practice, first it should be noted that we have focused on reviewing the evidence, arguments, and theoretical concepts of the "engine" of knowledge creation. We have not reviewed knowledge management projects that have been inspired by the SECI matrix, or other components of Nonaka and his colleagues' models. Just as the bread-making team was able to develop a functioning bread-making machine despite apparently false assumptions about the process of making bread (and Collins's studies showed that scientists' work proceeded to success on similar false assumptions), so it is possible that useful innovations in the management of knowledge have been inspired by the SECI matrix. We would argue, however, that any such successes could not be *explained* by Nonaka and Takeuchi's theory for the reasons given above. If there are any such cases, they would need to be studied in some depth to determine exactly *why* they came about.

A second practical point concerns the management of tacit knowledge. It is widely agreed that tacit knowledge is important and if it cannot be converted wholly into explicit knowledge, we need to be alert to other ways of managing it. Here, the fact that so many of Nonaka's examples are based on teamwork seems to the point since the use of multidisciplinary teams does appear to be a useful way of "unlocking" and sharing tacit knowledge through learning-by-doing together. This observation, in turn, suggests that perhaps some tacit knowledge can only be managed by particularly sensitive ways of managing people. The notion of communities of practice, natural or contrived, comes to mind in this context. Communities of practice can be seen as an attempt to leave knowledge where it is generated and used, and to control it indirectly by managing, motivating, and rewarding people. The idea that it might not be possible, or perhaps not fruitful, to attempt to separate "knowledge" from the context of its use also directs attention toward managing production processes and the design of work more generally, as well as to the management of people. Of course, this is not the only avenue open to managers—they can and do attempt to diminish reliance on tacit knowledge by redesigning products, production processes, or both, through what used to be called "deskilling."

Third, when generalizing about knowledge management it is all too easy to forget that the needs of organizations differ greatly one from the other. It is no accident that Nonaka and his colleagues developed their ideas through studying innovative organizations, and such organizations may have special knowledge management needs. An innovating organization, one that implicitly introduces changes to products, processes, or to both, must have management structures (in the widest sense) that facilitate the generation of new ideas and their evaluation and dissemination throughout an organization. Some of the kinds of management and work processes that might help are those discussed by Nonaka and his colleagues. If Nonaka is right to suggest that individual employees are or can be an important source of new ideas originating in working practices, and new ideas are important to an organization, then clearly means need to be established to capture those ideas and to bring them into the public domain. They probably will take the form, among others, of discussions, working together to learn from each other. We are simply suggesting that it does not appear useful to conceptualize such processes in terms of tacit–explicit knowledge transfer, or to confuse ideas with knowledge.

However, companies or enterprises that compete in ways that do not depend so highly on innovative practices implicitly might not need the same kinds of knowledge management practices. They will be less interested in generating new ideas than in the management of routine, by, for example, reusing knowledge and documenting best practice rather than reinventing the wheel to cope with repetitive problems. In this context, Nonaka and his colleagues' model and discussion probably holds little of interest. Snowden (2002) has described three generations of knowledge management, placing Nonaka's ideas in the second generation. Perhaps what Snowden has actually identified is that different models suit different kinds of firms, and firms that depend on innovation could do worse than to follow what seem to be the practical implications of the SECI model and related ideas. Firms that do not need to innovate in the same way, in contrast, can well stick with first-generation knowledge management, otherwise known as information management.

Finally, we believe there is another practical lesson for academic and managerial practitioners that arises from our investigation—claims to knowledge (including this chapter) should be treated with informed and critical skepticism. Consumers of academic research, and particularly of popularized versions, such as Nonaka and Takeuchi (1995), must become sophisticated critical consumers. This means that they must learn to ask questions about the nature of evidence being offered to support a claim; they must ask how that evidence was collected; they must question whether the methods of data collection used were valid and tested. If they are satisfied with the answers to these questions, they must then ask if the data has been analyzed adequately, or if it is open to alternative interpretations, and they must learn how to evaluate the linkages between evidence and claims. Nonaka and his colleagues did draw attention to some of the methodological limits of the original SECI model (Nonaka et al., 1994), but perhaps not forcefully enough, and their cautions went unheeded in a market for ideas that was crying out for a model like theirs in the mid-1990s.

NOTES

1.   The theory appears to have originally been developed by Nonaka (1991a, 1991b, 1994) and subsequently presented in several collaborative publications (e.g., Nonaka et al., 1994; Nonaka & Takeuchi, 1995). The chapter will refer to "Nonaka'" and "Nonaka and his colleagues" interchangeably except where it is necessary to be more precise.

2. The Nonaka and Takeuchi (1995) volume, for example, has been cited over 1,000 times between its publication in 1995 and October 2004. The number of citations has increased year by year, as has the range of categories of journals in which this publication has been cited (see the ISI Citation Indexes, searched April 2003).

3. The volume of citations of their work (see Note 2) makes it difficult to be certain that all significant criticisms of their model have been identified. For this chapter, abstracts of all the citations of Nonaka and Takeuchi (1995) (to December 2002) were searched for terms indicative of criticism or significant amendment: only six were found. Further criticism may have been published in edited volumes, which are typically not indexed. However, we assume that had any sustained criticism been published, it would have been cited. In the absence of any such evidence, we are left with the impression that no systematic critique of their model has been published.

4. It should be noted that the significance of Japanese management and social practices for the model of information/knowledge creation that Nonaka developed is evident in his papers (see, e.g., Hedlund & Nonaka, 1993; Imai et al., 1985; Nonaka et al., 1994).

5. It does not appear that Nonaka and his colleagues have responded, either directly or indirectly, to any of these criticisms.

6. The data were also analyzed using structural equation modeling, but the paucity of data precluded full development of this model (see Nonaka et al., 1994). We have therefore limited our discussion to the confirmatory factor analysis.

7. Nonaka's earlier studies focused on *semantic* information, as distinct from *syntactic* information, which, he argues, is usually meant when "information" is studied (see especially Nonaka 1991b).

8. It should be stressed that neither Nonaka nor, to the best of our knowledge, anyone else has made this explicit suggestion. The shift from semantic information to knowledge in Nonaka's work (e.g., Hedlund & Nonaka, 1993; Nonaka, 1991b, 1994) suggests he implicitly made this connection.

9. It should be noted that Nonaka uses the word "concept" to mean new product or process ideas. This is clearly different from the usual meaning of that word in the context of epistemology.

10. The distinction between technical and cognitive tacit knowledge is curious because it reinstates the body versus mind dualism that Nonaka and his colleagues are otherwise at pains to disavow. See Bereiter (2002, p. 176) for another example of "Western" dualism in their ideas.

11. Strictly speaking, Nonaka and his colleagues intend "socialization" to refer to the transfer of tacit knowledge from one person to another, but this must involve creation of tacit knowledge in or by the person who did not initially possess it.

12. Klein (1998, p. 268) in fact argues that "justification" is inadequate, and epistemologists now prefer to define knowledge as "true, warranted belief."

13. This idea continues to interest them (see Nonaka et al., 2001b, p. 15), but it plays no part in the SECI model development. The suggestion that knowledge is a process "toward" truth seems to imply the notion of truth as being outside human endeavor that they criticized.

14.   Nonaka and his colleagues do not discuss "belief," implicitly taking its meaning for granted—an unsound position since "belief" is an ambiguous word (see Dewey, 1986, p. 15). Luper (1998) also indicates that the relationship between knowledge and belief is unclear.

REFERENCES

Adler, P. S. (1995). Comment on I. Nonaka: Managing innovation as an organizational knowledge creation process. In J. Allouche & G. Pogorel (Eds.), *Technology management and corporate strategies: A tricontinental perspective* (pp. 110–124). Amsterdam: Elsevier.

Alexander, P. A., Schallert, D. L., & Hare, V. C. (1991). Coming to terms: How researchers in learning and literacy talk about knowledge. *Review of Educational Research, 61*(3), 315–343.

Barbiero, D. (2002). Tacit knowledge. In C. Eliasmith (Ed.), *Dictionary of philosophy of mind*. Retrieved February 15, 2005, from http://artsci.wustl.edu/~philos/MindDict/tacitknowledge.html

Barfield, W. T. (1947). *"Manna": A comprehensive treatise on bread manufacture*. London: Maclaren & Sons.

Becerra-Fernandez, I., & Sabherwal, R. (2001). Organizational knowledge management: A contingency perspective. *Journal of Management Information Systems, 18*(1), 23–55.

Bereiter, C. (2002). *Education and mind in the knowledge age*. London: Erlbaum.

Cherry, C. (1966). *On human communication: A review, a survey and a criticism*. Cambridge, MA: MIT Press.

Clancey, W. J. (1997). *Situated cognition: On human knowledge and computer representations*. Cambridge, UK: Cambridge University Press.

Collins, H. M. (1974). The TEA set: Tacit knowledge and scientific networks. *Science Studies, 4*, 165–186.

Collins, H. M. (2001a). Tacit knowledge, trust, and the Q of sapphire. *Social studies of science, 31*(1), 71–85.

Collins, H. M. (2001b). What is tacit knowledge? In T. R. Schatzki, K. Knorr Cetina, & E. von Savigny (Eds.), *The practice turn in contemporary theory* (pp. 107–119). London: Routledge.

Dewey, J. (1986). *Logic: The theory of inquiry*. In J. A. Boydston (Ed.), *The later works, 1925–1953. Volume 12: 1938*. Carbondale: Southern Illinois University Press.

Dewey, J., & Bentley, A.F. (1949). *Knowing and the known*. Boston: Beacon Press.

Dierkes, M., Antal, A. B., Child, J., & Nonaka, I. (2001). *Handbook of organizational learning and knowledge*. Oxford: Oxford University Press.

Doyle, J. L. (1985). Commentary: Managing the new product development process: How Japanese companies learn and unlearn. In K. B. Clark, R. H. Hayes, & C. Lorenz (Eds.), *The uneasy alliance: Managing the productivity-technology dilemma* (pp. 377–381). Boston: Harvard Business School Press.

Easterby-Smith, M., & Lyles, M. A. (Eds.). (2003a). *The Blackwell handbook of organizational learning and knowledge management*. Oxford: Blackwell.

Easterby-Smith, M., & Lyles, M. A. (2003b). Introduction: Watersheds of organizational learning and knowledge management. In M. Easterby-Smith & M. A. Lyles (Eds.), *The Blackwell handbook of organizational learning and knowledge management* (pp. 1–15). Oxford: Blackwell.

Engeström, Y. (1999). Innovative learning in work teams: Analyzing cycles of knowledge creation in practice. In Y. Engeström, R. Miettinen, & R.-L. Punamäki (Eds.), *Perspectives on activity theory* (pp. 377–406). Cambridge, UK: Cambridge University Press.

Glisby, M., & Holden, N. (2003). Contextual constraints in knowledge management theory: The cultural embeddedness of Nonaka's knowledge-creating company. *Knowledge and Process Management, 10*(1), 29–36.

Griffin, D., Shaw, P., & Stacey, R. (1999). Knowing and acting in conditions of uncertainty: A complexity perspective. *Systematic practice and action research, 12*(3), 295–309.

Hair J. F., Anderson R. E., Tatham R. L., & Black W. C. (1998). *Multivariate data analysis*. Englewood Cliffs, NJ: Prentice Hall.

Hedlund, G., & Nonaka, I. (1993). Models of knowledge management in the West and Japan. In P. Lorange, B. Chakravarthy, J. Roos, & A. Van de Ven (Eds.), *Implementing strategic processes: Change, learning and cooperation* (pp. 117–144). Oxford: Blackwell.

Imai, K., Nonaka, I., & Takeuchi, H. (1985). Managing the new product development process: How Japanese companies learn and unlearn. In K.B. Clark, R.H. Hayes, & C. Lorenz (Eds.), *The uneasy alliance: Managing the productivity-technology dilemma* (pp. 337–375). Boston: Harvard Business School Press.

Janik, A. (1988). Tacit knowledge, working life and scientific method. In B. Göranzon & I. Josefson (Eds.), *Knowledge, skill and artificial intelligence* (pp. 53–63). London: Springer-Verlag.

Janik, A. (1990). Tacit knowledge, rule-following and learning. In B. Göranzon & M. Floria (Eds.), *Artificial intelligence, culture and language: On education and work* (pp. 45-55) London: Springer-Verlag.

Jorna, R. (1998). Managing knowledge. *Semiotic Review of Books 9*(2). Retrieved September 17, 2000, from www.chass.utoronto.ca/epc/srb/srb/managing-know.html

Klein, P. D. (1998). Knowledge, concept of. In E. Craig (Ed.), *Routledge encyclopedia of philosophy* (pp. 266–276). London: Routledge.

Luper, S. (1998). Belief and knowledge. In E. Craig (Ed.), *Routledge encyclopedia of philosophy* (pp. 706–709). London: Routledge.

Nonaka, I. (1988a). Creating order out of chaos: self-renewal in Japanese firms. *California Management Review, 15*(3), 57–73.

Nonaka, I. (1988b). Toward middle-up-down management: Accelerating information creation. *Sloan Management Review, 29*(3), 9–18.

Nonaka, I. (1990). Redundant, overlapping organization: A Japanese approach to managing the innovation process. *California Management Review, 32*(3), 27–38.

Nonaka, I. (1991a). The knowledge-creating company. *Harvard Business Review, 69*(6), 96–104.

Nonaka, I. (1991b). Managing the firm as an information creation process. In J.R. Meindl, R. L. Cardy, & S.M. Puffer (Eds.), *Advances in information processing in organizations* (pp. 239–275). Greenwich, CT: JAI Press.

Nonaka, I. (1994). A dynamic theory of organizational knowledge creation. *Organization Science, 5*(1), 14–37.

Nonaka, I. (1995). Managing innovation as an organizational knowledge creation process. In J. Allouche & G. Pogorel (Eds.), *Technology management and corporate strategies: A tricontinental perspective* (pp. 73–109). Amsterdam: Elsevier.

Nonaka, I., Byosière, P., Borucki, C. C., & Konno, N. (1994). Organizational knowledge creation theory: A first comprehensive test. *International Business Review, 3*(4), 337–351.

Nonaka, I., & Kenney, M. (1991). Towards a new theory of innovation management: A case study comparing Canon, Inc. and Apple Computer, Inc. *Journal of Engineering and Technology Management, 8*(1), 67–83.

Nonaka, I., Konno, N., & Toyama, R. (2001). Emergence of "Ba": A conceptual framework for the continuous and self-transcending process of knowledge creation. In I. Nonaka & T. Nishigushi (Eds.), *Knowledge emergence: Social, technical and evolutionary dimensions of knowledge creation* (pp. 3–29). Oxford: Oxford University Press.

Nonaka, I., & Takeuchi, H. (1995). *The knowledge-creating company.* New York: Oxford University Press.

Nonaka, I., Toyama, R., & Byosière, P. (2001). A theory of organizational knowledge creation: Understanding the dynamic process of creating knowledge. In M. Dierkes, A.B. Antel, J. Child, & I. Nonaka (Eds.), *Handbook of organizational learning and knowledge* (pp. 491–517). Oxford: Oxford University Press.

Nonaka, I., Toyama, R., & Konno, N. (2000). SECI, *Ba*, and leadership: A unified model of dynamic knowledge creation. *Long Range Planning, 33*, 5–34.

Nonaka, I., & Yamanouchi, T. (1989). Managing innovation as a self-renewing process. *Journal of Business Venturing, 4*, 299–315.

Nonaka, I., Umemoto, K., & Senoo, D. (1996). From information processing to knowledge creation: A paradigm shift in business management. *Technology in Society, 18*(2), 203–218.

Poell, R. F., & van der Krogt, F. J. (2003). Learning strategies of workers in the knowledge-creating company. *Human Resource Development International 6*(3), 387–403.

Polanyi, M. (1969a). The logic of tacit inference. In M. Grene (Ed.), *Knowing and being: Essays* (pp. 138–158). London: Routledge & Kegan Paul.

Polanyi, M. (1969b). Tacit knowing: Its bearing on some problems of philosophy. In M. Grene (Ed.), *Knowing and being: Essays* (pp. 159–180). London: Routledge & Kegan Paul.

Ratner, S., & Altman, J. (1964). *John Dewey and Arthur F. Bentley: A philosophical correspondence 1932–1951.* New Brunswick, NJ: Rutgers University Press.

Snowden, D. (2002). Complex acts of knowing: paradox and descriptive self-awareness. *Journal of Knowledge Management, 6*(2), 100–111.

Stacey, R. D. (2001). *Complex responsive processes in organizations.* London: Routledge.

Teece, D. J. (2001). Strategies for managing knowledge assets: The role of firm structure and industrial context. In I. Nonaka & D. J. Teece (Eds.), *Managing industrial knowledge: Creation, transfer and utilization* (pp. 125–144). London: Sage.

Tsoukas, H. (2003). Do we really understand tacit knowledge? In M. Easterby-Smith & M. A. Lyles (Eds.), *The Blackwell handbook of organizational learning and knowledge management* (pp. 410–427). Oxford: Blackwell.

Yolles, M. (2000). Organizations, complexity, and viable knowledge management. *Kybernetes, 29* (9-10), 1202–1222.

CHAPTER 14

TEN YEARS OF KNOWLEDGE MANAGEMENT

Ramifications for Consultants[1]

Nicolas Rolland, Alice Guilhon, and Georges Trepo

While research continues to contribute to our understanding of the knowledge management (KM) arena, it has also had an unintended, harmful effect. Many practitioners criticize the theoretical research that characterizes the KM field as being largely disconnected from actual practice in corporations. At the same time, practitioners tend to unify KM initiatives into a "knowledge as possession" perspective, despite the reality that knowledge is "owned" by individuals—with varying goals and objectives—rather than their organizations. Universally applicable solutions therefore remain problematic. Indeed, if the gulf between theory and practice widens further, it will soon make more sense to talk of KM as a "symptom" rather than an organizational practice.

This chapter examines the main trends in KM over the last 10 years, and how these trends can be understood by consultants to facilitate the ability of their clients to bridge the gap between theoretical approaches and practitioner perspectives.

Challenges and Issues in Knowledge Management, 317–335
Copyright © 2005 by Information Age Publishing
All rights of reproduction in any form reserved.

TAKING STOCK:
A DECADE OF KM RESEARCH AND PRACTICE

As Trepo (1987) has argued, knowledge management may be no more than a fad. While this characterization may be true, it does not mean that KM is bound to disappear. As was the case with quality initiatives during the 1980s, reengineering in the 1990s, and business intelligence and organizational design at the turn of the millennium, researchers and practitioners regularly debate key KM challenges—ranging from renewing knowledge, creating new knowledge, and distributing knowledge, to establishing procedures best suited to its management.

People have always been fascinated by knowledge due to its eminently strategic character. Very early on, knowledge was associated with capturing information created and used in markets, largely through technology. This view is particularly true in the realm of economics. In the social sciences, especially in psychology, in contrast, knowledge acquires an individual dimension and is used as the basis for strategic reflection within organizations. The precursory work done by Polanyi (1958), which was carried on by evolutionists (e.g., Nelson & Winter, 1987) and management researchers (e.g., Boisot, 1995; Nonaka, 1991, 1994; Spender, 1996a, 1996b), suggests that the concept has achieved maturity and has become much more than a mere form of control. Knowledge management has become a management philosophy, a means of differentiation and innovation and a method of organization.

This chapter attempts to synthesize the main results of the work done by researchers and consultants in the KM field. Our main objective is to illustrate that while the efforts of researchers and practitioners have both progressed through several key stages, the results of this research and the proposed implementation models remain trapped within the perspectives of these two professions. As such, they limit the extent to which we have an adequate frame of reference for the conceptualization and implementation of KM.

As illustrated in Figure 14.1, KM is a continuum that stretches from the processes of information management (such as business intelligence) to the creation of organizational knowledge. Its definition is based on the development of the organization through the development of its knowledge. This process can be defined as a managerial philosophy that promotes continuously the creation, acquisition, and sharing of individual and organizational knowledge (cf. Bateson, 1979; Boisot, 1995; Drucker, 1993; Grant, 1996; Nonaka & Takeuchi, 1995; Sanchez & Heene, 1997; Spender, 1996a, 1996b, 1998; Varela, 1984; Von Krough, Roos, & Slocum, 1994; Wiig, 1999; Zack, 1998).

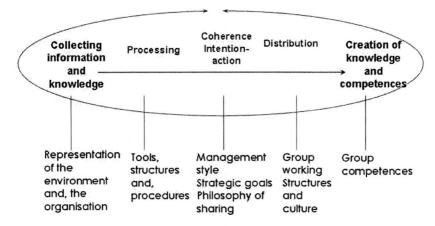

Figure 14.1.   The knowledge management continuum.

This process aims to raise the level of knowledge of individuals to achieve operational targets, create new organizational processes, and/or encourage and facilitate innovation. It is an organizational process resulting in the socialization of knowledge and a continuous learning process offering flexibility and change (Nonaka, 1994).

Even though, for many, the origins of KM are not new, the concept has become a field of research in its own right. The growth of articles in research is also based on the results of the theory of knowledge,[2] which gives the concept both an organizational and strategic dimension. The shift in the KM world is mainly due to globalization, a reality that obliges firms to have a global view of what is developed in every part of their organization, which most of the time is decentralized in business units and/or in country divisions. It is also due to the volatility of most business environments. Companies must be flexible and have quick access to relevant information and knowledge—the "know earlier, respond faster" doctrine. Both trends lead firms to focus on the management of their core competences, focusing on what they know and how to better coordinate this knowledge (Prusak, 1997).

Research Contributions in KM

Wiig (1999), Earl (2001), and Sveiby (1997) all explain that KM has its roots in different schools of thought and the concept has developed in several stages. The first wave of papers on KM explained the concept of knowledge, its dimensions, its role, its transformation, and why knowledge is strategic (cf. Drucker, 1993; Grant, 1996; Nonaka, 1994; Spender, 1996a, 1996b; Winter, 1987). These works distinguish information from knowledge and describe the weight of this "intellectual capital" in global production processes and competitive position. The second wave of papers analyzed how knowledge can be shared and its relation with organizational learning and strategy formation (cf. Leonard-Barton, 1995; Senge, 1990; Starbuck, 1992; Sanchez & Heene, 1998; Teece, Pisano, & Shuen, 1997; Weinstein, 1995; Zack, 1998). An emphasis in this wave focused on the role of trust, with researchers concentrating on the knowledge used in day-to-day "job living" (see Davenport & Prusak, 1999). The third wave is based on knowledge networks and social networks (Brown & Duguid, 1991; Hansen, 2002; Inkpen, 1998; Snowden, 2002; Wenger, 1998) and focuses on nurturing communities of practice and managing organizational space.

Knowledge management also has it roots in different schools of thought (see Earl, 2001): the technocratic school focused on technology and the cartography of knowledge; the economic school concentrated on knowledge management within organizations; and the behavioral school focused on communities of practice and corporate strategy. Researchers initially attempted to make this new discipline "scientific" within firms by using the technologies that enabled knowledge in the corporation to be accumulated, stored, and mapped. Once that knowledge was recognized within organizations as an intangible asset and a rare resource (the economic school of thought), researchers began to take interest in the owners of knowledge, that is to say, individuals themselves. Trust and cooperation then became key factors in the creation of knowledge.

The most significant results achieved over the last 10 years in the field of KM can be summarized by three major achievements:

- the creation of a theory of organizational knowledge;
- the role of organizational learning; and
- an embryonic reflection on the organization of KM.

The Theory of Organizational Knowledge

The frame of reference for KM processes was developed through a corpus of theories relating to resources and competences (cf. Barney, 1986; Collis, 1991; Grant, 1991; Prahalad & Hamel, 1990; Rumelt, 1982; Wernerfelt, 1984). The knowledge-based approach (Drucker, 1993; Nonaka & Takeuchi, 1995; Spender, 1996a, 1996b) follows this logic and demonstrates that knowledge has become a strategically important asset. Managers, accordingly, must focus on the production, acquisition, and movement of knowledge, inhibitors to knowledge, and the application of knowledge (Spender, 1996, 1998). The ability to acquire, share, and apply knowledge was thus viewed as the most important single factor in maintaining a competitive advantage (Cohen & Levinthal, 1990).

The theory of knowledge proposes that organizations are made up of resources, with knowledge being a key resource that enables firms to sustain competitive advantage. Such competitive advantage is conceptualized as the result of specific knowledge that the firm owns and that affords added value to its factors of production. Within this context, knowledge is a "nondelectable resource," which means that it can be used without being consumed. When owned by a firm, knowledge is a dynamic entity that changes and increases in value whenever new information is added to it. In essence, the firm's organizational knowledge and its ability to generate knowledge define the theory of the firm (Spender, 1996a, 1996b).

This version of the "knowledge-based view of the firm" impacts the "top-down" effect of existing management theories that perceived firms as hierarchical structures organized around the superior knowledge of management or shareholders who own tangible assets (Spender, 1998). This theory also explains the essential role played by the "middle manager" as an intermediary and a catalyst in the knowledge exchange process, which indirectly indicates the need for mediation (Nonaka, 1994). Mediation, in turn, explains the need for independent yet interdependent coordination in the overall organization of the company.

This theory concentrates on defining the forms of knowledge in the organization (Spender, 1996a, 1996b) as well as the process of conversion of knowledge through interaction between tacit and explicit knowledge (Boisot, 1995; Nonaka, 1994). Knowledge is analyzed as the result of a process of collection, selection, and distribution of information. This theory takes its roots in the fields of cognitive sciences and systems, biological systems (Varela, 1989), and genetic epistemology (Piaget, 1959). The *knowledge-based view of the firm* grew around the very concept of knowledge in the 1990s.

Organizational Learning as the Knowledge Creation Mechanism

The theoretical debate on knowledge management gradually evolved toward attempts to describe and explain the mechanisms of creating and renewing knowledge in an organizational context. The process of knowledge creation or renewal requires individuals, either alone or in groups, to regularly learn to develop knowledge on three different levels: professional, environmental, and behavioral knowledge. These forms of knowledge are highly tacit and they require researchers to investigate how they are created and transferred.

Organizations are defined not only as complex social systems, but also as organizational learning systems (Argyris & Schön, 1978; Kolb, 1984; Senge, 1990). Within this context, organizational learning is broadly defined by academics as the process of change in structures and knowledge, as well as a form of response by organizations that have historical and cultural foundations (Crossan, Lane, & White, 1999; Guilhon & Trepo, 2001).

However, as Spender rightly notes (1996a), while organizations develop processes that promote learning, they do not always reap the intended benefits. Learning must exercise an influence on strategy, management must be involved, and it must have a strategic significance for the organization. Yet, even if organizations implement processes that work in these directions, they must still be a source of sustainable competitive advantage (Rolland, 2003). Therefore, companies are showing a growing interest in learning, which just like knowledge, has now become a management imperative and suggested to be one of the keys to organizational success (Huber, 1991).

The Organization of KM

While many articles highlight the advantages and limits of the KM process, few investigate its structural aspects, which constitute an important key to its successful implementation. An effective KM process must match the coordination, structure, culture, and strategy of the firm (Snowden, 2002). To be truly effective, a KM process must be integrated into the culture of the organization that is promoting its development. This culture is implicitly founded on management's recognition of the importance of knowledge, and a clear strategic intention promotes a philosophy of sharing and communicating. *De facto*, frequent structural changes create opportunities for sharing and innovation. The virtual deincarnation (Child & McGrawth, 2001) of organizations is further underpinned by the control of information and knowledge flows that promote coordination methods suited to KM, ranging from project teams and communities of practice, to expert networks and discussion forums. The application of tools to KM comes at the end of the process as a way of assisting the conversion of information into knowledge.

Recent studies have explored the organization of knowledge networks and ways to nurture communities of practice (Hansen, 2002; Wenger, McDermott, & Snyder, 2002). These studies demonstrate the role of existing social networks and the role of trust as an informal coordination dimension.

Practitioner and Consultant Contributions

Although KM research provides insight into the underlying dynamics and processes associated with knowledge creation and knowledge sharing, the result of this work has not been systematically transformed into models (apart from conceptual methodologies, for example, Snowden, 2002, and Sveiby, 2002), methods, and tools. Consultants and software engineers, in contrast, focused much more fully on the "tool box" aspect of KM, typically neglecting the more dynamic problems associated with knowledge creation and organizational coordination. Work done by consultants was largely directed toward two streams: (1) the establishment of sharing and distribution platforms, mainly using information technology; and (2) the development of decentralized project processes. Consultants mainly focused on how to implement KM in specific parts of a company, without having a global perspective. This method was—and is still—successful *if* the focus is on a specific product, practice, country, and so forth.

Consultants and practitioners also focused on techniques for the quantitative measurement of KM process performance, often similar to return on investment analyses. Among the methods most widely adopted by firms are: (1) the Skandia Browser (IC), which focuses on intangible resources and the interconnections between them (e.g., the measurement of intellectual capital involves the functional measurement of the sum of human and structural capital); (2) the DOW method, which applies to patents and innovation and more qualitative methods, such as the American Productivity & Quality Centre method based on benchmarking; and (3) the most widely applied method, Kaplan and Norton's (1996) "Balanced Scorecard" (BSC), in which the measurement system is organized according to four perspectives (*financial* [profitability, cash flow], *customer* [satisfaction, market share, strength of relationships], *internal* [cycles, time, quality, productivity, innovation], and *learning* [the relationship between the employee and the system]).

Despite the advancements of these methods and measurement models, many companies continue to use techniques they have developed themselves.[3] Most of the methods are business oriented and they include both *financial approaches* that associate KM with revenue, profit or cost reductions (the company calculates trends in these measurements relative to the products or services impacted by the KM process), and *marketing-based* methods that focus on levels of customer satisfaction and loyalty. The interest shown by firms in marketing-based approaches has substantially increased in the last 5 years. When our research started in 1998, the reported interest level was 21%, compared to 72% in 2002.

As examples of these approaches, some companies calculate the annual savings achieved by avoiding duplication in R&D, capturing new sales, reducing overhead, and demonstrating how the efficiency of horizontal communications has improved. Beyond the notion of cost, this approach is based on the search for organizational links and synergy between individuals or departments. Other methods calculate the possibilities afforded to engineers, designers, or the sales force to quickly find quality information, thus enabling the company to save time and money.

Practitioner contributions also include two-dimensional learning-based approaches that (1) attempt to determine the reduction in the duplication of mistakes and (2) the extent to which individuals taking part in this process have progressed within the organization, reflecting a human resources management orientation to KM. Other approaches focus on the acceptance of the process. Since many KM processes are highly complex, their scope of use is limited. Thus practitioners have also attempted to measure the use of KM tools, for example by compiling the number of connections to company intranet sites and various databases.

A STUDY OF KM REQUIREMENTS

For 5 years, we conducted research into KM practice and developments in 102 international companies. Our research methodology followed a grounded theory approach in which we conducted interviews at each company a minimum of three times between 1998 and 2002. Most of the time, we questioned two people in each company for a total of 351 respondents (see Table 14.1). The study was designed in two stages, based on exclusively qualitative methods.

Table 14.1.   Characteristics of the Firms Surveyed

Regions	Number of Firms	Percentage
Europe	59	55
United States	37	38
Australia	4	4
Asia	2	3
Total	102	100

Industry	Number	Percentage
Telecommunications	39	35
Computer	20	20
Health	17	18
Aerospace	11	12
Chemical	10	11
Environment / Water	5	5
Total	102	100

Note: Firms interviewed are mainly European firms and U.S. firms. Roughly one half of the European companies are French multinationals. Some of the interviews at the U.S. companies were conducted at their European headquarters.

The purpose of the first stage of interviews was to understand the context of KM development and how companies viewed KM by (1) taking stock of KM practices and their evolution over the last 4 years and (2) defining key dimensions that would enable us to classify theses practices in terms of KM strategies. The objective of the second stage was to understand company expectations of KM initiatives and how these processes might be enhanced through the utilization of consultants.

The selection of cases follows the logic of theoretical selection, typical for theory building through case study (Eisenhardt, 1989), and our data gathering activity continued until we reached a point of "scientific saturation" (Miles & Huberman, 1988). Data were collected based on a triangulation strategy, through interviews, analyses of internal and external documents, and participant observation. Based on a review of the literature, data were categorized into different dimension matrices (Miles & Huberman, 1988) and analyzed according to an open coding technique (Corbin & Strauss, 1990). The data were first broken down by taking apart observations and interviews, identifying different ideas and events. The data were then regrouped into categories, pulling together groups of ideas and events into subcategories. The next step was axial coding, which identified main categories and made connections between them and their subcategories.

Company KM Requirements: The Survey Results

We attempted to identify and differentiate both formal, structured KM processes as described by Davenport (1997) and the more informal, potentially hidden processes that influence their development.

KM Motivation: A Will to Learn Rather Than a Strategic Goal

Our study suggests that KM initiatives are not explicitly used as decision-support tools and are not part of any formal strategic process. As summarized in Table 14.2, we found a number of motivations and goals underlying the development of KM:

- *To learn what the company "knows."* Key goals included identifying the sources of knowledge, who "owns" the knowledge, and what the firm needs to learn. More than 60% of the firms believed that KM was implemented to promote learning.
- *To save time.* If knowledge is to be easily accessed and used in an efficient manner, respondents noted that it must be mapped out or organized in readily understood ways.

- ***To know customers better.*** Key goals included enhancing the firm's ability to provide customized responses to their needs and to meet their future expectations. Just under half of the firms (47%) developed KM with a view to building a customer knowledge base.

- ***To train.*** Key goals focused on problems related to staff rotation and the transmission of strategic knowledge throughout the organization. This motivation was far more prevalent in small companies (78%) than in large ones (22%). In smaller companies, the loss of knowledge when key employees leave can have serious consequences.

- ***To innovate.*** Twenty four percent of the firms used KM as a way of creating new products and processes.

- ***To identify competitor knowledge.*** In our early interviews, over half the respondents associated KM with business intelligence that aimed at accessing information/knowledge outside the company.

As illustrated in Table 14.2, company motivation for KM gradually evolved to include other aspects of management, such as marketing and HR. By 2002, the main motivations were associated with *learning* and *marketing* more than with quality management, decision support, or strategy. The motivations changed in 18% of the companies between 1998 and 2002, with the shift in most instances toward learning. It appears that if the first attempts at knowledge management fail, the companies still find benefits that may differ from their original motivation. Overall, however, the will to create a global process from the outset that is useful for the entire company seems to be one of the keys to the ultimate success of the process.

Table 14.2. Company Motivation for KM Initiatives

Motivation	1998	2000	2002
Identify what the company knows	91%	88%	82%
Save time	47%	52%	61%
Develop collective intelligence	22%	44%	56%
Enhance customer relationships	12%	34%	47%
Staff training	9%	26%	39%
Innovation	51%	32%	24%
Identify what other companies know or do	56%	33%	12%*
Other	2%	3%	3%

*This figure reflects a steady decline in the number of companies that view KM and economic/industrial intelligence practices as largely the same.

KM Strategies and Foci

The theory of KM has been evolving over the last 10 years and has passed through several phases (cf. Earl, 2001; Sveiby, 1997; Wiig, 1999). The first of these was the *philosophical phase* in which academics focused on the entity of "knowledge" and gave this concept a strategic dimension. The second phase was the *technological phase*, where the IT dimension took the lead. The third was the *networked phase*, where academicians stressed the need to link individuals together through trust building and dialogue. The latest wave is the *strategic-learning phase*, which aligns the learning priorities with business strategies and emphasizes that KM should be integrated into the decision-making process.

Within this context, and following the results of Hansen, Nohria, and Tierney's (1999) research, our interviews pointed to three key KM strategies (KMS).

- **Technological KMS**. This strategy, also referred to as a codification strategy (Hansen et al., 1999) or the technocratic school (Earl, 2001), is designed for the structure and cartography of organizational knowledge. This approach emphasizes technological applications, systems, and databases. It focuses on information and explicit knowledge. Individuals have to make their knowledge explicit in order to transfer it to a database.

- **Personalization KMS**. This approach, which is also referred to as the spatial school (Earl, 2001), is designed for the emergence of knowledge. With this strategy, knowledge is closely tied to the person who developed it (Hansen et al., 1999). Firms focus on dialogue and face-to-face techniques for knowledge sharing. The purpose of this KMS is to facilitate learning through shared experience.

- **Socialization KMS**. This perspective combines both technological and personalization approaches. Emphasis is placed on knowledge communities, groups of people inhabiting the same knowledge space and interacting with each other through relationships, and socialization. This KMS is designed to exchange and to pool knowledge.

From a practitioner's point of view, our interviews suggest that companies are disappointed with the technological strategy and have turned toward building and attempting to sustain knowledge networks and learning communities (see Table 14.3). Many companies (67%) in our study emphasized the importance of developing relationships for knowledge creation and sharing, taking form as communities of practices and knowledge networks.

**Table 14.3. Evolution of
Knowledge Management Strategy in Study Firms**

Knowledge Management Strategy	1998	2000	2002
Codification	72%	66%	33%
Personalization	8%	6%	12%
Socialization	12%	26%	55%

These networks, or knowledge communities, are social structures whose shared practices, identities, and common engagement serve as a living curriculum for new organizational members (Wenger, 1998). Some authors complete this concept with the notion of work and define communities of practice or self-organized communities as collections of individuals (informal groups) bound by informal relationships that share similar work roles and common context (Lesser & Prusak, 2001). This means that individuals or groups interact on a regular basis around work-related issues and challenges. The notion of practice, of course, does not have to be limited to the "work" dimension as corporate enterprise (Wenger, 1998), also reflecting Ouchi's (1980) description of "clan networks" where members operate on an informal basis of shared information and personal trust. A common theme across these discussions is that communities of practice differ from teams or groups that only have a task-oriented approach. To be truly effective, these communities must have a clear identity that provides individuals with the opportunity to associate themselves with others who share the same interests or functions (Lesser & Prusak, 2001). Collective action and social knowledge claims are thus legitimized in terms of community identity. With co-specialized knowledge and collective expertise, the community can both solve business problems and build personal knowledge. Indeed, communities help retain critical expertise and can improve an organization's responsiveness by enabling the rapid location of knowledge across the organization. Another benefit of these intraorganizational networks is their positive contribution to building a sense of trust, a common language, and mutual commitment critical to the knowledge-sharing process.

Expectations of KM

The changes in organizational expectations of KM initiatives are substantial. In the past, firms sought to centralize and capitalize on their intellectual capital. Today, it appears they are trying to give it a more fluid organizational dimension in the shape of people *and* structures. Our interviews revealed that expectations of KM processes are very different and vary greatly in terms of their intensity. For some, KM is just another way of accessing information or knowledge, while for others KM represents a new organizational orientation and an opportunity to generate new synergies and change working practices.

One of the most striking results found in the responses to the question about expectations is the change in behaviors in relation to these expectations. At the beginning of the research, we observed short-term expectations and emphasis on immediate productivity gains. Companies were seeking to measure knowledge as if it were a conventional asset. In the last 2 years of our research, the expectations became more social. Notions of learning (which is often the result of initial efforts to conserve knowledge and develop human resources), training, and culture began to appear more frequently in the interviews. Sharing knowledge, especially in order to be aware of what is happening elsewhere (including benchmarking and attempts at best practice transfer), seemed to be increasingly important as a way of framing effective solutions to complex situations. Companies are also changing their expectations because they have understood that KM must be a part of the organization itself, not simply part of any general policy and clearly not on the periphery of the company.

Against this new background, one of the most frequently mentioned motivations is the desire to establish dialogue within the organization. Many of our respondents (56%) thought that the development of collective intelligence based on dialogue would help in making decisions that were focused on the real problems in the company. More than just a question of strategy, such dialogue also contributes to the improvement of the atmosphere at work and company–employee relations. From a more productive perspective, KM is also a means for saving time for many respondents (61%). The structuring of knowledge saves time in solving problems, executing tasks, and responding to customers.

LESSONS LEARNED: RAMIFICATIONS FOR CONSULTANTS AND RESEARCHERS

From both research and practitioner perspectives, KM does not yet seem to be a genuine management discipline. Moreover, we are still in search of true consensus on its definition and underlying theory, preventing the development of a unified model. The research borrows from psychology, organizational theory, and cognitive sciences in different proportions depending on the selected approach. Unfortunately, the outcome of all this work thus far falls well short of a "global" perspective on the management of knowledge within organizations, as demonstrated by the limited solutions proposed by consultants to HR, audit or Information Systems departments. *Stricto sensu*, KM has evolved substantially and independently of the other processes in the organization. It appears that KM is trapped in an ivory tower, reserved for decision makers and operational staff, without any involvement or links with middle management.

The most striking result of our survey is that the motivations, expectations, and ultimately the requirements of KM have moved toward a more global awareness. Knowledge management has progressed from being a search for information about competitors (and partners) toward becoming a management philosophy based on a realization of the importance of communicating, sharing, and distributing information. Over half (56%) of the firms in our sample reported the need to implement KM at the very heart of the organization, with a view to providing support for strategic decision making. There seems to be, however, a wide gap between such intentions and organizational practices.

Researchers, consultants, and practitioners have still not agreed on the approaches that should be developed to make KM processes more effective and efficient. While research may be contributing to our concepts about knowledge management, it also tends to have a harmful effect, literally pushing researchers and practitioners apart. Practitioners are increasingly lamenting the fact that theoretical research is far more "advanced" than actual practice in corporations, and that current research tends to overly intellectualize the KM process. More than 70% of the respondents noted that the creation of mere typologies does not serve any useful purpose, especially compared to more "pragmatic" research into key success factors or clear implementation processes. If the gap between theory and practice continues to widen, it may soon make more sense to talk of knowledge management as a "symptom" rather than a "process."

The organizational approach to KM can be defined as the process of knowledge creation that involves structure, culture, management practices, tools, and the expected results. As reflected in Figure 14.2, implementing a KM process is influenced by the harmonization of key stages involving different players. Recognition from the CEO (or his management team) and the philosophy that he or she promotes in terms of sharing and dialogue are the starting point for successful implementation. Mediators must then disseminate this philosophy, ensuring that the knowledge is traceable and that information can be converted into knowledge in teams and projects. The mediator acts as a catalyst to motivate and involve individuals in the process, either alone or in the shape of group competences. In essence, the mediator is the link between the different stages in the implementation of a KM initiative.

This process begins with the collection of useful and relevant information (internal or external) and established knowledge (including the "dormant capacity," which is often a source of competitive advantage; see

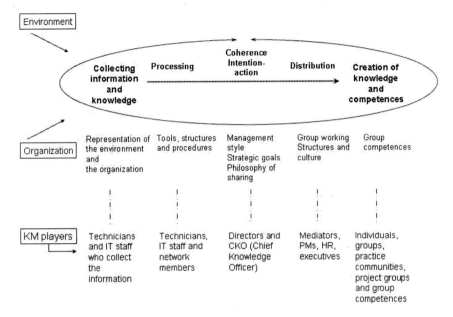

Environment					
	Collecting information and knowledge	Processing	Coherence Intention- action	Distribution	Creation of knowledge and competences
Organization	Representation of the environment and the organization	Tools, structures and procedures	Management style Strategic goals Philosophy of sharing	Group working Structures and culture	Group competences
KM players	Technicians and IT staff who collect the information	Technicians, IT staff and network members	Directors and CKO (Chief Knowledge Officer)	Mediators, PMs, HR, executives	Individuals, groups, practice communities, project groups and group competences

Figure 14.2.   Knowledge management process diagram.

Baden-Fuller & Volberda, 1997). Technicians and IT specialists can work with managers and team leaders to update the requirements for information and map out knowledge against engaged projects. This collection phase will only be effective if it is based on a representation of the environment and the organization that is shared, at least among the teams. For example, if individuals do not interpret the strategic directions the same way or do not all agree with them, great difficulties will be forthcoming. Only with this shared vision can clear requirements emerge from the KM structure.

The processing phase consists of simplifying the collected information and knowledge, and, where possible, rendering it explicit. Tools and organizational procedures used in conjunction with the IT structure can be very helpful in sorting, summarizing, and transferring the relevant elements to the right players. At this stage, technicians clearly play a key role and consultants often intervene through training or the implementation of tools. As suggested earlier, however, the processing phase is dependent on the clarity and coherence of the CEO's intentions and actions.

The latter stages of the process rely on an organizational culture that promotes the distribution and sharing of knowledge. The keys to success in the transformation and creation of knowledge are mediator roles, such as the project manager (PM), chief knowledge officer (CKO) as project co-

coordinator, and CEO who is a role model. This goal is often achieved by a reduction in the number of hierarchical layers and the redeployment of staff to horizontal mediating functions or PM roles such that their knowledge is secured for the organization in project memory.

Consultants should focus on developing approaches and models that highlight the role of the individual in the distribution and creation of knowledge in different contexts. Implementation of a KM process must start with an analysis of the structures, roles, and culture of the organization. Only then will it be possible to determine which stages of the KM process have already been implemented and which courses of action should be followed to meet the goals defined by the organization.

Consultants should also ensure that the client firm undertakes (1) sufficient analysis of the tools, practices, goals, and roles of key stakeholders in the KM process; (2) a cultural and structural analysis; (3) identification of individual and group competences and related communities of practice; (4) common representation of the KM process in the local context; (5) implementation of missing stages and the creation of mediator positions as needed; and (6) the promotion of knowledge networks rather than a technology-based approach. By more fully integrating academic/researcher and practitioner/consultant perspectives on KM structures, processes, and outcomes, knowledge management might one day become a true management discipline.

NOTES

1. An earlier version of this chapter was presented as part of the Management Consulting Division program at the 2003 Academy of Management meeting in Seattle, Washington.
2. Academic success essentially began in 1996 with the publication of a special Winter edition of the *Strategic Management Journal* entitled "Knowledge and the Firm."
3. It is important to note that while many corporations use numerous indicators, others use none at all.

REFERENCES

Argyris, C., & Schön, D. (1978). *Organizational learning: A theory of action perspective.* Reading, MA: Addison-Wesley.
Baden-Fuller, C., & Volberda, H.W. (1997). Strategic renewal: How large complex organizations prepare for the future. *International Studies of Management & Organization, 27*(2), 95–120.
Barney, J.B. (1986). Organizational culture: Can it be a source of sustained competitive advantage? *Academy of Management Review, 11*(3), 656-665.

Bateson, G. (1979). *Mind and nature: A necessary unity.* New York: E. P. Dutton.

Boisot, M.H. (1995). *Information space: A framework for learning in organizations, institutions and culture.* New York: Routledge.

Brown, J. S., & Duguid, P. (1991). Organizational learning and communities of practice: Towards a unified view of working, learning and innovation. *Organizational Science, 2*(1), 40-57.

Child, J., & McGrath, R. G. (2001). Organizations unfettered: Organizational form in an information-intensive economy. *Academy of Management Journal, 44*(6), 1135-1148.

Collis, D. J. (1991). A Resource-based analysis of global competition: The case of the bearings industry. *Strategic Management Journal, 12,* 49–68.

Cohen, L., & Levinthal, D. (1990). Absorptive capacity. *Administrative Science Quarterly, 35,* 28–152.

Corbin, J. M., & Strauss, A. (1990). Grounded theory research: Procedures, canons and evaluative criteria. *Qualitative Sociology, 13*(1), 3-21.

Crossan, M. M., Lane, H. W., & White, R. E. (1999). An organizational learning framework: Form intuition to institution. *Academy of Management Review 24*(3), 522-537.

Davenport, T. H. (1997). *Information ecology.* New York: Oxford University Press.

Davenport, T. H., & Prusak, L. (1999). *Working knowledge.* Boston: Harvard Business School Press.

Drucker, P. F. (1993). *Post-capitalist society.* Oxford: Butterworth Heinemann.

Earl, M. (2001). Knowledge management strategies: Toward a taxonomy. *Journal of Management Information Systems, 18*(1), 215–233.

Eisenhardt, K. M. (1989). Building theories from case study research. *Academy of Management Review, 14*(4), 550.

Grant, R. M. (1991). The resource-based theory of competitive advantage: Implications for strategy formulation. *California Management Review, 33*(3), 114–135.

Grant, R. M. (1996). Toward a knowledge-based theory of the firm. *Strategic Management Journal, 17,* 109–122.

Guilhon, A., & Trepo, G. (2001, August). *Using organizational learning to successfully implement a corporate change program: Lessons from the experience of Shell's complex at Berre.* Paper presented at the annual meeting of the Academy of Management, Washington, DC.

Hansen, M. T. (2002). Knowledge networks: Explaining effective knowledge sharing in multiunit companies. *Organizational Science, 13*(3), 232–248.

Hansen, M. T., Nohria, N., & Tierney, T. (1999). What's your strategy for managing knowledge? *Harvard Business Review, 77*(2), 106–116.

Inkpen, A. (1998). Learning, knowledge acquisition, and strategic alliances. *European Management Journal, 16*(2), 223-229.

Kaplan, R. S., & Norton, D. P. (1996). *The balanced scorecard: Translating strategy into action.* Boston: Harvard Business School Press.

Kolb, D. (1984). Experimental learning: Experience as the source of learning and development. Englewood Cliffs, NJ: Prentice-Hall.

Leonard-Barton, D. (1995). Managing creative abrasion in the workplace. *Harvard Business Review, 73*(4), 2-4.

Lesser, E., & Prusak, L. (1999). Managing creative abrasion in the workplace. *Sloan Management Review, 43*(1), 101-102.

Miles, M. B., & Huberman, M. (1988). *Qualitative data analysis: An expanded sourcebook.* Thousand Oaks, CA: Sage.

Nelson, R. R., & Winter, S. G. (1987). *An evolutionary theory of economic change.* Cambridge, MA: Harvard University Press.

Nonaka, I. (1991). The knowledge creating company. *Harvard Business Review, 69*(6), 96–104.

Nonaka, I. (1994). A dynamic theory of organizational knowledge creation. *Organization Science, 5*(1), 14–37.

Nonaka, I., & Takeuchi, H. (1995). *The knowledge-creating company.* New York: Oxford University Press.

Ouchi, W. G. (1980). Markets, bureaucracies and clans. *Administrative Science Quarterly, 25,* 129–141.

Piaget, J. (1959). *The language and thought of the child* (M. Gabain, Trans.). New York: Humanities Press.

Polanyi, M. (1958). *Personal knowledge: Towards a post-critical philosophy.* New York: Harper Torchbooks.

Prahalad, C. K., & Hamel, G. (1990). The core competence of the corporation. *Harvard Business Review, 68*(3), 79–91.

Prusak, L. (1997). *Knowledge in organizations.* Oxford: Butterworth-Heinemann.

Rolland, N. (2003). *Taking the stock on knowledge management.* Working paper, Ceram Graduate School of Management.

Rumelt, R. P. (1982). Diversification strategy and profitability. *Strategic Management Journal, 15*(3), 303-317.

Sanchez, R., & Heene, A. (1997). Reinventing strategic management: New theory and practice for competence-based competition. *European Management Journal, 15*(3), 303-317.

Senge, P. M. (1990). *The fifth discipline: The art and practice of the learning organization.* London: Century Business.

Snowden, D. (2002). Complex acts of knowing: Paradox and descriptive self-awareness. *Journal of Knowledge Management, 6*(2), 23–28.

Spender, J. C. (1988). Pluralist epistemology and the knowledge based theory of the firm. *Organization, 5*(2), 233-256.

Spender, J. C. (1996a). Making knowledge the basis of a dynamic theory of the firm. *Strategic Management Journal, 17,* 45–62.

Spender, J. C. (1996b). Organizational knowledge, learning and memory: Three concepts in search of a theory. *Journal of Organizational Change Management, 9*(1), 63–78.

Starbuck, W. (1992). Learning by knowledge-intensive firms. *Journal of Management Studies, 29*(6), 713-740.

Sveiby, K. E. (1997). *The new organizational wealth: Managing & measuring knowledge based assets.* San Francisco: Berrett-Koehler.

Teece, D. J., Pisano, G., & Shuen, A. (1997). Dynamic capabilities and strategic management. *Strategic Management Journal, 18*(7), 509-533.

Trepo, G. (1987). Introduction and diffusion of management tools. *European Management Journal, 5*(4), 287–293.

Varela, F. J. (1984). Two principles of self-organization. In H. Ulrich & G. J. B. Probst (Eds.), *Self-organization and management of social system* (pp. 113-130). New York: Springer Verlag.

von Krough, G., Roos, J., & Slocum, K. (1994). An essay on corporate epistemology. *Strategic Management Journal, 15*, 53–71.

Weinstein, K. (1995). *Action learning: A journey in discovery and development.* Glasgow, United Kingdom: HarperCollins.

Wenger, E. C. (1998). *Communities of practice: Leanring, meaning, and identity.* New York: Cambridge University Press.

Wenger, E. C., McDermott, R., & Snyder, W. C. (2002). *Cultivating communities of practice: A guide to managing knowledge.* Boston: Harvard Business School Press.

Wernerfelt, B. (1984). A resource-based view of the firm. *Strategic Management Journal, 5*, 171–180.

Wiig, K. (1999). What future knowledge management users may expect. *CMA Management, 73*(7), 13-15.

Zack, M. (1998). Developing a knowledge strategy. *California Management Review, 41*(3), 125–145.

CHAPTER 15

THE WONDERFUL WORLD OF KNOWLEDGE MANAGEMENT

Does Knowledge Management Really Add Value?

Peter Holdt Christensen

When entering the wonderful world of knowledge management (KM), companies often ask themselves: "Is the cost of knowledge management really worth it?" And, admittedly, the answer is often "No, it isn't"—or that it's simply "too difficult" to document savings related to new KM initiatives (Lucier & Torsilieri, 2001; Rigby, 2001). Even though the KM literature promises—perhaps overpromises—billions of savings when implementing KM tools, the reality seems to be more about rhetoric than actual savings. In other words, the value of knowledge management is questionable.

This point, of course, raises a number of questions about the overall utility of research on knowledge management. Can research help bridge the gap between *knowing how* to practice knowledge management and what one can expect by *actually practicing* knowledge management? Is research on knowledge management somehow valuable for practitioners

Challenges and Issues in Knowledge Management, 337–364
Copyright © 2005 by Information Age Publishing
All rights of reproduction in any form reserved.

and their organizations? The chapter explores the realm of knowledge management, delving into its content—both theoretically and empirically. The initial interest for this study began when I was working with a number of Danish companies, introducing them to the academic world of knowledge management. My understanding of knowledge management was very much influenced by the vast amount of writings on the subject, but during the introduction of various KM perspectives, I noticed some serious discrepancies in relation to how these companies perceived and practiced knowledge management. The theoretical perspectives on knowledge management were less valuable for the companies—and they seemed to be somewhat distant from the company's perception and practice of knowledge management. This observation prompted me to explore the relationship between theoretical and practical KM perspectives as a way of testing the value of KM theory.

This chapter is an outcome of that project. It was no easy task, and I am not sure whether I succeeded in identifying the actual practice of knowledge management, and hence the value of theoretical approaches to KM practices. The chapter does, however, identify a number of discrepancies between academic perspectives on knowledge management and more practice-based approaches.

Research runs the risk of becoming obsolete if the only thing it produces is more and more accurate discussions of less and less important matters. If research on business studies is not able to reflect on and elaborate the understanding of either how business has been run, is run, or should be run, then the research is obsolete in the sense that it is not able to improve the practice of business. On the other hand, researchers and research institutions often run the risk of being little more than markets seeking funding, a tendency that could have devastating consequences for both the reasons and quality of the research. In these instances, research becomes the means for funding, and the freedom to pursue research is, to a considerable degree, transformed into a marketing strategy (Bok, 2002; Kirp, 2003).

The chapter explores the issue of whether KM research produces useful reflection on KM business practices. The question goes beyond *what* reflections are produced, and focuses on the extent to which these research findings not only *reflect* practice but are actually *applied* in practice. The analysis focuses on whether knowledge management has turned into a theoretical concept with little or no relation to how knowledge management is being practiced in companies. In essence, does the reality of knowledge management reflect KM theory—and does KM theory reflect the reality of knowledge management?

To my knowledge, there have not been any prior attempts to answer this question, and this may be due to a couple of reasons. First, the KM field is still in the making. The primary focus thus far has been on (1) making the field theoretically robust by combining it with various disciplines such as organization theory and organization economies, and (2) finding empirical evidence—often in the form of case studies—for the vast number of perspectives and processes included in these theoretical developments. Second, there are some basic methodological problems in ascertaining the coherence between theoretical and practical realities. The challenge is to initially extract the theoretical realities of knowledge management, and then to find KM's practical realities—ultimately comparing and contrasting the two perspectives. This analysis is in itself quite ambiguous, and—it may be argued—could only add to the confusion of the concept of knowledge management.

Given these concerns and limitations, the analysis focuses on *how* and *whether* KM theory can actually be visualized in the context of KM practice. First, drawing on a comparative review of peer-reviewed journal articles, the chapter creates a theoretical framework that encompasses the central contexts and outcomes for managing knowledge. Second, based on more than 150 "images" drawn from practitioners in 10 companies, a practitioner view of the central key drivers for knowledge management is developed. The analysis then compares these theoretical and applied views of knowledge management, exploring the extent to which theory reflects practice.

KNOWLEDGE MANAGEMENT AND ACTIONABLE KNOWLEDGE

In the introduction to a special issue of *Management Learning* on the knowledge-based perspectives on organization, Tsoukas (2002, p. 419) asks the question, "What value do we gain by viewing organizations from a knowledge-based perspective?" Although he never fully explains who "we" actually are—allegedly, it could be the academic world, the world of practitioners, or both—or how "value" is to be understood—or even measured—Tsoukas (2003, p. 420) draws the conclusion that:

> Viewing an organization from a knowledge-based perspective draws our attention to both the organizational routines and experiences on which individuals draw in order to carry out their tasks and the inherently creative potential of human action, which stems from when past organizational knowledge is applied in open-ended contexts.

Thus from Tsoukas's perspective, it appears that the underlying value is about drawing attention to certain elements that are assumed important in today's society, and therefore relevant to business conduct. A lingering question concerns the extent to which that attention is drawn to the "wrong" issues—issues that have little if any importance in practice.

Both researchers and practitioners are continually searching for tools and methods to navigate the knowledge-based company in the knowledge-based society. Unfortunately, it appears that the increased focus on knowledge management—visualized in the increased number of books, articles, conferences, workshops, and seminars on the topic—has fallen short of providing us with a consensus understanding of what knowledge management is. On the contrary, there appears to be many different ways of both conceptualizing and practicing knowledge management. So, at the same time that knowledge management has become a popular management technology, it has turned in to a somewhat problematic, faddish concept.

Knowledge management is a cross-disciplinary enterprise, encompassing anthropology, social psychology, organization theory, and economics (among others). Such conceptual diversity makes it somewhat difficult to exactly determine the history of the KM concept. Recent publications on knowledge management even include the philosophical subdiscipline of epistemology, dating back thousands of years, to explain exactly what is being managed (see, e.g., Fuller, 2002; Patriotta, 2003). As a consequence, the KM concept remains quite ambiguous, and its popularity may be explained as stemming from a "band wagon effect" rather than its ability to positively affect organizational performance (Rigby, 2001). Discussion about knowledge management has even evolved into its own rhetoric—from something that was essentially conceptualized as building an intranet, to become a symbol of the modern knowledge-based company. The question that remains, of course, is whether the KM concept has become more of a symbol than a technology and approach that can positively affect organizational performance.

Schendel (1996, p. 2), in his introduction to a special issue of the *Strategic Management Journal* on "Knowledge and the Firm," expressed confidence in the ability of knowledge management to contribute to organizational performance, referring to the potential of the concept: "A new theory of the firm, better still, a new theory of competitive advantage creation and maintenance would be of enormous value to the practice of management." This almost decade-old statement, which was made during an upsurge in writings on knowledge management, has been followed by much more moderate enthusiasm for the concept—and the belief in its ability to positively affect organizational performance. In their introduction to another special issue on KM in the *Journal of Management Studies*, for example, Swan and Scarbrough (2001, p. 915), acknowledged that: "The papers in this issue tend to be agnostic about knowledge management, seeking not to propel this particular discourse into further stardom but, rather, to redress its more narrow, functionalistic tendencies."

A similar stand is taken by Argote, McEvily, and Reagans (2003, p. vii) in their introduction to a special KM issue of *Management Science*, stressing that the practice of knowledge management in great part has been substituted by theory, to the point of creating theory for its own sake: "Because we felt that conceptual papers had outpaced empirical evidence in the area of knowledge management, we were particularly interested in empirical papers that provided new evidence about the phenomenon."

As these more recent quotations illustrate, there is reason to believe that academic writings on knowledge management have become—and perhaps still are—sidetracked in relation to what is actually happening in practice.

There is no direct evidence, however, that this is necessarily the case. Yet, if academia is to produce results that are applicable outside its "ivory tower," there must be some minimum coherence between what is being done (in practice), what research "sees" is being done, and what research suggests could be done better to improve organizational performance. If there is one thing more practical than a sound theory it is the successful application of theory in practice.

Knowledge Management: A Theoretical Perspective

Knowledge management has many labels and many foundations—stretching from the KM movement and the knowledge-based theory of the firm, to a new management discourse and the fad of knowledge management. One might even argue that knowledge management is not just solely about relabeling old management techniques, but also about relabeling its own rise (or fall).

Judging by the number of publications, in recent years the KM concept has supplanted such management trends as total quality management (TQM) and business process reengineering (BPR) as the dominant research field within organization and management. While there has been a significant decline in the number of publications that focus on TQM and BPR since 1995, the number of publications dealing with knowledge management has significantly increased from 1995 to 2002 (Christensen, 2003).

There is something reassuring about the KM concept, as the prevailing semantic interpretation of the phenomenon suggests that it can ensure an organization's survival. But although an organization engaging in knowledge management may validate itself in the eyes of an array of stakeholders, as Lucier and Torsilieri (2001) suggest, there is only a minor correlation between the application of knowledge management and the company's bottom line.[1] Critics thus question the extent to which knowledge management is about relabeling and adjusting to institutionalized norms rather than about activities that can affect the organization's technical core and have a positive impact on organizational performance.

In the early 1980s, knowledge management was first and foremost a "thing," in essence a technology that provided organizations with the opportunity for storing and disseminating information. Over the past two decades, the concept has evolved into being less about technology and more about—what may be termed—softer issues, such as culture, motivation, empowerment, communities, and learning. As Alvesson and Kärreman (2001, p. 1014) note, the KM concept itself is somewhat ironic: "An interesting irony is that knowledge management probably has a strong rhetorical appeal because of the promise to manage knowledge at the same time, as the point of using the term knowledge is to indicate something that cannot be managed."An underlying problem with the KM concept is that there is no agreement on the appropriate unit of analysis. Knowledge management basically deals with everything, and thereby vaporizes into being nothing special.

This section of the chapter attempts to clarify these issues by creating a theoretical foundation for defining and understanding knowledge management. Admittedly, this is no easy task, and a relevant question concerns the sample that should be used to develop this foundation. The chapter draws on peer-reviewed academic journal articles that focus on the concept of knowledge management. More specifically, the review is based on articles that have appeared in special journal issues on knowledge management from 1995–2003. The review focused on 1995 as a starting point because of the publication of Nonaka and Takeuchi's highly influential (1995) *The Knowledge Creating Company*, which represents the upsurge of academic writings on knowledge management. I have identified a total of nine special journal issues on knowledge management—five of them are included in the content analysis.[2] The five special journal issues included in the study contained a total of 50 articles (not including editorial introductions or conclusions; see Table 15.1).

A framework developed by Argote and colleagues (2003) was used as an initial guide for the content analysis of these articles. In their conclusion to a special KM issue of *Management Science*, Argote and colleagues categorized the articles by their focus on different perspectives within two KM dimensions: (1) the "knowledge management context," which basically deals with KM components and processes; and (2) "knowledge management outcomes," which focuses on the goals of managing knowledge.

The context dimension focuses on properties of units, properties of the relationships between units, and properties of knowledge. The property

**Table 15.1. The Study Sample: Special Issues of
Academic Journals Devoted to Knowledge Management**

Journal	Number of Articles
Strategic Management Review, 1996, vol. 17, Special Winter Issue	10 (2)
California Management Review, 1998, vol. 40, no. 3	13 (4)
Journal of Management Studies, 2001, vol. 38, no. 7	6 (1)
Organization Science, 2002, vol. 13, no. 3	7 (2)
Management Science, 2003, vol. 49, no. 4	14 (2)

Note. The (number) indicates editorial introductions and conclusions

of units relates the key driver of knowledge management to a specific unit, such as the individual or the organization. The property of the relationships focuses on what is going on between two or several units. The property of knowledge emphasizes the content of the knowledge itself, which some consider as capturing the essence of knowledge management.

In terms of KM outcomes, Argote and colleagues (2003) focus only on creation, retention, and transfer of knowledge. These processes, however, may reflect the KM outcomes in that particular issue of *Management Science*, and may therefore be too restrictive. Thus, the analysis in the present study uses the Argote and colleagues outcomes as a starting point and explores several other KM outcome possibilities.

In addition to the context and outcome dimensions, the present study also examines the empirical focus of the articles and additional visual artifacts associated with key KM drivers. The empirical focus has been included to explore the extent to which a particular theoretical KM approach is slanted toward particular types of companies (e.g., biotechnology, consulting firms, and computer companies). Additional emphasis is also placed on those KM drivers that make it easier—or more likely—that KM outcomes will be fulfilled. In sum, the content analysis in this study focuses on four categories:

- knowledge management context
- knowledge management outcome(s)
- empirical setting
- key drivers for knowledge management

The sample of articles in this study represents a vast array of methods, empirical settings, and theoretical foci (see the Appendix for a summary of the content analysis of the 50 articles). Although there is a lot of rhetoric "buzzing around," making it difficult to clearly delineate KM outcomes, enablers, and barriers, the content analysis of the 50 articles reveals six different knowledge management outcomes: integrating, producing (productivity), creating, transferring, measuring, and retaining. A seventh category—reflecting—is not directly linked to an outcome of knowledge management, but emphasizes a more theoretically based discussion. One could argue that the category is an outcome of researchers dealing with knowledge management, and not necessarily influenced by, or having direct consequences for, the practice of knowledge management. The reflecting outcome, however, is included in subsequent analysis, since it represents reflections on knowledge management that may contribute to a better understanding of the foundations for practicing knowledge management.

- *Integrating* knowledge focuses on how companies can become better at exploiting the knowledge that already exists, in terms of installing rules, standards, and routines that are useful in applying existing knowledge and making knowledge accessible through databases.
- *Producing* (increasing productivity) is both about protecting knowledge from competitors, and—within the organization—restructuring the physical and social workplace so that the holders of knowledge—such as employees—feel more comfortable about sharing and creating knowledge.
- *Creating* knowledge emphasizes combining knowledge differently than in the past, allowing for "creative abrasion" and new ideas on how to solve specific problems more innovatively than they have previously been solved.
- *Transferring* knowledge is about getting access to knowledge that already exists, but that was previously not accessible.
- *Measuring* the application of knowledge is an attempt to positively link KM efforts to organizational outcomes.
- *Retaining* knowledge is the process of either documenting knowledge or retaining the holders of knowledge—such as employees—by offering them either financial or nonfinancial incentives.
- *Reflecting* on knowledge and knowledge management encompass discussions focused on establishing a better foundation for understanding key KM drivers rather than providing specific advice on how to practice knowledge management.

Table 15.2 categorizes the 50 articles in terms of the context of knowledge management focused on and the outcome(s) emphasized as central

**Table 15.2.   Knowledge Management Outcomes:
The Theoretical Analysis**

Outcome/Context	Unit	Relation	Knowledge
Integrating	Grant, 1996 Teece, 1998 Becker, 2001 Tsoukas & Vladimirou, 2001 Orlikowski, 2002 Weber & Camerer, 2003		
Productivity	Das, 2003		

Creating	Bierly & Chakrabarti, 1996
	Sanchez & Mahoney, 1996
	Brown & Duguid, 1998
	Leonard & Sensiper, 1998
	von Krogh, 1998
	Nonaka & Konno, 1998
	Brusoni, 2001
	Hargadon & Fanelli, 2002
	Zollo & Winter, 2002
	Zellmer-Bruhn, 2003
	Sorenson, 2003
	Nadler, Thompson, &
	  Van Boven, 2003
	Chang & Harrington,
	  2003
	Lee, Lee, & Lee, 2003
		Almeida, 1996
		Appleyard, 1996
		Lincoln, Ahmadjian,
		  & Mason, 1998
		Powell, 1998
		Hargadon, 1998
		Uzzi & Lancaster,
		  2003	

Transferring	Szulanski, 1996
	O'Dell & Grayson, 1998
	Menon & Pfeffer, 2003
	Thomas-Hunt, Ogden, &
	  Neale, 2003
		Mowery, Oxley, &
		  Silverman, 1996
		Davenport & Klahr,
		  1998
		Takeishi, 2002
		Hansen, 2002
		Sine, Shane, &
		  Di Gregorio, 2003
		Borgatti & Cross, 2003
		Song, Almeida, & Wu,
		  2003	

Measuring	Glazer, 1998		
Retaining	Liebeskind, 1996		

Reflecting	Tsoukas, 1996
	Fahey & Prusak, 1998
	Ruggles, 1998
	Alvesson & Kärreman,
	  2001
	Postrel, 2002
	Birkenshaw, Nobel, &
	  Ridderstråle, 2002
			Spender, 1996
			Lanzara & Patriotta,
			  2001
			Thompson, Warhurst,
			  & Callaghan, 2001
			Gittelman & Kogut,
			  2003

**Table 15.3.   Key Drivers for Knowledge Management:
The Theoretical Analysis**

Outcome/Context	Unit	Relation	Knowledge
Integrating	Rules, routines Job rotation, yellow pages, coordination mechanisms Sharing identity, interacting face to face, culture		
Productivity	The physical and social environment of the workplace		
Creating	Organizational forms Communities of practice Group work Incentive systems Mentoring programs Trust. Loosely coupled systems Interruptive events	Interaction Communication channels Relations Culture Intensive communication such as brainstorming	
Transferring	Technology, culture, rewards, leadership, measurement, social ties	Relations, knowledge storage and delivery, prestige, know-who, human mobility	
Measuring	Methods and models		
Retaining	Incentives		
Reflecting	Mapping internal expertise		Social processes

for practicing knowledge management. Table 15.3 lists the key drivers for knowledge management.

These tables suggest a number of points about theoretical approaches to knowledge management. First, it is important to acknowledge that from a theoretical perspective KM can be conceptualized in almost endless ways—the different approaches to outcomes and key KM drivers have been, and still are being, applied to establish ever more complex conceptualizations that seek to illustrate or grasp the essence of KM (see, e.g., Orlikowski, 2002). These contributions, however, seldom succeed, with the exception of adding to the sheer volume of KM articles.

Second, KM writings seem to focus on how to *create* knowledge and—to a lesser degree—how to *transfer* knowledge. The preference for creating new knowledge emphasizes the strong tie between the KM literature and the literature on innovation and entrepreneurship. In the knowledge-based economy, an organization's success depends on its capability to create knowledge, which, in the past, had been referred to as innovation. In the knowledge company, this has been relabeled as "the creation of knowledge." Recently, KM's focus has started to include the transfer of knowledge, attempting to enable companies to become better at exploiting the vast potential of knowledge that already resides in the organization.

A third point concerns the drivers that support knowledge creation and knowledge transfer. While one might assume that these drivers would be different, it appears that the key KM drivers—such as organizational forms, incentive systems, culture, and social ties—are quite generic and applicable to both the creation and transfer of knowledge. The explanation for this is twofold. First, KM theory prefers to explain knowledge-related problems with reference to socialization, which is suggested to establish more (and better) social ties, improve the organization's knowledge-sharing culture, and increase communication and trust. Second, KM theory is also dominated by what may be termed "black boxes"—for example, culture, trust, and communication. The precise content of these "black boxes" is not explained, but they are nevertheless used as an explanation for how companies can improve knowledge creation and transfer.

The question of course remains as to whether the categorization in Tables 15.2 and 15.3 adds to our understanding of KM or simply increases our confusion. Admittedly, the two tables represent yet another categorization of KM perspectives, and as such they might increase the confusion as to what KM actually is. On the other hand, since KM theory is still in the making we must accept confusion as a premise for exploring KM approaches. As such, the tables represent an attempt to present informed confusion based on a sample of KM perspectives.

Knowledge Management: An Applied Perspective

Knowledge workers are often portrayed as being difficult to manage, because they typically create the knowledge they apply. In the knowledge society, the production of knowledge has shifted from being a highly centralized activity to being decentralized (Gibbons et al., 1994). The knowledge worker is, thus, an important part in the production of knowledge, and within companies this is partly recognized by decentralizing authority and decision making. Decentralizing decision making also acknowledges the tacit dimension of knowledge and the inherent difficulties in attempts to transform that tacit knowledge into explicit, easy-to-control knowledge. The practices of managing organization—as emphasized above—are also changing as a consequence of changes in our understanding of what knowledge *is* and *who* contributes to its production. Nevertheless, KM research ignores these fundamental realities about the foundations of knowledge.

Researchers, of course, maintain a pivotal role in collecting data: they create the questionnaires, conduct the interviews, and observe and capture organizational practices. Yet, even the realization that knowledge is often tacit does not seem to influence *how* researchers collect data. Traditional approaches to collecting data—questionnaires, interviews, and observation—fall short of truly capturing something that is not visible. It is rather paradoxical that at the same time we acknowledge the many faces of knowledge and the problems in defining, understanding, and "seeing" it, we rely on very traditional ways of collecting data on the subject.

Visual Methodology

This project undertakes a different approach to gathering data—visual methodology. In recent years, the interest in visual methodologies has steadily increased, which is reflected in the growing literature on the subject (see, e.g., Banks, 2001; Rose, 2001; Sturken & Cartwright, 2001; van Leeuwen & Jewitt, 2001). The potential of visual methodology is directly related to the importance of images in daily life. As Banks (2001, p. 2) emphasizes, we need to place much more emphasis on such visualization:

> Paradoxically, while social researchers encounter images constantly, not merely in their own daily lives but as part of the texture of life of those they work with, they sometimes seem at a loss when it comes to incorporating images into their professional practice.

Visual methodology is basically about collecting data in the form of images. Similar to other data collection methods (interviews, questionnaires, observation), there are a number of potential errors in the process that can lead to a misrepresentation of reality. One of the central barriers to visual methodology is the participant's reluctance to expose others—or being exposed—to a camera. During our discussions of the images in this study, for example, it became apparent that participants often felt uncomfortable taking pictures of their colleagues, or were unable to portray the situations they intended to. The lack of comfort in taking pictures of colleagues can be partly explained by the introduction of a new approach to gathering data within the context of business studies. Respondents in companies typically prefer interviews or questionnaires, since these mainstream tools yield a higher degree of certainty as to what has been said. Occasionally, the participants felt that it was impossible to portray KM drivers—in one situation a participant wanted to capture a meeting, but since the meeting involved several managers, she did not feel it was appropriate to use the camera. Thus, the comfort level and appropriateness of using cameras can create barriers to the data gathering process.

A related problem is that the images are far from a transparent window to the world around us (Rose, 2001, p. 6). In fact, different meanings are often projected onto an image. In looking at a picture, for example, a viewer might see it in a very different way than intended by the photographer—even though they are viewing the same image (Banks, 2001). One way of overcoming this potential error is to let the photographer explain what he or she intended to capture—or illustrate—with the picture (image), a process that could be understood as an attempt to justify the interpretation of images (Rose, 2001). An alternative approach is to establish an explicit methodology with clear-cut categories—or tokens—to search for, though there could still be some uncertainties as to what the photographer actually wanted the image to illustrate.

Based on the experience in attempting to portray key KM drivers, I must admit that even though today's world is dominated by images, and KM often deals with implicit factors—such as tacit knowledge, the "doing" of knowledge, and culture—that are difficult to capture in interviews and questionnaires, there are difficulties in applying visual methodology. The main difficulty lies in the use of cameras in a context where cameras, more often than not, cause suspicion. The other difficulties relate to the more generic problems of actually portraying what you intend to portray.

These limitations, however, can be overcome. First, visual methodology should not be the only way of gathering data, but must necessarily be supplemented with interviews with the photographers and the people in front of the camera. Second, the use of cameras must be thoroughly planned and accepted, meaning that the data gatherers must receive a clear problem statement as to what they are supposed to portray, and the context in which the cameras are to be used. It also takes time to feel comfortable with this new medium.

One way of getting started is to make sure that the project is properly introduced in the company. I have found it useful for the researcher to launch the project with a thorough introduction to visual methodology. This can be supported by running a "camera test"—before shooting the images that are intended as part of the study, the data gathers are instructed to portray situations covering the problem statement. This process is not intended to produce images that are part of the data, but instead is focused on creating a supportive and comfortable context for photographing organizational activities and surroundings.

Managers' Visual Images of Knowledge

To explore the practice of knowledge management, the study focuses on 10 managers who had signed up for a one-week KM seminar. Prior to arriving at the seminar, the participants were asked to portray key drivers of knowledge management in their organizations. Each participant was given a single-use camera, and asked to photograph images that they felt captured central KM drivers that they believed improved their organization's KM practices. During the workshop, we discussed the essence of the images and performed a content analysis of their data. The purpose of the content analysis was to empirically identify key KM drivers and explore the extent to which the theoretical distinctions identified earlier reflected the visual images captured by the managers. If the theoretical discussions of knowledge management were reflected in the key empirical KM drivers—or vice versa—KM theory would thus have value for KM practice.

The 10 managers submitted a total of 179 images. Twenty three images had to be rejected due to technical difficulties in recognizing the content, leaving a total of 156 images for the visual analysis. As summarized in Table 15.4, these images were divided into seven groups of key drivers: meeting rooms, colleagues, seminars, technology, physical structures, manuals, and the physical workplace.

Meeting rooms were portrayed as formal rooms where groups meet, for instance, to coordinate ongoing projects, or where organizational departments meet to brief each other on current happenings and what was planned for the near future. Images of *colleagues* are rare, but this does not necessarily mean that colleagues are unimportant for the process of managing knowledge. *Seminars* refer to meetings, either inside or outside organizational boundaries, that focus on a subject not directly linked to ongoing daily activities. The main purpose of the seminars is education.

Table 15.4. Key KM Divers: An Empirical Perspective

KM Drivers	Percent
Meeting rooms	3.5
Colleagues	6.0
Seminars	14.6
Technology	14.6
Physical structures	16.4
Manuals	19.8
Physical workplace	25.1

Technology is often portrayed in images of computers, but telephones are also considered an important part of the organization's technology. In this sense, technology is both a communication channel allowing persons—either through face-to face or face-to-interface interaction—to bridge the gap between not knowing and knowing. Technology can also encompass virtual holders of knowledge, such as manuals or databases. *Physical structures* represent the means through which the contact between organizational subunits is either hindered or fostered. Such physical structures, which are represented by pictures of organizational headquarters and offices, tend to influence employee movements, thereby increasing (or decreasing) the possibility of knowledge sharing. *Manuals* are holders of knowledge, and are often portrayed in images of shelves with lots of briefcases of files—in contrast to the manuals in the technology driver (noted above), manuals in this group refer to nonvirtual holders of knowledge. *Physical workplace* displays "local contexts" (e.g., the employees' cubicle and the nearby cubicles) and represents the inside of the physical structures.

Comparing the findings in the theoretical analysis (Table 15.3) with the seven groups of key drivers should enable us to answer whether KM theory actually reflects KM practice and reality. Only a few drivers are, however, exactly the same, suggesting a gap between theoretical and empirical perspectives on KM. A closer look, though, reveals that the KM drivers are basically the same, but they do have different levels of abstraction. The empirical findings do not emphasize trust, culture, interaction, and social ties—what might be thought of as generic KM drivers—but rather more practical enablers. Culture, for example, is a key driver in KM theory, but it is not directly represented in the empirical analysis—although specific factors that can build a KM-supporting culture—interaction with colleagues, meeting rooms, and the physical workplace—were noted. The same applies to interpersonal relations—it is not relations as such that are portrayed, but rather enablers that promote good relations, such as seminars, and facilitative physical structures. Similarly, coordination mechanisms are portrayed with enablers for diffusion, such as manuals and technology.

The theoretical and practical key drivers are quite similar, but their level of abstraction is different. Whereas theory deals with a high level of abstraction, and focuses on generic terms such as trust, interpersonal ties, and shared identity, the practical perspectives focus on what actually enable the generic drivers. The empirical analysis also stresses the difficulty in distinguishing between KM activities and other organizational activities, since these different activities blend in to each other in practice. In other words, the images clearly illustrate that the practice of knowledge management is not decoupled from daily activities, but is precisely an integral part of ongoing daily activities.

Drawing on these visual images, empirically key KM drivers focus on the context of a unit and a relationship. Colleagues and manuals represent the context of a unit, whereas meeting rooms, seminars, technology, physical structures, and the physical workplace focus on the context of a relationship—or the possibility of creating and nurturing that relationship. Thus, fostering KM is both about supporting a *unit* that holds knowledge and supporting a *relationship* that creates ties between knowledge holders. From a practitioner's perspective, key KM drivers do reflect some of the theoretical issues discussed in the KM literature, but on a somewhat different level. Not surprisingly, the theoretical level has a higher degree of abstraction, and the contrary applies to the empirical level. Still, it seems that KM theory does reflect—albeit in generic terms—those practices that support KM activities. Thus, one can argue that theory actually has value for the practice of knowledge management—or can one?

THE VALUE OF KNOWLEDGE MANAGEMENT THEORY

This chapter started out questioning the value of theorizing about knowledge management. The 50 articles that were reviewed for this chapter are rich with perspectives, discussions, cases, advice, and reflections on knowledge management. The basic question, however, still remains—to what extent are these different viewpoints any value for practitioners seeking to improve their KM practice?

The practitioner images portraying key KM drivers appear to validate the theoretical key drivers in the sense that they portray enablers and proxies for the generic KM key drivers. The images emphasize technology, face-to-face interaction, and rules (embedded in manuals) as important key drivers—exactly the same factors as mentioned in Table 15.3. Thus, theoretical discussions focusing on how these drivers relate to knowledge management seem to reflect practitioner experience—these drivers contribute to both practicing and improving knowledge management.

There are, however, some basic differences, especially in terms of implicit KM drivers. The more implicit proxies for knowledge management are key drivers that are not easily defined and recognizable, such as culture, communities of practice, trust, relationships, and social ties (see Table 15.2). The visual images in the study did not portray these drivers, but rather what enables them. The same problem essentially exists in the KM literature—what actually enables KM in practice (key drivers) remains relatively unexplored. What theory and practice agree on is what the key drivers are—not how they are created, supported, retained, and enabled. Nevertheless, generic key drivers remain quite popular in the literature, and without exploring how they can actually be put into practice, they have, at best, rhetorical value for managers seeking advice in their KM practices.

To conclude, theory has value for KM practice, at least to the extent to which practice focuses on the same key drivers that KM theory recognizes. Theory seems to prefer generic KM drivers, but these drivers appear to have more symbolic than actual value. One of the main challenges in increasing the value of knowledge management is to explore the application and effect of these seemingly quite popular—nevertheless difficult to observe—generic drivers for knowledge management.

Appendix starts on next page.

APPENDIX: THE 50 REVIEWED ARTICLES ON KNOWLEDGE MANAGEMENT

Author	KM Outcomes	KM Context	Empirical focus	Key KM Drivers
Strategic Management Journal (1996)				
Almeida	**CREATION:** Learning through knowledge sharing	**RELATIONS:** Interfirm knowledge flows	US semiconductor industry	Interaction of employees, interfirm relations
Appleyard	**CREATION:** Knowledge creation through knowledge sharing	**RELATIONS:** Interfirm knowledge sharing	US and Japanese semiconductor industry	Communication channels
Bierly & Chakrabarti	**CREATION:** Organizational learning	**UNIT:** Knowledge strategies (external–internal learning vs. radical–incremental learning)	US pharmaceutical firms	None
Grant	**INTEGRATION:** Knowledge integration	**UNIT:** Mechanisms for integrating	None	The individual Rules + directives, sequencing, routines, group problem solving and decision making
Liebeskind	**RETAINING:** Protecting valuable knowledge	**UNIT:** Organization's institutional capability	None	Incentive alignment, employment, reordering
Mowery et al.	**TRANSFER:** Transfer of technological capabilities	**RELATIONS:** Transfer within strategic alliances	Bilateral alliances involving at least one US firm and established 1985–1986	Relation
Szulanski	**TRANSFER:** Internal transfer of best practices	**UNIT:** Barriers in the relation between source and recipient	122 best practice transfers in 8 companies	Recipient's lack of absorptive capacity Causal ambiguity Arduousness of the relationship between source and recipient

Tsoukas	**REFLECTION:** Utilization of knowledge	**UNIT:** Managing the distributed knowledge system	None	Individual in a distributed knowledge system
Spender	**REFLECTION:** Creation, storage, and application of knowledge	**KNOWLEDGE:** The epistemology of knowledge	None	Collective knowledge-based activities
Sanchez & Mahoney	**CREATION:** Product creation	**UNIT:** Organizational structure	None	Organizational forms
California Management Review (1998)				
Brown & Duguid	**CREATION:** Knowledge creation	**UNIT:** Communities of practice	None (sporadic)	The doing of knowledge
Fahey & Prusak	**REFLECTION:** Avoiding errors	**RELATIONS, UNIT, KNOWLEDGE**		
Lincoln et al.	**CREATION:** Knowledge creation and learning	**RELATIONS:** Keiretsu networks	Japanese manufacturing companies	Relations
Powell	**CREATION:** Knowledge seeking and creation	**RELATIONS:** Interorganizational linkages	Biotech companies	Relations
Hargadon	**CREATION:** Continuous innovation	**RELATIONS:** Inter- and intraorganizational relations	Engineering design consulting firms, management consulting firms, HP, Boeing Company, Edison & Co. (historically)	Access (relations); Intensive communication (e.g., brainstorming, hallway conversations); Culture
Davenport & Klahr	**TRANSFER:** Capture, share, and reuse knowledge	**RELATIONS:** Relation to customer	Customer support organizations within the information technology industry	Knowledge representation (storage); Information technology (delivery)

Author	Focus	Unit	Cases	Aspects
Glazer	**MEASURE**: Measure knowledge	**UNIT**: The knower (the possessor of knowledge)	Yes, but no particular cases	Formal measurement methods and models
O'Dell & Grayson	**TRANSFER**: Transfer of best practice	**UNIT**: The process of transferring	Mix	Technology Culture Rewards Leadership Measurement
Leonard & Sensiper	**CREATION**: Innovation	**UNIT**: Creative cooperation	Mix	Group work
von Krogh	**CREATION**: Creating knowledge	**UNIT**: The management of knowledge (workers)	No particular emphasis	Incentive systems (focused on access to help) Mentoring programs Trust Learning how to help (training programs) Learning-oriented conversations Social events
Ruggles	**REFLECTION**: Managing knowledge	**UNIT**: Knowledge processes	431 US and European organizations	The actual KM practice itself Creating an intranet, knowledge repositories, implementing decision-support tools, groupware to support collaboration The "should-dos" of KM Mapping internal expertise Creating networks of knowledge workers Establishing new knowledge roles

Author	Category	Unit / Knowledge	Empirical setting	
Teece	**INTEGRATION**: Deployment and use of knowledge	**UNIT**: The strategy of companies in a knowledge-based economy	None	None
Nonaka & Konno	**CREATION**: Creation of knowledge	**UNIT**: The ba (the shared space)	Sharp, Toshiba, and Maekawa (industrial freezers) Cos.	Physical, virtual, and mental ba

Journal of Management Studies (2001)

Author	Category	Unit / Knowledge	Empirical setting	
Becker	**INTEGRATION**: Managing knowledge	**UNIT**: Dispersed organizational knowledge	No particular	Job rotation, company yellow pages, coordination mechanisms, decomposition
Tsoukas & Vladimirou	**INTEGRATION**: Managing organizational knowledge	**UNIT**: Individual appropriation of knowledge / The "becoming" of organizational knowledge	A Greek call center	Reflective practice
Brusoni & Prencipe	**CREATION**: Innovation	**UNIT**: Knowledge and production boundaries	None	Loosely coupled systems
Lanzara & Patriotta	**REFLECTION**: Knowledge making (epistemologically)	**KNOWLEDGE**: Knowledge in the making	Six Italian courtrooms	Social processes
Alvesson & Kärreman	**REFLECTION**: Managing people or information	**UNIT**: Understanding the concept of knowledge management	A Swedish subsidiary of a large international consulting company	Managing people / Managing information
Thompson & Callaghan	**REFLECTION**: Critiquing the idea of a knowledge economy	**KNOWLEDGE**: Knowledge ability in work	Interactive service sector (UK) / Call center (UK)	Social and aesthetic skills

Organization Science (2002)

Hargadon & Fanelli	**CREATION:** Creation of new knowledge	**UNIT:** Conversion of latent knowledge into empirical knowledge, and vice versa	Two product development consultants in the US (idea and design continuum)	Social and physical artifacts from the surrounding environment in shaping the dynamics of individual and organizational knowing
Postrel	**REFLECTION**	**UNIT:** Islands of knowledge		
Takeishi	**TRANSFER:** Outsourcing knowledge (in product development)	**RELATIONS:** Supplier relations	Japanese automaker industry	Supplier relations
Hansen	**TRANSFER:** Accessing knowledge (through knowledge sharing)	**RELATIONS:** Intrafirm knowledge sharing (between units in multiunit companies)	New product development team; 120 new product development projects in 41 business units of a large multiunit electronics company	Linkages
Orlikowski	**INTEGRATION:** Effective distributed organizing	**UNIT:** Organizational knowing	A large software company headquartered in The Netherlands	Sharing identity, interacting face to face, aligning effort, learning by doing, supporting participation
Zollo & Winter	**CREATION:** Developing dynamic capabilities	**UNIT:** Learning mechanisms; Experience accumulation, knowledge articulation, knowledge codification	None	Articulation and codification processes (of knowledge)
Birkenshaw, Nobel, & Ridderstråle	**REFLECTION:** Dimensions of knowledge influence on organization structure	**UNIT:** Observability; System embeddedness	110 R&D unit managers in 15 Swedish multinational firms	Knowledge observability and system embeddedness

Management Science (2003)

Sine, Shane, & Di Gregorio	**TRANSFER:** Interorganization knowledge transfer	**RELATIONS:** Technology licensing (from universities)	102 US universities	Prestige
Menon & Pfeffer	**TRANSFER:** Internal versus external knowledge transfer	**UNIT:** Knowledge valuation	Two salad buffet chains Xerox	Perceived valuation
Zellmer-Bruhn	**CREATION:** Knowledge acquisition	**UNIT:** Team acquisition of new knowledge (as opposed to routines)	98 individuals representing 46 teams	Interruptive events
Sorensen	**CREATION:** Organizational learning	**UNIT:** Interdependence in vertical integrated firms	Computer workstation manufacturers	Vertical integration (interdependence)
Borgatti & Cross	**TRANSFER:** Organizational learning (knowledge transfer) Seeking and sharing	**RELATIONS:** Information seeking – know who to approach	37 information scientists in a global pharmaceutical organization 35 researchers in a genomic research function in a different pharmaceutical organization	Know-who (social networks)
Nadler, Thompson, & Van Boven	**CREATION:** Learning (through knowledge creation and transfer)	**UNIT:** Individual learning	122 undergraduate psychology students	Analogical and observational training
Chang & Harrington	**CREATION:** Learning (through the transfer of new ideas)	**UNIT:** Organizational structure	A computer simulation model	Organizational structure

Author	Category	Unit/Relation/Knowledge	Study context	Focus
Lee, Lee, & Lee	**CREATION**: Firm growth by exploring new opportunities or exploiting old opportunities	**UNIT**: The emergence of a superior but incompatible technology	A computer simulation model	Customer market segments
Das	**PRODUCTIVE**: Knowledge that enhances work productivity	**UNIT**: The call leading to locating, adapting or generating knowledge	Technical support center of a leading supercomputer vendor	Tools for finding knowledge – the physical and social environment of the workplace
Weber & Camerer	**INTEGRATION**: Knowledge culture's ability to perform tasks	**UNIT**: Culture Corporate mergers	Laboratory experiments	Culture
Uzzi & Lancaster	**CREATION**: Knowledge transfer and learning	**RELATIONS**: Informal interfirm relationships	Chicago-area banks	Social relationships
Gittelman & Kogut	**REFLECTION**: Does science lead to valuable knowledge?	**KNOWLEDGE**: Epistemic culture	Publications and patents of 116 biotechnology firms during the period 1988–1995	Patents Publications
Song, Almeida, & Wu	**TRANSFER**: Knowledge transfer (acquisition of knowledge)	**RELATIONS**: Interfirm knowledge transfer	US patent and patent citation from the global semiconductor industry (1980–1999). Focus on engineers who have moved from US firms to non-US firms.	Human mobility
Thomas-Hunt, Ogden, & Neale	**TRANSFER**: Knowledge sharing	**UNIT**: Within heterogeneous groups	111 undergraduate students in either engineering or business schools at a private US Midwestern university	Status as expertise and social ties

NOTES

1. A similar trend is underlined by Rigby (2001). In a 1999 study among 214 American companies that used a variety of management tools—including TQM, BPR, and KM—the average satisfaction with management tools was (on a scale of 1–5) 3.76. TQM scored 3.82, BPR 3.66, and the worst score in the study was KM 3.22.

2. The following journal issues were excluded from the sample of articles in the study: (1) *Long Range Planning*, 1997, vol. 30, no. 3, has several articles on knowledge management and intellectual capital, but the volume is not specifically devoted to KM; (2) *Organizational Behavior and Human Decision Processes*, 2000, vol. 82, no. 1, focuses on knowledge sharing rather than the broader KM concept; (3) *Management Learning*, 2002, vol. 33, no. 4, focuses solely on situated knowledge and communities of practice; and (4) *Organization Studies*, 2003, vol. 24, no. 6, focuses solely on knowledge issues in professional service firms.

REFERENCES

Almeida, P. (1996). Knowledge sourcing by foreign multinationals: Patent citation analysis in the U.S. semiconductor industry. *Strategic Management Journal, 17* [Winter Special Issue], 155–165.

Alvesson, M., & Kärreman, D. (2001). Odd couple: Making sense of the curious concept of knowledge management. *Journal of Management Studies, 38*(7), 995–1018.

Appleyard, M. M. (1996). How does knowledge flow? Inter-firm patterns in the semiconductor industry. *Strategic Management Journal* [Winter Special Issue], 137–154.

Argote, L.McEvily, B., & Reagans, R. (2003). Managing knowledge in organization: An integrative framework and review of emerging themes. *Management Science, 49*(4), 571–582.

Banks, M. (2001). *Visual methodologies in social research*. London: Sage.

Becker, M. C. (2001). Managing dispersed knowledge: Organizational problems, managerial strategies, and their effectiveness. *Journal of Management Studies, 38*(7), 1037–1051.

Bierly, P., & Chakrabarti, A. (1996). Generic knowledge strategies in the U.S. pharmaceutical industry. *Strategic Management Journal, 17*[Winter Special Issue], 123–135.

Birkinshaw, J. Nobel, R., & Ridderstråle, J. (2002). Knowledge as a contingency variable: Do the characteristics of knowledge predict organization structure? *Organization Science, 13*(3), 274–289.

Bok, D. (2003). *Universities in the marketplace: The commercialization of higher education*. Princeton, NJ: Princeton University Press.

Borgatti, S. P., & Cross, R. (2003). A relational view of information seeking and learning in social networks. *Management Science, 49*(4), 432–445.

Brown, J. S., & Duguid, P. (1998). Organizing knowledge. *California Management Review, 40*(3), 90–111.

Brusoni, S. (2001). Managing knowledge in loosely coupled networks: Exploring the links between product and knowledge dynamics. *Journal of Management Studies, 38*(7), 1019–1035.

Chang, M., & Harrington, J.E. Jr. (2003). Multi-market competition, consumer search, and the organizational structure of multiunit firms. *Management Science, 49*(4), 541–552.

Christensen, P. H. (2003). *Knowledge management: Perspectives and pitfalls.* Copenhagen: Copenhagen Business School Press.

Das, A. (2003). Knowledge and productivity in the technical support work. *Management Science, 49*(4), 416–431.

Davenport, T. H., & Klahr, P. (1998). Managing customer support knowledge. *California Management Review, 40*(3), 195–208.

Fahey, L., & Prusak, L. (1998). The eleven deadliest sins of knowledge management. *California Management Review, 40*(3), 265–276.

Fuller, S. (2002). *Knowledge management foundations.* Boston: Butterworth-Heineman.

Gibbons, M., Limoges, C., Nowotny, H., Schwartzman, S., Scott, P., & Trow, M. (1994). *The new production of knowledge.* London: Sage.

Gittelman, M., & Kogut, B. (2003). Does good science lead to valuable knowledge? Biotechnology forms and the evolutionary logic of citation patterns. *Management Science, 49*(4), 366–382.

Glazer, R. (1998). Measuring the knower: Towards a theory of knowledge equity. *California Management Review, 40*(3), 175–194.

Grant, R. M. (1996). Towards a knowledge-based theory of the firm. *Strategic Management Journal, 17*[Winter Special Issue], 109–122.

Hansen, M. T. (2002). Knowledge networks: Explaining effective knowledge sharing in multiunit companies. *Organization Science, 13*(3), 232–248.

Hargadon, A. (1998). Firms as knowledge brokers: Lessons in pursuing continuous innovation. *California Management Review, 40*(3), 209–227.

Hargadon, A., & Fanelli, A. (2002). Action and possibility: Reconciling dual perspectives of knowledge in organizations. *Organization Science, 13*(3), 290–302.

Kirp, D. L. (2003). *Shakespeare, Einstein, and the bottom line: The marketing of higher education.* Cambridge, MA: Harvard University Press.

Lanzara, G. F., & Patriotta, G. (2001). Technology and the courtroom: An inquiry into knowledge making in organizations. *Journal of Management Studies, 38*(7), 943–971.

Lee, J., Lee, J., & Lee, H. (2003). Exploration and exploitation in the presence of network externalities. *Management Science, 49*(4), 553–570.

Leonard, D., & Sensiper, S. (1998). The role of tacit knowledge in group innovation. *California Management Review, 40*(3), 112–132.

Liebeskind, J. P. (1996). Knowledge, strategy, and the theory of the firm. *Strategic Management Journal, 17*[Winter Special Issue], 93–107.

Lincoln, J. R., Ahmadjian, C. L., & Mason, E. (1998). Organizational learning and purchase-supply relations in Japan: Hitachi, Matsushita, and Toyota compared. *California Management Review, 40*(3), 241–264.

Lucier, C. E., & Torsilieri, J. D. (2001). Can knowledge management deliver bottom-line results? In I. Nonaka & D. Teece (Eds.), *Managing industrial knowledge: Creation, transfer and utilization* (pp. 231–243). London: Sage.

Menon, T., & Pfeffer, J. (2003). Valuing internal vs. external knowledge: Explaining the preference for outsiders. *Management Science, 49*(4), 497–513.

Mowery, D. C., Oxley, J. E., & Silverman, B. S. (1996). Strategic alliances and inter-firm knowledge transfer. *Strategic Management Journal, 17*[Winter Special Issue], 77–91.

Nadler, J., Thompson, L., & Van Boven, L. (2003). Learning negotiation skills: Four models of knowledge creation and transfer. *Management Science, 49*(4), 529–540.

Nonaka, I., & Konno, N. (1998). The concept of "ba": Building a foundation for knowledge creation. *California Management Review, 40*(3), 40–54.

O'Dell, C., & Grayson, C. J. (1998). If only we knew what we know: Identification and transfer of internal best practice. *California Management Review, 40*(3), 154–174.

Orlikowski, W. J. (2002). Knowing in practice: Enacting a collective capability in distributed organizing. *Organization Science, 13*(3), 249–273.

Patriotta, G. (2003). *Organizational knowledge in the making.* Oxford: Oxford University Press.

Postrel, S. (2002). Islands of shared knowledge: Specialization and mutual understanding in problem-solving teams. *Organization Science, 13*(3), 303–320.

Powell, W. W. (1998). Learning from collaboration: Knowledge and networks in the biotechnology and pharmaceutical. *California Management Review, 40*(3), 228–240.

Rigby, D. (2001). Management tools and techniques: a survey. *California Management Review, 43*(2), 139–160.

Rose, G. (2001). *Visual methodologies.* London: Sage.

Ruggles, R. (1998). The state of the notion: Knowledge management in practice. *California Management Review, 40*(3), 80–89.

Sanchez, R., & Mahoney, J. T. (1996). Modularity, flexibility, and knowledge management in product and organization design. *Strategic Management Journal, 17*[Winter Special Issue], 63–76.

Sine, W. D., Shane, S., & Di Gregoria, D. (2003). The halo effect and technology licensing: The influence of institutional prestige on the licensing of university inventions. *Management Science, 49*(4), 478–496.

Song, J., Almeida, P., & Wu, G. (2003). Learning-by-hiring: When is mobility more likely to facilitate interfirm knowledge transfer? *Management Science, 49*(4), 351–365.

Sorenson, O. (2003). Interdependence and adaptability: Organizational learning and the long-term effect of integration. *Management Science, 49*(4), 446–463.

Spender, J. C. (1996). Making knowledge the basis of a dynamic theory of the firm. *Strategic Management Journal, 17*[Winter Special Issue], 45–62.

Sturken, M., & Cartwright, L. (2001). *Practices of looking: An introduction to visual culture.* Oxford: Oxford University Press.

Szulanski, G. (1996). Exploring internal stickiness: Impediments to the transfer of best practice within the firm. *Strategic Management Journal, 17*[Winter Special Issue], 27–43.

Takeishi, A. (2002). Knowledge portioning in the inter-firm division of labor: The case of automotive product development. *Organization Science, 13*(3), 321–338.

Teece, D. J. (1998). Capturing value from knowledge assets: The new economy, markets for know-how, and intangible assets. *California Management Review, 40*(3), 55–79.

Thomas-Hunt, M. C., Ogden, T. Y., & Neale, M. A. (2003). Who's really sharing? Effects of social and expert status on knowledge exchange within groups. *Management Science, 49*(4), 464–477.

Thompson, P., Warhurst, C., & Callaghan, G. (2001). Ignorant theory and knowledgeable workers: Interrogating the connections between knowledge, skills and services. *Journal of Management Studies, 38*(7), 923–942.

Tsoukas, H. (1996). The firm as a distributed knowledge system: A constructionist approach. *Strategic Management Journal, 17*[Winter Special Issue] 11–25.

Tsoukas, H., & Vladimirou, E. (2001). What is organizational knowledge? *Journal of Management Studies, 38*(7), 973–993.

Weber, R. A., & Camerer, C. F. (2003). Cultural conflict and merger failure: An experimental approach. *Management Science, 49*(4), 400–415.

Uzzi, B., & Lancaster, R. (2003). Relational embeddedness and learning: The case of bank loan managers and their clients. *Management Science, 49*(4), 383–399.

van Leeuwen, T., & Jewitt, C. (Eds.). (2001). *Handbook of visual analysis*. London: Sage.

von Krogh, G. (1998). Care in knowledge creation. *California Management Review, 40*(3), 133–153.

Zelmmer-Bruhn, M. E. (2003). Interruptive events and team knowledge acquisition. *Management Science, 49*(4), 514–528.

Zollo, M., & Winter, S. G. (2002). Deliberate learning and the evolution of dynamic capabilities. *Organization Science, 13*(3), 339–351.

CHAPTER 16

KNOWLEDGE AND CONSULTANCY

Hans Siggaard Jensen

When discussing knowledge issues and the knowledge-based claims made by consultants, a question that often emerges concerns the difference between research and consultancy. In this concluding chapter, I will try to throw some light on this issue, exploring the similarities and differences between the practice of medicine (as done by the general practitioner) and management consulting. The discussion will draw out some important differences between consulting based on mainly natural science and consulting based on knowledge about humans, their actions, and organizations.

KNOWLEDGE, RESEARCH, AND CONSULTANCY

It is quite clear that there are forms of consultancy that are not research. This is the "doing" part of consultancy that draws on existing knowledge. Without knowledge—in some form or other—such "doing" is impossible. In deciding what to do, management consultants need to know what is possible and something about possible and potential effects. But this dynamic is also true of many other knowledge-based work roles, from

Challenges and Issues in Knowledge Management, 365–375
Copyright © 2005 by Information Age Publishing
All rights of reproduction in any form reserved.

being a surgeon to being the captain of a ship. They are all examples of people doing things based on various forms and areas of knowledge. Consultants, just as teachers, sometimes do what they are supposed to do and, by simply giving advice, telling others what to do. Then again, they sometimes also get involved in implementation, in essence giving the client a "hand." An interesting, underlying issue is how they decide what should be done, how to provide advice, and how to provide or produce knowledge.

Just like researchers, consultants are supposed to provide knowledge, either in the sense of actual (and even potentially radical) new knowledge or by drawing on old knowledge that had not been noticed or perceived as relevant or pertinent in the specific case. Consultants thus provide new knowledge of a sort that is relevant as advice about what to do. To be considered useful, the knowledge should be relevant to actual and practical problem solving.

Research, on the other hand, is often perceived as being concerned with theoretical rather than practical problems. An important reason for peoples' interest in theoretical problems, however, is that the solution is relevant, perhaps even necessary, for the solution of practical problems. In navigation and medicine, for example, one can succeed by using actual experience, but it seems that when the problems get really difficult, one needs more than that. At this point, one needs research. So one might, as a preliminary answer, posit that consultancy is about solving practical problems by using established methods to procure knowledge that is relevant to the solution—knowing what to do to solve the problem. Research, in contrast, is about solving hitherto unresolved problems by providing new knowledge that is relevant to the solution.

Research is necessary when the going gets rough, when we run into problems where tried and true methods do not work or established theories fail to point a productive path. We can thus describe the situation as a sort of continuum, from (1) solving common problems by providing relevant knowledge, to (2) the solution of difficult problems by investigating the situation (but still drawing on established theories and methods), to (3) situations where problems resist established solutions. This latter point is where new theories or methods have to be formulated and developed. Diagnosing a case of pneumonia and prescribing a relevant drug may be fairly straightforward, whereas a doctor seeing a case of AIDS for the first time in the early 1980s faced a much more difficult problem. Thus one end of this continuum (point 1 above) is the domain for consulting, and the other end (point 3) constitutes research, especially in the sense of "doing" science (i.e., not in the sense of "research" that might be used in journalism).

The provision of knowledge is also different. In each case, new knowledge may be provided. The knowledge that a specific person is suffering from pneumonia, for example, while fairly specific is still new knowledge if it was not known before. The knowledge that pneumonia is caused by a certain microorganism is of a different type, as it is more general and contributes to the theory that certain diseases are caused by microorganisms. In the case of AIDS, one needs both a new category—the recognition of the disease itself—and a new causal agent, in this case the HIV virus. Related to the question at the beginning of the chapter, consulting may concern itself with the solution of specific problems that have a relatively low level of generality, while research has to do with more generic or general problems.

This analysis, of course, has flaws. Much of what counts as research is based on the use of established methods to solve a general class of problems. Controlled randomized trials are a case in point. We want to find out whether a procedure is effective for solving a problem—or rather a type of problem. We select two groups at random that have the problem, and by using a standard procedure for one—or doing nothing (which is itself a standard procedure)—and applying the procedure we are testing to the other, we obtain certain results. By using standard statistical tests, we then try to determine whether the tested procedure is effective—in the sense of being significantly "better" than doing nothing or doing "the usual." Methods of medical treatment are often thought of as research-based (or evidence-based) if the results from controlled randomized trials support their effectiveness (or whether one procedure is more effective than another). So research could also be characterized as the solution of a well-known type of problem by application of a well-known method. Consultancy, on the other hand, often points to new types of problems, often to the deficiency of theories or established methods. A number of cases of a problem may be discovered and a new problem—sometimes of high theoretical importance—can thereby be discovered. For example, established methods of reasoning and policy formation (and even established theories) were challenged by the failures and deficiencies of economic policies during the Great Depression of the 1930s. This gave rise to the development of new theories in economics—such as that of Keynes—and new research programs—such as that instigated by the Cowes Foundation (leading eventually to a significant number of Nobel Prizes in Economics).

Consultancy no doubt involves different forms of knowledge. Experience, insight, understanding, and at times even intuition often play a role. The relationship between the consultant giving advice and the client receiving it is also a complex one. It is a relationship involving trust, communication, and the relevant forms of knowledge. In this sense, the experienced can help the inexperienced. Increasingly, however, we see that consulting involves the use of new knowledge that is based on research. The use of theories—the "right" theories—and certain methods—the "right" methods—could shortcut experience because they are based on research. In this sense, consultants become a type of scientific expert. Of course, the relevant choice in the concrete case of theories or methods may depend on experience and forms of understanding that are not themselves scientific in a simple sense. The use of a scientific theory to solve a concrete problem is not itself something that is done according to a scientific theory. It involves a certain competence, which is different from just knowing the theory in question. Driving a race car or flying a fighter plane involves more than the knowledge of Newtonian mechanics—although such knowledge is extremely relevant in understanding certain relevant and important phenomena, which can be useful to solve certain significant problems.

A simple type of problem solving, which is of high practical relevance, concerns the phenomenon of causality. If we know that certain types of events are caused by certain other types of events, we can either produce (or prevent) certain desired (or undesired) events by using that knowledge (at least in those circumstances where we can influence that situation through our actions). Lots of work in agriculture, medicine, and engineering fall into this category. We are in trouble when we have to deal with phenomena where causal relations are not very clear or where causality is at best something we can ascribe at higher levels of aggregation or as a metaphor. We are then unable to predict and control, or even influence in controlled ways to produce desired results. This is the case as soon as we are in the realm of human behavior, where intentions, volitions, desires, and decisions are involved. While certain types of causal knowledge may be relevant and useful, they are not sufficient. Causal laws are only formulated at high levels of abstraction, and, as such, are not very useful in solving particular practical problems. This is the reverse of the situation in, say, engineering, where we assume that the natural laws operating are always in force, because they are in a certain sense universal and without exceptions.

THE MEDICAL TRADITION

The very old medical tradition provides an important model for the use of knowledge, a tradition that goes back to the Hippocratic era in ancient Greek medicine (see, e.g., Crombie, 1994). The model was dominant until a large array of "objective" medical tests was developed. The clinical situation consists of the medical doctor and the patient. When they meet for the first time, the initial part of the consultation is the "anamnesis." In this the patient recounts the history of the problem that led to the consultation. We can refer to this as *narrating the problem*—questioning and specifying when the signs or symptoms first occurred, under what circumstances, and so forth, until the story ends.

The next step is the examination of the patient, which takes two forms—one objective and one subjective. The objective examination concerns the signs or symptoms that the doctor can actually see, hear, or feel. It could be a rash, a strange sound from the heart, or a lump or growth. The subjective examination concerns the actual experience of the patient in relation to the problem, probing what the patient feels or experiences. On the basis of the objective and subjective information gathered, the doctor then comes up with a "diagnosis"—in essence, a classification of the problem.

The process is often likened to the botanist classifying a specimen of a plant. Diseases come in types, as do problems. A concrete case, in this tradition, is always seen as a manifestation of a given type. The types of classification that are available, of course, is another matter, just as how they are found or produced (a point we will explore later). With the diagnosis obtained, the next step is the "prognosis," a prediction about the future development of the problem. It might of course disappear by itself—as many diseases do—or it might take a turn for the worse, potentially turning out to be a chronic condition. Depending on the prognosis, the doctor may propose a "therapy." This means doing something to change the spontaneous development of the problem. So the doctor, through therapy, tries to influence the course of events.

Many theories of various types of diseases have been proposed, and very often specific forms of therapy will follow from these theories. If the disease is seen as a result of lack of harmony between parts of the body, then therapy would naturally concern reestablishing this harmony; if the cause of the disease is a microorganism, then removing it or negating its influence could be viable forms of therapy. The goal of therapy is to return the patient to a state of health, or at least to a more optimal state than would be the case without the therapy. We could say the goal of therapy is actually to change the situation of the patient, so he or she is no longer a "patient," but rather a person. Of course, this also relates back to the beginning of the whole affair, because without some indication that something is wrong—that there is a problem at all—the whole process would never get started. There has to be some sort of distinction between what is normal and what is not for the process to be initiated.

This brief description of medical consultation should be familiar to most readers. Today, however, it seems that doctors increasingly check off a number of boxes on a form to indicate which clinical tests should be performed. Upon receiving the results of measurements—x-rays, CT-scans, and so forth—the physician will then make a diagnosis. But the process itself goes on, and most physicians aim for a close relation between the diagnosis and therapy. The ideal is that for each disease-entity, there is a specific therapy that will influence—at best cure—the disease. This is connected to the idea that a disease has a specific cause that produces the disease, and that the therapy should consist of removing or countering the effects of that causal agent.

MANAGEMENT CONSULTING AND THE MEDICAL TRADITION

If, for the sake of argument, we accept this medical model as a good and tested model of consulting—a sort of ideal type—we can explore a number of factors concerning the role of knowledge in consulting. What knowledge is used and what knowledge is produced in this type of process? Before answering, let us briefly transpose this process to the management consulting arena. A company has a problem; its managers call in a consultant, who will try to understand how the problem arose, the nature of the problem, its potential consequences, and so forth. Through diagnosis (which comes from the Greek word for knowledge, *gnosis*), the situation will be seen as exemplifying a certain type of problem. When the problem has been classified, some "cure" or course of action is prescribed in an attempt to solve the problem and/or prevent its recurrence. This is often done by trying to predict what will happen if nothing is done—prognosis—and what happens if a cure is administered—therapy. Implementation of the prescribed changes can, of course, also call for work by consultants. This role is typically filled by process-consultants—that is, people with a good deal of experience in ensuring that things actually get done.

What role does knowledge play in this process? First, there has to be an ability to identify a specific problem-situation as a given type of problem. Thus, there has to be a typology of problems—either explicitly or implicitly—that the consultant draws on. In medicine, attempts have been made to make the list of problems explicit by creating a classification of diseases. In management, the process is somewhat different and it relates to some important differences between a clinical situation and the reality of management. The ability of prescribing or doing something involves knowledge, a type of knowing what happens when "such and such is done." This assessment usually takes the form of "we have seen that when X is the case, then Y happens..." Again a form of typology is presupposed, because one can only transfer experience from one case to another if the cases are somehow similar—which means that they are of similar type.

We know this type of knowledge from situations involving artifacts that are created in types. A mechanic, for example, knows that the brakes on certain types of cars manufactured over a specified period tend to have a certain problem, a problem that can be resolved by following a given protocol. The mechanic might know that the brakes on a particular model are of a certain type—and that such brakes always create this type of problem. The car, as a mechanism, is considered to be a "nomological machine," in essence a physical system (see Cartwright, 1999). But as an artifact—it is also used by humans—there is often a presupposed assumption, for example, that the car has been used in "normal ways under normal conditions." Things that normally do not cause problems can do so if they are used in extreme ways—in ways they were not designed for. So regularities are presupposed and serve as various forms of limiting conditions. These are parts of the assumptions underlying the medical model.

For a very long time, the list of therapies available to the medical doctor consisted of a few general therapies—bloodletting, laxatives, vomiting (mostly based on the notion of getting "the bad" out of the body)—and prescriptions for a healthy, balanced life. The intent was to stimulate the body to get rid of the disease by itself. Disease was often understood as a form of disharmony, and prevention and therapy were related to the protection and restoration of harmony. Thus, the interest in diagnosis had mostly to do with the possibility of making a prognosis. Actual therapy was relatively limited, and could be boiled down to healthy living. With the advent of medical practice, which was increasingly influenced by natural science, this of course changed. The typologies of diseases were related to causal knowledge, and thus prevention and therapy were based on causal knowledge.

CONSULTING USING KNOWLEDGE ABOUT HUMANS AS SOCIAL BEINGS

From the perspective of management consulting, with people suffering from social and organizational problems rather than diseases, the situation is very different. There are very few relevant causal phenomena. Of course, there has been a long tradition of developing general theories of organization or management, which have made it possible to turn consulting into a sort of engineering, an applied science. As with the medical model, there are a number of presuppositions involved, which are even more important since they are not governed by causal laws. There may be other forms of regularities, but the element of contextuality is much more important than with physical and even biological systems (where they are actually also very important).

In organization theory, we can distinguish between two main traditions. One is sociological and sees humans in all their cultural and social diversity, and their behavior and decisions as based on many sorts of considerations—some rational and some nonrational. The other tradition is based on forms of economics that assume people to be rational agents trying to maximize the fulfillment of certain preferences and desires. The "therapy" one can apply in these two traditions is very different. One tradition focuses on values, norms, leadership, and so forth, while the latter emphasizes the creation of incentive-structures that will lead to the desired forms of behavior. The economical model is an attempt to create a sort of nomological machine as a model of the social system. The sociological view is very different as it relies on a different form of understanding of how knowledge works. Instead of creating incentives that can have predictable effects given certain assumptions of human action, it leads to a model where knowledge must be internalized in the actors if they are to start acting in different ways. They have to be persuaded, involved in new types of interactions, new types of situations, and they have to accept new norms and values. And it must be recognized that the persons involved will not always act in purely rational ways. In this case, the essential competence for using knowledge is the ability to relate to the specific situation without having a causal or nomological model. It is simply not seen as a machine, and an ethical or phronetic element—something involving norms and virtues—is present (for an exposition of these issues, see Fukuyama, 2004).

If we look at the relationship between a human problem and one that occurs in a mechanical context, we can see some important differences. In the mechanical case, the identification of the problem and the conception of the solution will be constant over time (the time from the problem is identified until it is perceived as solved). In the human context, this is not normally the case. The attempt at a solution will influence the perception of what the problem is, and the solutions proposed or enacted will sometimes fail to be real solutions, because, in essence, they focus on the wrong problem. A good example of this dynamic is the so-called "garbage can" model of decision making in organizations (Cohen, March, & Olsen, 1972). This point is further reflected in Simon's (1976) critique of the assumption that organizations have precise goals. One could argue that by making a decision one finds out what the issue actually is. Related to consultancy, it is through attempting to solve a problem that one finds out what the problem actually was.

MODELS OF CONSULTING, KNOWLEDGE,
AND THE ROLE OF RESEARCH

In the case of the medical model, it is fairly obvious how research emerged as it did. If one were to claim that a certain procedure was efficient in solving a type of problem, then one might, of course, ask for documentation of this claim. This need led to research in the form of controlled trials. A related issue concerns the generality of the solution—under what circumstances can it be transferred to another context? In those situations where one expects a proposed solution to work and it fails, further investigation is typically undertaken, with the potential for deeper understanding.

In management consultancy, these same dynamics might help to uncover social phenomena that were previously unnoticed. This is often the case when development in an organization occurs without any deeper previous understanding, but rather as a response to challenges or as a sort of "natural development." The classical dissociation of ownership and management, which has come under increasing criticism of late (see, e.g., Ghoshal, 2005), could be a case in point.

If consulting becomes increasingly based on established general scientific theories, it also becomes increasingly decontextualized and the consultant becomes a scientific expert. This role has been the ideal for many doctors and engineers, described in recent studies of research and knowledge production as "Mode 1" knowledge production (see Gibbons et al., 1994). The alternative approach is "Mode 2," a model that refers to a situation where knowledge production and knowledge application are not separated, where research problems arise in context of application, and research is more problem-oriented than discipline-oriented.

With respect to the Mode 2 approach to knowledge, one might think that there would be a confluence of research and consultancy. This would be a departure from Mode 1, where researchers provide the scientific theories that are applied by consultants, to more of a partnership model. In this latter approach, the consultant has the domain knowledge of the problems and the researcher tries to understand what the problems "really" are in practice, and how they might be solved or prevented, especially if there are no "best practices" that exist for handling them. In this context, research is more of a process in which tacit knowledge is made explicit. It is important to notice that the Mode 2 model has been formulated to a large extent on the basis of models of research that we find in new artifact-producing research areas, such as research in information technology and software.

A Mode 2 approach could provide a new understanding of the relation between research, knowledge, and consultancy. The model would be analogous to a medical model in which one assumes that the body already has healing capacities, and that therapy is about bringing those capacities "to life." This can be done by therapists who know—in the sense of knowing how—*what* to do, whereas they may not know *why* they are doing it. The *knowledge-producing* researcher is then the person who tries to come up with answers to why certain procedures seem to work. In the case of management consulting, this approach is similar to conceiving research as a study of what makes a particular series of events that are prescribed by a consultant, who in a sense of knowing "knows" what works, actually work in practice. This process provides knowledge of not only *how* to do a certain thing, but also *what* is involved and *why* a given procedure works. We can say that knowledge production is creating conceptualizations of what actually goes on in certain social processes that are being studied, and thus make implicit knowledge and capabilities explicit and available for analysis, discussion, and criticism.

The consultant, through processes of reflection and analysis, tends to become a researcher, and the researcher, as being involved with the actual problems and the processes surrounding their solutions, tends to become a consultant. Still, the basic distinction between research and what constitutes knowledge remains. Research, although practice- and evidence-based, has also to be conceptualized and made meaningful through being placed in a theoretical framework. Scientific knowledge depends on the ability to answer "why" questions, to provide explanations, and create understandings. Such knowledge provides an experience of coherence and wholeness, providing a vision of the concrete case that is part of a pattern, a meaningful whole.

The problems in organizational life, however, are seldom sufficiently simple for a single theory to provide leads to a solution. Thus, we have to be able to handle a plurality of knowledge types in attempting to provide solutions. The fact that we deal with human organizations places a limit on how formalized solution-procedures can be. One might say that there is a limit as to the extent to which we can turn the art of management consulting into a science. There has to be a competence—not necessarily formalized—that makes it possible to see a problem as exemplifying a certain type of problem situation. The competence to interpret and act in social situations is crucial, especially in *real* situations that are essentially open and problematic. There may be a lingering preference for modeling with nomological frameworks that make prediction and control possible, but these approaches reflect the difference between the way Frederick Taylor (1911) and Chester Barnard (1938) viewed organizations and their management. We need to move much closer to a Mode 2 approach to research and knowledge in management consulting. But this also has to be done in such a way that we not only tell about what is going on, but reflect on it by creating new theoretical understanding.

REFERENCES

Barnard, C. (1938). *The functions of the executive*. Cambridge, MA: Harvard University Press.
Cartwright, N. (1999). *The dappled world*. Cambridge, UK: Cambridge University Press.
Cohen, M. D., March, J., & Olsen, J. P. (1972). A garbage can model of organizational choice. *Administration Science Quarterly, 17*, 1–25.
Crombie, A. C. (1994). *Styles of scientific thinking in the European tradition* (Vol. 1). London: Duckworth.
Fukuyama, F. (2004). *State building*. Ithaca, NY: Cornell University Press.
Ghoshal, S. (2005). Bad management theories are destroying good management practices. *Academy of Management Learning & Education, 4*(1), 75–91.
Gibbons, M., Limoges, C., Nowotny, H., Schwartzman, S., Scott, P., & Trow, M. (1994). *The new production of knowledge: The dynamics of science and research in contemporary societies*. London: Sage.
Simon, H. (1997). *Administrative behavior: A study of decision-making processes in administrative organization*. New York: Free Press.
Taylor, F. (1911). *The principles of scientific management*, New York: Norton.

ABOUT THE AUTHORS

Antti Ainamo is coordinator of the Global Project Strategies of Finnish Firms research consortium, with the Helsinki School of Economics, VTT National Research Centre of Finland, Helsinki University of Technology, and Stanford University. His publications include "Coevolution of Organizational Forms in the Fashion Industry" in *Organization Science* and the *Handbook of Product and Service Development in Communications and Information Technology*. Ainamo's current research interests focus on project-based organizational forms, knowledge brokering, and strategy

Anne Bang has worked as a consultant since 1998, first as a senior consultant at Ernst & Young within knowledge management and people development, and most recently as the knowledge manager at Avenir/Ementor. Since 2002 she has done research on the consulting industry and is currently pursuing her doctorate at the Copenhagen Business School. Bang's research focuses on the possible forms and flows of efficiency in different applied management consulting approaches.

Jos Benders is a senior researcher at the Nijmegen School of Management, Radboud University Nijmegen, Netherlands. A member of the editorial board of *New Technology, Work and Employment,* he has written numerous books, the most recent of which is *Mirroring Consensus: Decision-Making in Japanese-Dutch Business* (2000). Benders's research interests include knowledge transfer in technological alliances, organization concepts, and the history of cellular manufacturing.

Elena Bou is assistant professor in the Operations and Innovation Management Department at ESADE. Her current research and consulting interest focus on organizational change, knowledge management, and service operations. Bou's previous work has focused on the consultancy field and in European research projects.

Per Nikolaj Bukh is professor at the Aarhus School of Management. He holds a PhD from the University of Aarhus. His current research interests focus on knowledge management and intellectual capital accounting as well as supply chain accounting and new costing models. Bukh has published more than 10 books and 100 articles in these areas, and has consulted with a number of private and public sector firms in the Nordic countries.

Anthony F. Buono, series editor, has a joint appointment as professor of management and sociology at Bentley College and coordinator of the Bentley Alliance for Ethics and Social Responsibility (BAESR). He holds a PhD with a concentration in industrial and organizational sociology from Boston College. Buono's current research and consulting interests focus on the management consulting industry, organizational change, and interorganizational alliances, with an emphasis on mergers, acquisitions, strategic partnerships, and firm–stakeholder relationships.

Peter Holdt Christensen is assistant professor in the Department of Management, Politics and Philosophy at the Copenhagen Business School. His current research focuses on knowledge-based activities, enlightened by organization economics and organization theory and practiced in both private and public companies.

Markus Ejenäs is a researcher at the Center for People and Organization at the Stockholm School of Economics. He is currently completing his PhD thesis on learning and knowledge management in mergers between consulting firms.

Jens Gammelgaard received his PhD from the Copenhagen Business School (CBS), Denmark. He is associate professor at the Department of International Economics and Management at CBS. Gammelgaard's research topics focus on international mergers and acquisitions and knowledge management in multinational corporations.

Stephen N. Gourlay is principal lecturer and director of doctoral training at Kingston Business School, Kingston University, Kingston upon Thames, UK. He holds a PhD in history, and has been involved in research projects on technical change, work organization, and industrial relations. Gourlay's current research interests are in knowledge management and organizational learning, with an emphasis on conceptual frameworks and their practical implications.

Alice Mathidle Guilhon is deputy director of CERAM Sophia-Antipolis, European School of Business in France. She holds a PhD in management from Montpellier University (France). Guilhon was Professor in Management at the Mediterranean University from 1993 to 2000, and since 2000 she has been professor in management at CERAM Sophia-Antipolis. Her current research and consulting interests focus on competitive intelligence, organizational learning, and change.

Lotte Henriksen is a knowledge manager at Deloitte Denmark. She holds a PhD with a concentration in knowledge management from Copenhagen Business School. Her current consulting interests focus on change management and knowledge sharing, with an emphasis in human behavior and communication. Henriksen also works within the human resource development area as a consultant at Deloitte.

Stefan Heusinkveld is a research fellow at the Nijmegen School of Management, Radboud University Nijmegen, Netherlands. His research interests include the diffusion of organization concepts, management consultancies, and the sociology of management knowledge.

Kenneth Husted received his PhD from the Copenhagen Business School. He is professor in innovation and research management and head of the TamakiDivision at the University of Auckland Business School, New Zealand. Husted's research focuses on the management of knowledge creation and utilization in networks, and research and innovation management.

Hans Siggaard Jensen is executive research director at Learning Lab Denmark, The Danish University of Education. The Lab is a Mode 2–oriented research institute focused on learning, knowledge creation, and competence development. He holds degrees in philosophy, mathematics, and psychology. Jensen's research focuses on the issues concerning the development of usable knowledge, and he has also written on the philosophy of medicine and technology. Before joining the Learning Lab Denmark, he was professor at the Copenhagen Business School. He is also director of the European Doctoral School on Knowledge and Management.

Sisse Siggaard Jensen is associate professor of communication studies at Roskilde University in Denmark. She holds a PhD with a focus on reflective practices in interactive and net-based media from Roskilde University. Jensen's current research interests focus on knowledge management and knowledge sharing in 3-D environments and avatar-based social interaction, and their use in team-building and organizational role-playing games.

Snejina Michailova received her PhD from the Copenhagen Business School. She is professor of international business in the Department of International Business at the University of Auckland Business School, New Zealand. Michailova's most recent research focuses on knowledge sharing and its links to organizational behavior.

Mette Mønsted is professor in knowledge management at the Copenhagen Business School. She is a sociologist and has a PhD in management from the Copenhagen Business School. Mønsted's current research focuses on knowledge management, with an emphasis on research and innovation management, and organizing knowledge-based firms and complex network relations.

Jan Mouritsen is professor of management control at the Copenhagen Business School. His research is oriented toward understanding the role of management technologies and management control systems in various organizational and social contexts. Mouritsen's interests include intellectual capital and knowledge management, technology management, operations management, and accounting and management control. Widely published, he serves as an editorial board member of 14 academic journals in the areas of accounting, operations management, IT, and knowledge management.

Sue Newell is the Cammarata Professor of Management at Bentley College. She is also a visiting professor in the School of Management at Royal Holloway, University of London, UK, and has taught at Birmingham University, Warwick University, and Nottingham Trent University. Newell holds a PhD from University College Cardiff, and is one of the founding members of ikon (the Innovation, Knowledge and Organizational Networking research unit), based at Warwick Business School. Her research interests focus on innovation processes using knowledge and organizational networking perspectives.

Andrew Nurse is a research associate in the doctoral program at Kingston University. He is also a lecturer at Kingston University and a partner in an organization development consultancy. Nurse is a chartered engineer and holds an MBA. His main research interest is the role of artifacts as the link between organizational capability and the capabilities of the people who work in it.

Sille Øestergaard is currently living in Thailand, working as a freelance consultant and an exporter of Asian products to Europe. She has previously worked as a management consultant and has, among other projects, conducted a study on knowledge management for a large Danish engineering company. Øestergaard has a MSc in communication and psychology from Roskilde University, Denmark. Her current research interests focus on research methods, knowledge sharing, and narratives.

Nicoline Jacoby Petersen is a freelance communication consultant. She has previously worked at the Copenhagen Business School as a researcher (focusing on KM within the consulting industry) and project manager (primarily on the development of executive master programs). Petersen has an MSc in communication and psychology from Roskilde University. Her current research interests focus on research methods, knowledge sharing, research communication, and new ways of conducting conferences.

Flemming Poulfelt, volume editor, is professor of management and strategy in the Department of Management, Politics, and Philosophy, vice dean of research communication, and director of the LOK Research Centre at the Copenhagen Business School where he earned his PhD. Poulfelt's current research and consulting interests focus on managing professional service firms, knowledge management, strategic management, change management, and management consulting.

Nicolas Rolland is professor in strategy and management at CERAM Sophia Antipolis, where he is responsible for the specialized master in competitive intelligence and knowledge management. His research interests focus on the management of communities of practice, the organization of knowledge management, and the impact of knowledge management on decision-making processes. Rolland is a member of numerous international associations, and is a partner of Plyxis, with which he develops research action and executive education programs for multinational corporations such as Eli Lilly, Boeing, Johnson & Johnson, Pirelli, and CIBA *Specialty Chemical*.

Alfons Sauquet is professor of learning and knowledge at ESADE at Ramon Llull University. He holds doctorate and master's degrees from

Columbia University as well as an MBA degree from ESADE and a master's degree in clinical psychology from the University of Barcelona. Sauquet is also vice dean of research and knowledge at ESADE Business School, where he has directed the university programs unit, and serves on the board of the Iberoamerican Foundation for Knowledge Management. His current research focuses on the meaning and practice of expertise and ecologies of learning.

Georges X. Trepo is professor of management at HEC School of Management in Paris. He holds an MBA from the University of Chicago and a doctorate from the Harvard Business School. Earlier in his career, Trepo was head of human resource development at France Telecom. His present research interests include change management, performance appraisal, and management development.

Andreas Werr is associate professor at the Stockholm School of Economics, where he also earned his PhD with a dissertation focusing on the functions of methodologies in the work of management consultants. His current research interests focus on the rhetoric of management consulting; the procurement, use, and consequences of management consultants in client organizations; and the management of consulting companies, specifically the management of knowledge and knowledge processes.

Printed in the United States
72353LV00001BB/19

9 781593 114190